THE BATTLE FOR THE UNIVERSITY OF ALABAMA

THE BATTLE FOR THE UNIVERSITY OF ALABAMA

The Perilous Path *of* Higher Education *in the* Reconstruction South

William Warren Rogers Jr.

The University of Alabama Press
Tuscaloosa

The University of Alabama Press
Tuscaloosa, Alabama 35487-0380
uapress.ua.edu

Copyright © 2025 by the University of Alabama Press
All rights reserved.

Inquiries about reproducing material from this work should be addressed to the University of Alabama Press.

Typeface: Janson

Cover image: Cadets in formation in front of the first building erected after the destruction of the University of Alabama campus at the end of the Civil War; The University of Alabama Libraries Special Collections
Cover design: Lori Lynch

Cataloging-in-Publication data is available from the Library of Congress.
ISBN: 978-0-8173-2228-1 (cloth)
ISBN: 978-0-8173-6200-3 (paper)
E-ISBN: 978-0-8173-9552-0

For my mother, Miriam Arnold Rogers

Contents

List of Figures   ix

Acknowledgments   xi

Introduction   1

Chapter 1   "I Do Not Know that the Un__y of Ala. Will Ever Be Rebuilt"   7

Chapter 2   "Peace Is the Indispensable Condition of Education": The Reinvigoration of Southern State Universities, 1865–1868   29

Chapter 3   Faltering Renaissance   47

Chapter 4   "A Position Connected with the University Is Not at Present a Very Pleasant One"   66

Chapter 5   In Search of a President   92

Chapter 6   "Mrs. Partington and the Sea"   113

Chapter 7   "The Revered Old Intellectual Mother Will Weather the Storm"   131

Chapter 8   "We Have a University to Resuscitate"   151

Chapter 9   Courting the Commodore: The University of Alabama Lures a President   173

Chapter 10   Aftermath   191

Conclusion   194

Notes   203

Bibliography   239

Index   255

Figures

1.1. The University of Alabama campus before its destruction   8
1.2. Ku Klux Klansman   23
1.3. Ryland Randolph   25
2.1. Louisiana State Seminary of Learning and Military Academy   38
3.1. The University of Alabama's main building in 1869   48
3.2. Gustavus Adolphus Smith   54
3.3. *Independent Monitor* cartoon envisioning the hanging of the university's leaders   62
4.1. John Calvin Loomis   71
4.2. DeForest Richards   72
4.3. Vernon Vaughn   73
4.4. A faculty residence   77
4.5. The new university building seen through the ruins of the antebellum campus   80
4.6. *Independent Monitor* cartoon ridiculing Vernon Vaughn   85
4.7. *Independent Monitor* cartoon mocking Republican alliances   86
5.1. Nathaniel Lupton   110
6.1. Nathan Chambliss   115
8.1. William Russell Smith   152
9.1. Matthew Maury   177

Acknowledgments

MANY INDIVIDUALS HAVE BEEN INSTRUMENTAL IN MAKING THIS BOOK possible. What follows falls short of a foolproof listing. I have missed some who extended help, and I apologize in advance for any omissions. A great deal of the research was undertaken at the Alabama Department of Archives and History in Montgomery. Among the archivists there is Ken Barr, who went well beyond the call of duty on various occasions. John Hardin combines affability and a broad understanding of the archives' holdings. Roland McDonald as well makes visiting researchers' trips productive. When a visit to the archives was not possible, Carlie Burkett provided reels of microfilm through the interlibrary loan office. Meredith McDonough called on her extensive knowledge and located many of the photographs that appear in the book. I am also indebted to archivists at the Special Collections Library at Duke University and the Southern Historical Collection at the University of North Carolina. I visited or worked with staffs from a number of university archives. The most time was spent at the University of Alabama's Special Collections Library. Kevin Ray showed interest in the project from the outset, and until his retirement I turned to Kevin repeatedly and always found hospitality and help. Alex Boucher is typical of the solicitous staff at the University of Alabama Special Collections, and I thank him for locating a single but highly revealing letter. Helping much with materials that enabled the description of Reconstruction developments at other schools were the staffs at the university archives of Dartmouth, Georgia, Louisiana State University, Mississippi, Oberlin, Samford, Sewanee, Virginia Military Institute, Vanderbilt, Washington and Lee, and Yale. The staffs at the Briscoe Center for American History at the University of Texas and the Tennessee State Library and Archives in Nashville were also instrumental in my research.

Acknowledgments

Colleagues at the University of North Georgia have contributed in different ways. The list begins with Jeff Pardue, chairman of the history department, fast friend, and a native son of Wyoming who took genuine interest in this Alabama study. I have benefitted from my friendship and association with George Justice, Clay Outz, and Ben Wynne, all of whom have set a fine example as historians and classroom teachers. Two individuals at the University of North Georgia library are truly unsung heroes. Chris Andrews, who heads interlibrary loan services, went to incredible lengths to borrow microfilm from various institutions. That sometimes took the form of personally calling interlibrary loan departments at other schools and retrieving obscure Alabama newspapers. I simply cannot thank Chris enough. And similarly, I am at a loss to repay my debt to Kristine Stillwell. Kristine is a reference librarian at the university library, a PhD in history, an author herself, and a born researcher. Through her efforts, many digitized out-of-state newspapers came my way and enabled a much fuller examination of universities outside of Alabama. Kristine has an incredible, precise eye for referencing material correctly, a weakness of mine, and she has been a savior. In the final stages, Kristine was of inestimable importance in helping to format the manuscript.

I appreciate the interest of others who contributed differently. My sister, Katie Berry, and her husband, Jim, enjoy history and invariably asked about the travails besetting the University of Alabama during Reconstruction. So did my longtime in-laws, Rick and Beth Farr. Bawa and Karrie Singh are longtime family friends; Karrie is a classicist who translated a Latin phrase that confounded me. John Inscoe and Sally Hadden, scholarly friends of many years, were kind enough to inquire as to the project's progress. Guy Hubbs has written extensively of Tuscaloosa, and he extended help, as did Robert Gamble, the state's authority on historic architecture. I also appreciate the advice of Mike Fitzgerald, close student of Alabama Reconstruction. Paul Pruitt is a law librarian, a professor at the University of Alabama Law School, and a historian who writes of Alabama. Paul's own fine publications I have turned to in this study, as I have done previously, and his longstanding friendship and our mutual identification with Alabama's past continue to mean a great deal to me. Neither have I forgotten the efforts of Paul's wife, Julie, who somehow found a parking place on the University of Alabama campus one day and took pictures of primary documents for me at the Special Collections Library. Claire Lewis Evans is my editor at the University of Alabama Press. When I first mentioned the topic of the University of Alabama during Reconstruction, she was extremely receptive and encouraging. That was the beginning of Claire's friendly and

Acknowledgments

efficient stewardship, which has made the task of turning a manuscript into a book enjoyable and has also significantly increased the study's merit. Along the road to publication, Jenna Portnoff also effectively contributed as copy editor. And I would be terribly remiss if I did not express my deep appreciation to Carol Connell, project editor.

My wife, Lee, and our two sons, Warren and Benjamin, have provided nice company on research trips. Without darkening the door of any archives, they found plenty to entertain them in Auburn, Birmingham, Columbia, Chapel Hill, Montgomery, Oxford, Tuscaloosa, and elsewhere. On these occasions their mother is an enthusiastic escort and coordinator of activities, and for me, she remains a great companion and wife.

My father, William Warren Rogers, was a historian and knew of my hopes of writing about the University of Alabama during Reconstruction. He would be pleased. My mother, Miriam Rogers, who survived him by a number of years, often expressed interest and encouragement. I am very sorry that she, along with my dad, is no longer here to see the book's publication. It is to her, a wonderful mother, that I dedicate *The Battle for the University of Alabama and the Perilous Path of Higher Education in the Reconstruction South, 1865–1871.*

THE BATTLE FOR THE UNIVERSITY OF ALABAMA

Introduction

THE ESTABLISHMENT OF REPUBLICAN CONTROL OF STATE GOVERNMENTS in the South during Reconstruction opened an era of unprecedented partisanship less than a century into the Republic's establishment. What accounted most elementally for that division—the elevation of some four million ex-slaves to citizenship status—provided a pivoting point for the young country. The evolving scholarly treatment of Reconstruction continues to attract considerable historiographical contemplation. A subject which remains largely unscrutinized, however, is how higher education was impacted in the South once Republicans came to power. In Alabama, the heavy focus of this study, Republican direction of the state university inspired implacable opposition. An alleged politically motivated hijacking of the University of Alabama provoked extreme revulsion among Democrats. The ancillary consequences of Republican stewardship also accounted for confrontation at the University of Mississippi and what would become Louisiana State University, and far more draconic repercussions at the Universities of North and South Carolina. Higher education became a flash point of Reconstruction conflict.[1]

No school faced as formidable a path to recovery in 1865 as Alabama's state university. The war took a toll on all Southern universities and colleges, but at least they were standing. The University of Alabama lay in ruins. The cause of the university's destruction could be traced to a legislative decision made six years earlier. Partly in an attempt to establish better discipline among rather refractory young men and also a reflection of increasing martial spirit as civil war loomed, legislators in 1859 designated the school at Tuscaloosa as a military institution. Hundreds of cadets trained there during the war to fight the presumed Yankee infidel. Less than a week before the Appomattox Court House surrender, Union troops under General John T.

Croxton overran Tuscaloosa. The town suffered comparatively little damage, but the military school offered a symbolic target. On April 4 soldiers summarily destroyed the university in several hours. So began a period of eclipse for an institution that had stood since 1831. The campus would be intellectually silent for the next four years. Most state universities in the South had, out of necessity, closed during the conflict, but they reopened in 1865 or 1866. The University of Alabama did not do so until 1869. I address the impetus for and fact of rebuilding the university, but this is not an institutional history, and those efforts are not emphasized. Moreover, James Sellers accomplished that task in the *History of the University of Alabama 1818–1902*. My focus is the critical period between the school's reopening in the spring of 1869 and the beginning of a new administrative tack in the fall of 1871. This two-and-a-half-year time frame encapsulates the explosive conflict surrounding the university.[2]

What took place in Alabama was predicated upon events in Washington after the Republican Party seized control of Reconstruction and passed the First Reconstruction Act in the spring of 1867. The Republican egalitarian ethos directly contradicted the foundational premises of Southern society. The battle lines in Alabama became clear between the recently formed state Republican Party and the Democratic or Conservative opposition. Following the dictates of congressional Republicans, a state constitution was written complying with the First Reconstruction Act guidelines. After the constitution's acceptance, and despite Democrats' strong objections, the legislature ratified the Fourteenth Amendment, and Alabama was reinstated in the Union in the summer of 1868. That Ulysses Grant carried the state several months later testified to Republican power. Even more grating to Alabama Democrats than the party's domination of national government in distant Washington was the power and place Republicans held in the state. Republicans controlled every courthouse and also the legislature in Montgomery, where William Hugh Smith presided as the state's first Republican governor. Republican legislators soon raised taxes and attempted to force whites to mix with Blacks on integrated railroad cars. The world had changed seemingly overnight and, according to Democrats, much for the worse.

The University of Alabama was caught in the following infiltrating political cross fire. The Republican Party controlled the board of education and through it the administrative direction of the school, which reopened in 1869. As conventional thinking went, just as Radical political domination ill-served the state, so did board of education policy regarding the university. Its members, referred to as "regents," malevolently directed the university with an eye toward politics and Republican aggrandizement. In the view of detractors, the University of Alabama became a Radical enclave where unqualified individuals—often Republicans—masqueraded as professors. The presence within a mile of the university of one of the most pugilistic editors in the Reconstruction South inflamed the situation. Of Ryland Randolph, editor of the *Independent Monitor*, much more follows. He condemned the "carpet-bag and scallawag Faculty."[3]

This study most specifically concerns the extraordinary circumstances at the University of Alabama. More generally, in far less detail, the status of other Southern state institutions of higher learning is examined between 1865 and 1871. In the former Confederacy, eight state universities existed when the war ended. Alabama, Georgia, Louisiana, Mississippi, North and South Carolina, Tennessee, and Virginia had previously established a state school. State universities had not yet been established in Arkansas, Florida, and Texas, however. Administrative oversight at the state universities in varying degrees provoked strong dissent. Democrats responded by training their fire on university presidents, professors, governors, and those making school policy, usually a board of trustees. As for the recently installed Republican professors at the University of North Carolina, a critic recommended "the whole troop ought to be led to the extreme eastern verge of the State and dismissed into the Atlantic with a harmless but ceremonious kick."[4] Much harsher invective was often employed: "If the University is to become a Radical machine," the widest circulating Democratic newspaper in Mississippi promised that residents will "shun it as a pest-house."[5] The ensuing tumult between 1868 and 1871 weakened universities, drove down enrollment, and threatened to close the schools, and, indeed, that happened in North Carolina.

Setting up a public school system and extending education to a long-neglected white underclass and the previously totally ignored former enslaved persons was fundamental to the Republican promise in a remastered South. Historians have understandably focused on the foundational establishment of public education, and that effort represents the party's vision at its shimmering best. Higher education in the South has received much less scholarly attention. In the William A. Dunning school treatments of Reconstruction, Republican management takes on a predictably sordid image. The passage of time scarcely provided any historiographical revision. Authors of comprehensive studies of the American university, its development and evolution, have not examined the unique challenges Reconstruction posed to Southern universities. What does provide some light are institutional monographs, however dated and of varying quality, whose authors piecemeal and sketchily address the subject.[6] More recently, encouragingly, the interplay of Reconstruction politics and higher education have commanded the attention of historians. In *Bearing the Torch: The University of Tennessee, 1794–2010*, T. R. C. Hutton establishes how Republican control of the legislature crucially advanced the struggling state university at Knoxville. At no place were passions more profoundly displayed than at the University of South Carolina, where Black men gained admittance to the school in 1873. "The entry of formerly enslaved people was a flashpoint for southern white critics," Tyler D. Parry writes in *Invisible No More: The African American Experience at the University of South Carolina*, "as it embodied the society shifts they most feared during Reconstruction." How the Civil War changed Northern universities, and even more fundamentally Southern institutions of higher learning, is the subject of *Reconstructing the Campus Higher Education and the American Civil War*, authored by Michael David Cohen. Southern universities emerged in a more complete form—offering a wider curriculum and a student body less top heavy with those of affluent backgrounds. Cohen describes a time of crucible, but by design his is a selective work. What remains is a need for a comprehensive study collectively examining higher education in the Reconstruction South.[7]

This study is in no shape or form that, but rather a book limited in scope and time. Alabama Democrats date the university's supposed "redemption" from 1871, when the school's decline was arrested and reversed, and I have closed the narrative in that year because that is when the University of Alabama ceased to be a source of political contention. Two of the nine chapters are devoted to the circumstances at other state universities in the South between 1865 and 1871. In order to maintain the focus on Alabama's state university, I have not addressed developments elsewhere after 1871, no matter how seminal, such as the integration in 1873 of the University of South Carolina. The status of numerous private and denominational colleges also lies outside my purview because control of those institutions had no connection to state government and was not shaped by the political environment. By way of further disclosure, the universities where Reconstruction strife flamed most fiercely gain disproportionately more treatment than those that were comparatively quiet.

The first of ten chapters concerns the university's destruction and efforts to rebuild the University of Alabama. The adjustments brought by Reconstruction, which deeply complicated the school's regeneration, are laid out. Chapter 2 delineates efforts at other state universities in the South to regain their academic footing in the war's wake. How the intense partisanship of

Introduction

Reconstruction affected the reborn University of Alabama, most specifically in relation to faculty selection, concerns chapter 3. A university thrust into public disrepute by alleged "Radical" political machinations makes for an inauspicious reopening in chapter 4. The following chapter details largely unsatisfactory attempts to find a president to steady and legitimize the institution. Despite hiring a Democrat as president, the downward trajectory of the state university continues in chapter 6, underscored by a sensational crime involving parties connected to the school, and the resulting consequences for the university. Returning to the larger picture of Southern state universities in chapter 7, the discussion examines how and why some schools avoided Reconstruction-generated political consternation and others did not. In chapter 8, following Democrats' return to political power, a bold, new course at the university is adopted. Chapter 9 involves efforts to restore the school's flagging reputation by attracting Matthew Maury, a renowned Virginia scientist, to become president of the University of Alabama.

Conceptualization of this project gradually took form when I was working on a book concerning Alabama Reconstruction. While researching, I continued to encounter mention of controversy at the state university. The dominant state Democratic press presented a narrative whereby Radical Republican professors assumed teaching posts and board of education members subverted education's Holy Grail for crass political ends. It occurred to me that the intriguing storyline might make for an article in a professional journal. I paid passing attention and recorded some preliminary notes. Returning to the subject later, after deeper research, I realized what unfolded could conceivably warrant a small book. I visualized a monograph concerning the university's experiences as a vignette redolent of the deep alienation that characterized Reconstruction. So a subject, initially imagined as a possible article topic, assumed the potential of a book. Then the prospectus became more ambitious. *What was the situation at other universities in the former Confederacy?* posed a natural question. I initially planned on providing some passing context by rather faintly addressing events at the University of South Carolina, University of Mississippi, and other schools. Yet, as with everything else about this project, what I found regarding adversity there begged for fuller exploration. And so what was initially intended, parenthetically providing some cursory comparisons to other universities, has become a more detailed (but still modest and circumscribed by the termination date of 1871) look at state institutions of higher learning in the Reconstruction South.

Dark and aberrant forces emerged on the Reconstruction stage in Tuscaloosa, where men holding racial convictions set in the antebellum South

Introduction

bitterly resisted a much-altered postwar society. Questions regarding race contributed to the turmoil at the University of Alabama, but the more immediate question involved that of sovereignty. Who would exercise control of Alabama's state university? Searing controversy followed, thrusting decisions regarding higher education to an unaccustomed place—the political battlefield. And as a paradigm, the wrenching narrative uniquely silhouettes and frames the passions Reconstruction summoned. *The Battle for the University of Alabama and the Perilous Path of Higher Education in the Reconstruction South, 1865–1871* charts those travails, addressing what devolved and why. The University of Alabama's resurrection was uniquely "perilous" among Southern state universities. The time, place, and prevailing winds made it so.

Chapter 1

"I Do Not Know that the Un__y of Ala. Will Ever Be Rebuilt"

D<small>EVELOPMENTS AT THE</small> U<small>NIVERSITY OF</small> A<small>LABAMA AND IN THE TOWN</small> of Tuscaloosa during this highly inflammable phase of Reconstruction are intertwined and indeed inseparable. Setting the scene seems appropriate. On the eve of the Civil War, the town served as the county seat of Tuscaloosa County and the home (some estimates are larger) of over two thousand people. A preponderance of oak trees lent the misnomer "the city of oaks." Tuscaloosa was not a city, but it was justly renowned for numerous water oaks and other Druid family varieties. The place was best described as a mature town. Its modest size belied an important past as the state capital between 1826 and 1847. Geography favored Tuscaloosa. Perched just north of the Black Belt—a central tier of counties stretching across the state and distinguished by dark alluvial soil and a heavy concentration of enslaved persons—Tuscaloosa County in some senses shared its defining traits without truly belonging to the Black Belt. The Black Warrior River provided more benefits. Tuscaloosa was situated at the fall line, and the town was connected by way of the intersecting Tombigbee River directly to Mobile and its cotton market. That was not insignificant. Almost half of the county's thirteen thousand residents were enslaved persons in 1860, and most labored in cotton fields. The historical confluence of Old South power—wealth, enslavement, and fertile land—classically intersected in this setting.[1]

In a physical sense, typical of other places about the same size, Tuscaloosa's mercantile section lay along a central byway, Broad or Main Street (terms sometimes used interchangeably). Other prominent streets, without a commercial emphasis, highlighted by impressive homes, churches, and public buildings, captured the admiring eye, as did the domed three-story

Chapter 1

former capitol. Greensboro Avenue was unrivaled. More than its share of affluent people resided in Tuscaloosa. A number of them lived in fine homes, tucked back from wide thoroughfares, obscured and shaded by abundantly flowering gardens and the enveloping oaks. If the gentry set a high tone, a much larger white underclass led a different life, and Black residents, the vast majority enslaved persons, composed a highly regimented laboring caste. An extremely finite number of free persons of color represented an anomaly, given the status of fellow African Americans.

An appreciation of the cultivated mind and education had always recommended Tuscaloosa. Several authors were previously responsible for a flowering of poetry and literature in the 1840s and accounted for what one scholar described as a literary school. Young women attending the Alabama

FIGURE 1.1. The University of Alabama campus before its destruction. As a general rule, colleges and universities in the South were not targets of the Federal Army, but the University of Alabama's designation as a military school accounted for its destruction just as the war ended. The razing of the university by US Army forces represented the most devastating physical loss suffered by the state of Alabama during the Civil War. University of Alabama Libraries Special Collections.

— 8 —

Central Female College and the Alabama Female Institute lent a certain intellectual mien. In this setting a pronounced streak of introspection was befitting. John Quist perceptively documented local residents' embracing reforms of the day and, among other causes, that of temperance. And it was here, in that spirit of enlightening improvement, that construction began in 1853 of the state insane asylum established to provide patients medically informed and humane treatment.[2]

The location of the University of Alabama at Tuscaloosa provided the clearest evidence of an intellectual mindset. Students from throughout Alabama and other states had made their way to the state university since its establishment in 1831. The campus lay a mile east of town. The impressive domed and columned rotunda, the lyceum (also graced by a neoclassical portico), and various buildings named for early notable Americans—Franklin, Jefferson, Madison, and Washington Halls—largely composed an architecturally pleasing campus. About half a dozen professors composed the faculty in 1854 when an out-of-state visitor steamed up the Black Warrior River and spent some time in Tuscaloosa. "A more intelligent or refined body of literary and scientific gentleman," he observed of the professors, "I have never seen anywhere." In the vacuum left by the much-regretted loss of the capital, the University of Alabama offered a source of pride and, not insignificantly, a boon to the local economy.[3]

Although Tuscaloosa could claim preferred advantages, the town was in other respects very similar to other Southern settings. The immutable laws of race concerning the inferiority of those of African descent composed local orthodoxy. As for any advantages of living in Tuscaloosa on the Civil War's eve, those individuals who were enslaved knew nothing. Their lot was clear: toil for their white owners. Some chaffed restlessly, and freedom's vision accounted for attempts to escape bondage. Advertising locally his "Negro Hunting" services in 1861, J. W. Thompson set a searching fee for five dollars a day, and if the fleeing enslaved individual "is caught on the first day my price will be $15." The individual who visited in 1854 and praised the university faculty also observed that the masons and carpenters laboring on the rising insane asylum were enslaved people. It may be assumed that the list of impressive private homes and public structures that enslaved persons did not have a hand in constructing was either short or nonexistent. The most important reform movement of the day, abolitionism, attracted virtually no disciples (at least among whites). Such was the social and physical topography of a town that was at once distinctive but also reflective of a slave society.[4]

Visitors often remarked on the aesthetic qualities of Tuscaloosa, but the observer was far less inclined to attribute a bustling quality to the town. In fact, although steamboats on the Black Warrior facilitated contact with the outside world, a certain somnolence characterized Tuscaloosa. Losing the capital to Montgomery accounted partly for that status. One contributing reason for the removal—Tuscaloosa's profound isolation—remained a source of frustration. Various methods of travel—river, wagon, stage—conveyed one to the ex-capital, but all were slow and often uncomfortable. Following an all-night forty-mile stage ride from Greensboro, a traveler complained of having traversed an "uncertain road" in "imminent danger of bodily injury." The absence of a connecting railroad left Tuscaloosa frankly stranded and, compared with places visited by the iron horse, rather quiet. Frederick A. P. Barnard traveled in 1838 from New York to fill an appointment as the university's professor of mathematics and natural philosophy. The last leg of his water voyage started at Mobile. Barnard's steamboat voyage up the Tombigbee River to Demopolis, and then the final stretch, via the Black Warrior to Tuscaloosa, took three days. That was during the presidential administration of Martin Van Buren. Nothing had changed over twenty years later, when Abraham Lincoln came to office and civil war broke out.[5]

Residents by 1860 well understood the Union's fragility. Threats posed by abolitionists and the Republican Party to the peculiar institution, and parenthetically to society as it was known, had increasingly alarmed local white residents. Early in the 1850s, incrementally, and later in the decade, exponentially, Tuscaloosans became anxious as to enslavement's life expectancy. By the presidential election year of 1860, nothing less than the Union's divisibility lay in the balance. The triumph of Abraham Lincoln made plausible something most white Tuscaloosans had previously rejected—cutting ties with the United States. As in other Southern communities, opinion as to pursuing independence divided white residents; Tuscaloosa County voters sent Cooperationist delegates (who opposed leaving the Union) to the secession convention in Montgomery. Despite significant dissent, Alabama seceded in January 1861 and became part of the Confederate States of America. Following events in Charleston Harbor on April 12, 1861, the large majority of white Tuscaloosans put aside any previous doubts. A number of local men joined Confederate armies, and some gave their life in pursuit of Southern independence. Yet the trying war years proved prescient those who had warned against breaking ties with the Lincoln government, and the conflict's attendant wrenching home-front anxiety and economic hardships eventually yielded in Tuscaloosa to an acute war weariness. The situation became much more dire as the war neared an end in the spring of 1865. Federal soldiers commanded by General John T. Croxton, crossing the Black Warrior River, overran the town on Tuesday, April 4, 1865, easily pushing aside token opposition. They inflicted some damage on manufacturing establishments but little on the town or residences.[6]

The University of Alabama easily suffered the worst devastation. Although purely symbolic given the anemic state of the Confederacy, destroying the school as a military institution where Southern soldiers received training was part of Croxton's orders. Maybe with relish, or possibly exhibiting simple business-like procedure, Croxton's troops set about their work. Flames crackled, brick walls fell, and the University of Alabama disappeared. Little was left standing by that afternoon. Critics decried the pillage as wanton and unjustified and compared the Union troops to the barbarians who destroyed Rome. Those protestations ignored the role the school played in preparing Confederates for taking up arms against the United States. General Croxton later allowed that the university "met the fate of war. We were not Vandals, invading the peaceful retreats of the Muses."[7] Landon C. Garland had served as president of the university for the previous decade. Six weeks after the devastating visit of federal forces, Garland wrote to his sister in Virginia, "The university buildings are all burned. Nothing was saved." The exact letter of his statement was inaccurate, but the central fact of carnage was indisputable. Alabama had claimed a state university since the administration of Andrew Jackson, but several catastrophic hours on April 4 suddenly and definitively altered that reality. A period of limbo began. The university ruins for the next few years offered a misbegotten relic of fire-eating Southern nationalism gone awry.[8]

Across Alabama a white population, generally disappointed by a failed attempt at independence but relieved that the war had ended, faced an uncertain future. The reality of adversity could be measured differently. Somewhere between thirty-five thousand and forty thousand Alabama soldiers had lost their lives, and many more had been wounded. Confederate veterans were identified well into the twentieth century by a missing limb or halting step. Alabama had suffered less directly from militarily inflicted wounds than most Southern states, but Athens, Selma, and other places lay in virtual ruins. The war brought economic chaos, and its cessation did not offer immediate improvement. What most critically determined stability, as before the conflict, involved the state of agriculture, and the prospects of farming and planting were highly problematic. What the future held without mandated enslaved labor provided endless speculation but, at least among white people, little optimism. Destitution prevailed from the state's southern Piney

Chapter 1

Woods to the Tennessee mountain valleys. Alabamians would continue to pay a high price for the war long after the Confederacy's capitulation.[9]

Freedpeople also understood deprivation, but hope dominated among the formerly enslaved people as the implications of Confederate defeat and emancipation became clear. On the war's eve, some 435,000 enslaved individuals lived in Alabama, making it the fourth-largest slave-holding state in the country. Thousands of freedpeople, enjoying the fruits of liberty, set out for places they perceived as more desirable and providing opportunity, leaving for Mobile, Montgomery, and possibly Huntsville. Josiah Gorgas returned to Alabama by the early summer. The former Confederate Chief of Ordnance decided freedpeople seemed in "great commotion" and "a state of excitement & jubilee."[10] When the New York *Herald* journalist Whitelaw Reid visited Alabama late in 1865, he spoke with former enslaved people. "I's want to be a free man," one Black man explained, outlining the most fundamental basics of emancipation. "Cum when I please, and nobody say nuffin to me, nor order me roun." Those words and freedpeople's subsequent actions, notably as voters, reflected both the enormous relief that slavery had runs its historical course and a race's determination for further advancement.[11]

Reestablishing some sense of normality posed a variety of challenges for Black and white Tuscaloosans. Economic collapse, impoverishment, and other difficulties captured the local situation. Recovering from the Union raid acutely compounded circumstances. As perfunctory an act as crossing the Black Warrior River now required much more effort following the bridge's destruction by Federal soldiers. Local government struggled to carry out even elemental functions. The insane asylum, the impressive Italianate-styled building near what had been the university, remained open despite the war-imposed stringency. Superintendent Peter H. Bryce traveled that summer to Washington and appealed personally to President Andrew Johnson for federal financial help on behalf of that institution—to no avail. Meeting with Dorothea Dix in the nation's capital was equally futile. Basil Manly Sr., evangelist, Baptist minister, and formerly president of the university, lived in Tuscaloosa. The man who had sworn Jefferson Davis into office owned a plantation near town where he worked enslaved persons. Force of habit accounted for Manly's reference to "my negroes," even as he acknowledged the ex-slaves as "freed men and freed women."[12] White residents surely did not interpret a devastating fire in November as the Deity's wrath for abiding slavery, but the blaze destroyed Washington Hall, a popular hotel and gathering point, adding to despair. The plight of Johnathan Gibbs framed matters in a personal sense. Leaving Virginia Military Institute as the war began, Gibbs became the quartermaster at the University of Alabama. The school's destruction, Gibbs remonstrated, meant he was "thrown out of employment" and pressed to support a large family.[13]

As for the University of Alabama, nothing was sure. The finite inventory of standing structures consisted of the president's mansion, Steward's Hall (which served as a dining hall and faculty residence), an observatory, five professors' homes, and what was termed the "Guard Room," a small structure built recently to protect sentinels from inclement weather. The estimated financial losses for destroyed buildings and their contents and forfeited investments in the Confederacy (notes and bonds) amounted to some $350,000 (the equivalent of over $11 million by 2021 standards). Landon Garland gloomily informed his sister, "I do not know that the Un__y of Ala. Will ever be rebuilt."[14]

Reopening the school drew attention within months of its burning. The fall term traditionally began each October, and over the summer the board of trustees laid plans to resume educational efforts at the conventional time. What proved to be hopelessly optimistic formulations were based on having several faculty members offer instruction for an undetermined number of students. As for their lodging, improvisation was required since the former living quarters lay in rubble. That some students could presumably find boarding house accommodations formed part of the operating premise. Landon Garland intended to make more space available by moving into one of the professor's homes and allowing others to share quarters at the president's mansion. In a published announcement, Garland further assured that the surviving campus structures and educational apparatuses (e.g., the telescope in the observatory and several thousand books cobbled together to form a library) would mean that students could expect an education equal to that which students received before the war. The plans were ambitious, even bold, but totally unrealistic. Setting up the barest framework of a university was impossible given postwar exigencies. An extremely finite number of young men (the university's historian puts the number at one) made their way to Tuscaloosa late in September. It was an unfeasible situation, considered logistically, financially, or any other way, and reopening was indefinitely postponed. Any timetable for restoration was highly uncertain. The university, a mile from town, had always been somewhat isolated; one fixed the school's geographical location as "out yonder." And now the formerly busy campus took on a desolate and somewhat eerie quality. The curious or those simply seeking solitude and reflection who ventured out to the school grounds gazed at the piles of charred bricks lying in haphazard fashion, lonely columns, and leaning shards reaching skyward. The unbuckled pillars of the former rotunda projected a seeming defiance. Just as surely the scarred campus conjured lamentations over the price of the South's disastrous bid for sovereignty.[15]

Four years of war had catastrophically detoured the young nation of less than a hundred years, and Reconstruction adjustments would come in the immediate years ahead. Although slavery had ended, what rights accompanying emancipation should be extended the former bondsmen provoked wide differences of opinion and dominated the national debate. The Republican Party had lost its leader, but many Republicans took inspiration from Abraham Lincoln's memory and understood a compelling responsibility, indeed the moral obligation, to make freedpeople full citizens. Only then could four million ex-slaves realize the benefits of emancipation and the United States become an interracial democracy. Nothing could compensate for the war's tragic loss of life, cruelly exacerbated by Lincoln's assassination, but Republicans contended that freedpeople's elevation offered a sense of redemption.

Andrew Johnson and most Democrats took exception to that vision. Johnson's plans for the immediate postwar South became clear that spring when the president established a temporary form of government in the ex-Confederacy. In each state Johnson set up a provisional government and appointed a provisional governor. His plan promoting states' rapid readmission to the Union was intrinsically based on the former Confederate states ratifying the Thirteenth Amendment. The prescription for Reconstruction notably did not include any path to citizenship for freedpeople and inferentially consigned the race to indefinite subordination. Andrew Johnson came to symbolize Democratic opposition to the profound changes Republicans envisioned.

That involuntary servitude had ceased to be the lot of African Americans was one of the few certainties in the immediate postwar South. What had been the de facto reality since the war's conclusion—slavery's demise—was formalized by the Thirteenth Amendment's ratification late in 1865. The more intricate question of the exact status of formerly enslaved persons defined differences between the two parties and became obvious when Congress reconvened in December. Southern legislatures had by then carried out the requirements set by Johnson and elected individuals to Congress. Republicans controlled Congress, and their refusal to seat the Southern representatives was due largely to Democrats' rejecting meaningful racial reconfiguration.

A highly irregular period followed in the South, and not until 1868 would any ex-Confederate state (except Tennessee) rejoin the Union. Contributing to the unprecedented situation across the region were United States Army soldiers who established posts and provided a sense of order by assuming various functions of local and state government. Part of their responsibility involved overseeing the formerly enslaved people's transition to freedom. The Freedmen's Bureau became critical to that task. Acclimating freedpeople to their changed world, the vast majority of whom were abjectly poor and illiterate, defined the agency's fundamental purpose and bureau offices opened throughout the South.[16]

Developments in postwar Alabama conformed to this pattern elsewhere in the South. Lewis E. Parsons became provisional governor in June 1865. A Talladega lawyer who had opposed secession presided for the next half-year, and the provisional state legislature carried out the readmission requirements. Doing so most crucially involved ratifying the Thirteenth Amendment. Some eighteen thousand soldiers were spread out over Alabama five months after the war. Freedmen's Bureau offices opened, and agents confronted the myriad tasks associated with a state laid low by four years of war.

Reconstruction adjustments registered most profoundly in areas where large numbers of former slaves resided. Tuscaloosa eminently qualified, for African Americans composed almost half of Tuscaloosa County's population. Federal soldiers established an outpost locally, and a Freedmen's Bureau office began operations. Oversight was needed. The view of white people concerning the African Americans' inferiority did not die with the war and accounted for the conviction that the formerly enslaved persons were hopelessly miscast as full citizens. John S. Kennedy warily anticipated the intentions of national Republicans. Writing to Governor Lewis Parsons late in 1865, the local lawyer conceded the Thirteenth Amendment's ratification but predicted the Republicans would demand more for freedpeople than simple emancipation. Anticipating efforts to extend further the rights of the formerly enslaved persons, Kennedy labeled the amendment a "Trojan horse."[17] Kennedy's fears reflected those of almost all white Tuscaloosa residents. Charles Manly pastored the First Baptist Church. The son of Basil Manly privately likened what he perceived as the limited intellectual capacity of Africans to Indians in the United States, whom he also considered an innately inferior race. In the spring of 1866, Republicans passed the Civil Rights Act granting citizenship to freedpeople. "I do not fear the effect of the Civil Rights bill, in disposing the whites," Manly wrote a relative. The University of Alabama graduate allowed "those Radicals have seen their best days. They will be overthrown this fall." Charles Manly indubitably possessed certain traits—devoutness, devotion to family, moral probity—esteemed by contemporaries. The Baptist minister was not, however, gifted with clairvoyance. National Republicans' strength would increase rather than diminish as a result of the fall elections in 1866.[18]

Some white men in Tuscaloosa advanced a different view. Among them was Elisha Woolsey Peck. The man born during the presidential administration of John Adams was sixty-six years old in 1865. A lawyer and devout Episcopalian, Peck had never believed in the Confederacy. After the war, Peck continued to defy the conventional, eventually converting to the Republican Party. Thomas P. Lewis also dissented from the determinist view regarding the Black race's subordination. A former legislator and secession opponent, Lewis became sheriff in 1865. William Miller offered another example of a former secession opponent who later became a Republican by virtue of accepting the citizenship of Black Americans. David Woodruff, proprietor of the Waverly, a longstanding bookstore, pledged "not to be undersold by anybody." Woodruff also expansively interpreted the consequences of the war's verdict for freedpeople. Lewis, Peck, Miller, and Woodruff would play a role in the coming storm.[19]

G. Ward Hubbs in his book concerning the swirling Reconstruction winds in Tuscaloosa contributes much to an understanding of colliding cultural and political forces through the prism offered by four individuals who either lived in the town or were part of what unfolded there. Hubbs emphasizes each man's contrasting definitions of "freedom." As for the ex-slaves, "freedom" was defined by a basic trinity: individual autonomy, citizenship, and the resulting opportunity of advancement.[20] An emerging Black community was gaining an identity, and the former slaves' pursuit of that "freedom" was measured individually and collectively. Cutting their ties with Basil Manly, twenty-four freedpeople struck out on their own. Other restless formerly enslaved persons, once part of the local Baptist church, left the flock presided over by his son, Charles Manly. Freedpeople often realized the connection between a better future and becoming educated. Under the auspices of the Freedmen's Bureau, a half dozen schools had opened by the spring of 1866, and a Bureau agent concluded "the better class of colored people are anxious to send their children to school."[21] By then, also, freedpeople were demanding a political voice. Among those leading them was Shandy Jones. Born into slavery, yet freed as a child, the mixed-race individual became a local barber well before the Civil War. Jones's race consciousness predated the war, for he had promoted the movement to have free Blacks colonize Liberia in Africa. Emancipation provided him deep satisfaction, and Jones joined the Republican Party and impressed on freedpeople the relationship between political participation and their future. All along, Jones barbered, maintaining a shop on Broad Street, where the light-skinned proprietor guaranteed a shave, shampoo, and hair cut "in the most finished style." Jones's credentials were well established, but other Black men emerged as influential advocates. Charles Williamson had or soon would open a blacksmith shop. He, too, realized and made fellow freedmen understand the promise of Republicanism.[22]

The clashing dynamics of a Black population seeking advancement and resisting white people made for irrepressible conflict. Lawrence Berry's visit in the spring of 1866 illustrated the potential for volatility. Berry was Black, a resident of Mobile, and a man who had rapidly developed as an effective speaker and advocate of freedpeople. Promoting the Mobile *Nationalist*—the first Republican newspaper in the state—brought him to Tuscaloosa in April. One year had passed since institutionalized slavery for all practical purposes died, but freedpeople's status as full citizens was anything but guaranteed. Some took strong exception to reports that Berry urged local Black residents to demand equal rights and protect themselves. On the morning of April 17, 1866, a group of "roughs" repaired to a local freedman's residence where Berry was staying and, finding him absent, told the freedman they would hang Berry if he remained another day in town.

Extrapolating from Berry's experience, a certain receptiveness to his message among local freedpeople is possible, and even more discernable is the white opposition to what the Mobile freedman stood for. Local residents violently indisposed to Republicanism, always a rather small number, ranged across a wide cross section of residents. John Glascock and Robert Yates, both prominent businessmen, contributed to inciting those searching for Lawrence Berry. They and others seem to have been emboldened by the recent departure of soldiers stationed in Tuscaloosa. William H. Peck thought so. Wounded in 1862 during Seven Days' campaign, he returned to action in time for the Federal debacle at Chancellorsville. His personal odyssey brought him to Tuscaloosa with the Freedmen's Bureau after the war. "Troops seem to me necessary to the protection of lives among some blacks," Peck wrote on the day the white men sought Berry, "to say nothing of a *few* loyal whites including myself."[23] He maintained several days later that "this town is in more need of a Garrison than any other town in the State."[24]

If questions about freedpeople's status remained open, some light was emerging regarding a reconstituted University of Alabama. In November 1865, as Provisional Governor Lewis Parsons left office, he addressed the school's restoration in a final message to the legislature. Parsons pointed to the university's destruction and a pressing need to provide opportunity within the state for those seeking higher education. He called attention to the institution's formulative role in launching some of Alabama's most influential men. Noting that the war had forced the collapse of denominational schools of higher learning, the governor maintained reviving the university offered the "only hope." Parsons endorsed appropriations for rebuilding. Just days later, on December 4, 1865, Landon Garland addressed the legislature. The university president maintained that food for subsistence constituted Alabamians' first need, but education represented the next greatest priority. Garland connected an advanced civilization to education and the corollary mandate of developing intellect.

Early in December 1865, when the university board of trustees convened at the state capitol, its members officially retained Garland as the university president and general superintendent. The consuming task was as obvious as it was formidable—rebuild the school. To that end, under board of trustees' instructions, Garland turned his attention to settling on plans and gaining construction bids. The trustees assigned the president with another responsibility that might facilitate those tasks—a request directed to Congress petitioning for financial restitution for damages inflicted on the university by Union troops.[25]

Lewis Parsons's successor as provisional governor, Robert M. Patton, also championed the state school. The Lauderdale County merchant/planter, who had opposed secession but cooperated with the Confederacy, held office for over two years until Alabama rejoined the Union. In January 1866, addressing the legislature, Patton made clear the importance of the university's restoration. In somewhat understated terms, he related that at the war's close, the university "sustained a most serious loss." The governor endorsed a $70,000 appropriation, described reviving the school a "duty," and stated he considered nothing of "more importance." The efforts of two governors and the school's president achieved the desired outcome. Within weeks, in February, the legislature approved loaning the school $70,000 for rebuilding the University of Alabama.[26]

Although some financial underwriting had been approved, and a building committee formed early in 1866, progress remained slow for much of the year. Settling on a specific construction design was delayed by the understanding that any architectural blueprint should be predicated on plans to continue or discontinue the university's military orientation. A visitor to Tuscaloosa that summer took note of some sixty patients at the insane asylum and the inspiring work of Peter Bryce but pronounced the former university a "mass of ruins." In November 1866, when the board of trustees met

"I Do Not Know that the Un__y of Ala. Will Ever Be Rebuilt"

in Montgomery, Landon Garland spoke persuasively in support of extending the military emphasis, and the trustees consented. The board also settled on a design for the envisioned school. On the night of November 22, in room 104 of the Exchange Hotel (Jefferson Davis stayed there for a time when Montgomery was the Confederate capital), the board voted to accept James Thomas Murfee's the architectural blueprint.[27]

James Murfee resided in Tuscaloosa. A Virginian, Murfee had graduated with distinction in 1853 from the Virginia Military Institute. While at the school, he studied civil engineering and developed an expertise in architecture. His relationship with the University of Alabama dated from 1860, when Murfee joined the faculty as a mathematics professor. The following year, when the war began, he became the commandant, and Murfee also for a time served as a colonel in the field. No one would be as crucial to developments at the university than the individual who a former student recalled as a "man of details" and "untiring energy." James Murfee was thirty-three years old in 1867. His rise coincided with Landon Garland's fall from influence. At Montgomery, when the board of trustees was in session, Garland graciously, but without explanation, resigned as president. The university would indefinitely do without a president.[28]

Setting the stage for rebuilding had been accomplished in 1866, and significant progress followed the next year. Early in 1867, the building committee settled on a contractor. George Figh was a well-respected builder and resident of Montgomery. He would devote much of the next two years to bringing to reality James Murfee's design.

Murfee envisioned essentially a square and three-storied castellated Tudor Gothic brick structure enclosing an open courtyard. It would resemble the university building he had known at the Virginia Military Institution. The board of trustees instead, mindful of financial constraints, approved a scaled-down version. Erecting a central building flanked by shorter east and west wings took first priority. The configuration could be likened to the capital letter E, but without the middle extension. Preliminary preparations included selecting a location to raise the large structure, and the building committee settled on a site at the extreme northern edge of the campus, close to where the lyceum had stood. The vantage point fronted the former campus and commanded an impressive view of an oak grove and beyond that the president's mansion. James Murfee established an architect's office on the grounds and soon informed the building committee of "working night and day."[29]

April 12, 1867, marking the sixth anniversary of the firing on Fort Sumter, was for the vast majority of Tuscaloosa residents a decidedly unremarkable

Friday. Early on, down at the river, fishermen tested their fortunes. Farmers and traders that morning guided wagons loaded with their wares, assorted produce, venison, chickens, eggs and more, into town. Dossie Roberts, a formerly enslaved man now barbering and providing competition to Shandy Jones, opened his establishment with a reasonable expectation of profit. At the Mansion House, the small but best-appointed place to stay in town, guests rose and ventured forth, possibly tempted by the scents wafting from J. Hausman's bakery. If the pedestrian set the tone, events distinguished that day out at the university grounds. Laborers laid the first bricks for the projected several-storied building. Almost exactly two years had passed since the school's destruction. Something else signified that a time had come and gone. Enslaved people had long worked for the university. Enslaved people trod the campus before students. Their efforts had previously been instrumental in raising university buildings, and as property of the school, they carried out on a daily basis a wide range of duties. The university's relationship with slavery had been long, one-sided, and sometimes brutal. That past conveyed a transformative twist on the workforce rebuilding the school. Some of the laborers were Black, but now they labored voluntarily and received compensation.[30]

In the months ahead, under the supervision of George Figh, construction proceeded steadily. Only weeks into April, a member of the building committee wrote Governor Robert Patton, "Our university progresses well." The trustee described James Murfee as "vigilant & attentive" and noted Figh's "diligent" efforts.[31] Construction had been underway almost half a year in August 1867, when Patton visited Tuscaloosa. The governor spoke publicly and referred optimistically to the rising structure. And by Christmas the brick work had been completed, a nearly finished roof provided protection, and less was left to the imagination with each passing week. The impressive edifice became a point of curiosity, and those making the mile journey from town found an expansive three-storied (four at one point) structure. Turrets not dissimilar in shape to chess rook pieces marked the point of intersection between the shorter wings and the main building. Along the east and west walls, providing architectural dressing, ran a line of battlements. Far from gilded, but hardly devoid of ornamentation, the Tudor Gothic building struck one as highly proportional. If a lack of enclosing walls discouraged comparisons to a fort, the edifice presented a martial pose. Some might conjure the vision of a moat even though the closest body of water, the Black Warrior River, was not within sight. James Murfee described the structure as "peculiarly expressive for a military establishment"[32] and further alluded to a "masculine expression of neatness, simplicity, and strength."[33]

Although possessing a military insistence on order, Murfee was a person of cerebral bent. The architect foresaw the building as the centerpiece of a virtual constellation where students and local residents engaged in "social conversation, mental and physical recreation." Murfee visualized a setting where "every tree and flower that may be planted will flourish" and, in replacing the war's scars with a campus, hoped to create "one of the most beautiful landscapes in the South." His cosmos represented the intersection of the practical and the aesthetic and a compromise overindulging in neither.[34] Thomas Clinton, a young boy living near the campus in 1865, witnessed the university's burning and later recalled, "It was a dry day and I watched the buildings as they gave way to the angry flames, and it made an impression in my youthful mind that was lasting in its effects." Creating and blending the environs with the handsome new structure to produce a seeming arcadia could not erase the devastating loss of April 4, 1865, but it could dim the memory of that horrible day and help lay to rest the ghosts of John Croxton's raiders.[35]

Murfee claimed a wide purview. Landon Garland recognized Claiborne Harris's carpentry skills and employed him in various capacities. One of Murfee's decisions was continuing the freedman's services at the university. An examination of financial records revealed that over 122 former students had outstanding financial accounts with the university. Making the young men aware of their delinquent obligations, Murfee wrote and apprised each of their arrears. Only twenty-three students responded, eighteen denied the debt's legitimacy, and one had the temerity to maintain that the university owed him money! The architect also became a driving force in restocking the library. Collateral damage to civilian or private property, in this case state property, is a transcending and inevitable fact attending military conflict, no matter the continent or century. The fate of the library at the University of Alabama reaffirmed that truism. General Croxton later regretted that the burning resulted in the loss of art works and books and remonstrated they would have been removed "had their existence been within my knowledge and had opportunity offered." When the war began, the library counted at least eight thousand volumes. The overwhelming majority were destroyed when the university burned. Landon Garland, and then Murfee began soliciting donations of books to rebuild the collection.[36]

In the meantime, events holding profound consequences for Alabama, and not incidentally, its state university, were transpiring nationally. Republicans added to their majority in the midterm elections of 1866 and seized absolute control of Congress. Ratification of the proposed Fourteenth

Amendment had by then become the rallying Republican battle cry. The amendment, broadly defining citizenship to all Americans irrespective of race and guaranteeing "equal protection" and "due process" of the law, lay at the heart of that insistence. In March 1867, Republicans passed the First Reconstruction Act, which established terms for the ex-Confederate states' readmission. Ratifying the amendment and drafting a state constitution enfranchising all males of age (twenty-one) was required in each state. Meeting those prerequisites guaranteed readmission, but until then states were subject to military control, and the former Confederacy (excepting Tennessee, which had returned to the Union) divided into five districts, and an army commander was installed in each. In Alabama, the civil government—presided over by Robert Patton—as elsewhere in the South, was subordinate to military oversight. The First Reconstruction Act represented the triumph of a Republican consensus and laid the foundation for what constituted Reconstruction.

A complementing development involved the establishment of the Republican Party in the South. Northern men (often having moved south since the war) and Southerners (frequently former Unionists) directed the forming party. Freedpeople, inspired by the party promise and the symbolism of Abraham Lincoln, provided its foot soldiers. Across the South the Republican Party quickly became powerful in 1867–1868. These circumstances set the stage for unprecedented political conflagration, for the Republican ethos denied calcified notions of race and provoked extreme resistance. Democrats reviled Southern Republicans, whom they denounced as "scalawags," and held in equal contempt his Northern counterpart, the "carpetbagger." Social ostracism followed for those who challenged the maxim of white supremacy. In its worst manifestation, with the rise of the Ku Klux Klan and other nightriding orders, beginning at least by 1868, opposition to Republicanism degenerated into violence. Throughout the South, disguised men organized, often riding at night, intimidating and wreaking physical punishment on Republicans, white and Black, but mostly the latter.

The turn of events made for shattering political upheaval in Alabama. In 1867 a limited number of white men, many former Unionists, and a small but influential contingent of those who had moved from the North formed the state's Republican Party. Freedpeople provided Republicanism traction. State Democrats, overwhelmingly white, stoutly opposed the egalitarian vision. That would, in some cases, take the form of violence, for by early 1868 Klansmen and political vigilantes were making their fearsome appearance.[37]

What took place in Tuscaloosa offers a revealing look at the dynamics of Reconstruction grassroots politics. The even demographic complexion of the

FIGURE 1.2. Ku Klux Klansman. Nightriders mercilessly terrorized Black people and white Republicans throughout Reconstruction. From *The Invisible Empire* by Albion W. Tourgée (1880). Smithsonian National Museum of African American History and Culture.

town and county presented a ready environment for confrontation. A large Black minority provided the Republican Party instant political heft. Some freedmen did, or soon would, talk politics at the shop of Charles Williamson, a former slave who listed among the inestimable benefits of freedom the opportunity to make a living as a blacksmith. Among the very few white men who acted with the Republican Party were Elisha Peck, David Woodruff, Thomas Lewis, Henry McGown, William Miller, and Robert Blair, the latter connected with the Freedmen's Bureau. The establishment of a Republican newspaper, *The Reconstructionist*, further evinced the new party's presence. In the summer of 1867, Hampton S. Whitfield, a local lawyer, began publishing the newspaper. At a meeting of Republicans at the courthouse on January 28, 1868, Elisha Peck confided to his predominantly Black audience, "I am, and always was, the friend of the colored man." As a white Republican, he belonged to a very small local minority.[38]

The vast majority of whites claimed identification with the Democratic Party. That included prominent men—such as Henderson M. Somerville, Sterling A. M. Wood, Charles M. Foster, Charles Manly, Peter Bryce, John Glascock, John M. Martin (son of a former governor), and Benjamin F. Meek. Sterling Wood voiced the sentiments of some. The lawyer and former Civil War general wrote Governor Patton that compliance with the Fourteenth Amendment represented the only option and later reported that locally the mood was one of "acquiesce[nce]."[39] Even so, any number of perceived threats to the old order—for instance, placing Blacks on juries or ex-slaves' enfranchisement—gained strident condemnation. One local white man labeled Shandy Jones an "impudent haranguer,"[40] and another described the Republican barber and his son, Bill, as "Radical niggers."[41] The notion that a white man was remotely sympathetic to Republicanism was highly insulting to almost all white Tuscaloosans. When imputations to that effect circulated about Richard C. Parish, he avowed publicly, "I am no radical, in any form or shape, and cannot nor will not support their doctrines." The local merchant assured, "I believe in a white man's government."[42]

It was a relative newcomer to Tuscaloosa who generated the most opposition to the changes congressional Republicans forced. Edward Ryland Randolph spent his formative years in Alabama and attended the university for a time in the 1850s without graduating. He served in the Confederate Army and remained fiercely Southern in outlook. In his early thirties, Randolph moved to Tuscaloosa in the fall of 1867 and embarked on a tempestuous tenure editing the *Independent Monitor*. An incendiary, who was also a talented journalist in a distorted sense, he denounced Radicalism in the most caustic terms and personally maligned individual Republicans. Both Randolph's appeal and bane lay in his ability to vicariously capture the outrage felt by many whites. The *Independent Monitor* masthead read "White Man Right or Wrong Still the White Man." Randolph had no journalistic experience, but favorable reception of early editorial tirades encouraged him to continue in a shrill vein the raw denunciations. Neither was he above using physical force against the despised political enemy. Ryland Randolph would contribute more than any other single man to Tuscaloosa's future emergence as one of the state's most troubled locales.[43]

FIGURE 1.3. Ryland Randolph, editor of Tuscaloosa's *Independent Monitor*. Arguably the most virulently anti-Republican editor in the Reconstruction South, Randolph was a Klansman and contributed more than any other single person to the vilification of the professors at the University of Alabama as well as of the institution itself. Alabama Department of Archives and History.

Chapter 1

Alabama became the first Southern state to initiate the readmission process required by the First Reconstruction Act. Whites and Blacks registered to vote in the summer of 1867, and the newly created electorate in October approved holding a constitutional convention. Thousands of formerly enslaved men casting ballots across the state marked the election's historic nature. Elected delegates, almost all Republicans, met in convention at Montgomery between November and December of 1867 and drafted a constitution enfranchising Black men. In February 1868, the state's electorate, now including the freedmen, would vote to ratify or reject the document. Various aspects of the contemplated constitution, and nothing as much as a provision disfranchising a class of white voters, provoked extreme opposition. The proposed constitution's ratification, requiring one-half of registered voters approval, provided opponents a chance to deny its implementation by registering but not voting. Although over seventy thousand Alabamians voted to approve the constitution in the February election, a larger number of those registered boycotted the polls, and ratification failed. Alabama's path to readmission was arrested, and the state remained outside the Union.

In Tuscaloosa County, as elsewhere, residents had participated in the October constitutional referendum and then several months later the ratification election. Well aware of opposition and the potential for election day trouble, Sheriff Thomas Lewis assembled a large detail of supervising policemen. History was peacefully served on Tuesday, October 1, 1867, when freedmen voted for the first time, many traveling to town from outlying areas of the county. They cast the vast majority of the 1,954 ballots in favor of holding a convention and elected Elisha Peck and Henry McGown as delegates to help draft that document. On that first day of October, the extra police "had no work to do but to walk the streets with their hands in their pockets." And the freedmen in the county returned to the polls several months later, early in 1868, supporting ratification. Few white men participated in either election and, at the latter contest, defiantly boycotted the polls in hopes of defeating a constitution they considered highly objectionable.[44]

Opposition to the Republican vision in Tuscaloosa, no matter the uneventful election days, was primal and brutal. One local Democrat offered the consensus, "This is a white man's government, and none but white men should be allowed to participate in its control." When Albert Smith and Allen A. Williams were placed on the grand jury as Circuit Court convened in the spring, extreme local outcry led to the Black men's removal. Any white Republican faced immediate notoriety.[45] "Some of the men that I esteemed my personal friends before," Elisha Peck stated, "declined to have social intercourse with me." A darker streak of resistance also emerged. A former enslaved person, Allen Williams, taught freedmen and served as a voter registrar. He drew the ire of come local Democrats, and when some disguised men threatened Williams, he left Tuscaloosa, fearing for his safety. Disguised white men seized a less fortunate freedman in the dead of night, took him into the woods, and administered a merciless whipping. A series of crimes lay ahead, often politically connected and usually directed at freedpeople.[46] The man who had commanded Union forces at Gettysburg, General George Meade, was in charge of the Third Military District to which Alabama belonged. In March 1868 Elisha Peck apprised Meade of threatened violence against white and Black men in the town and Tuscaloosa County. He referred to a "rebel element here," related the withering mistreatment directed at men receptive to congressional Reconstruction, and forecast without protection, "It will grow worse, instead of better." A deteriorating situation proved him correct.[47] Some carried out acts individually, perhaps satisfying some personal spleen. Other men acted in concert and reflected a collective and general anti-Republican mentality. The Ku Klux Klan formed locally. About twenty men organized Tuscaloosa's version of the nightriding order that spring. Among them was Ryland Randolph, who later recalled that "impudent and overbearing negroes" were high on the Klan's list of enemies. He belonged to a coterie of white men who, usually disguised and almost always at night, abducted those considered objectionable and forced them to the town cemetery, where they beat their victims, often leaving them tied to a tree. Such was the fate of freedmen, whom Randolph described as "offensively conspicuous and unbearable."[48]

Ellen L. Benton confronted this mindset. Removing most immediately from Virginia, where she had taught freedpeople, she arrived in Tuscaloosa in the spring of 1867 as an American Missionary Association instructor and began educating freedpeople. Benton could not miss the brewing acrimony. She sympathized with Allen Williams and rued the events that drove the fellow teacher away. Much to her horror, Benton learned of crimes against freedmen and wrote late in March 1868, "Can it be possible that there is no way to prevent midnight assassinations and cold-blooded murder in open day on the public streets?" As a Northern woman intent on teaching Black students, Benton drew disfavor. "I am told that my life is threatened," she remonstrated to Henry M. Bush, the acting superintendent of Freedmen's Bureau schools in Alabama, "but I cannot believe they will trouble a defenseless woman."[49] The unflinching teacher singled out Ryland Randolph as particularly disruptive. Robert Blair recognized a certain danger. The Tuscaloosa resident and bureau agent advised another bureau official that Benton might be forced to leave town for "the very *Devil* himself has taken possession of the Rebels."[50]

What was largely unforeseen in the spring of 1868 were events that dramatically and controversially linked Reconstruction and the University of Alabama. As the construction of the school continued in 1867–1868, James Murfee expedited recovery in widely diverging ways. At one point, preparing to make arrangements for books that had been donated to the library, he informed the building committee, "I leave this afternoon for Mobile on Business for the Uniy." Several days later, after putting down his bags at the well-known Battle House Hotel, Murfee earnestly began those efforts.[51] On another occasion, he volunteered that experience as a professor, commandant, and student of architecture provided him a perspective to design a building that "possesses rare advantages for a university of the highest order." That statement lay beyond contention.[52] It was George Figh, however, who gazed beyond raising of the building to another challenge. The man entrusted with constructing the university mentioned possible (but unspecified) future consequences for the school given "the present revolutionary condition of political affairs." His expectation of complications proved prophetic. An uncanny sense of historical timing would make for a spectacular convergence of events well after Murfee and Figh had completed their tasks. The task of physically resurrecting the University of Alabama would pale in comparison to the battles attending the school's successful relaunching.[53]

Chapter 2

"Peace Is the Indispensable Condition of Education"

The Reinvigoration of Southern State Universities, 1865–1868

THE BLAZING ELAN DISPLAYED ACROSS THE SOUTH AS SECESSION AND the war came played out enthusiastically on university campuses in the Confederacy. The large number of students abandoning their studies and enlisting expressed an effervescing patriotism. So did the exit of some of their professors to the battlefield. Other faculty not taking an active role emphatically supported the Confederate States of America.[1] As questions regarding slavery and state sovereignty became paramount in the national discussion, University of Virginia professor Thomas Bledsoe sometimes strayed in his mathematics courses and expounded on states' rights. Reflecting on the crescendoing Southern nationalism in 1860–1861, Joseph LeConte described a "spiritual contagion" and elaborated how "we breathed it [Southern patriotism] in the air." The professor of chemistry at South Carolina College put aside his initial reluctance regarding leaving the Union. Others never entertained any doubts. But now the long conflict was over. And as a component of a suffering South, in the aftermath of a failed war, universities faced extreme adversity. Some schools were physically broken, financial support was highly problematic, and the prospect of attracting students was uncertain. Achieving or approximating prewar status was not accomplished seamlessly at any university, yet the task was steeper in some places. This chapter concerns efforts at reviving the existing state universities in the former Confederacy.[2]

The universities in North Carolina and Virginia managed to remain open during the highly irregular war years, but those elsewhere closed. The conflict necessitated suspending operations at South Carolina College in 1862, and the Army of the Tennessee razed much of Columbia three years later, but the school escaped serious damage. Fortune also favored the University of Mississippi. Union troops under General Ulysses Grant had occupied Oxford briefly and innocuously in 1862, and two years later the enemy returned and destroyed much of the town but not the university. Despite the havoc General William Sherman's troops wrecked on the state, the University of Georgia continued to enjoy its prewar dress, although the school at Athens shut down in the year of the Confederate debacles at Gettysburg and Vicksburg. Near Pineville, Louisiana, at the most recently designated state university, the Louisiana State Seminary of Learning and Military Academy, war interrupted the school's brief life in 1863.[3]

A cluster of buildings picturesquely located several miles south outside of Knoxville had constituted East Tennessee University since 1840 (the school became the University of Tennessee in 1879). With the exception of the University of Alabama, that school suffered the most military destruction of any state university. Federal armies controlled more of Tennessee during the war than any other Confederate state, and East Tennessee University suspended classes early in 1862. In the fall of 1863, when troops commanded by General James Longstreet attempted unsuccessfully to break the Union occupation of Knoxville, the campus formed part of the Federal's enveloping defense. By the time of the war's close, one building had been entirely destroyed, others languished in seriously damaged condition, and rifle pits littered the campus grounds, which a witness described as "mutilated."[4]

Incrementally, over a period of months at Knoxville, and in a matter of mere hours at Tuscaloosa, the war's ancillary consequences for higher education became graphically obvious. On balance, however, it was not cannonades or cavalry charges that accounted for the depleted condition of most Southern universities. The compromised state of university buildings owed much more to the war-imposed period of heavy wear and neglect. Confederate and Union forces had at one time or another occupied and appropriated campus structures in almost all the schools. The appeal was one of functional convenience. What had been the living quarters of students, for instance, proved particularly well suited for conversion to hospital wards. Soldiers in both armies displayed something less than scrupulous respect for university property. The experience of the Louisiana State Seminary of Learning and Military Academy offers a certain appreciation. At different intervals of the war, Confederate and Union troops bivouacked on the remote campus in the pine forests of central Louisiana. Their hard stay took a toll on the school, and some local residents were not above pilfering the abandoned institution. A similar situation existed at Columbia. "I am very sorry to say," Professor Maximilian LaBorde reported to South Carolina College trustees in October 1865, that the college buildings "have suffered greatly from their occupation by the Confederate and United States Authorities." In the main, campuses lay in a trampled state, academic buildings begged for attention (some were gone), and valuable and critical scientific accoutrements had been broken or simply vanished.[5]

Bleak financial realities added to the infrastructural weaknesses. State universities had previously depended on annually remitted legislative appropriations. The continued flow of money was now circumspect given the depleted status of state treasuries. The considerable investments universities had made in the Confederate States of America, often involving the purchase of Confederate bonds, vanished as completely as the hopes of Southern independence. Tom Dyer points out in his treatment of the University of Georgia that by the war's end the school was "absolutely destitute."[6]

A wanting physical and financial infrastructure only partially measures fragility. The pipeline of state funds would be reopened, buildings repaired or rebuilt, grounds refurbished, libraries restocked, and scientific equipment replaced. But other war-incurred costs could not be calculated in terms of dollars. Students in the immediate post-bellum years often bore scars of Confederate service—a missing leg, arm, or some limiting disability betrayed their immediate antecedents. Some made a greater sacrifice. Charles Phillips taught mathematics before and after the conflict at the University of North Carolina. He remorsefully observed, "A very great number of my pupils have perished during the war." About 270 soldiers who had previously wandered Chapel Hill's campus would not return. As many as five hundred former University of Virginia students lost their lives. Some professors likewise did not survive the conflict. Lewis M. Coleman had spent 1859–1860 teaching Latin at the University of Virginia before joining Confederate forces in the field. He was among the casualties at the Battle of Fredericksburg. The year 1861 found the Reverend Robert W. Barnwell of South Carolina College ministering to Confederate soldiers in Richmond hospitals. Two years later, the professor of moral philosophy and sacred literature contracted typhoid fever and died at the Confederate capital.[7]

These circumstances impeded but did not prevent the resumption of education at these universities in 1865–1866. Former professors resumed their positions, and new colleagues joined them. Some students returned to an academic life interrupted by the war, and other young men, many coming of age during the conflict, enrolled for the first time. A recognizable student profile emerges. All were white, at least fifteen years of age, and the vast majority were residents of the state, depending on the school. A noticeable number were older than students before the war, since some were ex-soldiers. As a general rule, conceding that time in the army came at the expense of some preparatory education, these students were also academically weaker than those before them, often unprepared for true university-level work. The circumstances varied from state to state. Scale should be kept in mind. No school had an enrollment of over three hundred students, and some institutions counted less than one hundred attendees. And, correspondingly, though never exceeding ten, the number of professors varied. Some faculty claimed a longstanding relationship with a school, while other professors were recently appointed. The faculty, like their students, were male and white.

The large majority of students sought a bachelor of arts degree and, doing so, required following a rather rigid academic map. The ancient languages, physics, chemistry, general science, logic, mathematics, and ancient history had composed, and continued to compose, a heavily weighted classical curriculum. Not honing skills for a profession but developing a young man's mind, as Michael Sugrue, among others, has pointed out, constituted the guiding intention of education. Although a movement toward broader and more practical courses was nationally underway, a curriculum offering modern languages and natural sciences remained the future. So it was, for instance, that students continued to translate texts from the original Greek and Latin. Professors presented their subject largely as it had been conveyed to them. Some form of a lecture was pedagogically de rigueur. And invariably, in almost all disciplines, there was the recitation. This time-honored exercise involved a student responding orally at the professor's cue and then a peer replying to another question. More heavily weighted examinations, often ending a term, provided a more telling academic reckoning. These tried one's physical fortitude as well as intellectual aptitude for examinations and might last much of the day and occupy an entire week. Such were the general academic contours of higher education in Athens, Charlottesville, and elsewhere.[8]

In the case of South Carolina, that South Carolina College was even standing as the war ended provided the most fortuitous fact. Dead trees and solitary standing chimneys testified to the thoroughness of Union troops who had destroyed much of Columbia on February 17–18, 1865, and the blaze nearly reached the university. Even so, quickly the groundwork for resuming class began. Meeting several months after the conflict, the school's board of trustees determined to convene classes in the first month of 1866. Among the proponents of doing so was Provisional Governor Benjamin F. Perry, describing the closed school as having been the "pride of the State." A unique situation confronted officials. Many residents had lost their homes in the February fire and were joined by other refugees, sheltered in school buildings, some indefinitely remaining there. Union soldiers who had established quarters on campus soon after the war ended added to the highly unusual circumstances.[9]

About twenty students were present in January 1866 when the recently rechristened University of South Carolina emerged from four years of war-imposed dormancy. Seven professors, representing a blend of former and new faculty, covered the classical curriculum offerings. Maximilian LaBorde and William J. Rivers provided a sense of continuity. Far more recent was the connection to the school of Edward Porter Alexander, who had served on Robert E. Lee's staff and now became instructor of mathematics and engineering. Almost fifty students eventually enrolled as the term progressed. Students dutifully attended classes, morning and evening prayer, and gave little cause for reprimand. The academic readiness of this first postwar class, given the waiving of entrance examinations, was more debatable. William Rivers struggled to familiarize students with Greek and Latin, but the ancient languages and literature professor admitted, "The desire of the men to improve has been very great."[10] Adjustments were also in order for Professor Porter Alexander, who put the number of those prepared to take engineering or higher mathematics courses at exactly zero. Joseph LeConte carried on as best as possible in science classes. As General William Sherman's army had moved toward Columbia, LeConte anticipated harm to the university and oversaw moving scientific equipment by railroad to a safer setting. That was the last he saw of what the chemistry professor described as "absolutely indispensable" scientific accoutrements basic to the most "ordinary experiments."[11] The refugees created by the war's havoc provided a different challenge. A full year after the conflict's conclusion, some displaced individuals remained in college buildings, and their refusal to leave constituted what Maximilian LaBorde described as a "very serious annoyance."[12]

A fluid number of students, which steadily increased, occupied themselves variously. Literary societies had long provided part of the intellectual and social development of the young men. At the University of South Carolina, students revived the Euphradian and Clariosophic societies. Some enjoyed the camaraderie, and the elocution competitions attracted others, but the societies appealed to a wide cross-section. In the spring of 1866, the Euphradians disagreed sharply over the appropriateness of executing Mary Queen of Scots. Consistent application to their studies seems to have best recommended this first postwar class. Professor LaBorde congratulated that among the young men "absent for recitation without a sufficient excuse has been almost unknown."[13]

The school gained more students and a surer footing in the next couple of years. A trend identified by Michael Cohen in *Reconstructing the Campus*, offering a wider and more practical curriculum, was evidenced at the University of South Carolina, where a construction or engineering component was added. By 1867 over a hundred young men were circulating on the campus. Matriculating from the South Carolina hinterland, D. Z. Dantzler was representative of a student population fielded from the Palmetto state. Dantzler was anything but typical in other respects, for the young man accrued various academic honors and, at the university chapel, delivered the valedictory address before the Euphradian Society on June 29, 1867. At about that time, students completed a series of examinations, and the academic year closed. Facing the realities of reviving the school, Professor John LeConte referenced the obstacles posed by "contingencies of war," but even so, a path to prosperity could be imagined at the University of South Carolina.[14]

At Oxford, Mississippi, where a year earlier Union troops had destroyed much of the courthouse square, Provisional Governor William L. Sharkey presided in the summer of 1865 when the board of trustees met. The hiring of a faculty numbered among the outcomes of the meeting.[15] No one was as important as John N. Waddel, long associated with the university and now the chancellor. In the fall 1865 term, the first since the school closed in 1861, over one hundred students began a trend of healthy enrollment. Some were former soldiers and often lacked what would previously have been considered sufficient academic grounding. University of Mississippi officials had also put aside entrance examinations. Chancellor Waddel diplomatically described the class as "not advanced." Whatever their ability and background, all students assembled daily at the chapel. Holding commencement exercises as the academic year ended marked a certain point of institutional rejuvenation.[16]

Several months later, when the fall session of 1866 began, over two hundred young men were present. Among the faculty were Claudius Sears and Eugene W. Hilgard. Sears was a former Confederate general who lost one of his legs at the Battle of Franklin. He maneuvered to his mathematics classes with the aid of crutches. Hilgard's association with the school predated the war. The Bavarian-born and University of Heidelberg–educated chemistry professor was also the state geologist and by early 1866 had resumed fielding letters from Mississippians concerning artisan wells, fertilizers, and, in one instance when several people suddenly died in the small village of Duck Hill, calmed residents' fears that a local well had been poisoned. "I see from the Press of the State," one correspondent commended him that fall, "that you are still exerting yourself to educate, and direct the farmers in the proper channel—to open their eyes to the fallacy of old notions." Hilgard, Sears, and several other faculty formerly associated with the school promoted a largely smooth resumption at the University of Mississippi.[17]

The campus lay a mile west of town, and students often negotiated that distance by relying on plank sidewalks of varying quality. Young women attending the Union Female College also depended upon the sometimes-undependable walkways. Late in 1866 a male student protested their disrepair to the city fathers, calling attention to "planks settled in elegant confusion without any regard for mathematical precision." And to the female students, he reasoned, "If you wait until the City Council fix your walk you will yet see a good many winters pass by without it being fixed." Power lay in collaboration, and he suggested that those at both schools raise money for the sorely needed improvements. Late in June 1867, twenty-four students were awarded diplomas at commencement. Following the ceremony, students and local young women (surely some from Union Female College) enjoyed a ball that extended into the early morning hours.[18]

Unlike the University of Mississippi, North Carolina's state university had remained open for the war's duration. On April 17, the day after Easter in 1865, Union troops uneventfully entered the village of Chapel Hill. Theirs was a brief stay. Just weeks after Appomattox, although students were few, professors forming a largely unchanged faculty reconvened classes. Various developments blemished the standing of the proud institution. Among them were the circumstances of Eleanor (Ellie) Swain's marriage. She was the daughter of the school's president, David L. Swain. During the brief occupation of Chapel Hill, Ellie met Union General Smith B. Atkins, and their betrothal several months later in August reflected poorly on the university locally.[19] Deeper-seated problems worked more critically against the school. The war accounted for the loss of the university's endowment and an accruing debt. Cornelia Phillips Spencer became a close observer of developments. "We are all so dependent on the prosperity of the Univ," the local woman wrote privately in 1866, "its decline carries the whole village down"; and Spencer described the faculty as "greatly straightened."[20] That included her brother, Charles Phillips. Writing an acquaintance in the spring of 1866, the mathematics professor described the school's situation as "lamentable." Phillips welcomed the North Carolina legislature's recent appropriation of $7,000, but given needs, that was hardly adequate. He did not fear for the "life of the University," yet worried that competing denominational schools would use their influence to sway legislators from "calling on the public of N.C. to support the University with vigor." Many students were ex-soldiers who, Phillips allowed, "try to redeem some of their lost time" but academically "need assistance."[21]

Even so, between 1865 and 1868, anywhere from eighty to one hundred students each year attended the University of North Carolina. As had those before them, they settled into East, West and South Buildings, and roused early by the unwelcome clanging bell in the belfry above the latter structure, students repaired for prayer and recitations. The activities of the Philanthropic and Dialectic societies provided a distinct pulse. In the fall of 1866, unknown forces in play caused the reevaluation of a seeming form of hazing. Members of the Philanthropic Society resolved to resist the tradition of subjecting first-year students to "the evils of the practice of treating [freshmen] with contumely."[22] Almost a year had passed since the surrender when Professor Charles Phillips noted that collectively "we work on in hope that something good may turn up for us here." That proved to be a false hope. By 1868 worsening financial strains threatened to close the faltering university.[23]

Among the most successful schools navigating the path of academic regeneration was the University of Virginia. Located on the western edge of the Blue Ridge Mountains in the small town of Charlottesville, the school gloried in the name of Thomas Jefferson. Granting that Virginia provided the setting for the war's most crucial fighting, the university had remained open and avoided serious physical damage.[24] By the fall of 1865, over two hundred young men, some new to the school and others resuming a war-paused education, were walking the distinctive arcade-lined halls. Routines resumed with comparatively few complications on the campus designed by Jefferson. Fraternity, elocution, and enlightenment were served by the long-standing Washington and Jefferson societies. Both societies cooperated to erect a monument to unknown Confederate soldiers who had died on the university grounds. And here, too, among students, baseball appealed and clubs formed. Among the Alabamians counted there was Charles Cabiness, a young man of Huntsville antecedents. In a series of letters to his father back home, Charles assured that he was keeping body and soul together—the boarding accommodations were comfortable and he had a warm coat—and that with the exception of algebra, academics posed no difficulties.[25] Commencement exercises on June 29, 1866, closed the academic year, and a large crowd turned out at the Public Hall in Charlottesville. As chairman of the faculty, the aptly named Socrates Maupin presided, and he proudly called attention to the number of enrolled students, which far exceeded expectations. Before a crowd disappointed by the war's outcome, Maupin by consolation offered, "Peace is the indispensable condition of education." Some sixty students received diplomas that day.[26]

In October 1867, as the next academic year began, large crowds of visitors and students gathered on the campus grounds. One intrigued observer contrasted the "dark skinned young men of the South" with the "fair-complexioned, lightly-dressed youth of the North." Among the latter group was a former federal officer who the onlooker forecast (perhaps naively) would be treated by fellow students "with perfect courtesy whenever the duties of college life bring them in contact with him." The opportunity that year to study Sanskrit, although one probably resisted by most students, provided a certain worldly cachet.[27] Basil Gildersleeve contributed to the school's esteem. The classics took on vibrancy in the classes of the professor of Greek, who recalled his time serving the Confederacy and at one battle losing a horse, pistol, and "my pocket Homer." Held in awe by students, the brilliant and darkly bearded Gildersleeve became a familiar figure walking (with a catch in his stride resulting from a war wound) the university campus.[28]

Peace breathed life into the Louisiana State Seminary of Learning and Military Academy. Established in 1859, near the middle of the state, the school was most often approached by the Red River. Many students reached their destination by steamboat, arriving at Alexandria, then crossing the river to the village of Pineville, and after piling their belongings on some conveyance, making the three-mile overland trip through a dense pine forest to the school. A three-storied building with touches of the fashionable Italianate style served as the university. William Sherman, the seminary's first superintendent (1859–1861), likened the edifice at the top of a hill to a "gorgeous palace." Now directed by David Boyd (formerly ancient languages professor), the Louisiana State Seminary of Learning and Military Academy reopened in its former military guise in October 1865. Four former Confederate officers and a priest composed the faculty.[29]

Extremely trying circumstances confronted Boyd, who filled the position of superintendent. At the outset fewer than ten students were present, but as the term wore on, their numbers grew, and over fifty cadets had enrolled by the first month of 1866. A lack of scientific equipment and library

Chapter 2

Figure 2.1. Louisiana State Seminary of Learning and Military Academy. This impressive structure served as the state university of Louisiana between 1859 and 1869. The diplomatic course of its president prevented the school, unlike some other Southern universities, from becoming part of the contentious Reconstruction debate. LSU University Archives Photograph Collection.

books formed but part of an expansive inventory of glaring needs. Among Boyd's first acts was issuing a public notice demanding the return of items taken earlier by local residents while the building had been vacant. He had taught at the school during William Sherman's tenure, and their friendship survived the differing paths they took during the war. After reading a grim summarization of the school's situation that Boyd forwarded him early in 1866, Sherman conceded the formidable problems but consoled "the greater your difficulties now, the greater will be your pride and satisfaction at some future day when they will be in the past." Boyd worked indefatigably, making ties with legislators at Baton Rouge, and promoted legislation creating what became a robust beneficiary program. (Beneficiaries were students whose college expenses were assumed by the state.) As 1866 drew to a close, the school could count over 150 students.[30]

The central building housed the barracks, library, and classrooms, and the mess hall represented the cadets' cosmos. They rose early, took breakfast, repaired to the parade ground for roll, and then marched to class. Drilling without weapons reflected the spare realities. Cadets understood demanding expectations regarding deportment and order in their living quarters. Providing another source of discontentment were a lack of beds—the young men slept on the floor. Under the direction of professor of Greek James Garnett, they delved with various degrees of enthusiasm into Horace and Xenophon. Garnett would fondly recall the cadets who posed few discipline problems and remembered, "I could have taught them some Greek if I had been there longer."[31]

An unmistakable sense of the school's remoteness emerged in this early formative period. Pineville was at best a village, and Alexandria, not much more. Over three hundred miles separated the seminary from New Orleans and a similarly imposing distance from the school's future home at Baton Rouge. Recalling his brief time at the isolated school, Professor Garnett allowed, "There were no distractions," and he described the setting as "intolerably dull."[32] Samuel H. Lockett settled in as commandant in the spring of 1867. He quickly gained a favorable impression of his fellow teachers, whom Lockett complimented as "hard students" who "study a good deal to be in fashion."[33] His colleagues' scholarly habits may have had less to do with dedication than a lack of alternatives. Early in 1867, Raphael Semmes became the professor of naval philosophy and English literature. "We know something of the difficulties of coming and settling in the Pine Woods," David Boyd wrote the Confederate naval hero. The superintendent understandably promoted "hops" for students and faculty. Women from Alexandria and the vicinity arrived for a much-anticipated dance one April evening that year. After a break for a late-night meal at the mess hall, the dancing resumed, carrying over until dawn.[34]

The status of the Louisiana State Seminary of Learning and Military Academy remained precarious. Among developing obstacles in 1867 was the relationship with military authorities who assumed supervising authority with the passage of the First Reconstruction Act. Louisiana belonged to the Fifth Military District, commanded by General Phillip Sheridan, a man of strong Republican convictions. The former Union cavalry general's refusal to grant Superintendent Boyd's request to issue uniforms and guns to cadets for drilling provided a running conflict. At a higher level, the prospect of the United States Army assuming direction of the seminary became a topic of worry. Commandant Samuel Lockett wrote doubtfully of the chances to his wife that spring: "But this being a military academy may possibly attract their attention." General Sheridan had pursued a vigorous policy of removing public officials he associated with opposing the letter or spirit of Reconstruction change.[35] Although Raphael Semmes taught at the seminary for only a couple of months in 1867, the *Alabama*'s commander continued to correspond with David Boyd after leaving the school. He feared a Republican coup d'état and "hungry Yankee schoolmasters" replacing the current faculty. Semmes hoped the "military rascals" would leave the seminary alone, but posed, "Sheridan is such an ass, that there is no telling what he may do."[36]

It was a tenuous situation, and President Boyd tread carefully, wary of the consequences for the seminary and hopeful the school could operate above the fray generated by political differences. Contributing to that possibility was the removed location of the seminary from Baton Rouge and New Orleans and the maw of Reconstruction conflict. Boyd was a resolute Democrat and privately reviled Republicans, but he also understood as the seminary's president the necessity of working with the political opposition.

Various problems nevertheless threatened in 1867 to overwhelm the school. Financial difficulties endangered its solvency. Following the establishment of military oversight, officials temporarily refused to honor school warrants, plunging affairs into deep uncertainty. Yellow fever spread to the area, driving away students and leading to strict quarantine measures. Late in the year Boyd wrote to a New Orleans acquaintance from his distant outpost of hopes that the number of cadets would increase, although "the fever is still in this country and it wd seem as if it has a notion of making this neck of the woods its permanent house."[37]

The university came in for a public raking in the summer of 1867 when an observer adopting the pseudonym "Loyalist" authored a series of letters published in the *New Orleans Republican*. He portrayed Louisiana's state university as an unreconstructed Confederate bastion. Rather than reflecting "the new order of ideas," the school represented a "stronghold of rebel spite and resistance." "Loyalist" trained fire on a faculty composed of former Confederate officers, and Raphael Semmes's previous departure from the school did not prevent "Loyalist" from labeling the former naval commander a "pirate."[38] Neither was the school at Pineville, according to him, a place of moral probity. The university's critic made allusions to the hops, women spending the night on the premises, and some local females "fighting for the privilege of being regarded as the favorites."[39] Angered by the attack that he blamed in part on the *New Orleans Republican*'s editor, Boyd privately expressed a desire to physically retaliate. "But if I caned the scoundrel now," the supervisor expressed to a sympathetic Democrat, "up goes the seminary."[40]

General Winfield S. Hancock replaced Phillip Sheridan later in 1867 as Fifth Military District commander, and Boyd welcomed the arrival of the less partisan general. The seminary's superintendent anticipated Hancock would administer "conservatively" and spare the school "Radical interference." Despite extreme trials between 1865 and 1868—yellow fever, financial distress, political threats—enrollment continued to increase at the Louisiana State Seminary of Learning and Military Academy.[41]

No school emerged from the war as physically sound as the University of Georgia. Andrew Lipscomb, a man long associated with the nation's first chartered state university and now the chancellor, declared, "We have sustained no material losses in the property upon the campus."[42] Among the undisturbed campus structures was the chapel, where, on November 12, 1865, Brigadier General Davis Tillson of the Freedmen's Bureau explained to assembled freedpeople that with emancipation came responsibilities. Five days into 1866, education resumed on the Athens campus with somewhere approaching eighty students. Rather than residing on campus, a number of students initially lived in private residences with families, which one observer optimistically concluded meant that "they are unconsciously restrained from every act of impropriety."[43] Students pursued academic tasks in a library room described as "delightful"; the book arrangement, "admirable"; and the volumes' "state of preservation, perfect." Chancellor Lipscomb was an early advocate of deviating from the straitjacket classical curriculum. A new emphasis on a civil engineering curriculum reflected that vision. Making the institution more accessible were Georgia legislators who passed a statute assuming the tuition of maimed (presumably ex-Confederate) soldiers.[44]

Adjusting from a soldiering life to that of a student came harder for some than others. Nathaniel E. Harris enrolled in the fall of 1867. Harris later recalled his first year as one of "tribulation" because he had "mingled in great armies" and in the balance of things underestimated academic demands.[45] For all students, both those with or without war experience, there was a certain bracing indoctrination to new circumstances. Walter B. Hill was too young to serve in the conflict but by 1868 was of college age. Making the trip by railroad from Macon, Hill reached Athens on January 14. Examinations in Greek, Latin, and mathematics emphatically introduced him to academic life the next morning, and further orientation to the rigors ahead were provided in successive days by a clanking sunrise waking bell, followed by early morning prayer, and an hour-long recitation—all before breakfast. University of Georgia students holding the badge of the Phi Kappa and the Demosthenian societies frequently engaged in debate. A certain rivalry did not prevent

Chapter 2

Walter Hill, a Demosthenian, from pronouncing a Phi Kappa affiliate as the school's finest declaimer, who had recently in debate "tore all the shingles off the hall." Hill and other students confronted considerable academic challenges. They took different positions in the spring of 1868 when asked, in composition form, to argue whether Julius Caesar's assassination was justified. And here, too, students engaged in extracurricular pursuits—that included baseball, several teams formed, and soon the "Dixie Club" exerted its dominance. Almost three hundred young men (the number included about 130 attending an attached high school) were by 1868 enrolled at the University of Georgia.[46]

Events surrounding commencement exercises in the summer of 1867 would seriously jeopardize the successful relaunching of the university. Students and a public audience gathered for the ceremony. One of the speakers, Albert H. Cox, a student known for his extreme partisanship, faulted Republicanism and the state's Civil War governor, Joseph E. Brown, who had recently broken ranks with most state Democrats by recommending cooperation with Congressional Reconstruction. Indirectly more than directly, but nevertheless unmistakably, Cox took issue with the subordination imposed by what he portrayed as a victimized South. At Cox's conclusion, the crowd broke into applause, and a band struck up "Dixie." The fallout was immediate. General John Pope presided over the Third Military District in Atlanta, and he learned quickly of the commencement oratory. Much like General Phillip Sheridan in Louisiana, Pope was a committed Republican. He turned his ire on the university for what he interpreted as a defiant Rebel manifesto. Pope blamed in part Benjamin H. Hill, who belonged to the board of trustees. A former member of the Confederate Congress and present law professor at the university, Hill was an outspoken Democrat. On the night before commencement, Hill passionately presented the case for Southern defiance in a speech delivered at Athens. General Pope accused Hill of using commencement as a forum to attack Congressional Reconstruction. He moved to punish the university by cutting off the $8,000 state stipend to the school. Pope described to Secretary of War Ulysses S. Grant the University of Georgia as a "rebel Institution."

Andrew Lipscomb well understood what the loss of revenue would mean to a school attempting to regain academic traction. The deeply worried chancellor traveled to Atlanta and to General Pope repentantly plead the university's case. Only through the intervention of Grant and President Andrew Johnson were matters smoothed over and the flow of state money assured. In the aftermath of the political tempest that gained statewide attention, the board of trustees banned any references to political subjects in future commencement exercises. Disaster had narrowly been averted and a lesson learned.[47]

The trouble at Athens reflected an empathy for the Confederacy that existed at Southern universities. Four of the five professors at the Louisiana State Seminary of Learning and Military Academy were former Confederate officers. Although Senator Carl Schurz did not visit the school on his fact-finding mission for President Andrew Johnson in the summer of 1865, he noted critically the faculty's top-heavy Confederate composition. Little had changed two years later when Raphael Semmes briefly joined the teaching corps. His colleagues called on him to regale them with accounts of the *Alabama*'s exploits. Any number of situations pointed to continued sectional loyalties. Charles Phillips, professor of mathematics at the University of North Carolina, was contemplating authoring some textbooks. Well aware that doing so might require approaching Northern publishing companies, Phillips admitted a hesitancy to associate even in a business capacity "with the victorious." When Jefferson Davis was freed from Fort Monroe in 1867, the Jefferson and Washington societies at the University of Virginia passed joint resolutions expressing their approval. An already fermenting, lost-cause school of thought did not lack for devotees.[48]

A vastly different environment existed at East Tennessee University. At the war's outset, campus sentiment leaned toward the Confederacy, and students often joined Southern armies. Even so, eastern Tennessee was one of the most Unionist regions in the South, and developments at the school during and after the war reflected as much. In 1862 the Confederate-leaning university president resigned, and East Tennessee University soon closed. As the war ended, Thomas W. Humes, a recognized secessionist opponent who lived in Knoxville, became president.

Humes confronted a supremely elemental challenge: to rebuild the shambles of a university. Such was the extent of the war's damage to the campus that when the school reopened in March 1866, professors convened classes at the nearby Asylum for the Deaf and Dumb. The university could at least draw from a reservoir of local good will. Marking the end of that session in July at the Knox County courthouse, nineteen students declaimed, and the attending audience exceeded the number of seats available. When classes resumed on what was referred to as College Hill later that year, Thomas C. Karns was one of the students. He later recalled efforts to salvage part of "the wreck of the war."[49] Removing breastworks around the buildings bluntly framed the extraordinary times. A preparatory program for several years carried an

— 43 —

exceedingly fiscally strapped school, and by 1867 some one hundred students were circulating on the gradually recovering campus. The Philomathesian and the Chi Delta literary societies provided a measure of increasing vitality. On the evening of April 10, 1868, a capacity crowd witnessed a "very spirited" debate between representatives of the societies. Competition of another type, on the baseball field, also pointed to coming stability. On June 17, visiting nearby Louisville, the "University Nine" defeated the "Hunki Gory" club 55 to 25 in a high-scoring affair. A true freshman class (only eleven belonged) was established in the year of Ulysses Grant's election. East Tennessee University remained a functioning but limited institution. Commencement week, June 1869, offered a telling commentary. Declamations and public examinations marked the occasion, but no diplomas were extended to graduates. Up to that point, four years after the war's last shots had sounded, not a single student had graduated from the school.[50]

If work of a physical scaffolding nature proceeded slowly, the political arc of the university shifted more dramatically. In the summer of 1866, Tennessee became the first Southern state to rejoin the Union when the legislature ratified the Fourteenth Amendment. In Governor William "Parson" Brownlow, Thomas Humes found a man of like-minded political convictions who shared a determination to rejuvenate East Tennessee University. Addressing the state legislature shortly after his election in 1865, Brownlow insisted on revitalizing the "time-honored Institution." The Republican executive lamented the school had "been almost destroyed by the Federal Army." Brownlow also realized that rebuilding demanded more than brick and mortar. The governor regretted the presence of "rebels" on the board of trustees and advised replacing them with "loyal men."[51] An increasingly Unionist- and Republican-dominated board took form between 1865 and 1868. So did a small but unquestionably loyal faculty. Frederic W. Allen, Oberlin-educated, joined the faculty in 1866. Allen's connections to the leading abolitionist school in the country may have recommended him to a Unionist-controlled board of trustees eager to repudiate the former Confederate regime. It was a strikingly different political environment than that at Athens or Oxford. At the University of Georgia, trustees offered a political science/history professorship to Alexander Stephens, and grateful University of Mississippi trustees granted free tuition to the son of the lawyer who had pro bono defended Jefferson Davis against treason charges. Thomas Humes paid deference to a far different man. He held Abraham Lincoln in high esteem. As 1866 ended, before the state teachers' association at Nashville, the school's president approvingly spoke of "a new era." Humes's past and present political positions, and the wisdom of portraying East Tennessee University as a school loyal to the United States government, T. R. C. Hutton writes in his recent history of the school, eventually resulted in significant dividends.[52]

In the last month of 1866, just days before the University of Georgia reopened, the *Southern Banner* in Athens declared that "we now need, more than ever, the advantages of a fully developed University." That statement held no relevance for the vast majority of Georgians, since the status of a removed state university had absolutely no application to their lives. The connection was equally tenuous in other states between residents and some dimly perceived and distant academic institution. An infinitesimally small number of young men had before the war attended universities and an even fewer enrolled in the immediate years following the conflict.[53] Yet, in the present, and resoundingly for the future, providing higher education opportunities was highly significant. Reestablishing these state universities was accomplished despite considerable adversity. Among those visiting the ex-Confederacy in the immediate postwar period was John T. Trowbridge. The lack of students and financial backing for the university struck the author as he was traveling widely in the South and recording his impressions as he went. Writing from Columbia, Trowbridge decided, "South Carolina College is a striking illustration of the effect the war has had upon the institutions of learning at the South."[54] Even so, despair and empty classrooms yielded to optimism and enrollment. When Professor Porter Alexander joined the faculty at Columbia, an acquaintance forecast the small number of students, about fifty, would soon double. He predicted correctly. Such was the influx of young men in 1866 at the University of Mississippi that the board of trustees appointed two new professors. Governor William Sharkey acted to have $6,000 provided for the Mississippi school, sometimes referred to as Oxford University, and encouraged by Governor J. Madison Wells, the legislature likewise financially jump-started the Louisiana State Seminary of Learning and Military Academy. In the fall of 1867, Governor William Brownlow predicated his appeal for appropriations to East Tennessee University on the Republicans' status as a "party of progress." The University of Virginia, where several hundred students were attending by 1868, flourished like no other. Alexander Galt completed a marble statue of Thomas Jefferson shortly before the war began. And fittingly, as a new era in the institution's life began, the sculpture of the school's founder was ceremoniously dedicated during commencement in 1868.[55]

An overview of the path of higher education between 1865 and 1868 reveals a jagged but encouraging line. State universities in Georgia, Mississippi, and Virginia by most any measurement pointed to a hearty revival. More imposing challenges at the Louisiana Seminary for Learning and Military Academy did not prevent significant progress, and in South Carolina, where a broad-based university replaced the college, the future seemed favorable. The status of East Tennessee University is better described in terms of resiliency than rapid recovery. Only at the University of North Carolina did adversity dominate. The episodic outbreaks of partisan-inspired controversy at the state universities in Georgia and Louisiana offered ominous signposts, but they did not rewrite or even seriously revise a positive narrative. Chancellor Andrew Lipscomb pronounced the University of Georgia on a path to full recovery, having overcome "the ravages of the times."[56] And in degrees so it was generally elsewhere. In his memoirs, Joseph LeConte recalled directing a science course without sufficient materials and volunteered that what the students took from the course must have been "meager." But he also admitted that some students assured him otherwise. At the South Carolina university, as with other schools, the transition from wartime to peace was fitful rather than fluid, but progress, startling at some universities, foretold an academic renaissance.[57]

Chapter 3

Faltering Renaissance

On October 1, 1867, as the fall term at the University of Virginia began, several hundred students milling about what was traditionally referred to as the "Lawn," fronting the Rotunda, presented an accurate picture of a resurgent institution. One observer noted the young men wearing "big legged breeches," complemented by a sack coat and often a broad-brimmed hat. Most were Virginians, but he identified the next highest number of matriculates as Alabamians.[1] With no state university to attend, young men from Alabama figured disproportionately in the student population at the Charlottesville school and elsewhere. In that same year, at the University of Mississippi, one out of every ten students was an Alabamian. F. M. Grace, a resident of Elyton, Alabama, joined the faculty in 1868 at a slowly recovering East Tennessee University. The Rhetoric and English literature professor and a contingent of enrolling students from the state were large enough to become known on campus as the "Alabamians." The number of young men in 1868 from Alabama at the University of North Carolina exceeded that of all other out-of-state students combined. At the University of Mississippi, matriculates came from Selma, Florence, Marion, even Tuscaloosa itself. And they did so also at private institutions, like Washington College (later Washington and Lee University) in Lexington, Virginia, where a steady stream of young men from outposts such as Eufaula, Florence, Lafayette, and again, Tuscaloosa enrolled. After federal troops burned down part of the University of the South, the school at Sewanee, Tennessee, reopened in 1868. More Alabamians were soon walking the campus than were sons of Tennessee.[2]

That the exodus would slow considerably once the University of Alabama reconvened composed the expectation. The resumption of education at the school seemed within sight by the summer of 1868, when Governor

Robert Patton addressed the university's status. The man who had viewed the building in an earlier construction stage hailed an imminent reopening. Explaining the recent attendance of young men to other schools in terms of necessity, Patton promised the restored university would provide the "amplest facilities for acquiring a finished education."[3] A certain elemental state pride drove that sentiment. The *Montgomery Mail* agreed the time was approaching when "there shall be no longer a necessity for our young men to go out of state in order to obtain the highest education advantages."[4]

Governor Patton forecast the university reopening for October. That seemed a reasonable prognostication because, after a year and a half of steady labor, the impressive structure was approaching completion. Those making their way to the campus well past the town's perimeter came away with the impression that life would soon be restored. The edifice that would essentially constitute the University of Alabama rose three (four, at one point) floors. On

Figure 3.1. The University of Alabama's main building in 1869. Postwar campus construction at the University of Alabama conformed to a military design. Later named Woods Hall, the structure erected between 1867 and 1868 essentially became the University of Alabama. Cadets attended class, drilled, dined, slept, and led their lives as students within its walls. Even the school's enemies, of which there were many, conceded the building's functional assets. University of Alabama Libraries Special Collections.

approach one beheld tiered galleries or corridors, defined by iron railings and staggered iron columns, looking out on an open court. Classrooms and science laboratories, a chapel, library, space for literary societies, and the mess hall largely composed the first level. Accommodations for some 188 students dominated the second and third floors. The honey-combed rooms, spacious with high ceilings, opened onto the galleries. Above the central building, but not the east and west wings, was a shorter fourth floor reserved to care for the sick or incapacitated. A tin roof crowned the structure. As the work neared an end, James Murfee reiterated the desirability of removing the ruins in front of the building and, ever practical, advised enclosing a garden behind the mess hall and cultivating winter turnips. Anticipating the fall reopening, the *Independent Monitor* in Tuscaloosa forecast, "We hope the University will now begin a career of uninterrupted prosperity."[5]

Assembling a faculty and determining a president became relevant concerns. The wartime faculty's relationship with the university expired in July 1865. Various names were projected to assume professorships and that of Henry Tutwiler gained favorable mention as president. A graduate of the University of Virginia, his experiences as a student included dining on various occasions at Monticello as a guest of Thomas Jefferson. Back in 1831, when the University of Alabama opened, Tutwiler became the ancient languages professor, and he remained for seven years on the faculty. He was most known, however, for founding the Greene Springs School in the 1840s at Havana, a Black Belt hamlet about twenty miles south of Tuscaloosa, where Tutwiler had attracted much praise for presiding and teaching at the boys school, which grew in repute.[6]

Among those taking a special interest in the faculty's composition was Elisha Peck, the local Republican, who recently had presided over the constitutional convention. In February 1868, he had received a letter from E. F. Bouchello, a resident of Pickensville in nearby Pickens County. Bouchello allowed that the war had left him in a bad financial way and struggling to support a large family. The man who identified himself as a Republican asked Peck to support his candidacy for the professor of chemistry and natural philosophy. Throughout Reconstruction, across the South, men rendered unpopular by their Republican loyalties often paid an economic price. E. F. Bouchello offers an example. Using for leverage both his political convictions and his resulting employment needs, Bouchello's was a plea from one Republican to another. The Republican-authored state constitution, pending ratification until the summer of 1868, established a board of education, and its members would make hiring decisions. Peck replied to Bouchello that he hoped the board would remove the existing faculty and appoint an entirely new set of professors. The Tuscaloosa Republican worried about the installment of unrepentant former Confederates who sympathized with the Southern cause. Peck favored turning to professors who repudiated secession and by way of extension endorsed changes associated with Reconstruction. He envisioned a faculty composed of "good loyal men" and assured Bouchello that he would welcome him becoming a professor there.[7]

Other Republicans shared those concerns. Universities in the South had often been ideological bulwarks of support for slavery and Southern sovereignty; none more so than South Carolina College under the presidency of Thomas Cooper, between 1821 and 1834, and later Augustus Baldwin Longstreet, who also used the executive's forum to make the case for states' rights and slavery. In his groundbreaking study, Alfred Brophy has pointed to the buttressing foundation Southern schools provided the peculiar institution and how faculty by word and deed contributed to sectional polarization. Although questions regarding the end of slavery and the Union's indivisibility had been settled, Republicans feared a pseudo-Confederate presence in the halls of academia. Yesterday's racial determinist and secessionist was quite conceivably today's blistering Democrat, unreconciled to what was referred to as "the new order of things." Elisha Peck's reference to "loyal" men unmistakably inferred avoiding "disloyal" individuals. Those falling into the latter category were opponents of the Congressional Reconstruction framework and the Fourteenth Amendment. At the University of Alabama, where the thinking of many of the state's future leaders would be shaped, expunging all residual Confederate empathy and resistance to a biracial democracy seemed imperative to men of Peck's view.[8]

E. F. Bouchello was not the only man interested in joining the faculty who took into account the political complexion of those making the hiring decisions. Sidney Lanier, educated at Oglethorpe University in Georgia and beginning to establish a reputation as a poet, was living in Montgomery and considered seeking a faculty position. Yet he was circumspect about what lay ahead given the changing of the state's political guard and how that might compromise any decisions of the board of education concerning the faculty's composition. Lanier wrote his father in May of the possibility that any selections made by the board of trustees might be quickly reversed by those representing the new regime. If the trustees did settle on a faculty, Lanier declared, "I would not despair of getting a chair."[9]

At least temporarily, decisions regarding the faculty lay as they always had with the school's board of trustees. When the trustees met intermittingly in the spring and summer of 1868, they considered a wide variety of questions bearing on the university, including the faculty's composition. At Montgomery, on June 12, the board settled on Henry Tutwiler as president. An Alabamian, respected as an educator and administrator and with university ties, Tutwiler was a natural choice, but whether he would accept was in doubt, and in case he did not, they agreed to offer the office to William Wyman, who had taught at the university since 1852 as a tutor and then ancient languages professor. Tutwiler did decline, and the presidency devolved to Wyman. The trustees elected a faculty that included Landon Garland (natural philosophy and astronomy), A. Q. Thornton (modern languages), and John H. Forney (mathematics). James Murfee was called upon to resume the commandant duties he had carried out during the war. Each of these men was of Southern extraction, and several had previously taught at the university. The academic year, traditionally split into two terms, began in October, and the trustees projected that month for reopening.

Since the war's end the university's resumption had been contingent on the obvious lack of a physical classroom building and living quarters for students. These obstacles no longer existed for the building inspired by James Murfee and erected by George Figh's laboring force stood fortress-like and waiting. And presumably, some students beginning their college education, and others who had left Alabama in the absence of a state university, would enroll at the reincarnated school. These circumstances seemingly foretold the university resuming its constitutional mission as a "seminary of learning" after four years of dormancy.[10]

As it was, however, the interplay of Reconstruction developments and higher education thrust the university into the political realm and sharply detoured the projected resurrection. An understanding of the following evolution or perhaps devolution at the university requires a contextual appreciation of what transpired in Alabama in the first half of 1868. Following the constitution's rejection in February of that year, the timetable for the state resuming its place in the Union remained unsure. In March, in response to what had occurred in Alabama, the Republican-controlled Congress passed the Fourth Military Reconstruction Act. The legislation provided that the approval of a majority of voters simply *participating* in a constitutional referendum was sufficient for ratifying a proposed state constitution. The last of the Reconstruction Acts had profound significance for Alabama. Several months later, in June 1868, after considerable debate in Congress as to whether the law could be retroactively applied to Alabama, the state was readmitted.

Chapter 3

Since Democrats had concentrated on denying the proposed constitution's ratification and had not, unlike state Republicans, nominated a ticket, Alabama's return confirmed Republicans' total direction of state government. William Hugh Smith, a Randolph County Unionist, was inaugurated in July 1868 at the Montgomery capitol, and his installment marked the triumph of Republicanism. Republicans overwhelmingly controlled the legislature, all high-ranking state officials belonged to the party, as were the three individuals sitting on the state supreme court, which included Elisha Peck. The legislature convened in July and immediately ratified the Fourteenth Amendment.

The ramifications of Republican domination in Alabama held enormous consequences for education. Fundamental to the party's vision in the South was extending learning opportunities to both races, and Republican-authored state constitutions in the region established public school systems. Alabama's constitution made education available for those between the ages of five and twenty-one regardless of race. Administering the system was vested in the previously mentioned board of education, created by the state constitution. Twelve elected members (two from each congressional district) composed the board. A superintendent of education, also elected, presided over the board.[11]

Noah B. Cloud became the superintendent of education. Cloud had moved from South Carolina in 1838, settled near Tuskegee in Macon County, and began growing cotton. He became prominently involved in reforming cotton's cultivation, emphasizing a scientific approach, and in 1853 established *The American Cotton Planter*, a journal devoted to advanced farming methodology. A former Whig and a Unionist, Cloud opposed secession but seems to have briefly served the Confederacy as a surgeon. He later characterized secession as the tragic triumph of shortsighted and "rash" Southern elements.[12] Following the war, Cloud joined the Republican Party and, with Alabama's reinstatement in 1868, became superintendent of education. Between 1868 and 1870, during the William Hugh Smith administration, Cloud and the board of education oversaw a crusade to spread learning. Teachers began instructing white and Black children, often in rural, wooden one-room schoolhouses, invariably in segregated arrangements. Financial mismanagement, poor administrative oversight, and a lack of necessary resources partly accounted for an uneven performance. The virulent opposition among some whites to educating ex-slaves further impeded progress. But what early on raised controversy involved the board of education's oversight of the University of Alabama.[13]

The completion of the university building generally coincided with Republicans assuming direction of the state, and the school's revival became a significant subject of concern for the board of education. Superintendent Cloud found much fault in the institution's former guise as a training ground for young men to raise arms against the United States, and he somewhat callously represented its destruction as "the natural fruits of secession."[14] Even so, Cloud took a keen interest in the university, and in the summer of 1868, the superintendent urged the importance of resuming operation at "the earliest practicable moment."[15]

Doing so necessitated settling on a faculty. On the surface, at least ostensibly, a professorial corps was already in place. The board of trustees had in June elected a faculty and a president. The next month the situation dramatically changed when Republicans came to power. Making policy for the school, formerly reposed in the board of trustees, now a defunct body, shifted to the board of education. Its members were referred to as the "board of regents" when conducting business concerning the state university. (I will use the term "regents" more often than "trustees.") A critical function vested in the regents involved hiring the faculty and president. The board of education, under the aegis of a Republican administration, would meet in July for the first time. Only weeks earlier, the board of trustees had elected William Wyman as president and selected three professors and a commandant, but at the university, the future of Landon Garland, John Forney, A. Q. Thornton, and James Murfee lay in extreme jeopardy. These were Southern men and identified with the Democratic Party. The tenure of the faculty-elect, simply put, now rested with Republicans acting in their capacity as regents.[16]

Among the most influential men sitting on the board of education was Gustavus Adolphus Smith. The man presumably named for the noted Swedish king would figure prominently in the university's present and future. He previously resided in Illinois and enjoyed success as a carriage manufacturer. When the war began, Smith was instrumental in raising the Thirty-Fifth Illinois Infantry, and early in 1862 at the Battle of Pea Ridge in Arkansas, he suffered wounds that ended his active participation for the war's duration. But Smith remained in the army in various capacities and was eventually brevetted brigadier general. Before the war, Smith spent considerable time in the Southern states, conducting business relating to his carriage enterprise, and possibly the familiarity he gained prompted the family's relocation to the South. At any rate, by 1867, he and his family settled at Courtland, near Huntsville. His was the unswerving perspective of a mainline Republican. At one point, the man who had previously campaigned for Abraham Lincoln's reelection described educating Alabama freedpeople as an achievement rivaling the laying of the Atlantic cable and completing the transcontinental railroad. On the Pea Ridge battlefield, Smith fought valiantly, carrying the fight to the enemy, even as a horse was shot from under him. The Illinois Republican brought similar resolve to Alabama. As with the war, whose outcome was uncertain for a long time, he realized the changes associated with Reconstruction hung in the balance. And now in a South positioned at a pivotal crossroads, confronting a different type of foe, Gustavus Adolphus Smith understood that lofty Republican words and egalitarian principles meant little standing on their own. This was a man who held definite ideas as to who should and, equally critical, who should not belong to the University of Alabama faculty.[17]

Although twelve men apparently composed the board of education, not all regularly attended meetings, and some never did. What became clear, despite their mutual Republicanism, were differences among the regents regarding university policy. A Northern/Southern divide became clear in July 1868 when the board of education convened in Montgomery. Several men shared Gustavus Adolphus Smith's frame of reference. They had come south since the war. Several of them, and most prominently Smith, favored replacing the recently elected faculty. As matters stood, if the professors anointed

FIGURE 3.2. Gustavus Adolphus Smith, influential member of the board of education. A former Federal Army officer and man of resolute Republican convictions, Smith worked to ensure the revived state university did not compromise questions settled by the war. He was the most powerful of regents and played a major role in the battle for the University of Alabama. Wikipedia, "Gustavus Adolphus Smith," accessed August 1, 2023.

by the former board of trustees took their chairs, they feared a defiant and unreconstructed influence at the university. This faction considered it imperative to install men of unquestioned loyalty to the United States who repudiated secession and endorsed a remade South. It was implicitly understood that these individuals would be drawn from Republican ranks. Other regents had spent their lives in the South, and they took a different perspective. They opposed replacing the sitting faculty. Jesse H. Booth, William H. Clayton, and Thomas F. Jackson, long residents of Alabama, supported retaining the professors chosen previously by the board of trustees. Notions of unreconstructed Democrats presiding as professors did not haunt them. They considered far more potentially harmful putting in place a faculty with no connections to or understanding of the state. Booth, Clayton, and Jackson worried Alabamians would dismiss the school as a Radical and Northern institution and refuse to send their sons there.

Conflict flared openly as the board of education deliberated in the consulting room of the state supreme court at the capital. Noah Cloud presided. Late on the morning of August 1, William Wyman, university president and an ex officio board member, outlined the present status of the university. Wyman's presentation included listing the professors chosen by the previous board of trustees. By way of rebuke, Gustavus Adolphus Smith motioned that all the faculty positions be declared vacant and new elections held to fill each chair. His gambit anticipated replacing the existing professors. Several days later, on August 5, Smith's motion came to a vote. Jesse Booth objected to a second round of elections. None of the faculty, the Autauga County Republican protested, had given cause for removal. Booth described them as men who would attract students, and he conversely warned that appointing outsiders threatened discrediting the institution, diminishing enrollment, and stunting the university's growth. Booth laid out what he considered a likely scenario—professors presiding in virtual idleness for lack of students. Better than elevating unknown outsiders, the regent posed facetiously, was establishing a committee for laying torch to the new building. He warned against a course that would raise "a howl of indignation." Thomas Jackson and William Clayton agreed with him. The regents voted five to three in favor of vacating the offices. The board then selected a new faculty and president. Its members settled on Wyman as president, in effect reelecting him, and also endorsed the previous judgement of the board of trustees by reappointing John Forney to the faculty. Otherwise, however, they fundamentally reshaped the faculty, electing David Humphreys (ancient languages), Joseph M. Geary (mathematics), Hampton Whitfield (rhetoric and oratory), and Thomas M. Goodfellow (commandant). Three of the men, Humphreys, Geary, and Goodfellow, had moved to Alabama from the North since the war and participated actively with the Republican Party.[18]

Removing most of the faculty selected earlier by the board of trustees deeply disillusioned Wyman, who regarded them as sound academicians and men who were familiar with the university and, as such, were crucial to a successful relaunching. He lacked confidence in the men appointed in their stead. On August 6, the day after his election as president, Wyman resigned in protest. Hampton Whitfield, another Tuscaloosa resident, also apparently considered the course of action high-handed and declined to join the faculty. Regents Jesse Booth and Thomas Jackson, also far from reconciled, made plain their objections by drafting a short note to Noah Cloud opposing a faculty "unknown to the people." Restating their strong reservations against repudiating the sitting professors, Booth and Jackson labeled the course "unjust, unwise and tyrannical." Registering these objections had no practical effect. Wyman's resignation necessitated electing a president, and the regents did so several days later. They turned to Arad S. Lakin. He had attracted support for the office the previous day, when Wyman had been elected. A man with Northern antecedents who came to Alabama soon after the war as a missionary of the Methodist Episcopal Church, Lakin was a committed Republican.[19]

What had transpired immediately attracted scathing public notice. The unspooling Democratic version of events prominently featured partisan Republican regents bestowing the undeserved title of professor on incompetent fellow Radicals. Arad Lakin attracted the most fire. The *Montgomery Advertiser* condemned him for "preaching politics to the negroes ever since he squatted in Alabama."[20] Lakin had lived several years in Huntsville. The Huntsville *Democrat* recalled the resented Republican had contributed much "to poison the minds of negroes towards their former owners" and allowed Blacks to visit his family home "on terms of perfect social familiarity." Thomas Goodfellow, elected commandant, had also moved to Huntsville after the war and took a position with the Freedmen's Bureau. The biography of the former chaplain of the 101st Colored Infantry presented by a Democratic press was not intended to inculcate favor. Goodfellow's loyalties to the party of Lincoln accounted for his election as clerk of the recently convened state house of representatives. The Huntsville *Democrat* denounced him as "devoid of literary qualifications and unable to write good English,"[21] and when queried about his familiarity with military tactics, the *Montgomery Mail* added the "seedy, long-whiskered person" replied that he knew nothing but was prepared to learn.[22] Neither did the apparent credentials of David Humphreys inspire confidence. The man entrusted with conveying the subjects of Greek and Latin was identified as a former Union soldier and the resented Republican editor of the *Decatur Republican*. He became professor by default after reputedly losing elections for clerk, enrolling clerk, and engrossing clerk of the recently convened, overwhelmingly Republican legislature. Denied these sinecures, according to the *Montgomery Mail*, the office-hungry Northern ex-patriate sought the doorkeeper post but was defeated by a Black man. The *Mail* declared, "The University had as well close its doors. No gentleman will send his sons to be educated by knaves and fools."[23] William Wyman returned to Tuscaloosa and soon composed a public letter taking issue with what had transpired at Montgomery. Explaining his resignation, Wyman predicted the faculty's installment insured the university's failure. With the exception of John Forney and Hampton Whitfield, he described the slate of professors as either "unknown to our people" or "notoriously incompetent."[24]

This tone reflected a quickly forming storyline regarding the university's new guard. One school of thought emphasized that the university needed the continuity provided by the faculty originally chosen by the former board of trustees. Those men had previously taught at the school, or, at least as Southerners, conveyed to Alabamians an essential familiarity and confidence. Extending that logic led to the inverse conclusion that bringing in unknown individuals and Northerners foretold a harmful and badly timed disruption. The regents' course was also denounced as an act of partisanship crassly serving Republicanism and individual Republicans just as surely as it disserved the state. That a board of education composed totally of Republicans had placed like-minded men on the faculty with highly dubious academic standards emerged as the consensus. Viewed in this sense, what had transpired dovetailed with assumptions made by Alabama (and Southern) Democrats. That narrative featured aggrandizing Republicans opportunistically seizing places of power and influence. In these terms, the regents' actions were disseminated, received, and largely accepted. What had transpired in Montgomery, the citadel of Radical Republicanism, was perceived as a political hijacking of the state university. Democrats in the future decried the direction that Republican regents would take the University of Alabama. The first chapter was written at Montgomery in the summer of 1868.

Accepting the conspiratorial interpretation ignores a more nuanced understanding. The regents' decision to turn the presidency over to William Wyman calls into question imputed partisan motivations. He was a Democrat of the first order. So was John Forney, a former Confederate general, tapped by regents to instruct mathematics. And Hampton Whitfield, although briefly associated with the *Reconstructionist* in Tuscaloosa, vacillated politically and maintained social connections with local Democrats. His refusal to accept the professorship reflected that maverick quality. It is also noteworthy that Wyman did not in his public letter attribute political motives to the regents. Instead, he faulted them for selecting men who lacked a past connection to Alabama and/or academic standing. And, likewise, when regents Jesse Booth and Thomas Jackson protested the elections to Noah Cloud, their objections were not framed in terms of Republican favoritism.[25]

Some basic suppositions, for all the uncertainties regarding motivation, may be plausibly advanced. The faculty previously elected by the board of trustees did not reflect the postwar Alabama that a majority of the regents envisioned. Other men of Republican orientation seemed far more appropriate to a slight majority of the regents. Accepting that premise does not require conceding to the new regents' intention of installing a Republican faculty intent on indoctrinating students, but subjectively posed, it does reflect the regents' determination to guard against possibly providing a forum to men who reflected a hard Democratic obstructionist position. The board of education members who identified with Gustavus Adolphus Smith were men determined to honor an ideology. One person knowledgeable of the regents' thinking would soon advise a prospective candidate for the university presidency: "If they know that you believe that the *law* ought to make no distinction between white and black, it might make them more ready to vote for you." Elisha Peck had earlier expressed his feelings regarding the type of men he hoped would gain faculty appointments. Most of the regents thought likewise.[26]

Back in Tuscaloosa, most white residents agreed with Ryland Randolph. The editor referred to the "carpetbag-vultures" who viewed the professor posts as "spoils" and had hoisted on the university a set of "scoundrels." And in degrees they were sympathetic with his promise. In the *Independent Monitor*'s columns, Randolph further made known that if the latest version of faculty expected "to live quietly here, and draw their salaries form the sweating brows of the toiling tax-payers of Alabama, *we tell them, they are mistaken.*"[27]

It was against this backdrop that Arad Lakin made plans to visit Tuscaloosa. What type of reception he expected cannot be known, but the newly elected president was not an obtuse and naive outsider new to Alabama and therefore unaware of passionate opposition to men like him assuming positions of power. The fifty-eight-year-old man was previously identified with New York and Indiana but had lived in Huntsville since 1865. A minister in the Methodist Episcopal Church since the 1830s and a chaplain during the war for an Indiana regiment, Larkin spread the Methodist word as a missionary, which brought him to Alabama, where he settled with his wife and daughter in Huntsville. His life for a time followed the contours of the devoted missionary. Taking pains to wear jeans and a slouch hat common to plain folk, Lakin traveled hundreds of miles by mule, recalling his wanderings through the state's northern reaches "in my saddle; with the cares of my church resting on my mind." His proselytizing also took a partisan Republican turn. It was hard to distinguish where Lakin's efforts to make converts ended and those recruiting for the Republican Party began.[28] Well before becoming president of the University of Alabama, he came to an explicit understanding of the permeating revulsion to Republicanism and, even more precisely, the deep objections to men with his very credentials. Yet Lakin was rather strong willed, surely emboldened by a sense of Christian righteousness and possessed of an unshakable Republican resolve. This was the man who stated his determination to "put it [the university] upon its feet again." The first step involved gaining some familiarity with the school. He specifically intended to obtain the keys to the university, which was both practical and also a symbolic rite signaling the inauguration of a new administration. Former president William Wyman possessed the keys.[29]

Late in August, several weeks after being named president, directing a horse and buggy, Lakin set out from Huntsville for Tuscaloosa. Noah Cloud would meet him there. Both men must have been circumspect about their mission given the prevailing political climate. There was reason for concern. Installing an outspoken Northern Republican as president to many Democrats constituted a consummate act of Radicalism. Only three weeks had passed since the rightful (in Democrats' view) faculty had been displaced. Many Tuscaloosans read in agreement ex-president William Wyman's published letter. The presumption that erudite professors had been replaced by imposters, and Republican imposters at that, represented many white residents' version of the truth. Special antipathy was reserved for Arad Lakin, condemned as a Radical Republican and perceived as sharing with other outside "intruders" a thirst for power and personal reward. Although they might object, even protest vociferously, most remained peacefully inclined. Others were not. Some local men belonged to the Ku Klux Klan and, by definition, were violently predisposed. And others might not be affiliated with the nightriding order, but they were swept along by the wave of revulsion cresting in an election year. Most were young, highly territorial, and primed by their contempt for Republicanism.[30]

Chapter 3

On Thursday, August 27, Cloud and Lakin, arriving separately, reached Tuscaloosa and settled in at the Mansion House. They spent a comfortable night at the town's best-appointed hotel. The situation dramatically turned the next morning. As the president and superintendent moved about town, they noted posters and messages threatening those associated with Republicanism. The opposition had assembled. Some individuals, concealing themselves out of sight, screamed warnings and groaned, indulging in what Lakin interpreted as "unearthly sounds." The situation alarmed both men. Later that morning, arriving at the university, they met William Wyman. He realized the violent capacity of some local men and urged Lakin and Cloud to leave Tuscaloosa. Lakin needed no convincing. Making arrangements at the livery to get his horse and buggy, the university president exited on the Huntsville Road, which he had arrived on the previous day.[31]

Lakin may have exercised sound judgement. Wyman soon privately provided Governor William Smith with an account of what transpired. In a letter to the executive, he explained his decision against relinquishing the keys as precautionary rather than defiant. Wyman confided, "Mr. Lakin and the new professors would have been mobbed and driven from the town" by "some of our rash young men." That was quite possible. Whether the harsh reception had been orchestrated or was spontaneous is impossible to conclude.[32] It is suggestive that Ryland Randolph had publicized in the *Independent Monitor* the upcoming visit of Cloud and Lakin: "Let our boys be prepared to hoot them by day," he recommended, "and charivari [a loud and mocking serenade extended to unpopular elements] them by night." The editor urged "no quarter to the unconscionable scoundrels."[33]

Recent events profoundly shook Arad Lakin. In his study delineating widely diverging currents in Reconstruction Tuscaloosa, G. Ward Hubbs describes Lakin as an exceedingly devout man who was convinced the Deity had extended a spiritual and sustaining hand to him in personal hard times. Even so, Lakin concluded from his visit that there were limits to the Almighty's influence in the temporal world that was Alabama in 1868. The brief visit to Tuscaloosa, which was measured in hours, convinced him that serving as president seriously jeopardized his personal safety. Lakin determined to resign. Arad Lakin was a Northern man and as devout a Republican as he was a Christian, and that accounted for a presidential tenure described as eventful, controversial, and above all, short-lived. What transpired at Tuscaloosa would sensationally reemerge and gain national attention during the presidential election.[34]

Back in the spring in Chicago, Ulysses S. Grant had received the Republican nomination, and a man identified thoroughly with war paradoxically made political capital out of the party mantra "Let Us Have Peace." Horatio Seymour and Francis P. Blair represented the Democratic Party on a platform that denounced Congressional Reconstruction. Eight former Confederate states had been reinstated to the Union and would participate in the election. In those states Grant stood to run well given that freedmen across the region had flocked to the Republican Party. Democrats in Alabama and the South took their political enemy to task, and what most consistently defined their attacks were the underlying racial premises of Republicanism. Avidly and unapologetically, they championed white supremacy. An alchemy of forces, in no small part cultural, created a climate of unprecedented political volatility.

The intensity made for an eventful campaign in Tuscaloosa. That Grant's election would be highly detrimental to the country's interest was made clear when local Democrats met at the courthouse on July 25 and ratified the nomination of Seymour and Blair. An impressive display of solidarity took place two months later on Saturday, September 19. At around 10:00 a.m., men, women, and children, some perched on wagons, others lining up on foot, assembled in town at Glascock's Corner. The procession began up Main Street and continued out to the campus, where, in sight of the almost-finished university building, some eight hundred people enjoyed speakers who denounced Grant and castigated Radicalism. A month later, Republicans attempted to present a dissenting view. The election was but a week away, and feelings were intensifying by Wednesday, October 28, when several hundred Blacks and about twenty whites assembled at the courthouse. Charles Hays, who lived in nearby Greene County, had gained infamy among white folks by converting to Republicanism. In a second-story courthouse room, the notorious figure extolled the virtues of peace and connected that promise to Grant. As Hays continued, some contemptuous and intoxicated white men began taunting him, and when a shot rang out from downstairs, chaos temporarily ensued. That abruptly ended the Republican event.[35] The trouble formed but a part of campaign that took on a dark hue throughout Alabama. In the weeks before voting day, Klansmen and others violently disposed against Republicans beat, whipped, and shot freedmen in the name of white supremacy. The small town of Northport lay directly across the Black Warrior River from Tuscaloosa. A Freedmen's Bureau official regretted the brutal murder of a Black woman there and declared, "The plain truth is the Rebellion is flourishing in these parts."[36]

Chapter 3

In the meantime, Tuscaloosa had gained national exposure as a place of extreme political contention. In the aftermath of Noah Cloud and Arad Lakin's visit, Ryland Randolph reacted to it by denouncing Republicanism and Republicans in sulphureous terms. Within a week of the visit, on the *Independent Monitor*'s front page, he likened Cloud to a "pole cat," a prototype who surreptitiously met "negroes in dark dens and back streets" and drew from carpetbags "dirty election documents." Even more reprehensible was the scalawag, "the local leper of the community," betrayer of his native South, who was "possessed of the itch of office and the salt rheum of Radicalism." What indelibly distinguished the acidic diatribe and fueled its notoriety was the inclusion of a woodcut commemorating Cloud and Lakin's visit. The woodcut depicted two individuals hanging from a tree. The crude likeness

FIGURE 3.3. Newspaper cartoon envisioning the hanging of University of Alabama's new leadership team. Printed shortly after University of Alabama president Arad Lakin and State Superintendent of Education Noah Cloud's fateful visit, the *Independent Monitor*'s graphic woodcut and the acidic denunciation that accompanied it represent perhaps the most iconic published expression of resistance to Republicans and Republicanism in the Reconstruction South. Alabama Department of Archives and History.

clearly represented Lakin carrying a carpetbag on which was the stenciled word "Ohio," and the other image was that of Cloud, both men suspended from the same tree. The artist also etched a mule, tattooed with the letters "K. K. K.," identifying those responsible for the lynchings. In early March 1869, a new presidential administration would begin, and presuming the victory of Horatio Seymour, Randolph's caption read, "A Prospective Scene in the 'City of Oaks,' 4th of March 1869." The intent of the graphic and threatening message—the vigilante lynching of meddling Republican outsiders—was implied and promised.[37]

The most astute diviner could not have predicted the fallout caused by Randolph's scathing words and the accompanying woodcut. Since the war's close, the South's willingness to peacefully accept racial changes associated with Reconstruction had been the source of national debate. Republican spokesmen often portrayed a thoroughly recalcitrant ex-Confederacy where Republicans faced withering social rejection and physical violence. The vicious editorial and the complementing woodcut provided prima facie evidence of persisting Southern defiance. Editor Murat Halstead of the *Cincinnati Commercial* recognized a supreme opportunity to make political capital when he saw one. Eighteen days after their original publication, the *Cincinnati Commercial* of September 19 reprinted on its front page the shocking woodcut and Randolph's accompanying lacerating words.[38] Halstead's reproduction triggered a truly national reaction. Randolph's fiery assault, the woodcut, or both were picked up on and printed in newspapers in Missouri, Ohio, Vermont, Illinois, Michigan, and elsewhere. An Iowa editor printed Randolph's accompanying narrative and responded, "We commend the following manifesto to those Democrats who affect to ridicule the idea that the Southern members of their party meditate mischief." Readers of the September 21 edition of the *Pittsburgh Gazette* were greeted by a large front-page reproduction of Cloud and Lakin's imagined lynching and Randolph's message in full. Such was the widespread dissemination that the attack may have helped the Republican cause in the presidential contest by confirming the fact of an unreconstructed South.[39]

Ulysses Grant won the presidency by a sizeable popular vote and carried twenty-six states to Seymour's eight. The Republican prevailed in six Southern states where participation of formerly enslaved men accounted for his victory. That included Alabama, where he received over seventy-six thousand votes, and Seymour, some seventy-two thousand. Although Seymour prevailed in far more of the state's counties, Grant won by huge margins in the Black Belt, where freedpeople composed a large majority.

The freedmen who cast ballots for the first time in a presidential election at Tuscaloosa endowed the occasion with resounding historical significance. On election day, freedpeople began arriving early from outlying parts of the county. African Americans there and across the state felt safer voting at the county seat. Charles Williamson, a freedman and blacksmith, handed out Republican ballots. At the courthouse, former bondsmen cast three times as many ballots as white men. At other county precincts, white men matched the freedmen's solidarity, but on behalf of Horatio Seymour. The Democrat received 1,383 votes in Tuscaloosa County, and Grant tallied 1,167.[40]

The University of Alabama, tangentially through Randolph's notorious woodcut, had become an unlikely prop in the presidential election. Arad Lakin later provided identifying annotation. "The person represented in the cut in, hanging from the limb of a tree," the ex-president allowed, "is intended to represent myself."[41] The sordid episode framed the poisonous environment from which a university associated with "Radicalism" would soon reopen. Basil Manly Jr., another son of the Reverend Basil Manly and a University of Alabama graduate, was a professor at the Southern Baptist Theological Seminary at Greenville, South Carolina. Having learned of Arad Lakin's harsh reception, Manly exhibited no regard for a fellow man of the cloth whom he regarded as "an ignorant, impudent, cowardly scamp of a Methodist minister."[42] What lay ahead for the university could only be guessed. Alabama's state university would remain part of a political cauldron that simmered, seethed, and sometimes boiled over. Always, the institution's standing was tied to the interplay of Reconstruction politics. Amplification of the Republican position in Tuscaloosa fell partly to Dennis Dykous, editor of the recently established *Republican Banner*, having replaced the *Reconstructionist* as the local party newspaper. Dykous attempted to take the high road. He decried, "Let this cry against 'scallawags' and 'carpet-baggers' cease" and urged mutual cooperation to promote prosperity.

But in Tuscaloosa, at the state capital of Montgomery, indeed throughout the South, raw emotions made cooperation all but impossible. Dennis Dykous's plea went unheeded.[43] Benjamin Meek previously tutored at the university and more recently directed a boys school in town. He viewed what had transpired at the university through a filter of politics. Several weeks after Grant's election, the Democrat wrote the editor of the Mississippi *Democrat* in Jackson that the school "has risen proudly from its ashes, in even handsomer dress than old," but Meek qualified, "The scallawag authorities of our State have control of it, and consequently its doors are closed." Meek was correct in some respects. The university building was impressive, although it did not approach aesthetically the constellation of structures that previously adorned the campus. But, in acknowledging Republican direction of the institution, he was accurate. And for that reason, in a state where rattling Reconstruction adjustments made for an unforgiving and raw brand politics, the once-opened state university would become a partisan lightening rod of contention.[44]

Chapter 4

"A Position Connected with the University Is Not at Present a Very Pleasant One"

THE INTEREST THAT LOCAL RESIDENTS TOOK IN THE UNIVERSITY ranged widely, and in fact Tuscaloosa's pulse could be measured in any number of ways. Among the longstanding dilemmas was the periodically falling level of the Black Warrior River, which prevented boats from reaching the town for months out of the year. Residents greeted with relief the arrival of the *Mary H.*, which steamed up the Black Warrior early in October 1868. Merchants and their customers alike much appreciated the vessel that brought commodities to restock shelves depleted by the "low water" season.[1] A more permanent solution seemed near. Construction was underway of the Alabama and Chattanooga Railroad, which would slash diagonally across the state and pass through the town. "Soon will the whistle of the locomotive," the *Tuscaloosa Observer* assured, "infuse its life into the very air we breathe."[2] Almost every other person in Tuscaloosa was African American. Emancipation had dramatically changed the life of formerly enslaved individuals like Nat Lawson. He now drew pay working at a local foundry. The number of white men who compensated freedpeople for various services was numerous enough for Ryland Randolph to call on to them to boycott their enterprises. And the war's memory remained vivid. On April 26, 1865, General Joseph Johnston's surrender to General William Sherman had effectively ended the Civil War. That date became known as "Decoration Day," and on the ceremonial occasion in late April 1869, local women decorated the graves of Confederate soldiers in Tuscaloosa. In the former capitol building, now the home of the Alabama Central Female College, young women pursued their studies, as did their counterparts at the nearby Alabama Female Institute. A year after the war's conclusion, Catholic sisters had established the Ursuline

Convent, where women balanced spiritual and academic concerns in a handsome three-story edifice. In March 1869, the baptism of three individuals in the river gained attention, and several months later the Black Warrior provided the scene for tragedy when a soldier belonging to a small detachment of troops remaining on duty locally drowned while bathing in its waters. Given the local political adversity, the potential for trouble accounted for the presence of a nominal number of soldiers. The military-imposed removal of local government officials and their replacement with Republicans had recently stirred controversy. David Woodruff, one of the local white Republicans, became mayor. An observer noted the organization of various baseball clubs throughout the state and wondered why there was no local team. "During these dull times," young men playing baseball seemed far advisable to "remaining idle on the streets discussing politics, which is neither healthful or pleasant."[3]

As always, considered in the town's warp, stood the university. Charles Manly wrote to family relations from Tuscaloosa of his confidence in James Murfee and William Wyman in shaping developments. "If they keep the university intact from the scalawags," the minister ventured, both "will deserve the thanks of the state, & of future generations."[4] The overarching fallout from the recent visit by Arad Lakin and Noah Cloud obscured certain benefits. Following the university president's harrowing experience, Lakin immediately left town. Cloud did not. The superintendent of education remained for another day and soon reported, "I met with no obstructions whatever." He gained a familiarity with the campus's physical environs. The imposing new building struck him as "substantial, capacious and beautiful," but Cloud noted with appall the charred brick refuse of Croxton's raiders and labeled the surrounding campus a "common waste." An examination of financial records provided better insight into the school's debt. Meeting with James Murfee further advanced Cloud's knowledge. On the return trip to Montgomery, considerably extended by the lack of a railroad, the superintendent surely reflected on both the potential and the perils of the university's reorganization.[5]

Cloud had emphasized to Murfee the importance of resuming instruction at the university as soon as possible. The first projected target date, October 1868, had come and gone. Readying the institution for reopening was a priority when the board of education convened at Montgomery in December. Four months had passed since the August meeting that resulted in the election of a president and faculty. Finding a successor for Arad Lakin seemed crucial for the rudderless institution. The regents turned to Robert

David Harper. Approaching forty years of age, Harper had, for over the last twenty years, been the minister of a Presbyterian church in Xenia, Ohio. Harper was not an overtly political man, but he was a Republican, and he had during the war directed efforts to provide spiritual and physical support to wounded soldiers belonging to the Army of the Cumberland. Harper came south after the conflict and became the superintendent of education of the Freedmen's Bureau in Alabama. He soon celebrated advances and forecast for Black children "the future is hopeful."[6] Harper had made a generally positive impression on a recent trip to Huntsville. While admitting a preference for an Alabamian to direct the university, a representative of the Huntsville *Democrat* nevertheless discerned a man of intelligence, and in the columns of the *Mobile Register*, Harper was described as capable, intelligent, and a "quiet, unassuming gentleman."[7]

The regents at Montgomery also made decisions regarding the faculty. Since the last meeting, Thomas Goodfellow (commandant) and Professors David Humphreys and Joseph Geary decided against accepting the positions previously tendered them. The public backlash to those appointments may have contributed to their decisions, and conceivably each worried—considering the experiences of Lakin and Cloud—about their safety in Tuscaloosa. Whatever the circumstances, the regents declared every chair vacant and determined to hold new elections. They elected five professors and a commandant. John Calvin Loomis (ancient languages), Jonas DeForest Richards (natural philosophy and astronomy), John Forney (mathematics), Vernon H. Vaughn (history, logic, and metaphysics), and William J. Callan (rhetoric and oratory) gained faculty positions. Each was hired for one year at a salary of $2,500, and compensation included their use of one of several residences on campus set aside for professors. Exactly how these candidates came to the regents' attention and the subsequent cases made for or against them is not part of the board of education minutes, but the regents established a protocol requiring all applicants to present a diploma of graduation from a university and provide testimonials from former instructors attesting to their ability. A committee on credentials was also created. Taking these precautionary steps seemingly represented a tacit admission of the inadequate vetting of the previous faculty. The six men represented the third slate of professors chosen in half a year. Much is known about some of those entrusted to take the university forward and less about others. Almost all would understand an eventful tenure.[8]

The art of oratory had and continued to be a desirable complementing skill, and instructing young men in public speaking and persuasion became the responsibility of William Jasper Callan, who was named the rhetoric and oratory professor. Although born in North Carolina, Callan was more recently identified with Gaylesville, Alabama. In 1856 he was a sophomore at Cumberland University in Lebanon, Tennessee, and pursuing a theological degree, but he graduated in 1859 with the bachelor of arts degree. Ten years later, joining the faculty, Jasper Callan was approaching the age of forty, married to his second wife, Sarah Elizabeth Bradford (his first had died in 1863), and the father of at least five children.[9]

John Calvin Loomis claimed the most impressive academic pedigree. His father, Hubbel Loomis, had been the president of Shurtleff College, in Upper Alton, Illinois. Under his father's direction, Calvin started studying Latin when he was seven, and two years later began becoming familiar with Greek. By the age of eleven, the boy was reading scripture from the Greek Testament at family morning prayers. Calvin attended Western Reserve College in Hudson, Ohio, between 1838 and 1840 and, deciding on a teaching career, followed several sisters to Alabama, settling there later in the decade. The transplanted Ohioan married Caroline Voltz in 1848, but she died fifteen months later. His was a peripatetic and unsure life for much of the 1850s, moving from one school to another in the relentlessly rural landscape of south Alabama, understanding the pangs of loneliness and longing for what he forlornly referred to as the "society of a wife" and a "congenial spirit." Calvin conveyed these sentiments to his brother Elias, at the time a professor at the University of New York. Over thirty now, the bachelor dissented when a sister advised him to wait to remarry until his financial future was more secure. "I could always find more happiness in the company of one whom I know to be devoted to my welfare," he wrote Elias in 1854, "than in the reflection that I have a pile of rusty dollars laid up in some safe place."[10] Three years later, moving to the small community of Monterey in Butler County, he found employment at yet another school and, not incidentally, also a wife. Minerva Traweek Barge was a young widow in her early twenties and, according to her admiring husband, was "good looking" and possessed of an "amiable disposition."[11] They married on Sunday, February 8, 1857, in her family's home.[12] The family—Minerva had a young son named Thomas by her previous husband—moved by 1860 some fifty miles to Dallas County, where Calvin filled an appointment at Centenary College, ten miles outside of Selma. Centenary College was a Methodist-affiliated women's school of some academic standing, and it was here that Loomis gained his first college teaching experience. During the war, however, it became much more difficult to carry out Centenary College's motto that "to educate woman is to refine the world," and enrollment fell off. This probably accounted for Loomis leaving the college, and at least by 1869 the family had relocated to the small hamlet of Evergreen, in Conecuh County, where he began teaching at a recently created public school. In that Wiregrass setting he made the fortuitous acquaintance of William Miller, who belonged to the recently created board of education. Loomis made known his desire to teach at the restored University of Alabama and, with Miller's influence, was elected the ancient languages professor. A circuitous but ultimately satisfying route led John Calvin Loomis to Tuscaloosa. For the itinerant teacher, now nearing the age of fifty, who understood small compensation and the myriad challenges of instruction on a different level, the appointment represented a dramatic promotion. Loomis valued the extension of prestige, a home, and a better salary than he had ever known. He happily joined his brother in the exalted ranks of college professor. Elias Loomis was by now on the Yale College faculty and a notable author of textbooks concerning geometry and astronomy. Writing to him at New Haven, Connecticut, Calvin Loomis celebrated that "a considerable change for the better has taken place in my prospects."[13] Such was the trajectory of a man soon pronounced "a plain, unassuming scholar."[14]

DeForest Richards had spent almost all of his life in the North. Born in 1809 in Vermont, he graduated from Dartmouth College in 1836 and belonged to the class of 1840 at Andover Theological Seminary, in Andover, Massachusetts. An abiding devoutness was central to the man who the next year was ordained a Congregational Church minister. Two years later, in 1843, he married Harriet Bartlett Jarvis. She was the daughter of William Jarvis, a prominent man of New England who had served for a time as consul to Belgium in Thomas Jefferson's administration. For some twenty years, the Reverend DeForest Richards presided for congregations in New Hampshire, Vermont, and Ohio and, in the last two years of the war, served as principal of the Ohio Female Seminary at College Hill, Ohio. Any understanding of Richards acknowledges his deep spiritualism but also an interest in politics. And the two were related. It is highly likely that the frequently intersecting strains of Christianity and abolitionism gained classic illustration in DeForest Richards. He eventually became a Republican. When the Civil War ended, he and Harriet Richards had been married for twenty-two years and were the parents of four children. For unknown reasons, the family moved to Alabama, first purchasing a plantation in the Black Belt county of Marengo. Richards took his faith and politics with him. Within days of arriving, he declared that "the Lord has preserved us." A deep spiritualism did not preclude Richards's appreciation for worldly possessions. "I

Figure 4.1. John Calvin Loomis, professor of ancient languages, 1869–1871. A man of intellect and professional devotion, Loomis joined the faculty when the university reopened, but his strengths went unappreciated. His hopes of career advancement were instead swept away as he came to be ridiculed and even physically assaulted as part of a torrent of abuse directed at the school in its new guise. Calvin Loomis photo courtesy of Madeline Murfee David.

Chapter 4

am mightily pleased with my purchase," he wrote Harriet of the plantation, and allowed that he "could sell it now for several thousand dollars more than I have agreed to give for it." Richards may have done so, because the family soon moved again, this time setting down stakes at Camden, about fifty miles distant, in Wilcox County, part of the state's Piney Woods region. Increasingly, the tumultuous world of Reconstruction politics concerned Richards, and newly enfranchised Blacks in Wilcox and Dallas counties elected him to

FIGURE 4.2. DeForest Richards, professor of natural philosophy and astronomy, 1869–1872. Richards stands as the quintessential symbol of what Democrats charged was tragically wrong with the University of Alabama. He faced intense hostility. No matter the cost, the Republican professor was not a man to compromise principle. DeForest Richards photo courtesy of Ronald Millar.

the state senate in 1868. Richards belonged to the Republican-dominated legislature that convened at Montgomery in the summer of 1868 and cast one of his first votes in favor of ratifying the Fourteenth Amendment. And now, the next year, the regents elected him professor of natural philosophy and astronomy. In the Wilcox County hinterland, white Democrats would have vilified the man they condemned as an intruding carpetbagger. Jonas DeForest Richards would be even less popular in Tuscaloosa.[15]

FIGURE 4.3. Vernon Vaughn, professor of history, logic, and metaphysics, 1869–1870. Vaughn came to the university as the school reopened, but his Republican credentials and overindulgence in alcohol soon cast him into local disfavor. In 1870, Vaughn became part of a local firestorm, falsely implicated in an attempt to murder Ryland Randolph. Once acquitted, Vaughn and his family left campus and fled Tuscaloosa forever. Utah Historical Society.

Vernon Vaughn was the only faculty person claiming any previous ties to the University of Alabama. Raised in Mount Meigs, a community near Montgomery, he attended the Tuscaloosa school briefly in the 1850s. Vaughn left, however, and by 1857 was enrolled at the University of North Carolina, where he made a reputation for declaiming, graduating about 1860. In that year he married Cornelia Dandridge Bibb, who belonged to a prominent Montgomery family, and the next year he joined the Confederate Army. When the war ended Vaughn was twenty-seven years old, married, and the father of three small children. He soon began practicing law with R. B. Ryan, and the partners established an office on the second floor of a building on Market Street, near the capitol. On a late April night in 1867, honoring local deceased members of the Odd Fellows, Vaughn spoke eloquently to a crowd of some one hundred individuals who gathered at the local cemetery. Several months later, as a lawyer for the defense, Vaughn had the distinction of participating in the first case in the state where Black men sat on the jury. Vaughn's prospects—well married, educated, and a barrister—seemed promising. Another step he took, however, was highly unconventional. He joined the Republican Party. When the party formally organized at the state capital in June 1867, Vaughn represented Montgomery County as a delegate. Putting the practice of law and politics behind, Vernon Vaughn now prepared to return to Tuscaloosa, where higher education had begun for him over a decade earlier. He would assume the professorship of history, logic, and metaphysics at the University of Alabama.[16]

Regents had entrusted the teaching of mathematics to John Forney. An Alabamian and a West Point graduate, he had risen quickly in rank from colonel in the Confederate Army to major general. Forney's war record—wounded at the Battle of Dranesville in Virginia as 1861 ended, taken prisoner when Vicksburg fell, and later returning to command soldiers—was that of a committed soldier. When the professorship was conferred, Forney was living with his wife in Jacksonville, Alabama.[17]

In its resurrected form, the University of Alabama remained what it had been between 1859 and 1865: a military school. In *Reconstructing the Campus*, Michael Cohen establishes that adopting a military emphasis became more common at American universities following the war. As with similarly oriented institutions, and all were modeled on or at least inspired by West Point Military Academy, discipline provided a crucial component. "Military discipline will be enforced at all times," authorities promised. The burden of that charge fell most crucially to William K. McConnell as the commandant. His formative years had been spent in Talladega County, Alabama, but when the war broke out, McConnell was a cadet at the La Grange Military Academy in La Grange, Georgia. As did many fellow cadets consumed by patriotic fervor, McConnell joined the army. He served with the Sixteenth Alabama Infantry as a private, became color-bearer of his company, and saw extensive action with the Army of the Tennessee at Murfreesboro, Chattanooga, and later during the Atlanta campaign. In 1865, McConnell was young, single, and uncertain about his immediate future in a vanquished South. He boldly joined the exodus of maybe as many as ten thousand Southerners, leaving for Mexico and an imagined better future in Austrian Archduke and Emperor Maximilian's proclaimed Second Mexican Empire. Two years later, disappointed by the realities in Mexico, as were the vast majority who had departed, McConnell returned to the United States. He married Martha Ellen Smith in 1868. McConnell's soldiering experience included acting as drillmaster, which presumably recommended him as commandant.[18]

These six men constituted the faculty after a war-interrupted hiatus of four years. The school's reopening was reset for the first Monday in March. Tuscaloosa residents had before the war taken pride in the state university; many also benefitted—general merchants, boarding house owners, indeed a wide spectrum—from the enterprise generated by the university. The resurrection of the school under ordinary circumstances would occasion much celebration. But circumstances were far from ordinary. Many viewed the faculty as unqualified usurpers occupying the places of the rightful professors. Among the critics was John Warren, a man with a lengthy local journalistic pedigree who had recently assumed the editorial duties at the *Tuscaloosa Observer*. Warren anticipated President Robert Harper arriving "with a carpetbag in his hand and a huge desire in his heart for the spoils of office."[19] The editor recalled how the faculty selected by the board of trustees in the summer of 1868 had been "ruthlessly rejected" and admitted to a certain "repugnance" when he compared those erudite professors with the corps now assembling. Warren forecast misery and failure.[20] Much more intense opprobrium appeared in the *Independent Monitor*'s columns. Even before the educators had stepped foot on campus, Ryland Randolph denounced the "bogus faculty" and promised to "put our promising cartoon-artist at work, to reduce to wood their doubtless repulsive phizes and forms."[21] More alarming was the encouragement he offered a group of men who were geographically identified as residents of the Sipsey Swamp, a sprawling bog that defied precise dimensions but spilled over into several counties, including Tuscaloosa. Some Klansmen, or at least those described as violently anti-Republican elements, resided there. Randolph counseled against bothering

John Forney and William McConnell, Democrats and former Confederates, but advised the Sipsey Swamp contingent were "at liberty to do what they please with the others." The president's mansion, a three-storied Greek Revival structure, had been spared by the Union soldiers who had destroyed most of the university. Robert Harper would soon presumably move into the home. Ryland Randolph had other ideas. He warned president Harper against taking up residence and compared his safety unfavorably to that of Arad Lakin. A war that Randolph encouraged eagerly had begun.[22]

The suitability of the incoming regime provided one question and the legality of their appointment summoned another. Democrats operated from the premise that Alabamians had legally rejected the state constitution's ratification and that Congress had illegally forced the Republican-authored document on the state. That assumption led to the conclusion that all authority ostensibly mandated by the constitution, such as the creation of the board of education, lacked legal sanction. And derivatively, given that repudiation, board pronouncements and decisions did not carry legal weight.

It was not, however, an interpretation of the constitution's validity that explained the dramatic appearance of disguised men on the campus on Saturday night, January 9. Simple primal resentment accounted for what transpired. On that evening, under cover of darkness, a group of individuals eerily draped in white approached the removed campus. They stopped first at the president's mansion. The mere chance that Robert Harper had not relocated to Tuscaloosa prevented some confrontation. Yet, undeterred, the forbidding-looking group advanced the short distance to the professors' homes, but again the fortunate circumstance that none of the faculty had yet arrived avoided trouble. Rather than their academic targets, they encountered some freedpeople, who understandably fled. In anticipation of the expected professors, Randolph recorded, "It is supposed that the spirits of the Confederate dead are making themselves familiar with the premises." That the new regime was unwelcome and faced danger was the clearly conveyed message.[23]

Against this ominous backdrop, the faculty drifted into town over the first several months of 1869. William Jasper Callan arrived first. On January 22, the rhetoric and oratory professor directed a heavily loaded oxen-pulled wagon that included his wife, their numerous small children, and necessary belongings. The sprawling Callan family settled into one of the five spacious (often two-story) frame homes reserved for professors. Calvin and Minerva Loomis and their son soon followed. Disembarking early in March from a Black Warrior River steamboat, DeForest and Harriet Richards, two sons and a daughter, also took their place on the campus. Vernon and Cornelia

"*A Position Connected with the University Is Not at Present a Very Pleasant One*"

Vaughn, with three small children, did likewise. Leaving his wife in Jacksonville, John Forney began what would be a short stay in Tuscaloosa. The former Confederate general boarded locally. William McConnell had or soon would make his appearance. The commandant's duties required closely supervising the cadets, and McConnell likely quartered in the university building.[24]

The faculty quickly came to an understanding of their notoriety. Several days after arriving, Calvin Loomis wrote to his brother at Yale of prevailing circumstances. As Loomis explained, "There is in Tuscaloosa great opposition into the opening of the University." By way of explanation, he attributed

FIGURE 4.4. A faculty residence on the University of Alabama campus. There were five commodious homes for professors and their families within the campus constellation. That they were rent-free provided one of the few advantages for a faculty under fire. Alabama Department of Archives and History.

that feeling essentially to prevailing politics and the connection some made between the university and "those who cherish a deadly hatred of the present State government."[25] Neither was local sentiment lost on DeForest Richards. When the Richards family moved furniture into their home, Ryland Randolph wondered if the professor of natural philosophy and astronomy "actually intended to deposit his vile carcass out at the University for a series of years."[26] Richards had graduated from Dartmouth more than thirty years ago, and he maintained ties with the school's president, the Reverend Asa Smith. He soon wrote Smith of "the bitter disloyal elements around us."[27] Jasper Callan, described as a "modest, quiet, scholarly gentleman," nevertheless felt a sense of unease, and the rhetoric and oratory professor was inquiring about his security within days of arriving.[28]

These highly irregular circumstances compounded the professors' most fundamental responsibilities: advancing the knowledge of young men who possessed widely ranging academic backgrounds and levels of aptitude. In correspondence with Asa Smith, Professor Richards anticipated instructing courses in natural philosophy and astronomy, "branches of science I have given considerable attention of late years."[29] Calvin Loomis was the most intellectually dexterous. Although he would instruct Latin and Greek courses, Loomis had a keen and expansive mind; in correspondence with his brother at Yale, he sometimes posed and illustrated mathematical problems. The ancient languages professor determined on setting a high standard. In the weeks before classes began, Professor Loomis prepared, studying on his own, settling on Greek and Latin textbooks for class use. He consulted with colleagues about what textbooks they planned to provide and was not above pitching those his brother authored. The task awaited of presenting the works of Herodotus, Sophocles, Plato, Horace, and among others, Virgil and Cicero. "Even the most factious opposition of the present organization of the University," Loomis declared to Elias, "shall have no ground for saying that I did not discharge my duties with ability and fidelity." John Forney never had the opportunity to prove his merit. It was Forney's unique experience to have been elected by the board of trustees and then reelected by the board of education. But he was an unstable man. Arriving in early February, he soon demonstrated behavior that indicated a mental imbalance. On one occasion, shocked observers witnessed the Confederate general running down the street screaming the Ku Klux Klan was after him. These circumstances forced his return to Jacksonville and treatment at the insane asylum in Nashville, Tennessee. Although Forney did resume a normal life, he did not return to the university.[30]

"A Position Connected with the University Is Not at Present a Very Pleasant One"

In March, just weeks before the anticipated university reopening, events took another unexpected term. Robert Harper resigned as president. Some evidence indicates that his health figured in that decision, and it also seems that the devout man wished to return to the ministry in Ohio, which he did. It may be assumed that Harper was influenced by an understanding of the acute adversity he would face as president. Time in Alabama had schooled him all too well in the temper of the times. Addressing an audience back home in Xenia, Ohio, during the recent presidential campaign, Harper described a defiant Southern population that was violently resisting changes associated with the war. In his executive position with the Freedmen's Bureau, despite confronting innumerable problems, recourse often existed. At one point, Harper despaired for any funds from the state, yet legislators allowed him to draft a bill appropriating funds. By contrast, at the university, Robert Harper understood the challenges were of an insidious nature. That reality at least contributed to the decision of a man imminently qualified to lead the university to give up the presidency before the first day of his administration.[31]

These facts remained. In a month, the University of Alabama would reconvene, hardly sufficient time to find a president. Under the circumstances, DeForest Richards was appointed the president pro tempore. He also assumed direction, in John Forney's absence, of mathematics instruction. Only three men had served as the school's president between 1831 and 1865. Richards became the fourth executive to fill that office in the last seven months.

On April 1, four days before school opened, Professor Calvin Loomis projected to his brother, "We shall have a respectable number" of students. A very finite number of students had begun to make their way to Tuscaloosa in the first week of April. Some of the young men stepped off the *Jennie Rogers* or the *Reindeer*, having negotiated the trip's last leg on a steamboat up the Black Warrior River. Others came overland, often by stage, entering Tuscaloosa on what were referred to colloquially as the Greensboro Road or the Huntsville Road. A short trip out to the campus accomplished by hack or stage concluded a journey that might have taken several days. The weather was obliging, and the oak trees were beginning to regain their leaves and hint of the green patina blanket of shade they would offer in the hot months ahead. The vast majority of students were of rural backgrounds. They were unremarkable and no different from college students before and after them. Removed from their families and the familiar landmarks of their youth, the prospect of a new life summoned a mix of excitement, anticipation, and a degree of fear. As he arrived on campus, the prospective student could not have missed the unsightly piles of burnt brick left from the Federal soldiers' visit. Even so, it was the future, not the past, that he contemplated, as admittance through the perimeter gate was gained. And then the majestic building came into sight. For some it was the largest structure they had ever beheld. Only the next step was sure. The cadet disembarked and began the task of maneuvering his chest-filled belongings into a second or third story room.[32]

FIGURE 4.5. The new university building seen through the ruins of the antebellum campus. The unsightly signs of the catastrophic raid by Federal troops remained in evidence for quite some time before being removed to make way for the university's future. Alabama Department of Archives and History.

A surveying walk about the premises likely impressed the acclimating student. He found large classrooms filled with newly hewed desks, a library, science laboratories, a chapel, and the mess hall. If an environment for intellectual stimulation had been created, physical comfort had not been ignored. The hand of James Murfee was evident. The architect had inspired living quarter arrangements that maximized space and convenience and, not incidentally, promoted academic performance. His scheme provided for beds that could be rolled up out of the way and "cases" for storing bedding, clothes, books to minimize clutter and leave, according to Murfee, "the room clear for study—like a ship's deck when ready for action." Such was the physical environment that constituted cadets' new home.[33]

Although little of a personal nature can be determined about this first class of students, a general prototype emerges. The vast majority were Alabamians. All were white, male, and at least fifteen years old, the minimum age of admittance. F. W. Trawick, from the small community of Monterey in Butler County, fit that profile. Late in March, after disembarking from the *Reindeer*, he made his way out to the campus. A certain academic conversance was also expected of Trawick and his peers. Those with weaker backgrounds entered a preparatory department. Admittance to the freshman class was based upon demonstrating knowledge of English grammar, geography, arithmetic, and some familiarity with Latin, Greek, and among others, the Roman literary figures Virgil and Sallust. Knowledge of Caesar's timeless *The Gallic War's*, appropriate at the military school, was also required. A more subjective stipulation, evidence of "unexceptionable character," was based on submitted testimony from a recent teacher.[34] These standards were likely stretched or ignored at an institution in need of students. A letter from an unknown cadet reveals a shocking disregard for the most rudimentary skills. Several days after arriving in Tuscaloosa, he wrote, "Deer Farther, college is opened and we has about twenty-five Boys more nor less." He and other cadets for some reason briefly lived with the professors. "I bode with Mr. Loomiss and he don't feed well a bit. He have nothing but corn-dodgers and fish there times a day and no coffee except for hisself and his Ladey." The thoroughly ungrammatical cadet continued, "We get no bakon or other sorts of meets," and "those fellows what stays at the other professor's houses sais that they don't give even I does." Fellow cadets may have shared his poor living arrangements but hopefully not the student's spelling and syntax inadequacies. It may be assumed the young man took a place in the university preparatory department.

Most who enrolled, whatever their academic readiness, were from small towns or locales even less distinguished. Howells Crossroads in rural Cherokee

County was the home of M. L. Barnard, W. G. Butler, and J. T. Vandaver. M. Dick crossed the state from Tuskegee, and J. M. Wilson began the trip north at Grove Hill in Clarke County. Andalusia, Talladega, Tuscumbia, Courtland, these were also the homes of students setting out for Tuscaloosa. Most were farm boys. T. R. Thurston and H. D. Stearns, respectfully of Huntsville and Mobile, left sizable places. About a half dozen of the young men had little or no previous connection to Alabama. C. S. Brott (New Orleans) and A. S. Bates (Columbus, Georgia) numbered among them. What circumstances caused Edward Maury, H. Maury, and A. B. Shelton to matriculate from Kemper County, Mississippi, can only be imagined. Among their classmates was Jarvis Richards, the son of DeForest and Harriet Richards, and Thomas Barge, that of Calvin and Minerva Loomis.[35]

The students at the University of Alabama before the war, like their counterparts elsewhere, had largely been fielded from well-heeled Southern gentry. That was emphatically not the case as the school reawakened. It was indeed the university's affordability that drew many. The cost of attending, $125 annually, represented a modest sum. And some students did not pay that. The regents recently provided for the state to absorb the expenses of one cadet from each county. The number of those referred to as "beneficiaries" is uncertain, but it was considerable, and perhaps even a majority of pupils fell into that group.[36]

On Monday morning, April 5, guests, faculty, and somewhere between twenty and thirty "genteel looking" cadets assembled for opening ceremonies in a room on the imposing building's first floor. Professors Jasper Callan, Calvin Loomis, DeForest Richards, and Commandant William McConnell looked on, but Vernon Vaughn was not among them. Noah Cloud was present, and two women, one a sister of the superintendent's, were among the small number attending. Tuscaloosa residents were conspicuously absent. Taking the floor just after noon, Cloud emphasized with due historical importance the opening of the University of Alabama. Some of what the superintendent imparted represented the conventional—he charged the faculty as dispensers of knowledge and students as receivers of wisdom, in their respective roles. In a less traditional vein, Cloud assured that the school's direction would not be controlled by any political party. The very disavowal of partisanship offered a sign of the times. He then administered the oath of office to DeForest Richards, and the president pro tempore spoke. Acknowledging the honor conferred on him formed the basis of brief remarks, which drew applause.[37]

A university had been reincarnated. Almost to the day, four years earlier, John Croxton's exiting troops had left behind the institution in smoldering ruins. The contrast between then and now was more relevantly measured in events than by the calendar. The country was at peace. And Alabama was in the Union. Ulysses Grant, not Abraham Lincoln, sat in the Whitehouse. Some four million freedpeople independently carried on their lives and without bondage's constraints. An era had ended, and another begun.

Until late June, when the abbreviated spring term ended, education resumed at the University of Alabama. Somewhere between fifty and sixty cadets attended, but not all at the same time, during the academic 1869–1870 year. Of the school's present and future, pro tempore president Richards soon wrote the Reverend Asa Smith. He commended to Dartmouth's president the fine new building and the university's rise from desolation. Richards pointed to its sound financial standing, described the number of students as "fair," and noted optimistically a "very favorable beginning."[38]

It was with varying degrees of success in the weeks ahead that cadets acclimated themselves to a rigid routine. Much of the day was passed in class. Study of the Greek and Latin authors provided a heavy dose of the classics, and mathematics, natural philosophy, (physics and astronomy), and natural history (biology and chemistry) largely composed a rigorous academic diet. Each professor presented material differently, but some form of lecture was common. At other times, the student was asked on the spot to recite. Nothing was more central to prevailing pedagogical practice than the recitation. That entailed, at the professor's cue, a cadet orally responding to a question. Recitation took on various forms, depending on the discipline, and in the year the state university of Alabama reopened, a student at Yale outlined the procedure. "In a Latin or Greek recitation one may be asked to read or scan a short passage," and then "another to translate it, a third to answer question as to its construction." The reciting scenario played out countless times at the University of Alabama. Whatever the class, whoever the teacher, memorization was central. Opportunity for accomplishing that was provided in mandatory study hours.[39] A different form of learning took place in a laboratory environment associated with sciences, and officials promised that "the Laboratory will be kept up to the requirements of modern science." Students proved their merit or exposed their shortcomings during the designated examination period when formal tests were administered.[40]

Academic rigor provided but one of the challenges. The day-to-day activities of students at colleges and universities were rather carefully overseen, and even stricter regulations prevailed at schools of military orientation. The University of Alabama cadet understood a highly structured life. Reveille began the day and taps ended it. And in between, the cadets' day was guided by the periodic ringing of a bell. Nothing quite captured the essence of a military school than mandated drill. The young men attending during the Civil War had done so with the realization and determination of honing skills for impending combat. His postwar successor was not a Confederate soldier in waiting, but drilling remained obligatory. Marching in civilian attire rather than uniforms demeaned the activity. So did doing so without weapons. Promoting physical health largely accounted for the practice, and as Noah Cloud testified daily drill provides "the most practicable method of making it certain that all shall take exercise enough to keep them healthy." Established times for meals, study, and inspection further reflected military precision. Attention to neatness and order, directly applied to cadets' rooms, mess hall, and the general premises, was demanded, and an officer of the day provided accountability. Such was the typical day, heavy on time constructively spent and parsimonious with leisure that cadets came to know. It was the weary young man who climbed several flights of stairs to his room on the second or third floor. Early the next morning, with prayer and breakfast, the regimen began again.[41]

The faculty faced a different type of adversity. A week after class opened, Calvin Loomis informed his brother that thirty young men were enrolled, which was "not as many as we hoped to have, but more than our enemies expected us to obtain." All things considered, given the awkward opening time and the "fiendish" opposition of some, he wrote, "I think that we have done well."[42] Nobody was as "fiendish" as Ryland Randolph, who declared a seeming verbal war on the faculty. Loomis became a favorite target. When the ancient languages professor asked for a refund after a chair did not arrive by steamboat, Randolph reminded readers of Northerners supposed mercenary streak and labeled him a "thorough Yankee."[43] The editor observed few boundaries. Loomis apparently suffered from strabismus, an affliction preventing an individual's eyes from lining up in the same direction, sometimes taking the form of crossed eyes. Randolph described Loomis as "repulsive-looking" and judged his "hideous" countenance would frighten children.[44] It was less Vernon Vaughn's appearance than his reputation for imbibing liberally that Randolph leveraged as a point of attack. The editor referred to Vaughn as "Tanglefoot," an allusion to a term denoting cheap whiskey. Randolph attributed to drunkenness his absence from the university's opening ceremonies. Vaughn's habit of walking his dogs (which he also used to hunt quail) also gained unflattering attention, and the recently arrived professor soon became the subject of a cartoon. Randolph would continue to present him to *Independent Monitor* readers as a hopelessly miscast professor and "an ignoramus, an upstart, a drunkard, and a fool for staying in Tuscaloosa."[45] DeForest Richards inspired special venom. Randolph habitually referred to the eldest professor as "Old Dicks." The editor pointed to his "bitter and coarse denunciations" of Alabama while he was a state senator (no evidence corroborates that charge) and, assuming Richards's teaching incompetence, wondered that the so-called professor could possibly think that Alabamians would expose their sons to his instruction, "even if he were capable of imparting it."[46] Nothing about the natural philosophy and astronomy teacher escaped Randolph's ire. His stovepipe hat drew ridicule, Richards's gait became a "strut," and his personal projection one of "much importance."[47] Meeting Shandy Jones one day on Main Street, Richards embraced the Black barber. That act inspired a mocking woodcut, and Randolph decided "he is the best

FIGURE 4.6. Cartoon ridiculing Vernon Vaughn hunting with his dogs. Unflattering images of Ryland Randolph's enemies, often accompanied by eviscerating narratives, appeared frequently in the Tuscaloosa *Independent Monitor*. As seen here, the acerbic editor exhibited absolute contempt for Professor Vaughn, whom he also depicted as an embarrassing drunk. University of Alabama Libraries Special Collections.

Chapter 4

subject for Ku-Klux treatment that we have ever seen." DeForest and Harriet and their youngest children, Margaret (twelve) and her brother Bartlett (ten), enjoyed carriage rides down Greensboro Street and about town. Randolph noted the habitual trips and promised the Richards patriarch "a day of reckoning awaits you."[48]

The editor's antipathy spilled over into a physical altercation with Calvin Loomis only two weeks into the term. Randolph's decision to send copies of the *Independent Monitor* by a courier to the cadets provided the backdrop for confrontation. Circulation of a newspaper some faculty found highly objectionable contributed to banning its distribution during study hours, and on several occasions Randolph's representative was turned away. The

FIGURE 4.7. *Independent Monitor* cartoon mocking interracial ties between university faculty and Tuscaloosa's African American community. Slandering individuals whom editor Randolph branded objectionable was done by word and illustration, inflaming local hostile attitudes toward Republicanism, emancipation, and the university. This example targets DeForest Richards, Shandy Jones, and Jones's son using racist tropes. Richards and Jones had been seen embracing in public. University of Alabama Libraries Special Collections.

editor angrily took umbrage and, on failing to encounter Loomis in town, dispatched a note "in language unmistakably plain" promising that if the practice continued, "I would, on sight, proceed to give him a d__ good whipping." The courier was soon again denied entrance. On Wednesday, April 14, Randolph armed himself with a pistol and a solid stick and set out to confront Loomis. He staked out David Woodruff's bookstore, which the editor described as the "headquarters of Radicals." Randolph was an ex-Confederate soldier accustomed to bearing firearms. His adversary, an academician with no martial experience, did not even have a pocketknife. Loomis entered the bookstore that morning and Randolph followed. A one-sided encounter predictably followed. Randolph accosted the professor, struck him a glancing blow with his stick, and drew a pistol, apparently causing Loomis to plead for mercy. After sternly admonishing him against intervening with the newspaper's circulation, the satisfied editor departed.[49]

Neither was there security within the university confines. About the same time, one night early in April, a group of young men ventured onto the campus and, making hideous noises, caused terrorized professors, their wives, and young children to flee their homes. The visit had precedent. When Arad Lakin made his appearance several months earlier, local elements chased the president off, and more recently disguised parties had, under cover of darkness, congregated at the presidential mansion. This most recent band of hooligans, probably some Klansmen, further served notice to the academic community of their resented standing. The incident seems to have provoked the faculty to pass a rule to close the gates on the fence-enclosed campus. Several days later, Randolph and like-minded friends rode out by buggy to the campus and, as a "taunt," flaunted the newly imposed restrictions imposed by the "miserable 'fessers."[50]

The highly fortuitous survival of the letters Calvin Loomis wrote his brother between 1869 and 1871 provides an invaluable window into the university. Soon after settling in Tuscaloosa, Loomis recounted Randolph's incendiary bent and informed Elias he "pitches into all connected with the institution with an utter disregard of truth." When a colleague that spring asked the ancient languages professor if his brother would be interested in becoming the university president, he relayed the query but admitted, "A position connected with the University is not at present a very pleasant one." A month's residence in Tuscaloosa provided perspective. Some whites did support the school, but they composed the smallest class. The biggest group he characterized as largely apathetic. Those residents falling into a faction between the two groups Loomis referred to as "deadly enemies."[51] Loomis also described the bitter environment in letters to his father in Upper Alton, Illinois. Passing on his fears to Elias at Yale, Hubbel Loomis would observe that Calvin "complained of a political party bitterly opposed to the party which gave him a professor's chair in the Tuscaloosa University." The Loomis patriarch despaired, "I very much fear he will not sit long in the chair."[52]

Any understanding of the faculty's plight is dependent on recognizing that Tuscaloosa was a place of deep political alienation. The close of the presidential campaign later in 1868 did not noticeably defuse passions. Several weeks after Ulysses Grant's election, Merdy Crossland was shot to death passing through the forbidding Sipsey Swamp on his way to Montgomery to sit in the legislature. The murder of the Republican state senator constituted a political assassination. Without large numbers of troops patrolling the countryside, Sheriff Thomas Lewis wrote Governor William Hugh Smith, "I cannot see any way to put a stop to such outrage. A large reward for those responsible for Crossland's murder(ers) went uncollected."[53]

Unprecedented turmoil followed in the spring of 1869. Just two weeks after the university reopened, an altercation resulted in several freedmen threatening to kill some white men. In retaliation, a few nights later, on April 20, a group of white men sought them out on the Northport side of the Black Warrior River, shots were exchanged, several men were wounded, and a young white man, William Finley, was killed. The next day a large and angrily resolute crowd assembled, armed and mounted. Lead by Ryland Randolph, they returned to the skirmish's vicinity, burned the Black men's residence, and killed Ike Jenkins and Aaron Coleman, both freedmen. In the meantime, William Cochrane, a young freedman, wounded at the outset of difficulties, was arrested and on April 23 put in the two-story jail located across the street from the former capitol building. On the next night, Saturday, April 24, a party of white men forcefully took Cochrane from his cell and shot the young Black man to death within fifty yards of the jail. About the same time, a young white man who had been previously shot died of his wounds. The toll as April ended stood at five dead, three Black men and two white, and several individuals wounded. All of this took place within three weeks of the university's reopening.[54]

The shocking events triggered decisive action. A number of freedmen desperately wrote Governor William Hugh Smith and attributed crimes to the Ku Klux Klan. "It was known the K.K.K. are to go at night," they beseeched the executive, "but they go now in the day time."[55] Responding to Sheriff Thomas Lewis's previous letter, Smith acknowledged the letters he received from individuals deploring the situation and urging him to take

"A Position Connected with the University Is Not at Present a Very Pleasant One"

"rigorous measures."[56] An alarming situation prompted response in Montgomery. Early in May, Charles Miller, secretary of state, and David L. Dalton, the governor's private secretary, made an investigative trip to Tuscaloosa. Based on their observations, troops were sent to the troubled town. Soldiers had been in and out of Tuscaloosa for different periods of time since the war ended. The latest contingent, transported by the *Virginia* up the Black Warrior River, arrived on May 22. Captain William Mills commanded the company. Some residents indignantly condemned what they perceived as bayonet rule, but others approved of the soldiers in light of recent violence. In the meantime, Sheriff Lewis resigned, and the governor appointed Josiah J. Pegues to the office. The new sheriff wrote Smith that more than five hundred local residents had signed a document promising support for law and order—and he speculated that twice that number would do so. A week later, the governor reasoned to David Dalton that one thousand citizens surely could maintain peace and stated, "I sincerely hope we will hear no more of trouble in Tuscaloosa."[57]

Out at the university, the turmoil caused two professors to offer their take on the situation. Eleven days into May, Calvin Loomis wrote to Smith of grave concerns. The ancient languages professor identified two problems frustrating justice. Well-meaning residents could not feel confidently safe if they testified against the guilty due to a lack of protection, Loomis positioned. That was because men executing the law belonged to the same party of those transgressing it. Loomis also pointed to the impossibility of seating an impartial jury. Writing demonstratively for effect, Loomis posed, "How can we be sure that every white man on the jury does not belong to the KKK?" Loomis noted that this lack of impartiality posed special liabilities for freedpeople. He cited the recent murders of several Black men, presumably Ike Jenkins and Aaron Copeland, and informed that other freedpeople were so terrorized that only a necessary few attended to their burials.[58] Loomis received a reply from David Dalton several days later. Admitting that the governor recognized the "formidable difficulties," Dalton referred to his recent visit to Tuscaloosa and steps taken to provide unconditional law and order. The governor's secretary asked for "patience."[59]

DeForest Richards rejected that recourse as far too passive. Several weeks after Loomis corresponded with the governor, Richards also addressed Smith. Writing from the university, the natural philosophy and astronomy professor described an untenable situation where "murderers are walking boldly in our streets in open daylight and no one dares to move a finger towards their arrest and punishment." No discernable improvement had resulted since the visit of Miller and Dalton, and "if *possible* the wicked" are more "defiant." Richards pointed to cowed civil officials and explained the effectiveness of the soldiers was hamstrung because they could not intervene unless called upon by civil officials. The acting president shared Loomis's concerns as to the impossibility of impaneling an impartial jury. Only by declaring martial law could order be restored, Richards informed Smith, for that "is what alone these defiant out-laws fear," and otherwise "they *laugh* at our civil authorities and commit murder openly."[60] Two days later, again composing from the university, Richards addressed Elisha Peck. He had previously discussed the situation with the state supreme court justice and Tuscaloosa resident. Richards advised Peck of the recent whippings of several Black men and the impotence of civil officials and soldiers. He maintained that nothing less than "our salvation" depended on the invocation of martial law.[61]

A large majority of respectable residents strongly deprecated the violence and rued prevailing circumstances. Some townspeople considered Randolph's inflammatory words counterproductive and disapproved of him. Longtime resident and former Civil War general Sterling Wood informed the governor that "the whole community deplores that such things [crimes] should happen."[62] As a general statement, admitting significant exceptions, the Tuscaloosa lawyer's observation was true. But a dire situation existed in Tuscaloosa County in the spring and early summer of 1869. Several months earlier, a legislative committee had investigated and taken testimony from Alabamians and confirmed the fact of widespread political violence. The legislators concluded that conditions in five counties warranted declaring martial law. Tuscaloosa County was one of them. Robert Jemison Jr., planter, entrepreneur, and confirmed member of the gentry, had opposed the state leaving the Union as one of Tuscaloosa County's delegates to the secession convention. It was left to him to inform David Dalton that "the lawlessness and outrages of our county continue without abatement." A company of soldiers under Captain William Mills remained in Tuscaloosa indefinitely.[63]

It was the more pedestrian—academics, fraternity, pleasure—which dominated cadets' lives. On the morning of the school's reopening, students passed idle time playing the coming game of baseball. In the weeks ahead, becoming accustomed to a world defined by restrictions, a certain settling occurred. Some cadets began retreating to the university fence, crossing the enclosure, and practicing their pistol marksmanship by shooting at paper targets posted on trees. At most turns, however, they confronted rules, expectations, and academic challenges. Hot weather had arrived in Tuscaloosa, and the term, truncated by a late start, ended late in June. Students undoubtedly welcomed a break from early reveille, confining strictures, looming demerits, impromptu recitations, and academic preparation. Some felt suffocated by the environment, and for others the school provided welcome liberation from home and the grind of farm labor. Even so, on balance as the term ended in July, returning home beckoned. Some students did not intend to return.[64]

Less than one term had transpired, but some conclusions were obvious. Those embracing the school of thought identified with Noah Cloud viewed the imposing brick edifice as representative of a new Alabama and a monument to the state's progress after a disastrous war. But far more allowed that under Republican guidance, the University of Alabama had become the home of a few students best described as mendicants on the state dole and the refuge of pretended scholars, whose compelling prerequisite for gaining faculty status was their Republican brand. The thoughts of Barbara Little represented mainstream opinion among white Tuscaloosans. Apprising her son in New Orleans of developments in Tuscaloosa, the local woman wrote that the newly arrived faculty were "not so comfortable." That was not a reference to their living accommodations. She singled out Vernon Vaughn, who "drinks and gambles. What a Teacher!" Some protested strenuously with words, others stooped to slander and threats and, in the case of Ryland Randolph, even physical violence. Neither did some elements allow the law to deter them, resorting to forays of intimidation under the cover of darkness. The battle for the University of Alabama was just beginning.

Chapter 5

In Search of a President

OVER THE SUMMER OF 1869, A VISITOR TO TUSCALOOSA MADE REFERence to the oak trees, noted local anticipation regarding the coming of the Alabama and Chattanooga Railroad, and listened to the Methodist minister passionately inveigh against the sin of dancing. A trip out to the university evoked mixed emotions. He noted piles of burned bricks that testified to what had been but complimented the replacing structure as "magnificent" and lauded the "modern improvements." Recalling the school as an academic beacon, the observer attributed its present status to the "shameful" policy of Republican administrators and unfavorably compared the current professors to the former faculty.[1] Jerome Cochran also took a dim view. The prominent Mobile physician's familiarity with Tuscaloosa dated back to his time there during the war, caring for soldiers at a military hospital. Cochran chastised the professors who "pass their time in ease," referenced "the falling fortunes of the Radical University," and noted that prospective students "avoid it as they would the plague." Many across the state shared Cochran's estimation of the school.[2]

These shorthand observations reflected the partisan predispositions of those who made them. Beyond any frame of reference, however, was the undeniable need for a permanent and respected president at the university. In his encompassing study of American higher education, Frederick Rudolph has written that the nineteenth century college or university president "lived at the college, was not absent for long periods of time, probably taught every member of the senior class, knew most of the students by name, indeed probably made a practice of calling on them in their rooms." The absence of such a recognized and galvanizing individual gravely compromised the University of Alabama. Finding that person lay in the hands of the board of education. When Robert Harper resigned in March 1869 and DeForest

Richards became president pro tempore, it was established that he would step down in favor of a permanent executive. Late in June, as the abbreviated academic term ended, the board would meet at Tuscaloosa, and settling on an executive formed part of an agenda to accomplish before school resumed.[3]

Noah Cloud made finding a president a high priority. He had recently authored an advertisement published in some newspapers reaffirming the not so obvious: that the University of Alabama had indeed reopened. The superintendent of education praised the new building, the professors, and, more abstractly, peace and education. Cloud further promised that a president would soon be named.[4]

Among the candidates gaining mention was Raphael Semmes. Since the war, the former commander of the *Alabama* taught briefly at the Louisiana State Seminary of Learning and Military Academy and edited a newspaper in Memphis. He was now living in Mobile. Others championed another Confederate hero, William J. Hardee, author of the widely respected *Rifle and Light Infantry Tactic* and, for a time in the 1850s, the commandant at West Point Military Academy. The former Confederate general resided in Selma and served as the president of the Selma and Meridian Railroad. Hardee's enthusiasm for the presidency is uncertain, but Semmes heartily desired the appointment. The name of Matthew Fontaine Maury also surfaced. The former superintendent of the National Observatory was a scholar who had written masterfully on sea navigation and wind currents. A Virginian, Maury served the Confederacy in various appointed capacities, and the renowned scientist had been since 1868 a professor of physics at the Virginia Military Institute at Lexington.[5] Maury's interest could be described as tepid. Acknowledging to his son-in-law the overtures of the University of Alabama, Maury put the number of students at the ailing school as "right low," and advised, "I'm not anxious to go" but admitted that conditions could change.[6]

These men in varying degrees appealed to or repelled the regents. Until the general election of the 1870 altered the board's political complexion, Republicans held every seat on it. Administering the public school system created by the state constitution had primarily occupied them since the summer of 1868. At other times, deliberating in their capacity as regents, affairs connected to the university commanded attention. What constituted the institution's best interests had and would continue to provoke differences of opinion. The strong and contrasting views expressed when the board of education first met in Montgomery back in the summer of 1868 attested to conflict. At that time, a Northern and Southern split had emerged. Regents Jesse Booth, William Clayton, and Thomas Jackson, all Alabamians, failed to head off the attempt led by Gustavus Adolphus Smith to remove the previously appointed faculty. The alienated triumvirate branded the Northern regents' efforts to bring in outsiders "unjust, unwise," and nothing less than "tyrannical."[7]

In the larger picture of Southern higher education, differences of opinion among those making university policy would emerge in other states after Republicans came to power (largely the subject of chapter 7). How decisions, often involving hiring, could be intertwined with political point of view became clear in Louisiana, even before Republicans took control of state government. Those determining faculty appointments met late in 1866 or early in 1867 and divided over appointing Raphael Semmes to the faculty at the Louisiana State Seminary of Learning and Military Academy. Robert Ryland, a Republican, inveighed against the "Rebel" in his distinctive Irish accent. "Of all men," Ryland decried against honoring a man whose "hands were as yet red" from a war waged against the United States. Some of his colleagues agreed, although Ryland's argument did not carry the day.[8]

No such colorful account of closed-door deliberations involving the regents in Alabama seems to exist. The minutes of the board of education reveal voting tallies, fiscal calculations, and general business, but the antiseptic record provides no insight into regents' opinions, arguments, or, indeed, personalities. Clearly, however, they disagreed and at times stridently when discussing university policy, evaluating professors, or choosing a president. A shared Republican faith hardly made for harmony. In that respect the board mirrored the state Republican party itself, rent by factionalism and disagreements between moderate and Radical elements. The advisability of politically punishing some Alabamians for their Confederate past, for example, provided an early point of interparty contention. And similarly, among the regents, the administration of the University of Alabama summoned differences. They were opinionated men, whose views of the future university were informed by ideology, and some would contend blinded by it, who could take an entrenched position and, with great tenacity, hold it.

Late in June 1869, as the first term of the University of Alabama since the war ended, the board of education met at Tuscaloosa. Each of the men who by hook or by crook made their way to Tuscaloosa was a Republican. Meeting at the university was no accident, for the school's situation dominated the gathering. Electing a president was a possibility. Yet on June 25, when Superintendent Cloud convened proceedings, only five board members were present—William Clayton, Andrew Collins, James Nichols, George L. Putnam, Gustavus Adolphus Smith—and the lack of a quorum initially prevented conducting any business. A pattern for the next few days, convening briefly and then adjourning due to insufficient attendance, quickly became frustrating. Harriet Richards and several other faculty wives provided various refreshments to the men otherwise outdone by their fellow regents' truancy. Regardless of a quorum, the board began deliberations on the morning of July 1. DeForest Richards presented a report outlining the university's standing. The president's summarization could not have been overly optimistic. Even in this early stage of the school's second life, financial problems and the finite number of tuition-paying students, as opposed to beneficiaries, called into question the school's economic sustainability. The priority of saving money accounted for suspending the steward's salary for the summer and temporarily dismissing the kitchen staff, and an "embarrassed ... financial condition" also provided the rationale for dispensing with the university physician or surgeon.

Regents also turned their attention to selecting a president. The candidacies of Raphael Semmes, William Hardee, and Matthew Maury seem to have been discussed, but they decided against making a choice until the next meeting. Reproving those who did not come to Tuscaloosa was among the last actions taken before adjourning. Determining a president would have to wait. Two months later, at Montgomery, the board would reconvene.[9]

Some sense of what took place is derived from the correspondence of Hampton Whitfield. The local lawyer was the university's attorney and attended the deliberations at Tuscaloosa. On July 3, the day after the meeting adjourned, he wrote Raphael Semmes at Mobile of the failure to name a president and related, "All the Yankee members came, and all the Southern members staid home." Whitfield apprised the famous privateer that his chances of becoming president lay with the Southern faction and urged Semmes to write them of his aspirations. At the upcoming meeting in Montgomery, Whitfield predicted a president would be settled on, and before then the attorney advised Semmes to build a coalition. As for gaining the endorsement of the superintendent of education, he confided, "You need not depend on Cloud—he has no influence with them." Far more crucial, Whitfield emphasized, was winning the favor of George Putnam, the superintendent of education of Mobile County, who belonged to the board. "I think Putnam would have gone for you if it had come to a vote," the attorney informed Semmes and urged, "Hold him to you." A clear geographic divide had emerged previously. Whitfield's words underscored that running theme.[10]

As it happened, it was Hampton Whitfield, and not Raphael Semmes, who figured significantly in the school's future. The man who had graduated from the university in 1844 practiced law locally. A Republican, but very nominally so, he had recently sold his interest in the *Reconstructionist*, the Republican newspaper in Tuscaloosa that preceded the *Republican Banner*. His brother, Newton Whitfield, a local Democrat, would refer to him as a "Radical all over."[11] In fact, Hampton Whitfield was not that but rather an individual attempting to honor his somewhat malleable political inclinations and also to maintain local standing. He and his wife (Nannie) were well connected socially and had four children, and the man described as a "thorough, courtly southern gentleman" was anything but a partisan firebrand.[12] When the regents had elected him professor of rhetoric and oratory in the summer of 1868, Whitfield resigned (joining William Wyman) in apparent protest over the dismissal of the standing faculty previously elected by the board of trustees. He also soon authored a public letter defending Ryland Randolph against critics who blamed the editor for fomenting local trouble. David Woodruff owned the Waverly bookstore, which served casually as a gathering point for local Republicans. "If Mr Whitfield is a Republican," Woodruff privately wrote, "such men as Judge Peck, myself, & others are Democrats." Woodruff's party credentials could not be doubted.[13]

The university's solvency had been a topic of concern at Tuscaloosa, but its financial status only partly measured the school's standing. The public perception of the institution provided a better barometer. The most prominent state newspaper, the *Montgomery Advertiser*, decided any hopes of avoiding "the last sad rites of Sepulture" were based on selecting a faculty that commanded respect.[14] The *Gadsden Times* maintained the "State University is totally depraved under Radical management."[15] Robert McKee edited the *Southern Argus* at Selma. From his vantage point, the faculty had "been treated by the Tuscaloosans just as they ought to be treated and would be treated by any refined people in the world."[16] When John Warren described the university being "literally destroyed," he was not referring to the depredations carried out by John Croxton's command. A more appropriate faculty and a president "in harmony with the interests of the South," the *Tuscaloosa Observer*'s editor considered imperative, for otherwise "the bell of the University might as well be tolled."[17] Republican newspapers, badly outnumbered in the state, took a different perspective. Among the best was the *Southern Republican*, located in Demopolis, sixty miles south of Tuscaloosa. Pierce Burton, its editor, came to Alabama after the war from Massachusetts. The town's proximity to Tuscaloosa in part accounted for his interest in the melodrama that was playing out there. Burton agreed with Democrats that politics and the university's administration did not mix but drew the line at promoting Raphael Semmes to the presidency. Equating his naval exploits to "piracy," the editor shuddered at the thought of "an unrepentant rebel" leading the state university,[18] and the *Alabama State Journal* also dimly noted the military heft of several candidates, posing, "It will be better for the University to be locked up and the key thrown in the Warrior River" than to promote "heroes of the lost cause."[19]

In June 1869, at Tuscaloosa, efforts fell short to designate a president, but two months later at Montgomery, they would not. Over the summer, in the weeks before the convocation, Noah Cloud maneuvered behind the scenes to entice Matthew Maury to accept the presidency. Doing so took the form of asking H. L. Owen, a Tuscaloosa resident and an acquaintance of Maury's, to inquire of his interest. Owen wrote the Virginia Military Institute professor, describing Tuscaloosa as a healthy town and a place of refined and congenial society. Apologizing that the present means of traveling to Tuscaloosa were "limited," Owens explained that the Alabama and Chattanooga Railroad would soon connect the town. He confided to Maury that the superintendent of education preferred him to "any other person now spoken of." Maury also heard that summer from William Byrd. The former Alabama state supreme court justice wrote him from Selma in admiration of, among other works Maury had authored, *The Physical Geography of the Sea*, and urged the famed author to consider the presidency.[20]

Ten days into August, gathering at the Montgomery capitol, members of the board of education found a rain-starved town gripped by a brutal heat wave. Whether a much overdue and appreciated heavy torrent on the afternoon of August 17 offered a positive omen remained to be seen. University business consumed the much better attended meeting, and the regents soon turned their attention to electing a president. Well situated at Virginia Military Institute, Matthew Maury had taken some interest in the Alabama post but decided against pursuing the position. Raphael Semmes and William Hardee remained favorably disposed toward the office, and both claimed support. On Saturday afternoon, August 21, as the day's deliberations wound down, the board decided to adjourn and reconvene at five o'clock at the Carter House, where the declared and sole purpose was naming a president. And it was there, in the more comfortable confines of the Carter House, that a consensus was reached. The regents turned to a man who had not been mentioned publicly.

Cyrus Northrop had been, since 1863, the professor of rhetoric and English literature at Yale College. Accounting for the selection requires some conjecture. Calvin Loomis may have been partly responsible. At a regent's previous request, the ancient languages professor had asked Elias Loomis to gauge the receptiveness of fellow faculty at Yale to the presidency. "I do not think that one who has a reputation as a thorough scholar need fear much persecution here," Loomis soft-pedaled to his brother, "just because he comes from the north." Elias Loomis possibly acted as a liaison; through him Northrop conceivably indicated an interest, accounting for his election. Whatever the case, on August 24, Cyrus Northrop received by telegraph notification of his election as the president of the University of Alabama. It would be almost two weeks before the Yale professor made known his decision.[21]

The faculty's composition and tenure also gained attention at Montgomery. The regents retained each of the professors—Jasper Callan, Calvin Loomis, DeForest Richards, Vernon Vaughn, and Commandant William McConnell. In light of John Forney's medical problems, Richards had been pressed into teaching mathematics. That responsibility was now entrusted to Nathan R. Chambliss, a former Confederate officer presently living in Selma. His addition raised to six the number of faculty.

Another subject was potentially far more momentous. The feeling that the university would be better off in another location had been growing among regents. The venomous attitude some townspeople exhibited toward the school, students, and professors largely accounted for that determination. The resulting malaise endangered the school's very existence by discouraging enrollment. These circumstances explained regents' approval of a resolution stating the "best interests" of the University of Alabama required its relocation. The board asked that promoters of alternate sites provide proposals in the form of land, property, or money to secure the university. Jesse Booth, George Putnam, and Gustavus Adolphus Smith composed a committee to evaluate applications. Settling on a location other than Tuscaloosa, the regents unanimously recommended, should be accomplished "at the earliest moment practicable."[22]

In the meantime, some eleven hundred miles away in New Haven, Connecticut, Cyrus Northrop seems to have prevaricated. To colleagues and others, he denied having expressed interest in the appointment. It seems unlikely, however, that the regents would have randomly turned to him. And, disingenuously, Northrop did not immediately make his intentions known. As the days passed, far away in Alabama, Noah Cloud grew increasingly impatient. He had hoped to release an announcement promoting the fall term and the new president. As the presidency dangled in limbo, the choice of Cyrus Northrop gained public attention. The *Alabama State Journal* hailed a "wise" decision, describing the Yale professor as "scholarly" and a man further recommended by the fact he had not sought the appointment.[23] That was hardly the view of the *Mobile Register*. That a "Yale Yankee" had prevailed over former Confederate officers Semmes and Hardee angered editor John Forsyth, who attributed the choice to Northrop's "Radical" status.[24] Placing faith in an individual from a "distant Northern State,"[25] John Warren agreed in the *Tuscaloosa Observer*, constituted a mistake, and the Greensboro *Alabama Beacon* described the decision as a "death-blow."[26]

Early in September, Cyrus Northrop drafted a letter declining the invitation. Various considerations may have contributed to that decision. Northrop cherished teaching at Yale, his alma mater, and living in his native Connecticut. Other realities also factored. In conversations he must have had with Elias Loomis, Northrop would inevitably have come to an understanding of the political environment at Tuscaloosa. That was sobering for a man who had recently run unsuccessfully for Congress as a Republican and had at one point allowed it was "unsafe to go and talk freely in the South." Becoming a university president eventually did appeal to Northrop, and he would leave Yale fourteen years later to become the president of the University of Minnesota. How seriously Northrop considered that same office at the University of Alabama cannot be established, but he did not mention the opportunity in his memoirs.[27]

The outcome by any interpretation constituted a serious setback. Settling on a president over the summer and before the fall term started was a crucial priority for the precariously fixed university. Noah Cloud soon diplomatically described to the board of education attempts to find a president as "unfortunate" and, in a more pointed reference to the Northrop debacle, chastised in the future that before extending a candidate the presidency, "first to know, that he will accept it."[28] Democrats were even less forgiving. Northrop's decision caused the *Montgomery Advertiser* to unfavorably compare the school's status with the state universities in Virginia and Georgia and opined that a first step toward achieving their stability necessitated casting "Radical politics to the wind." According to the leading Democratic newspaper in Alabama, the regents must turn to a Southern man identified with the state. That contention was open to debate, but something else was not. Four men had been elected president since the school reopened—William Wyman, Arad Lakin, Robert Harper, and Cyrus Northrop—and that not one had spent a single night in the presidential mansion bordered on the unfathomable.[29]

In the aftermath of the gathering, the university's possible relocation gained attention. Boosters set on landing the university's relocation read opportunity into developments. Several possible places gained mention—Montgomery, Opelika, Selma, and Talladega among them. Changing the venue did not violate any law or constitutional provision. Fifty miles northeast of Tuscaloosa, at Elyton, soon to be renamed Birmingham, some residents envisioned the university settling there as part of the rapidly growing place's presumed expansive future. From his close vantage point at Demopolis, Pierce Burton speculated that Tuscaloosa could lose the university if faculty continued to face animosity. The *Southern Republican*'s editor admonished town residents to halt the "foolish conduct" and recognize that the university served their interests.[30] The Republican brain trust at the *Alabama State Journal* was less sympathetic. The Montgomery newspaper seconded removal, since Tuscaloosa residents "have abundantly shown that they do not want it [the university] there any longer."[31] A far shriller and amplified Democratic press branded relocation as spurious and seized the opportunity to denounce the school under Republican stewardship. The *Mobile Register* ventured that those favoring relocation missed the crucial consideration. What worked against the university was unrelated to geographic situation but rather was attributable to the direction provided by "ignorant Regents and an uneducated Faculty they style Professors."[32] And John Warren agreed that the school's failure had nothing to do with the people of Tuscaloosa. "There is not a spot on the green earth," the local editor projected, "where it could have been a success, under its present administration."[33] Robert McKee turned his pen on those who were amenable to accepting the university. The *Southern Argus*'s editor decided that doing so invited disgrace given the school's disrepute, and he responded to Elyton's courtship by volunteering, "We took it for granted that no town or city . . . would be willing to receive it."[34]

Whether the university would find a new home remained to be seen. What was certain, however, was the school's low ebb. Less than half a year had passed since the University of Alabama's resurrection, but some conclusions were inescapable. The optimistic hopes for revival had fallen flat. The spare number of students provided the most telling yardstick. Some mitigating circumstances accounted for the poor enrollment. The timing of the reopening, for instance, worked against a better showing. Fall term at universities began usually in September or October, and students subsequently returned for winter term in January of the following year. The University of Alabama's awkward opening time in April compromised attendance. So did a simple lack of awareness that the school was even in operation. One prospective enrollee would soon write from Shelby County, "Our county paper here never says a word about the University, so we ain't posted."[35]

Other potential students shared his ignorance of the school but, hopefully, not his choice of contractions. Bad timing and poor dissemination of information regarding the school contributed to the slight enrollment but what did so far more exponentially was the university's perception as a Republican enclave. That was a formidable, if not impossible, obstacle to overcome in Reconstruction Alabama. By way of sounding the depths of malignity directed at Republicans are the sentiments of Dick Riser. In 1870 the young man lived with his family in Talladega County. Ignoring his father's imprecations that "past favors" necessitated the family inviting several Republicans to dinner, the young man pointedly instructed that no place be set for him. Riser proposed drowning "every Rad" in a raging river of Pennsylvania oil and North Carolina turpentine. He did not dine with those he considered political vermin.[36] Another allegory involves the family of Benjamin Gardener, a Republican lawyer living in Eufaula. Gardner confided that his wife, who was "fond of society," had fallen precipitously in social standing locally, and the taint of Republicanism even extended to their eleven-year-old son, who, taunted by his classmates, confided to his father, "Pa, I wish you were a Democrat."[37] Many Democrats in truth did not balk at partaking of a meal with a Republican, and neither could the experiences of the Gardner family be described as universal. But the abiding and eviscerating enmity Republicanism summoned was unprecedented in the experience of Alabama politics. And indisputably, acknowledging the extremely small pool of young white men in Alabama who might potentially seek a college education, matriculating to a Radical university was not an option.

Repositioning the school's image demanded a faculty housecleaning, and at that point a majority of the regents were not prepared to do so. Another rehabilitative option, relocating the university to a more hospitable setting, they did favorably consider. The questions were as obvious as they were divisive. Was it incumbent that the faculty reflect the regional background of the students they taught? And the related query begged settlement: Who were the proper custodians of the University of Alabama? These questions returned to the larger dilemma of autonomy. No resolution was in sight in the summer of 1869.

Against this backdrop, Noah Cloud that fall drafted a treatise concerning the university with two purposes in mind. Publicizing that the university was actually open and that it offered opportunity to young Alabamians desiring a college education formed part of his intention. Cloud promised students a fine education at minimum financial cost. He also intended to correct misinformation. The superintendent realized that the Democrats were succeeding in defining the university in their distorted terms, and the all-important battle for public opinion was being lost. Pivoting to the defensive, Cloud refuted charges that the university was a "political machine" and, replying to those ranting about Republican influence, pointed out that a committed Democrat (William Wyman) had initially been offered the presidency. Cloud also felt compelled to dismiss any intentions to admit Black students to the university as part of a scurrilous and baseless campaign aimed at discrediting the school. In one sense, conveying the institution's advantages as a means of encouraging enrollment, the public letter was thoroughly unremarkable. Contemplated in another sense, the document was extraordinary. Cloud attempted to define what the state university *was*. Explaining what the institution *was not*, though, was more critical.[38] The name of Gustavus Adolphus Smith rarely appears in any secondary literature concerning Reconstruction in Alabama. And yet, between 1868 and 1871, he was the most controversial and powerful member of the board of education. The former Union Army officer also composed a public letter exonerating the embattled school. He, too, denied that partisan considerations drove the board's decisions. "We have studiously avoided politicians," and Smith maintained that a professorial candidate's character and education, not political affiliation, determined hiring protocol. And he also for the record stated that young Black men would not be attending the university. Although Democrats "misrepresented" the institution as a "Radical organization," Smith assured the university "still lives." How long it would do so posed an open question.[39]

Both Cloud and Smith felt it necessary to deny the possibility of an integrated state university. With the prevailing winds of Reconstruction at its back, the formerly unthinkable had become plausible. Admitting freedmen to the Tuscaloosa school and other Southern universities seemed possible given the thrust of Republican egalitarianism. If the very foundational motives animating the establishment of state universities concerned providing educational opportunities to a state's residents, how could that avowed principle be squared with denying the chance to residents of color? The enrollment of freedmen at the University of Alabama had been speculated upon even before the school reopened. Living in Greenville, South Carolina, Basil Manly Jr., had addressed the subject in a letter to his brother in the summer of 1868. "N.C. Univ is to be negroized," the minister predicted, "S. C. Univ will probably go same way," and Manly despaired, "I hope Ala. Univ. will escape." And, more recently, as the university returned to life, Ryland Randolph volunteered that William Henry Jones, son of Shandy Jones, planned to enroll.[40] In fact, neither William Jones nor any other freedperson had any chance of attending the school. Most if not all the board of education members were determined to avoid the firestorm integration foretold. At Montgomery, regents discussed higher education for Black Alabamians and establishing a university for young Black men. But the board minutes are typically sketchy. Providing young Black men with the opportunity to learning was commendable—but not at the University of Alabama.[41]

Few students, either Black or white, were enrolled at the outset of the fall term 1869. Between twenty and thirty cadets took their places when class convened on October 4. Some resumed their studies from the last term, and others were new to the school. The cadet profile—white, at least fifteen years old, and almost all Alabamians—remained the same. A significant number gained state support as beneficiaries. Some were from Republican families. "The boys in town is down on us for bein here," one cadet had complained. "Thy calls us scallerwags and such like." All cadets, regardless of background, continued to lack what was seemingly essential at military schools—uniforms. In her study of military education in the prewar South, Jennifer Green establishes the symbolic importance cadets attached to wearing uniforms. But at the University of Alabama, cadets went without, directly contravening that military ethos. Promises of uniforms, modeled on those at West Point Military Academy, were said to be coming. The first full session of the university lay ahead.[42]

Whatever one's perception of the reasons for the university's standing—a school gutted by Republican machinations or a credible center of learning derailed by conspiracy-obsessed Democrats—the university mission remained what it had always been. Professors and students, in their traditional roles, went about the businesses of imparting and receiving knowledge. The vast majority of cadets, if not all, were of freshman or sophomore standing. Under the direction of Professor Calvin Loomis, they applied themselves in various degrees to reading in the original Latin the *Six Orations of Cicero* and further demonstrated conversance with languages in ancient languages composition courses by translating English into Latin and Greek. The tragedy of *Antigone* bestirred some cadets, while others persevered with grudging resignation. And similarly, the spectrum of interest varied when Professor Vernon Vaughn enlarged on the conquests of Alexander of Macedon or the cultural splendor of the Greeks. All understood the rigors of mathematical courses. Among the students was Thomas Barge, the son of Calvin and Minerva Loomis, who demonstrated a certain familiarity with advanced algebra, but the greater challenge of calculus awaited.[43]

The cadets' deportment varied as widely as did their academic application and ability. Exacting rules at colleges and universities were common, and restrictions at military schools were, by definition, considerably stricter. That a deep streak of mischievousness at best and maliciousness at worst was endemic among young men represented a guiding tenet, and it followed, according to Noah Cloud, that a firm hand provided "the most efficacious means for correcting those irregularities and excesses into which young men are at times liable to fall."[44] Discipline provided the assumed antidote. Infractions involving punctuality, proper dress, order, and generally irregular deportment earned demerits. The commandant more than any other person represented authority. At the opening ceremonies the previous April, Noah Cloud had singled out William McConnell and expressed confidence in the commandant fulfilling his duties. A powerfully built man standing over six feet, McConnell exuded authority. Punishment fell swiftly, but that is not to discount the quotient of mercy. McConnell compiled conduct reports. One summation, presumably typical, early that fall term singled out ten cadets and the number of demerits they had accrued. McConnell might have placed others on the list, but the commandant excused them "under the promise to do better."[45]

The young men living together within the finite space understood a shared burden of academic demands and exacting military regulations. Robert Pace identifies the natural "we" versus "them" dynamic in a perceptive study of students at antebellum colleges and universities. At the University of Alabama, cadets referred to Calvin Loomis as "Cock-eye" because of his eye affliction and, for less obvious reasons, to Jasper Callan as "Shanghai." The alleged hard-drinking habits of Vernon Vaughn earned him the dubious "Tanglefoot" nickname, and a glance at the towering commandant explained William McConnell's appellation, "Big Indian." When DeForest Richards was not in hearing distance, cadets referred to the noticeably senior professor as "Old-Dicks." These men inspired respect, affection, fear, and possibly contempt but, regardless, in the life of each cadet, undeniable relevance.

Academic expectations and conforming to regimentation formed but part of a young man's experience at the University of Alabama. So did the challenge of social acclimation. For students, "college was a social experience," Oscar and Mary Handlin write, "shaped not by their elders or by the subject matter of instruction, but by contact with their peers."[46] The physical incarnation of the university building, which James Murfee designed and George Figh built, is accurately described as capacious. But the structure could also seem very small at times to cadets. A finite number of students randomly thrown together in close proximity made potentially for a strong sense of camaraderie or, considered more darkly, a forced intimacy that bred personal dislikes. Limited evidence suggests that the cadets' experiences were similar to other young men living together in a closely confined environment. Some were self-assured and boisterous and others less confident, reserved, unassuming. In this small world, cadets became fast friends, remained largely passing acquaintances, or sometimes developed frank animosities. As will be seen, those with Republican backgrounds understood an added burden.[47]

The living and working arrangements of professors and the families likewise contributed to a certain insularity. The short distance from one faculty residence to another promoted contact and, reasonably assumed, a sense of neighborhood. Domestic preoccupations drew the women together in a day when gender rigidly defined rules. Family concerns, there were numerous children, partly occupied the women's time. None more so than Sarah Callan, already the mother of several children, who gave birth to a baby boy just weeks after arriving in Tuscaloosa. Harriet Richards was about to turn fifty when she moved to Tuscaloosa. As a mother, Harriet devoted herself to daughter Margaret and her little brother, Bartlett. The Richards impressed on them the centrality of faith. Sunday morning found the family at the local Presbyterian church. Years later, when Bartlett moved West as a young man, he would write back to his mother of reading the Bible and a book of Psalms his mother had given him. The faculty and their wives took pleasure where they could find it. Active and independent, Harriet enjoyed riding horseback about town. Both men and women enjoyed croquet on the removed campus. Vernon Vaughn sought a certain peace walking his dogs and hunting quail. A shared interest in promoting learning encouraged collegiality among the men, and they gathered sometimes at David Woodruff's bookstore. In fact, for all the turbulence, the banal dominated the faculty's cloistered world. Writing to his brother, Calvin Loomis rarely failed to comment on his and Minerva's health. The weather and the crops conditions also drew attention. Minerva had been quite sick for some time when the family moved to town, but the ancient languages professor soon noted that a healthy appetite testified to her improving condition. "We have both gained considerable flesh during our stay here," he informed Elias, "and in fact Minerva is somewhat distressed about this."[48]

In another sense, the experiences of the faculty and their families classically illustrate the perils of a small minority living among a much larger population who resented their presence and, through numbers and power, made those deemed undesirable highly uncomfortable. When contemplated in an overarching worldly view, religious or ethnic differences have often accounted for mistreatment or worse of the vulnerable. It was rather the faculty's Republican affiliation, or their presumed academic shortcomings, that accounted for their denigration. Randolph's assault on Professor Loomis stands as the most obvious example of outward contempt. What can be assumed, however, are an infinite number of smaller incidents, ranging from subtle slights to open insult, which conveyed to the professors, and surely their wives, an unmistakable notion of their unpopularity. Tuscaloosa's small size and population denied a certain anonymity that would have provided some protection at larger places. DeForest Richards's unbowed demeanor and what Randolph described as his "brazen pluck" made him an inviting target. The bespectacled and often top-hatted professor became a familiar but hardly endearing figure. As Richards rode past on horseback, young boys yelled "Old Dicks." Richards was not the only the supreme object of ire. Such was the reality for these unwitting proxy figures forced into a role on a politically charged stage that they had neither sought nor desired.[49]

Sharing an embattled status did not always ensure collegiality, and disagreements among the faculty inevitably arose. DeForest Richards was a man of high expectations. "Your letter to Mother was, on the whole, a very good one," he would write Bartlett in the future, "but it was not as good as it might have been." Reciting "perfectly" was necessary, and he urged his son to pay "diligent attention to your books" and advised against becoming one of the "lazy boys that are always dragging at the foot of their class." That some of Richards's colleagues did not meet the approval of a man who had been a minister much longer than a teacher is easily imagined. It could only have been with serious disapproval that the man of God held a freely imbibing Vernon Vaughn.[50] It was Nathan Chambliss, not Vaughn, that Calvin Loomis faulted. He believed the recently hired math teacher underserved his students. The ancient languages professor wrote his brother at Yale that students complained to him that Chambliss did not fully comprehend some problems, and when he was asked for additional help outside of class, evasively replied, "I am too busy just now." Loomis may have lacked complete objectivity. Among the decisions confronting Chambliss involved selecting textbooks to require for students. Loomis hoped that Chambliss would choose a mathematics book authored by his brother. When the ancient languages professor approached his colleague about doing so, Chambliss politely conceded the book's merit but declined. Writing Elias, Calvin theorized that Chambliss preferred not to have to "study hard" and switch from books he had used at West Point Military Academy.[51]

The concerns of the present were preoccupying, but the faculty also understood the uncertainties of the future and their continued tenure. That the school would move or even close was a distinct possibility. Corresponding with family relations in Ohio, Calvin Loomis admitted his tenuous status. His father, Hubbell Loomis, responded by mentioning in a letter to Elias at Yale that Calvin remained the ancient language professor but qualified that "how long he may continue to hold it appears to me uncertain." If the present was precarious, the future could hardly be described as promising.[52]

It would be overly simplistic even so to assume that all white Tuscaloosans scorned the new regime and ostracized those connected to the institution. Several months into his tenure, Calvin Loomis confided to Elias, "A very great change has evidently taken place in the feelings of many of the citizens . . . though not many of them have become friends."[53] For a time, at least, Nathan Chambliss was accepted in local circles. His status as an ex-Confederate, a Democrat, and a man of social standing provided insulation. Anna Chambliss enjoyed warm relationships, and Ryland Randolph later recalled the daughter of General William Hardee as a "splendid woman."[54] Some local townspeople also befriended Vernon Vaughn's wife. Cornelia Spencer Bibb Vaughn belonged to a high-class Montgomery family. Randolph described the "elegant Montgomery woman" and how "her palpable mesalliance excited the sympathy of Tuscaloosa society."[55]

A passing but revealing public contretemps between John Read and Ryland Randolph also revises the narrative of social banishment. Read was a University of Alabama graduate, a local doctor, an inveterate inventor, and a Democrat in sound standing. Only in the last year he had run for Congress under the party banner. He did not allow political considerations to prevent a sociable relationship with DeForest Richards. Both men lived near each other and attended the Presbyterian church where they sat in proximate pews. Read had recently devised a method of producing paper from the okra plant, and with some pride he forwarded to Richards a newspaper printed on okra-based paper. When Randolph took exception to the friendly gesture, Read turned on the editor. In a public letter he downplayed a "small civility," which hardly constituted "any endorsement of [Richards] in his official capacity," and reasoned that political differences did not make the professor his mortal enemy. "To sacrifice indefinitely all the amenities of life, towards a neighbor, and a member of the same church," Read allowed, "is going too far." Some in Tuscaloosa agreed with that school of social thought—others did not.[56]

In the meantime, between October 1869 and January 1870, the fall term played out. Six weeks into the term, Loomis put the number of cadets at thirty and, skeptically mentioning the rumored arrival of more, decided, "I look up upon the prospects of the University for having a large number of students in attendance as having been well nigh destroyed for the present term."[57] Continuing to his brother, "There is talk of a great many changes here of moving the University—of shutting it up." That did not represent his reading of the future. Loomis predicted by the term's end some seventy-five students, "but for the present it is rather discouraging."[58]

Differences between Loomis and Randolph remained. Their enmity, Randolph had accosted and struck him months before at David Woodruff's bookstore, was well established. The editor soon seized on a chance to publicly humiliate Loomis. As the fall term began, under the ancient language professor's hand, a university circular was drafted, providing the curriculum study plan. The document contained several spelling errors. A reference to "Heroditus" rather than Herodotus provided one transgression. Several other mistakes marred the publication of what Randolph described as an "awful literary botch." He held Loomis responsible for these mistakes and acknowledged incredulously that he was the school's "boasted top scholar."[59] What that indicated about the other professors was unsaid but plain. Reacting in a public letter addressed to the editor, Loomis attributed the mistakes to the poor proofreading of others. Even so, he took Randolph to task. "I have been teaching Latin and Greek for more than twenty-five years," the outraged professor concluded, "and perhaps you may fail to convince that I am quite as ignorant of those subjects as your criticism shows that you are anxious to believe me to be."[60]

A visitor to the campus would inevitably come away with various impressions. The simple majesty of the university building first caught his or her eye. Its sheer size led to and magnified another observation—the limited number of cadets. Even so, form was served, and the appraiser quickly noticed rigid regimentation as the young men went about their day. Military protocol translated into precise observation of order, time, overlaying synchronization. Drill best captured the martial spirit. If the uninitiated onlooker was expecting dashing grandeur, they would be disappointed. The cadets maneuvered adeptly enough in close-order formations of the day, but something was lost given a lack of resplendent uniforms or polished guns and gleaming bayonets. Neither did a meal at the mess hall overly impress. The fare at universities in the nineteenth century was notoriously pedestrian and indeed often did not rise to that level. The food at the University of Alabama did nothing to suggest revisiting that generalization. If our guest inquired of the cuisine, the cadet would likely have described their fare as dull if serviceable and, above all, monotonous. Hickory shad was a heavy standard. Students tired of the boney fish—cheap and plentiful for they were gathered in box traps placed in the Black Warrior River—a far-too-frequent staple. Leaving the campus, the visitor likely pondered something else: Was the very finite number of cadets and the future of a suffering institution quite possibly living on borrowed time?[61]

The university's status accounted for dramatic developments when the board of education met at Montgomery in the last month of 1869. Under the capitol dome, the board addressed a backlog of state education business. Among their highest priorities was settling on a university president. In his opening remarks, Noah Cloud described naming an executive as "essential to the entire success of the Institution." On December 9 they turned to a man in the school's backyard.[62]

Nathaniel T. Lupton belonged to the faculty at Southern University, a private institution located at Greensboro, just forty miles south of Tuscaloosa. A native Virginian, Lupton graduated from Dickinson College in 1846 and attended the storied University of Heidelberg at Berlin, where he studied in the laboratory of the recognized chemist Robert Bunsen. Lupton had since instructed at four colleges or universities before settling more permanently in the late 1850s with his wife at Greensboro and beginning the instruction of chemistry and natural philosophy at Southern University. Lupton's academic credentials, however laudable, were likely not determinative in his hiring. His selection represented the regents' implicit admission that the university needed a president identified with the South. Lupton was emphatically that. He had been a committed Confederate and, drawing upon his scientific expertise, belonged to the Confederate Nitre and Mining Bureau, in which capacity he had personally climbed into caves in search of saltpeter or niter. The South's failure to gain independence, Lupton was certain, did not call into question the cause's righteousness. Several months after the surrender in 1865, Josiah Gorgas visited him at Greensboro, and over a cup of tea with the Confederacy's former chief of ordnance, Lupton expressed doubts as to a general amnesty proclamation. It may be assumed that the ex-Confederate did not think those who had raised arms against the United States had committed offenses that warranted seeking amnesty. At the age of forty, he assumed the university presidency.

The elevation of a Southern man to the presidency constituted but part of the university agenda addressed by regents. The regents dramatically reduced the number of faculty. They declared each chair vacant as of January

FIGURE 5.1. Nathaniel Lupton, president of the University of Alabama, 1869–1870. A Southern Democrat, Lupton's credentials raised the hopes of resetting the direction of a university under siege. But his presidential tenure proved brief and in fact was marked by increased controversy. University of Alabama Libraries Special Collections.

1, 1870, three weeks distant, and determined to fill only the professorships of mathematics, ancient languages, and a newly created Department of English Literature chair. Nathan Chambliss (mathematics) and Vernon Vaughn (English literature) retained their faculty posts, and David L. Peck became professor of ancient languages. Severing ties with half the faculty, seemingly sudden and unexpected, came at the expense of Jasper Callan, Calvin Loomis, William McConnell, and DeForest Richards, who virtually overnight found themselves without position.[63]

What can only be described as a faculty cleaving was bold and shocking. Officials associated with the school would explain the action in terms of saving money and financial realities, which certainly did account in part for the draconic change. Almost inevitably, however, other factors were at work. William McConnell advanced a theory based on the conspiratorial. The commandant blamed Republican regents for his dismissal. The Democrat bitterly referred to being "thrown out of my position by the Rads." The truth was something else. McConnell became expendable when it became the expectation among regents that the United States Army would provide a commandant, saving a hard-pressed state treasury from funding his salary.[64] A brooding and deeply disappointed Calvin Loomis could make a more compelling case for intrigue. Loomis looked to the composition of the board of education to explain his fate. Loomis was aware of the North/South factionalism that divided the board. The ancient languages professor explained to his brother that when he had first been hired, a faction of regents whom he referred to as "carpetbaggers" had opposed his appointment. More recently, however, several of them had confided to him that they regretted doing so and, in the future, that "I might count upon their support as long as they were on the Board." The promise was not kept. Northern regents remained opposed to him, and as Loomis recounted, one of the "scallawags" who originally had been responsible for his election joined the opposing "carpetbaggers." As for the "scalawag" who had crucially voted against him, Loomis wondered to his brother how the "carpetbaggers managed to induce him to vote with them against me."[65] The board of education minutes characteristically provide no enlightenment. These facts remained: the time left on the university faculty for Professors Callan, Loomis, and Richards and Commandant McConnell was measured in days.

The administration of Nathaniel Lupton would begin with the new year. His interpretation of what had gone wrong at the university conformed to that of other Democrats. Republican partisans had packed the faculty with Radicals or otherwise unqualified men, and the once-venerated institution had lost the respect of those who might otherwise have sent their sons there. In fact, such was the stigma of associating with the university that when approached about the presidency, Lupton initially leaned against accepting, fearing association with the school would compromise his social standing and call into question his political loyalties. Lupton relented when several well-placed Democrats convinced him of the opportunity of turning the university in a positive direction. It can be assumed that the attractions of power, prestige, and salary in degrees surely factored into his decision to accept the presidency. A sense of duty to right the badly off course ship may have figured prominently. And the regents accommodated him. Lupton was in the middle of an academic year at Southern University, and presumably for that reason it was agreed that he would finish the term before moving to Tuscaloosa and assuming the daily functions of overseeing the university. Robert McKee noted Lupton's fine reputation and predicted a restoration of public confidence and a resulting influx of students. The *Southern Argus*'s editor ventured, "The University is saved."[66]

Chapter 6

"Mrs. Partington and the Sea"

Novelist Thomas Wolfe wrote evocatively in *The Web and the Rock* of "a thousand points of friendly light," and it was in a similar luster that Nathaniel Lupton's appointment took on a consecrated grace.[1] If the University of Alabama profited by the addition of the new president, the process of subtraction further raised hopes. Severing ties with Jasper Callan, Calvin Loomis, and, most emphatically, DeForest Richards, gained wide approval among local white Tuscaloosans. A deep personal sense of gloom set in for Calvin Loomis. On the first day of class in January 1870, he pined to Elias, "I do not know what I shall do."[2]

As the final days at the university for Loomis and his fellow ousted colleagues counted down, David Peck prepared to assume his place on the faculty. In a sense, assuming a place on the faculty at the University of Alabama represented the completion of a circle. The university's most recently tapped professor had spent his childhood in Tuscaloosa. He was one of several children born to Elisha and Lucy Randall Peck. Leaving Alabama in 1860, Peck enrolled as a junior in 1860 at Trinity College in Hartford, Connecticut, where the transplanted Southerner made a mark as the president of Athenaeum, a literary society, and as a campus poet. The young man's background, his father opposed secession, and Peck's eventual affiliation with the Republican Party strongly suggests that from his perch at Trinity College he regretted the establishment of the Confederate States of America. In 1862, the year of the bloodletting at Antietam, Peck graduated from Trinity College. If he was opposed to secession, it did not follow that the Southern expatriate would lend a hand to preserving the Union. In 1863 Peck was teaching and living in Delaware and paid a commutation fee to avoid serving in the United States Army. In the year the war ended, Peck married Mary Brainerd, a woman with a Connecticut background, and he soon began to prepare to practice law. By 1867, having "read" law, as was the practice of many auditioning future attorneys, he was anticipating becoming a barrister in Rockford, Illinois. "I have had enough of studying in other men's offices," Peck wrote his father, "& always felt as if they didn't want me."[3] Hanging out his shingle in Rockford, judging from a subsequent move, may have not met with success. About 1870 Peck returned to Alabama and settled with his wife and two children in Tuscaloosa. His Republican principles were acknowledged. Ryland Randolph invidiously referred to him that summer as "freshly imported from Yankeedom" and, noting Peck's Republican loyalties and recent connection with the university, reasoned, "As dirty water seeks its level, so he should seek his in the gutter." On January 13, the day the appointments of the Callan, Loomis, McConnell, and Richards formally concluded, Peck assumed his duties as professor of ancient languages.[4]

As it turned out, for all its presumed promise, the administration of Nathaniel Lupton began in highly irregular fashion. What partly contributed was the arrangement made with the board of education apparently allowing him to finish the academic year at Southern University and postpone relocating to Tuscaloosa until the fall of 1870. When the regents elected Lupton in the last month of 1869, they instructed him to select a faculty member to serve as commandant until the United States Army provided the promised official. On January 12, 1870, early in the winter term, Lupton issued an order naming Nathan Chambliss as commandant and providing him with authority to direct the university. He would fill the void of power in the president's absence and effectively supervise the university's day-to-day operations during the winter/spring term of 1870.[5]

Time and circumstances thrust Nathan Rives Chambliss into a position he could not have imagined a few months earlier when he joined the faculty. Even so, in many respects, Chambliss's past prepared him for leadership. Born in Virginia in 1834, he had attended Giles College and Cumberland University in Tennessee, and demonstrative promise accounted for an appointment to West Point Military Academy in 1856. Part of his fine record included election as captain of the cadet corps. A photograph of him at West Point reveals a handsome, sandy-haired cadet with classic features. Chambliss graduated ninth in a class of forty-five in 1861. The timing could not have been more awkward. The Civil War was beginning. Nathan Chambliss faced the decision confronting other Southern men with a West Point background. Devotion to country was the deepest imbued principle of the military school's creed. Did the unprecedented circumstances that exploded into civil war justify violating that principle?

"Mrs. Partington and the Sea"

An underlying commitment to the United States did not prevent Chambliss (or the vast majority of Southerners with a West Point past) from resigning and becoming a dedicated Confederate. As an officer, he saw duty in Kentucky, Mississippi, Tennessee, South Carolina, and Alabama, and was promoted from captain to lieutenant colonel in an exemplary military career that spanned the war's duration. Chambliss was commanding the Charleston

FIGURE 6.1. Nathan Chambliss, professor of mathematics and commandant, 1869–1870, during his education at West Point before the war. A decade after graduating from West Point Military Academy, Nathan Chambliss began teaching math at the University of Alabama and soon assumed the duties of commandant. In an administrative capacity for a period of months in 1870, Chambliss acted with integrity during an incredibly challenging time. This had the ironic effect of his falling from local favor and soon resigning. 1861 Class Album, Special Collections, USMA Library.

Arsenal in South Carolina when the conflict ended. In the intervening years between the war's close and when Chambliss joined the University of Alabama faculty late in 1869, Chambliss lived in Selma. His residence there is apparently explained by the fact that during the war, while stationed for a time at the Selma arsenal, he had met and fallen in love with a local woman, Martha "Mattie" Matthews. They married in 1865, but only six weeks later, she died at the age of twenty. Chambliss remained in Selma, at some point becoming editorially connected to the *Selma Morning Times*, in addition to cultivating cotton. He also became romantically involved with Anna Dummett Hardee. Some years earlier, while a West Point cadet, he had become acquainted with the daughter of William Hardee, at the time the military academy's commandant. The man who had previously been considered to direct the University of Alabama was the president of the Selma and Meridian Railroad and living with his wife in Selma. Anna lived with them. The circumstances allowed for a blossoming romance. On April 24, 1867, the couple wed at the former Confederate general's home. If Chambliss had not been before, he now belonged to the Southern gentility. His connection to the *Selma Morning Times* had ended, or soon would end, and efforts at raising cotton went largely unrewarded. In the fall of 1867, aspiring to a new livelihood, he wrote Governor Robert Patton about joining the faculty at the soon-to-be opening University of Alabama. His efforts came to nothing. Neither were his prospects as a cotton planter promising. Thomas B. Roy, soon to become his brother-in-law, wrote distressingly in 1868 of Chambliss's short cotton crop, empathizing, "Poor Chambliss! He hasn't been able to find anything for him to do here." Chambliss was a restless man searching for a place when the regents extended him an appointment to teach mathematics at the University of Alabama. His time in Selma had been marked by personal loss, professional uncertainty, but ultimately rejuvenation. He, Anna, and their infant daughter moved to Tuscaloosa, where Professor Chambliss began teaching mathematics when the fall term opened in 1869. Several months later, at the outset of 1870, he was made commandant and assumed responsibility for overseeing the university.[6]

Following a Christmas recess, as 1870 opened, the university reconvened. Although the regents had decided in the last month of 1869 against extending the tenure of Professors Callan, Loomis, and Richards and Commandant McConnell, each continued to carry out their duties for several weeks and into the new year. Until January 12, as the lame-duck professor's time wound down, Chambliss wrote that "the usual role of recitations" continued. Thursday, January 13, 1870, offered a marking point. Following morning prayer at the chapel, the cadets were detained. Gustavus Adolphus Smith had traveled to Tuscaloosa in order to speak for the board of education. He announced to the cadets what they surely knew already—that Professors Callan, Loomis, and Richards and Commandant McConnell were departing. Economic realities, Smith explained, accounted for that development. Parting with them, the regent dutifully continued, the university did regretfully. Smith explained that a commandant from the ranks of West Point graduates would soon be selected. The former Union officer preached resilience, and even if their numbers remained small, he urged faculty and students alike to harmonize and resist demoralization. Gustavus Adolphus Smith remained vitally interested in the university's future and, before concluding his remarks to the cadets, projected prosperous days ahead. Among the assembled cadets that day was his son, William Smith, who, at least for the moment, was relatively unknown locally. That would soon change.[7]

On that Thursday morning, wasting no time, Professors David Peck, Vernon Vaughn, and Nathan Chambliss convened class under what the latter termed "the auspices of the new Faculty." The thirty or so enrolled cadets represented a slight improvement from the previous term. A daunting situation did not overwhelm Chambliss. Well aware of the precarious present and questionable future, he took some encouragement in the days ahead from students who mentioned to him "improved instruction." Nathaniel Lupton would remain largely if not entirely absent from the campus during the first half of 1870. Addressing him in monthly letters as "president," Chambliss kept Lupton abreast of developments.[8]

The cadets began a period of adjusting to new instructors, but much also remained the same in their daily lives. Rising early, they offered prayer at the chapel and then set off for breakfast, and a structured day unfolded from there. Nothing testified to routine more than daily breeches of the rules. On the morning of February 11, W. B. Cheney gained formal reprimand for talking while "marching to breakfast."[9] Neither were cadets always models of deportment once at the mess hall. On February 22, Edward Maury threw bread at a fellow cadet, and possibly in retaliation, M. H. Mahan did likewise. Early in March, after being reported for talking out of turn, W. Cheney was cited again for an early morning transgression, and he profanely replied to the officer as the cadets marched to, of all places, the chapel. Cadets could formally challenge alleged transgressions, but inflexible military protocol placed a premium on order rather than rights and reduced the young men to highly disadvantaged plaintiffs. Some would have found the logic of T. D. Osborne strained after he missed an early morning recitation in Professor

Peck's class and, by way of absolution, explained, "I was under the impression that we would not be required to speak."[10] Late for roll call, M. A. Kendrick cryptically justified to Chambliss that was due to "very pressing business."[11] Cadet M. H. Mahan also chose the route of supplication. Reported for appearing in night clothes at roll call, Mahan explained, "I over slept myself" and asked for forgiveness.[12] Study hours were over and the nine o'clock bell had rung on February 16 when John M. Wilson took the liberty of smoking. The officer of the day reported him for a seeming violation, but Wilson demurred that after the nine o'clock hour, "a cadet can be at leisure." On balance, for the University of Alabama cadet, there was little "leisure" time.[13]

And that was manifestly true of an understaffed faculty as well. The duties of Nathan Chambliss seemed to never end. President Lupton's directive of January 12 granted the commandant authority to draw funds necessary for the school's operation. Making certain that adequate stores of food were on hand composed part of his responsibilities. Chambliss placed orders with F. E. Stollenwerck & Bros., commission merchants in Mobile, for large quantities of rice, sugar, lard, over three hundred pounds of bacon, and a hundred pounds of "Rio" coffee. Maintaining personnel in the kitchen caused him in January to hire a freedman named Monroe Edwards as a cook. Some workers were more dependable than others. When a mess hall employee was determined to be intoxicated at work, the commandant replaced him with "a sober man." Early in the year, surely with some awkwardness, Chambliss accepted from Calvin Loomis the keys to the home he and Minerva had occupied. The large Callan family packed up, and soon William McConnell also departed. In the meantime, five hours each day, commandant Chambliss directed math courses.[14]

The status of DeForest Richards resisted a final solution. The former professor was pious, hardworking, and dedicated. He could also be imperious. On January 13, the day the professorial guard changed, Richards was sitting in the legislature in Montgomery. In her husband's absence, Harriet Richards looked after their two youngest children, Margaret and Bartlett, and they remained at the campus home, for Chambliss granted permission to rent the residence. Late in January, as part of a legislative committee charged with inspecting the insane asylum, Richards briefly returned to Tuscaloosa. Various topics accounted for a meeting between the commandant and the former professor at the home he had lived in since first coming to Tuscaloosa. Although Richards compliantly handed over the keys to the observatory, their conversation became contentious. Richards denied that the regents had authority to remove him from the faculty and on those grounds maintained his family's right to the residence. He adamantly reiterated that he remained the "Professor of Natural Sciences in the University of Alabama," that he would continue to maintain the home, and that anyone trying to force him to vacate "would be regarded and treated as an intruder." When Chambliss responded that would be decided by an interpretation of the law, Richards grew angrier and defiantly invited the law's application.[15]

Years of conforming to rigorous West Point standards had instilled in Nathan Chambliss an unswerving respect for protocol and procedure. While commanding the Charleston arsenal during the war, he had at one point protested interference from another officer as detrimental to "military discipline."[16] The circumstances he now confronted weighed heavily against precision and order. A burdened commandant delegated duties out of necessity. Above and beyond instructing ancient and modern language classes, David Peck served as officer in charge of what were termed the barracks and each day inspected them twice. Peck lived in the barracks. Neither did Vernon Vaughn enjoy the luxury of concentrating on academics, for the rhetoric and oratory and English literature professor acted as the university quartermaster. Commandant Chambliss, betraying his military acclimation, or possibly the professor's unreliability given his drinking habits, soon recorded that Vaughn "reported ready for duty." Between teaching and carrying out responsibilities as quartermaster, Chambliss observed Vaughn "has no more leisure than either Prof. Peck or myself." Weeks into his tenure as commandant, he remonstrated to President Lupton, "I have published orders but this avails nothing if there is not someone to follow them up every hour of the day and see them enforced." All that could be hoped for, Chambliss resigned, was preventing "boisterous noise" during study hours and "lessons tolerably learned." At least, living in the barracks, Professor Peck "keeps the cadets quiet at night."[17]

The first three months of 1870 cautiously encouraged the optimist. A tailor was engaged by the university to provide uniforms, and that well-overdue prospect generated favorable anticipation among the cadets. Chambliss also held out hope to issue more obligatory accoutrements at a military school—guns for drilling purposes. He welcomed the arrival of supplies from Mobile brought up the Black Warrior River, which included lard, pork shoulder, rice, sugar, and a barrel of "good molasses." In a letter to the president, the commandant proposed that April 11 be set aside for martial exercises. And so, under Nathan Lupton's absentee stewardship, generously characterized as nominal, events moved forward at the university. As March ended, a week-long vacation began. A period of relative calm was about to change dramatically.[18]

On Friday, April 1, in broad daylight, a cadet shot Ryland Randolph on a downtown Tuscaloosa street. The event would have extreme consequences for the editor and his assailant and tragic finality for an individual unconnected to the fray. And there were also definitive repercussions for the University of Alabama.

It seems highly likely that the events that led up to the shocking incident date from Randolph's most recent denunciation of Vernon Vaughn. Two weeks before the shooting, he had, in the columns of the *Independent Monitor*, advised Tuscaloosans to shun the professor whom Randolph referred to as a "drunken vagabond and sorry scallawag."[19] Out at the university, a number of cadets determined to defend him. Fourteen students signed resolutions branding the allegations "untrue, unjust, [and] uncalled for," and far from the miserable professor Randolph portrayed, they considered Vaughn a "thorough scholar" and an "efficient, successful and enthusiastic teacher." Neither was he the drunkard ridiculed as "Tanglefoot," but rather a "moral, high toned gentleman." The cadets who affixed their signature also demonstrated an understanding of the larger stakes involving the University of Alabama. They took Randolph to task for a campaign that collaterally damaged "the best interest of the institution." It cannot be substantiated that their protest had any relation to what transpired several days later, but the timing and the principal figures involved are suggestive.[20]

Friday, April 1, began similarly to other days in Tuscaloosa. Merchants opened their businesses, women and men milled about town, some with purpose and others not, often occupied in conversation. A cross section of the populace, Black and white, looked forward to a traveling circus that had arrived. Among those in town was a cadet named William Smith. Ryland Randolph was also circulating. About noon, as the editor was conversing with an acquaintance, Smith roughly brushed into the editor. Taking the stranger for an "insolent rowdy," Randolph angrily retaliated by striking Smith in the face. The cadet pulled out a pistol and began shooting at Randolph, who, also armed, fired back. The rapid fusillade ended when Randolph, struck at close range in the thigh, fell to the ground. William Byrd, a bystander hit by an errant bullet fired by Smith, also collapsed, mortally wounded. In the ensuing moments of chaos, there was confusion as to what had happened, but some certainties did emerge. Ryland Randolph was seriously wounded, and William Byrd's life had suddenly ended. In the immediate aftermath, William Smith fled on foot, bolting through a store's back door, and instinctively made rapidly for the university. The campus provided the most temporary of sanctuaries. Within hours Sheriff Josiah

Pegues and a party of men arrested him in the second-floor room of Vernon Vaughn's campus home.

When authorities took William Smith into custody, they also arrested Vaughn on suspicion of being an accessory to the crime. Allegations, innuendo, and hearsay allowed for a materializing storyline implicating the professor many already considered notorious. He had been in town at the time of the incident. Some townspeople credited reports that Smith and Vaughn had been seen together at the professor's home on the morning of the shooting, that Vaughn had driven a university wagon into town, carrying concealed guns, and that he had created a diversion at the time of the altercation. Vaughn's alleged erratic behavior just before the incident—specifically, pacing about oddly—also stoked conspiracy notions. The apparent friendly terms between Vaughn and Smith and the cadet's flight to the professor's residence further added to the subjective indictment. That Vaughn had struck at his bitter enemy through one of his students was a theory advanced, considered, and accepted by more than a few. These facts were beyond dispute. William Byrd, a saddler and the town weigher, was dead. Ryland Randolph's condition worsened in the following days, and saving the editor's life necessitated amputating his left leg. And William Smith and Vernon Vaughn, incarcerated at the jail across the street from the former capitol, awaited their judicial fates.[21]

One of the protagonists in the episode that commanded much attention for the next several weeks in Tuscaloosa, Vernon Vaughn, was a familiar figure. Most white residents regarded him as a heavily alcohol-indulging opportunist who owed an undeserved appointment as professor to his Republican affiliation. Vaughn's abysmal public standing managed to do the unthinkable—fall even further.

William Smith, by contrast, had no public reputation. He was merely one of the largely anonymous young men out at the university. A biography of the suddenly notorious cadet emerged in subsequent days. A curious public learned that William A. Smith was the son of Gustavus Adolphus Smith and was twenty years old at the time of the shooting, although some local residents erroneously thought he was older. His Northern background and past as a Union soldier during the war drew a sharper distinction. The former Union soldier's ironic enrollment at a university previously destroyed by federal troops was accounted for by his family's relocation after the war to Courtland, Alabama. Although a recommended physical profile for cadets did not exist, Smith fell well short of any desirable composite. A contemporary, but definitely not a friend, described him as "exceedingly stout, uncouth, and ruffianly in appearance."[22] Neither was Smith a stranger to trouble. In the summer of 1869, after suspending the university steward's services temporarily, regents entrusted him with looking after the building and generally policing the grounds. Taking advantage of that position, Smith and two others filed a counterfeit key to the quartermaster's room and stole supplies and sold them locally on some version of a black market. At the time William McConnell was the commandant, and he proved the cadet's guilt in a disciplinary hearing. McConnell considered Smith a "scoundrel" and recalled that before an examining board the cadet had profanely accosted DeForest Richards.[23] University records documenting the cadet's conduct in the weeks preceding the shooting further color a young man who attracted more than his share of negative attention. Over a period of weeks, Smith was cited for numerous offenses that included failing to rise from the dinner table at command and using improper language in the mess hall. Southern cadets at West Point Academy faced bitterness from their Northern classmates well into the nineteenth century. It is highly likely, reciprocally considered, that William Smith's past status as a Union soldier was held against him. On March 24, found "scuffling" with a fellow student during study hours, he was assessed six demerits. On another occasion, Smith defended himself against charges of using profanity. His forty-one-word explanation composes Cadet Smith's only known oral record. By way of defense, he related a conversation with a fellow cadet. Smith disingenuously explained, "I was giving a description of a mill being washed away the dam remaining," and continued, "I said there was a dam by a mill site but no mill by a dam site, I did not think there was anything improper in it." William Smith was hardly a model cadet. Whether he had attempted murder posed another question. In several weeks, when what was referred to as an "examining court" convened, some conclusions would be reached.[24]

Time must have passed slowly for the two prisoners during the first three weeks of April, but the length of a single day in a cell Vaughn described as "wretched" was hardly their greatest concern. Both men understandably feared for their safety.[25] Threats of the prisoners' lynching circulated. Public opinion among white Tuscaloosans lay against both men. William Byrd, a well-thought-of man, lost his life, and Ryland Randolph, to some an unflinching defender of the right, would never be the same man again. Recent precedent argued for strong preventive measures. From the same jail, a group of men had forcibly taken William Cochrane and shot the young Black man to death a year earlier. In fact, within hours of their arrest, Captain William Mills took action. The commanding officer of the small company stationed in town detailed several soldiers to guard the jail. Intensely worried, Cornelia Bibb Vaughn begged her husband to write Governor Smith of the danger. He did not, but she did, maintaining "not a scintilla of proof" implicated her husband. Neither did Cornelia and their children rest easily. On Friday night, April 16, hallowing and screaming men surrounded the Vaughn's campus home, terrorizing the family. All too aware of their vulnerability, she beseeched the governor, "They knew that my poor dear husband was in jail" and "that I was alone."[26] Gustavus Adolphus Smith also worried. William Smith's father had recently left Alabama and relocated to Santa Fe, New Mexico, where he took a position with the Internal Revenue Department. From his jail cell, Cadet Smith wrote to him there. The letter no longer exists, but the prisoner's trepidation is easily gleaned from his father's reaction. Alarmed by his son's words, the former regent urgently wrote Governor Smith, asking that he maintain the military guard and pleading, "Let me beg of you gov. to see that my son has protection and a fair trial." Neither security nor due process of law was sure.[27]

The charges against Smith and Vaughn gained preliminary evaluation between April 18 and April 20 in what was termed an "examining court." Local lawyers Dominique D. Fiquet and W. G. Cochrane presided. William Russell Smith, Judge W. Moody, and J. M. Martin represented the defendant, charged with murdering William Byrd and assaulting Ryland Randolph with intent to murder. Vaughn seems to have been formally accused of conspiracy. Local attorneys Henderson Somerville and A. B. McEachin prosecuted. In a very real sense, the University of Alabama was on trial. A lack of court records or other accounts of the proceedings preclude much elaboration, but it is certain that the proceedings at the Tuscaloosa courthouse attracted much attention. On April 18, and then for the next two days, Sheriff Pegues and the jailer escorted the defendants from the jail to the courthouse and back. While making the short walk, Smith and Vaughn would have drawn contemptuous looks if not open derision. It can also be assumed that local residents crowded a courtroom, which had been the site of its share of drama and bizarre trials—but nothing resembling this set of circumstances. Both the prosecution and defense produced witnesses. Apparently, Smith maintained that he shot at Randolph only after the editor fired at him twice, and the case his lawyers mounted rested on self-defense. On April 20, after over two days of examination, Vaughn was acquitted. The court remanded William Smith to jail without bond to await action by the county grand jury.[28]

It was hardly a vindicated and triumphant defendant who exited the courthouse. Fully appreciating the fact that the verdict did not absolve him of guilt in the eyes of many residents, Vaughn understood the importance of quickly leaving town. His lawyers advised departing, for they worried as well about the professor's safety, as did his wife, who had fearfully written the governor "*everybody* that speaks to me says that he must leave here at once or be murdered."[29] Anxious that he had little time to lose, Vaughn applied to Nathan Chambliss for a leave of absence. The commandant recognized the gravity of the situation and expeditiously granted the request. Well aware of Vaughn's personal jeopardy, he later justified to President Lupton, "I aided him all I could in getting off."[30] The Vaughns hastily packed their belongings, gathered their children, and left town within a day of the trial's close. Stopping over at Selma, Vaughn spoke with representatives of the *Selma Press*, a Republican newspaper. A man still experiencing the physical and psychological effects of several weeks of anxiety and incarceration described a dangerous state of affairs in Tuscaloosa. Grim but relieved, he took the opportunity to thank the soldiers who composed his guard for their kindness during the ordeal. Regarding a connection to the shootout, Vernon Henry Vaughn assured in his conversation at Selma that there was none, "save as a spectator."[31]

As it was, concerning the matter of William Smith's guilt or innocence, there would be no legal reckoning. Six days after the court adjourned, on Tuesday night, April 26, the prisoner escaped. It seems an opportunity arose when the jailer, Jesse Mabry, left the jail about midnight to go fishing, making it possible for one or more of the soldiers to free Smith. Elated at liberation but well aware of his acute danger, Smith made the campus his destination, as he had after shooting Randolph. There he rendezvoused with T. D. Osborne, a cadet who would leave town with him. Maybe there was a preconceived plan or possibly the situation spontaneously played out. Whatever the case, the cadets understood the necessity of putting distance between themselves and Tuscaloosa, and to do so they stole a horse and mule, both of which belonged to the university. That night or early the next morning, one astride the bay horse and the other riding the black mule, Smith and Osborne left town.[32]

An incredible drama had taken yet another astounding twist. Apprehending the fugitive concerned Governor Smith, and he telegraphed Sheriff Josiah Pegues on April 28, "Do your utmost to recapture him." In the wired message, the executive also asked Pegues if he believed William Smith had been freed by his "friends" or "enemies." That question was apparently based on the plausible theory that those responsible for the prisoner's escape, if they were in reality his "enemies," intended to harm Smith once he was beyond the jail's protective walls. A version of that scenario ended in William Cochrane's murder less than a year earlier. The governor offered a reward of $400 for apprehending Smith, the maximum that the state could provide.

The precise set of circumstances accounting for Smith's escape remains a mystery. It was not due to keen resourcefulness on the prisoner's part, or the result of a bungled trap set by those intent on administering to the cadet their version of vigilante justice. It seems likely the soldiers trusted to guard Smith felt compelled to aid a former comrade in arms in the heart of the former Confederacy. Less rather than more is known, but collusion seems certain. Captain William Mills tellingly ordered the confinement of several soldiers for their apparent roles, and at least one of the men remained locked up for months at Tuscaloosa.[33]

In the meantime, Smith and Osborne headed for what Chambliss soon referred to as "parts unknown."[34] Some general knowledge of their flight surfaced. Three weeks after fleeing Tuscaloosa, Osborne wrote his father at Tuscumbia on May 12 from Corinth, Mississippi. Corinth was some one hundred and seventy-five miles northwest of Tuscaloosa. Horace Osborne, the boy's father, forwarded the letter to Chambliss. Nothing is known about the letter's contents, other than revealing the fugitives' westward journey and that they had abandoned the horse and mule above Elyton. Apprehending William Smith was desirable, but so was recovering the animals that were school property, and the latter seemed more likely. On behalf of a financially pressed university, Chambliss wrote to Horace Osborne and asked for more precise information as to where the horse and mule had been left, for "recovering the animals is very desirable in every way."[35]

For the remainder of his life, Ryland Randolph held that Vernon Vaughn was implicated in the shooting. That is possible. As a Republican, Vaughn took much exception to the editor's extremism and held him accountable for much of the local volatility. On a personal level, the insulted professor deeply resented the man who had repeatedly slandered him in the columns of the *Independent Monitor*. Only two weeks before the shooting, Randolph had labeled Vaughn a "drunken vagabond" who should be "spurned and kicked out of every decent man's walk." About the same time, Vaughn bitterly denounced Randolph in a letter published in the *Alabama State Journal*.[36] On balance, however, Vaughn's involvement seems highly improbable. That a professor would murderously conspire with a student stretches credibility. The respect a former attorney would have held the magistery of the law in further discourages conclusions regarding his guilt. Even more convincing is the fact that a jury in a court of law heard testimony, weighed evidence, and on that basis acquitted Vaughn. Nathan Chambliss also absolved the professor. "The situation is one for which he should not be held responsible," the commandant informed Noah Cloud and, in the larger picture, praised Vaughn for carrying out "his duties with fidelity, and has in all respects conducted himself with the decorum becoming his position."[37]

The innocence or guilt of William Smith also invites speculation. The confrontation with Randolph plausibly resulted from a spontaneous altercation. Randolph was an extremely hot-headed man. In his unpublished memoirs written some twenty-five years later, the editor recalled mistaking the individual who ran into him that day for an unmannerly countryman in town for the circus and responding instinctively by hitting Smith in the face. Randolph's admission of striking Smith first suggests a theory. Angered by the assault, the cadet retaliated by drawing a gun and firing, and there was no premeditation. It is also conceivable that Smith, acting on his own, intentionally provoked Randolph, hoping to harm or kill him. That he carried not one but two pistols supports this theory. Smith plainly despised the editor. Three days before the shootout, when cadets drafted the resolutions defending Vaughn and condemning Randolph, Smith was the first person to sign the manifesto. Another subjective consideration, but possibly a revealing one, was Smith's behavior record, suggestive of a defiant and rebellious spirit. The simple laws of probability, that Smith would by remote chance run into a supremely hated foe, weigh further against pure happenstance. And if Vaughn's acquittal points to his innocence, the jury's decision to retain Smith in custody is incriminating. Neither can the profile offered thirty-four years later at Smith's death be dismissed. "He was a man of strong likes and dislikes," a friend judged, "always upholding that which he believed to be right and denouncing in no uncertain terms those things that to him seemed wrong." A younger version of that person was sure there was much "wrong" about Ryland Randolph. A tantalizing question remains: Did an impressionable and trouble-prone young man who admired Professor Vaughn assume the role of defender and avenger? Ryland Randolph would maneuver on one leg for the remainder of his life. And William Byrd's life was suddenly and tragically over.[38]

Whatever the origins of the gunplay, what had transpired inevitably attracted unflattering scrutiny to the University of Alabama. In the minds of many, a cadet who was the instrument of his professor had killed an upstanding citizen and grievously wounded one of the best-known journalists in the state. "Are Radicals to be permitted to murder our people with impunity," the *Montgomery Mail* asked, "and then to escape punishment through the connivance of our corrupt and inefficient rulers?"[39] The *Alabama State Journal* pronounced Vernon Vaughn innocent and decided that Smith and Randolph shared blame for William Byrd's death. The Republican newspaper conceded that the cadet fired the bullet that killed Byrd but pointed to Randolph's intemperate pen and reasoned "hate begats hate, and murder follows."[40] That was hardly the dominant interpretation.

The episode foretold devastating consequences for the university. Well before the trial, cadets began to leave out of a sense of disillusionment and quite possibly fear. Some received letters from parents instructing them to do so. Something resembling a collective panic resulted. Chambliss remembered "a stampede seemed to possess the students," many gathering their belongings and departing. An inability to concentrate on their studies in the charged atmosphere provided the most commonly cited reason. Chambliss and Peck tried to stop or slow the exodus, but their entreaties made no difference. "In vain did we fulminate," the commandant would later write Noah Cloud, "against those who were abandoning the school." He compared his situation to the plight of Mrs. Partington, a character popularized by an American humorist, Benjamin P. Shillaber. In his version of events at Sidmouth, England, Shillaber describes Mrs. Partington vainly attempting with a mop to keep out the flooding Atlantic Ocean waters. Chambliss avowed, "The struggle was like that between Mrs. Partington and the sea, although we might be good at a slop or a paddle we could not beat back the Atlantic Oceans."[41]

The situation steadily deteriorated during the remaining weeks in the spring term. The original faculty, reduced recently from six to three, now stood at a mere two professors, Nathan Chambliss and David Peck. Simply attempting to keep the university open caused Chambliss to draconically cut back services. He closed the mess hall to save money and released the entire staff except a carpenter and another individual who carried out the duties of porter, watchman, and gardener. Chambliss had based previous calculations for food and supplies on the needs of considerably more young men than were now present. The commandant was left with an overabundance of supplies. It was both a resourceful and desperate man who was reduced to selling locally some of the surplus previously obtained from Stollenwerck & Bros., the commission merchants in Mobile. Efforts to maintain a semblance of normality continued. Despite the few students, Professors Chambliss and Peck conducted classes. A certain familiarity with various fields had meant that university professors sometimes instructed in areas beyond their specialization. Yet Chambliss and Peck composed the barest skeleton of a faculty. They faced the unrealistic prospect of teaching courses far removed from their expertise. Events at the mess hall on the evening of April 21 offered at least a sense of continuity. Five cadets were cited for throwing bread at the dinner table. As May neared an end, Chambliss wrote Noah Cloud of the storm's passing and prevailing quiet. With the slightest of perspectives, he recalled the exodus and confessed, "The situation has been a trying one and I have had to do the best I could." That involved enforcing the rules. When several of the very finite number of cadets missed a 6:00 a.m. roll call, the officer of the day reported them. "The instruction of these 6 cadets continues daily as if there were 60," Chambliss dutifully informed Cloud. On April 1, the day of the Smith/Randolph shootout, twenty-eight students were attending. Only six remained a month later.[42]

The school had reached a new low. Some eighty miles away, in Shelby County, self-styled "Pencil" posed as an authority. He noted the small number of cadets and wryly observed the ratio of students to professors was about one to one. Such was the "effect of too much Republicanism."[43] When the final days of the term signaled a merciful recess, John Warren also directed comments at the institution, which was carrying on in the skimpiest guise of a university. Well-attended commencement exercises that June at the Tuscaloosa Female College and the Alabama Central Female Institute had reminded him of the formerly celebrated occasion at the university. Warren contrasted those festive times to the present desolation and compared the campus to Egypt after the "plague" of biblical lore. Until the "Radical professors'" banishment and the relinquishment of Republican political control, Warren prophesized a "pall of darkness."[44]

Nathaniel Lupton remained at Greensboro through all the turmoil. Six weeks had passed since the shootout when Chambliss informed the president by letter of extreme difficulties and prevailed on him to make the short trip to Tuscaloosa and gain a full appreciation of matters. As the academic term wound down in June, Lupton did return to the campus. Among his intentions was severing the university's ties with Vernon Vaughn. Over a month earlier, Vaughn had hurriedly left Tuscaloosa. At the very least, the president considered Vaughn a drunkard and morally unfit for the high mantle of professor. If he needed more justification, Vaughn had left the campus and was not fulfilling his academic responsibilities. Lupton determined to revoke the professor's leave of absence and instructed Chambliss to write to him of that decision. In fact, Vaughn never intended to reclaim his faculty post. He was in Washington attempting to gain a political appointment through the Grant administration. At some point, opening the commandant's letter at the Metropolitan Hotel where he was staying, the former professor learned of his leave's cancellation. So ended Vernon Vaughn's highly controversial relationship with the University of Alabama.[45]

Nathaniel Lupton's return to Tuscaloosa in June 1870 would be brief. His administration, in fact, was on the verge of ending. Well before the Randolph/Smith incident, conflict had arisen between Lupton and the board of education soon after he was made president. The differences concerned the faculty's composition and hiring procedure. When Lupton had been elected president late in 1869, it was his understanding that the regents would select professors from the pool of candidates he recommended. Lupton held that assembling an entirely new faculty was fundamental to reversing the university's direction. Yet, just days after he agreed to accept the presidency, the regents reelected Vernon Vaughn and placed David Peck on the faculty. Lupton apparently interpreted this as a breach of their agreement. Violation of the understanding to cede nominating responsibilities to Lupton, or the regents contrasting interpretation of the terms, accounted for extreme contention. Relations between the president and the regents, off to a poor start, would degenerate further.

Late in June, when Superintendent Cloud convened the board of education at Greensboro, Lupton repaired there to meet with the regents. Differences concerning the faculty's composition continued to be unbridgeable. According to one local resident, the regents intended "to fix up the State University with a Faculty." The unknown observer specifically referred to "Old Richards" and ventured that the regents "will split on men opinions and make a grand failure." Lupton remained determined to make wholesale faculty changes. A list of possible professors, all Democrats, had been presented to him. The regents refused to comply, and the impasse remained. The lack of a quorum prevented definitive action at Greensboro, and when the board met several days later, forty-five miles to the east at Selma on June 26, insufficient numbers again thwarted the transaction of business. Three days later, on June 29, Noah Cloud convened the board at the capitol in Montgomery. What had transpired at Greensboro and Selma widened disagreements, and the fruitless deliberations seem to have pushed Lupton to make a decision he had probably been contemplating for some time. At some point, before the meeting at Montgomery, Lupton provided Noah Cloud with his letter of resignation. The superintendent of education presented the letter, and the regents accepted the resignation.[46]

A tortured administration lasted six months or one academic term. The regents' refusal to surrender total control over faculty hiring accounted for alienation. Providing a definite explanation or assessing blame is impossible.

Democrats contended that the regents had not fulfilled their promise and cast Lupton's resignation as the noble course of an honorable man. From Greensboro, the editor of the *Alabama Beacon* faulted the "treacherous regents" and congratulated Lupton for "the fact that he has resigned."[47] Another take is also possible. The *Alabama State Journal* positioned that Lupton had resigned because the regents had balked at his partisanship and facetiously posed that Lupton's resignation was "eminently right, if he had no purer and better motive in accepting the Presidency than the aiding of a political party."[48]

Nathaniel Lupton soon rejoined the faculty at Southern University in Greensboro. In an otherwise erudite treatise concerning agricultural chemistry, Lupton offered a prosaic observation concerning the requirements of making a successful crop. "The wind and rain and sunshine are given or withheld by a power which human agency cannot effect," the scientist reminded, "and without their influence all our labor is fruitless." In a similar sense, without compliant regents, Lupton considered rehabilitative efforts futile.[49] When the president offered his resignation, George Putnam sounded the regents' general sentiment. At the Mobile Republican's behest, his colleagues added to the board of education minutes what they considered a fitting postscript. They accepted the resignation but pointed to an inherent redundancy, for "Prof. N. T. Lupton has never entered upon his duties as President." And so it was that Nathaniel Lupton joined the growing list of recent presidents whose tenure at the University of Alabama was either stillborn or described in terms of utter failure.[50]

Chapter 7

"The Revered Old Intellectual Mother Will Weather the Storm"

BETWEEN 1865 AND 1868 THE EIGHT STATE UNIVERSITIES IN THE FORmer Confederacy had achieved, on balance, some resemblance of their previous prewar status. The universities of Georgia, Mississippi, and Virginia chartered a clear path of recovery, and sister schools in South Carolina, Louisiana, and Tennessee demonstrated a determined resiliency. Only the University of North Carolina offered an exception to that decided trend. To be sure, students were fewer and sometimes not adequately academically prepared, but a foundation for higher educational progress had been put in place in the immediate postwar years. A critical tilting point nevertheless arrived at some schools after Republicans assumed control (as they did in all Southern states) of state government. The scorching partisanship accompanying Reconstruction created an environment of confrontation at several state universities. The "politicization" of university affairs drove the extreme controversy. Contributing to agitation was a perception of the placement of Republicans in positions to influence university policy, often as trustees, and in the classrooms as professors. The prospect of Republican-mandated integration further raised the stakes. In Mississippi, South Carolina, and emphatically North Carolina, Republican stewardship provoked severe consternation. Republican political control in Georgia, Louisiana, and Virginia did not significantly affect the state universities, and the circumstances at East Tennessee University, as will be seen, are uniquely different. How and why some campuses became political battlegrounds is encapsulated in this chapter, which resumes the timeline for state universities where chapter 2 ended (1868) and carries the narrative forward to 1871.

At varying intervals between 1868 and 1870, Republicans came to power.

Their administrative purview often included oversight of the state university. Making policy specifically was invested in men, possibly elected, and sometimes appointed, often designated as the board of trustees. The nomenclature varied. The board of visitors directed the University of Virginia, and the board of supervisors made policy for the Louisiana State Seminary of Learning and Military Academy. A superintendent of education, if there was one, might belong to the board of trustees and so could the governor. The number of individuals sitting on these governing boards varied. They met several scheduled times a year and, if circumstances warranted, in called special session. Settling on the faculty and president was basic to their duties. In the past, machinations and factionalism inevitably attended their deliberations, but decisions rarely attracted much public attention. That changed in some states when Republicans began making policy and changes.[1]

No institution of higher education, with the exception of the University of Alabama, underwent the travails as did the University of North Carolina. Under the President James Swain, the state university had struggled since the war's conclusion. In May 1868, Republicans won control of state government, and William Holden became governor. That development had enormous consequences for the state university. The Republican-authored state constitution created a board of education. These officials became ex officio trustees and shared with trustees the power to direct university policy. As it devolved, under a Republican administration, the executive officers were Republicans and so were the rather large number of Holden-appointed trustees.[2]

The arrangement worked against the interests of longstanding President Swain and the present faculty. Meeting at the capital of Raleigh in July 1868, the board of education declared vacant the presidency and faculty positions. What would unfold at Chapel Hill remained uncertain because the board temporarily closed the university. Among those taking interest in the school was Solomon Pool. A graduate and former tutor at the university, Pool was a Unionist during the war and had since embraced Republicanism. His brother, John Pool, represented North Carolina in the United States Senate as a Republican and belonged to the board of education. Writing him from Chapel Hill in August, Solomon Pool explained that Democrats blamed Republicans for shutting down the university and consequently costing local residents the revenue generated by the school. "The Conservatives are charging that we closed the University," he informed, and "without taking any step looking to its resurrection." Pool speculated that the university would remain shuttered for a year, and locally that possibility "cast a gloom."

In November 1868, when the reconstituted board of education met, its members completely replaced the established faculty. A new president and four professors were settled upon. Solomon Pool became president. Fisk P. Brewer, Greek and literature; James A. Martling, English language and literature; David S. Patrick, Latin language and literature; and Alexander McIver, mathematics, gained faculty appointments. All were Republicans. The selections confirmed Democrats' expectations of a partisan board resorting to a political divining rod for guidance. The assumption that the faculty owed their positions to their Republican loyalties contributed to the professors' overnight infamy. And their notoriety was also amplified by who they *were not*, the respected and, to many, rightful faculty whom they had replaced.[3]

Several months later, in March 1869, the University of North Carolina would reopen, but the Democratic state press did not wait to denounce the new guard. Forty miles away at Raleigh, the state's most powerful Democratic newspaper took aim. "When party spirit" determines a university's course, the *Raleigh Sentinel* responded, "its doom is sealed."[4] Denunciations took on a decidedly personal form. One observer soon described Solomon Pool as a "formal arrogant prig" and decided "the adventurers who make up the Professional corps are quite worthy of their head."[5] A recent teaching stint at a Black school in Raleigh threw Fisk Brewer into disfavor, and the Greek and literature professor drew more unfavorable attention for temporarily boarding with a freedman. James Martling's background in Missouri was sufficient for an observer to consign the English language and literature professor to the "carrion crow, carpet-bag order."[6] Presumably no less an opportunist was David Patrick, a University of North Carolina graduate who gained ingrate status as the professor of the Latin language and literature. Alexander McIver, set to teach mathematics, had recently resigned his position at Davidson College, a private North Carolina school. His standing had fallen considerably at Davidson after McIver made known his intention to vote for Ulysses Grant; he learned that a group of students had pledged "never to recite to me again if I voted for Grant."[7] A statement circulated, inaccurately, that on receiving the Chapel Hill appointment McIver responded, "The party needs my services & that gratitude to the party compels me to accept."[8] Nobody would attract the deep-seated antipathy that Solomon Pool inspired. He had recently declared the school as a former "nursery of treason," which must be "thoroughly loyalized."[9] A small man, crowned with curly hair, somewhat pompous in manner, the president was decidedly uncharismatic. A not unfriendly contemporary granted the president's considerable intelligence but observed that Pool's "face bore constantly a melancholy look." His was a highly tempestuous tenure.[10]

Chapter 7

A school seemingly under siege even before classes convened attracted few students. One young man considering pursuing his education at Chapel Hill based his decision not to do so on the grounds that he refused to recite for a professor (i.e., Fisk Brewer) who had roomed with a Black man. It was an extremely finite number of students who in March 1869 moved into their East, South, or West Building quarters. In that first term, which extended into June, any number of publicized incidents—false, embellished, or accurate—threw the president and the faculty into a compromising light. Alexander McIver drew public disfavor by cutting down some shade trees on his property. It was the alleged misappropriation of university property from one of the two elegantly furnished literary society "halls" that reflected poorly on David Patrick. A local tempest resulted when the Latin professor entered the Philanthropic Society Hall and reputedly took for personal use velvet rugs and armchairs. Alluding to the newly acquired appurtenances, Patrick's wife was quoted as promising to improve her parlor and "be as big a frog as any in the pond."[11]

Cornelia Phillips Spencer turned her caustic pen on the academics. The local resident was the sister of Charles Phillips, one of the displaced professors, and was further pedigreed as the daughter of the Reverend James Phillips, who had taught mathematics for over forty years at the university. In 1868 she was a forty-three-year-old widow and living in Chapel Hill. Phillips kept up a running commentary bemoaning the school's fate and excoriating those she held accountable in anonymous letters published in the *Raleigh Sentinel* and elsewhere.[12] Among her targets was Fisk Brewer. He graduated from Yale, studied archaeology and modern Greek in that country, was an authority on ancient coins, and had a brother on the United States Supreme Court, but Spencer accentuated the professor of Greek's supposed lack of character. "Successful men in any walk of life do not leave home, carpet-bag in hand, on the lookout for a job," she averred, and continued, "The well fed game cock rules his own dunghill, while the hungry carrion crow wanders about in search of some putrid carcass."[13] Spencer held Solomon Pool in supreme contempt. She incredulously quoted the president as declaring "that if no white students wd come here, he wd have negroes!"[14]

The university's status provoked discussion on the legislative floor in Raleigh when a bill appropriating $12,000 for school expenses gained consideration. One Democrat responded by relating what in his view represented a ridiculous pantomime—overpaid professors presiding before a handful of students. A fellow legislator identified himself as education's friend but, after visiting Chapel Hill, noted a dearth of students and concluded, "So far I can see, the present University is a failure."[15] When President Pool predicted the attendance of fifty to sixty students at the next session, Cornelia Spencer skeptically responded, "We shall see." In the meantime students carried on, neither oblivious to nor vitally affected by the overarching controversy. Factoring much more strongly and consistently in their daily life was the pealing bell that abruptly aroused them as the sun rose and signaled the outset of a day that began with offering prayer at the chapel. The students likely gave some consideration to their professors' political affiliation, but what their academic taskmaster demanded of them was far more germane. That included at least three daily recitations.[16]

In preceding weeks before commencement exercises on June 10, reports circulated that Ulysses Grant planned to attend and speak. The president did not come to Chapel Hill, but Governor William Holden did, and he spoke at the ceremony. The Republican portrayed a reincarnated university shedding the reputation as the exclusive domain of the wealthy and becoming a destination for young men of modest means. Young Black men should also have the opportunity of higher education, Holden averred, but not at Chapel Hill, for the university was reserved for white men. Few local whites heard the governor's remarks because they boycotted commencement, and Cornelia Spencer labeled the much-promoted event a "grand (and to our side, delightful) fizzle." The diminished ceremony, in comparison to previous graduation celebrations, ignominiously closed the academic year.[17]

Several months later, in August 1869, a slightly increased number of students enrolled as fall term began. Establishing attendance is complicated by the disproportionately large group of beneficiaries and those belonging to the preparatory department. It is certain, no matter the number of students, that some could be irreverent and enjoyed hijinks traditionally associated with undergraduates. Ringing the university bell in the dead of night offered a harmless diversion. One or more of the young men, good naturedly or not, aimed some doggerel at professors. Responding to his own question as to what would improve the health of Chapel Hill, the author answered, "Get rid of that low, stagnant Pool." Probably the same wit posed which tradesman in the town was most expendable? He replied, "The Brewer." Whether it was because of James Martling's company, or his choice of the promised main dish, students overwhelmingly deciding against attending the English literature's professor's "possum dinner."[18]

A lack of evidence largely precludes addressing the relationship between professors and students, but there can be no doubt as to the faculty's standing with townspeople. As the recent term had ended, a number of

Chapel Hill residents drafted resolutions calling on the board of trustees to replace the faculty. Growing familiarity with the recently elected professors hardly bred tolerance in the second term, which began in the fall of 1869. George Dixon, an Englishman and a Quaker, had joined the faculty as professor of agriculture. Well versed in scientific farming methods, Dixon proposed innovative techniques to establish efficient farms. Kemp W. Battle, a contemporary and objective Democrat, later judged him "proficient," but in the partisan present, Dixon's competence was of no consequence.[19] The man holding enlightened Quaker ideals concerning race received little brotherly love. One resident pointed to Dixon's previous association with Black schools and superciliously ridiculed plans to establish a "model" farm. George Dixon soon took leave to visit England—he did not return.[20] Not content to simply denounce the faculty, Cornelia Spencer disparaged their wives. She revealed that professor Martling's wife habitually walked about her house "stockingless," and the woman married to Professor Patrick qualified as "a great tobacco chewer & dipper."[21] As the academic year 1869–1870 ended, only somewhere between thirty and fifty students were present. "Of the university that you and I were proud of," a *Wilmington Journal* correspondent decided following a visit "nothing is left but the name!"[22]

South Carolina College had narrowly escaped destruction at the hands of William Sherman's army. Several uneventful years at the school had passed since the renamed University of South Carolina had reopened. Attendance had not increased exponentially, but the number of students by 1868 had risen from almost fifty to over one hundred. In 1868, the year that Republicans came to power in Alabama and North Carolina, South Carolina Republicans also assumed direction of state government. Robert K. Scott presided as governor. Late in 1868 he directed a message to the legislature entirely devoted to the university. Scott noted a consensus for reducing the number of board of trustees, lowering tuition to facilitate the entrance of young men with less means, and raising faculty salaries. The Republican legislature generally complied. Among the most crucial changes was cutting the number of trustees from thirty-eight to seven. Legislators early in 1869 filled each of the posts with a Republican, and two of the trustees, Francis L. Cardozo and Benjamin A. Boseman, were Black men. Restructuring the board was overdue, the large number of trustees had been unwieldly, but Democrats warily considered Republican motives.

Republican oversight of the university did not immediately translate into turmoil. A reconstituted board of trustees did not threaten the faculty's tenure. In sharp contrast to the scenario at Tuscaloosa and Chapel Hill, no faculty lost their positions. Professors John and Joseph LeConte, Maximilian LaBorde, and William Rivers, among others connected to the university before the war, enjoyed respect as academic men of letters. Making for a unique direct connection between the university and state government was the close proximity, a distance measured in yards, of the capitol and the university. In fact, when construction to the capitol in 1868–1869 prevented legislators from convening in the building, they deliberated in the university chapel.

The emerging possibility of the university's integration in 1869 began to have an unsettling effect. Integration was a real prospect, for the recently drafted and Republican-authored state constitution expressly opened public schools on all levels to all races. That included the University of South Carolina. As Provisional Governor James L. Orr left office late in 1868, he counseled against integration in his final address to the legislature. Orr proposed establishing a separate institution of higher learning for African Americans. In fact, in 1873, Black students would take their place at the university. Well before then, however, the possibility caused controversy. Early in 1869, some legislators supported a plan to close the state university at Columbia and establish an integrated institution at the Citadel in Charleston. Among the proponents was William J. Whipper, a Black Republican legislator who represented Beaufort in the state house. Nothing came of shutting down the school, but Whipper attached an amendment to university funding legislation that prevented making distinctions regarding admission on account of race. The bill became a statute. Fears of integration and the gambit to close the university seem to have shaken public confidence and accounted for fewer students. When winter term opened at the university, some sixty students were enrolled, about half the number who had attended the previous term.[23]

The finite number of students in 1868–1869 made their academic way with widely disparate degrees of success. What they gleaned from reading Tacitus and Horace in courses directed by William Rivers varied individually, but the ancient languages professor did pronounce the students "uniformly studious and strictly attentive in the lecture."[24] On February 19, 1869, senior students in Professor Porter Alexander's analytics and calculus class took what were referred to as intermediate examinations. The results ranged widely, but all presumably signed this promise: "Before entering the room, I did not know what questions would be proposed, and in preparing my answers I have received no assistances." Students pridefully wore their badges signifying membership in the Clariosophic or Euphradian literary societies. One year after Americans elected a second Republican president, the question of slavery's morality came under scrutiny in elocution exercises.

In the ensuing debate the Euphradians condemned involuntary servitude. That position did not betray any egalitarian streak. Its members, theoretically conceding the admittance of Black students to the university, soon went on record opposing any freedman's induction into the Euphradian Society.[25]

Strain at the university became more noticeable. John LeConte had for some time envisioned dire consequences if Black students gained admittance, and he pursued and gained an appointment to the newly opened University of California. His brother, Joseph LeConte, also worried about what might take place. A clash between a correspondent of the *Charleston Courier* and William Whipper pointed to agitation as 1869 began. The Republican legislator's designs concerning the university had alienated the journalist, and he apprised a group of university students of Whipper's indisposition toward the school. They organized outside the capitol to accost, if not attack, Whipper. Trouble was avoided, but the incident was revealing. Some legislators supported withholding funds for professors' salaries if integration was not carried out. As the academic year progressed, Joseph LeConte became more disillusioned. Later in 1869, the chemistry professor directed his final class at the university and soon joined his brother in Oakland at the University of California. "When the Negro legislature began to talk of what it intended to do to the University," LeConte remembered years later, "I thought it was time to quit."[26]

Losing two esteemed scholars harmed the University of South Carolina's standing, and the school's questionable future contributed to other faculty weighing their positions. One week into 1869, Professor Porter Alexander wrote his father of uncertain legislative support for the university and promised that even if a bill financially benefitting the school passed, "I will hold on here until I can get something better—no longer."[27] Doubts about the university increased. In a report to the board of trustees, Robert W. Barnwell addressed the university's status. The chairman of the faculty called their attention to the relationship between the public's flagging confidence in the university's future and falling attendance. A certain embattled status was obvious. A journalist representing the *Charleston Courier* visiting Columbia that summer noted that Democrats controlled the board of trustees and the faculty believed "the revered old intellectual mother will weather the storm."[28]

Far more than the professors, who enjoyed prestige and respect, the trustees provoked criticism. In the summer of 1869, with a view apparently toward hiring Republicans, James L. Neagle attempted to establish an entirely new faculty. Fellow trustees blocked the effort by the Republican state comptroller. Even so, decisions regarding prospective faculty exposed the board of trustees to criticism. Albert G. Mackey's appointment early that fall to the professorship vacated by John LeConte contributed to a growing perception of untoward Republican influence. Mackey was a learned man, but he possessed few academic qualifications for the post. The *Columbia Phoenix* pronounced the action partisanly inspired and called on the trustees to understand that the university was "outside of politics." The Democratic newspaper declared Mackey academically unqualified and asked what he really knew of "the sublime science of astronomy?"[29] The Chester *Reporter* also read politics into the decision and responded by blaming a board of trustees composed of "two negroes, two scalawags, two carpetbaggers, and a refugeed thief." Appointing the "old skunk" constituted an "act of damning shame" and advanced the notion that interaction with the hypothetical "Professor" would be highly detrimental to the character of any student. Albert Mackey declined the position, but in isolation the episode pointed to the increasing disrepute in which whites held the University of South Carolina.[30]

An observer allowed as the fall term of 1869 began that "few, if any of the sons of South Carolina gentlemen of financial standing will be sent." Only about forty young men walked the campus.[31] Most did not pay tuition and, as beneficiaries, conjured the epithet "Scott's pets," for Governor Robert Scott.[32] The *Sumter Watchman* warned readers that under "Radical" leadership the school was approaching the status of the state universities in Alabama and North Carolina, institutions defamed by Radical influence and inhabited by "bats and moles."[33] A few dissenting voices were raised. An anonymous individual that fall appealed to the reason of those fretting about the university's possible integration. After all, he rationalized, the fathers of the young men who might theoretically sit in a classroom with a Black student were taking their place on juries with freedmen. Why was it any different for their sons to take a seat in a classroom where a Black student was present? White South Carolinians resisted that logic. Chairman of the Faculty Robert Barnwell reported to the trustees as 1869 neared a close that a dramatic fall off in students due to "prejudices" constituted the biggest problem confronting the school.[34]

Avoiding similar politically induced decline at the University of Mississippi was the determination of John Waddel. In lieu of a president, the chancellor exercised the most administrative authority at the Oxford school. Waddel had held that position since 1865. He understood the school's image among Mississippians was crucial to its stature, enrollment, and, not incidentally, financial security. When an article in 1870 appeared in the Aberdeen

Examiner alleging that Union troops during the war had removed a valuable telescope from the university, Waddel quickly informed the editor that was not so. He asked for a retraction, and the chancellor insisted that the public realize "our attractions are as great, and our means and facilities as the same as before the War in the way of apparatus and Libraries, etc." Waddel also realized the importance of maintaining at least a working relationship with the Republican governor and Republican-dominated board of trustees. The chancellor's status as a longtime Mississippian and a Democrat did not prevent him from doing so.[35]

The Reconstruction timetable was different in Mississippi than it was in Alabama and the Carolinas. Not until March 1870, when James Lusk Alcorn became governor, did Republicans assume direction of state government. As did William Holden, Alcorn had a Southern background, but in contrast to North Carolina's controversial governor, who was eventually removed from office for overreaching executive powers, Alcorn attempted to avoid political confrontation. The governor's relationship with the University of Mississippi reflected that predisposition. Five years had passed since the war and the school had more than persevered, for increasing numbers of students and faculty pointed to a healthy situation. Even so, change was afoot, and inevitably controversy attended Republican oversight of the university.[36]

As was true sometimes elsewhere, the advent of Republican domination was followed by structural changes to the state university's administrative body. The legislature reset the board of trustees at thirteen. Governor Alcorn named eight Republicans and five Democrats. In the capital city of Jackson, the *Clarion* decided that reconfiguring the board anticipated converting the school into "a nursery of the political and social abominations of the Radical party,"[37] and predicted Mississippians would "shun it as a pesthouse."[38] The envisioned apocalyptic collapse did not take place. The trustees made no sweeping faculty changes. As at the University of South Carolina, the carryover of professors from before the war projected credibility and continuity. Alexander J. Quinche, Eugene Hilgard, and Claudius Sears, with standing connections to the University of Mississippi, remained on the faculty. The politically diverse board of trustees carried out a decidedly nonideological agenda. Meeting in the summer of 1870, they revived a scholarship program, waiving from each county the tuition of one meritorious but needy young man, appropriated $5,000 to the library, and established a reading room providing students and faculty access to newspapers and magazines. These initial gatherings of the revamped board set a pattern of seeming harmony, or at least shared purpose. Among the trustees was Jonathan Tarbell, one of the state's most polarizing political figures and chairman of the Republican State Executive Committee. He later stated, "No political question or consideration has ever intruded itself into deliberations of the trustees."[39]

Republican oversight nevertheless created considerable dissonance. The removal initially of some longtime trustees and their replacement by Republicans raised objections. Among those joining the board of trustees was Alexander Warner. His presumed infamy dated at least to the 1868 national Republican convention at Chicago, when, acting as the Mississippi delegation's spokesperson, he supposedly boldly announced on the convention floor, "Mississippi, the home of that *arch-traitor* Jeff. Davis, casts her seven votes for Gen. Grant."[40] In Democratic circles such a man hardly reflected well on the state university. Neither did the credentials of trustees Jonathan Tarbell and Charles Clarke, who were described as "carpet-bag Radicals of the deepest dye." The assault continued. The dominant and prolific Democratic newspapers generally drowned out a far weaker Republican press.[41] That did not deter the *Mississippi Pilot* from refuting aspersions. The Jackson-based Republican newspaper concluded that the university could not receive a fair hearing because state Democrats so deeply resented Republican political control. "If the twelve apostles constituted the board, and Christ himself dictated the management of the University of Mississippi," the *Pilot* rationalized, "their unreasonable opposition would be the same."[42]

Much like at the University of South Carolina, the recurring image of a young Black person taking a place at the hallowed institution conjured outrage. That possibility gained considerable public attention in the weeks before the fall semester began in 1870, when Robert S. Hudson, a Yazoo City judge, addressed a public letter to Chancellor Waddel inquiring about the chances of a freedman attending the university. Waddel immediately solicited the faculty's advice. In another public letter replying to Hudson, the chancellor and the faculty maintained the university was the exclusive domain of white students. The defiant response, which took on the feel of a manifesto, positioned that the board of trustees intended to make a categorical statement as policy and further declared that should a freedman apply, "we should without hesitation reject him." In the unlikely event that the board insisted on forcing integration, the faculty further promised to immediately resign.[43] A week later Governor Alcorn weighed in. He confirmed that the University of Mississippi was reserved for white men but promoted establishing an institution of higher learning for Black students. The Republican executive rejected the Democrats' position that it was absurd to make higher education opportunities available to young Black men. Alcorn resented the political edge of the trustees' letter and publicly responded by inviting them to resign if they felt so inclined. The Hudson/Waddel/board of trustees exchange of correspondence gained wide circulation in state newspapers and with public opinion among whites rebounded to the university's credit. A prominent Democrat confided to Chancellor Waddel that the letter "saved the University."[44]

Robert W. Flourney resentfully followed the correspondence trail. A former secessionist, the well-to-do resident of Pontotoc had joined the Republican Party and edited the *Equal Rights* newspaper. From the trustees' strong words, Flourney discerned a determination to "look into [an applicant's face], and if they discovered that he had negro blood, they would refuse him admission." Editor Flourney defiantly proposed that a young Black man apply and test the constitutionality of barring freedpeople from the state university.[45]

The faculty fiat opposing integration did not insulate the university from attack. It did not matter that enrollment continued to increase or that there were no faculty appointments that could be construed as politically motivated. The *Fayette Chronicle* mourned the university's alleged partisan tack and anticipated "some greasy colored chap to take a seat in the school."[46] The *Columbus Democrat* rued the Alcorn-engineered changes and predicted a fate similar to that of the state universities in Alabama and North Carolina. "When the State is redeemed from Radicalism," a private citizen conjectured, "then we can save the University."[47] Thomas E. B. Pegus, a highly prominent planter and former enslaver in Oxford, did not think the school needed "saving." The Democrat and trustee noted the postwar carryover of proven professors and expressed mystification at critics who encouraged Mississippians to leave for schools in other states. Implacable foes and opposition were unconvinced. "If I send my son to state University, will any influence be brought to bear on him to make him a Radical," one Mississippi parent rhetorically asked. He answered, "I fear there will." And many fellow whites agreed.[48] On the campus, however, Chancellor Waddel and others vigilantly tamped down partisanship. Samuel C. Caldwell entered the university in 1869. He later reflected "states' rights and secession were forbidden words."[49]

On the evening of November 15, 1870, Robert Barnard wrote his father from the university of regretting "to learn that La. had gone radical, it seems like the yoke will never be lifted from the neck of the good old State." The young man reflected the strong political lean of his fellow students. Barnard was writing from his campus quarters and mentioned his roommate reading the Roman classic "Agricola" by the light of a coal lamp and a "magnificent wood fire in the place."[50] Other students boarded locally. Any young man, wherever they resided, could for eighteen dollars a month take meals at Stewart Hall. Paying a nominal sum for one's wash to be done offered more convenience. Academics dominated the lives of Robert Barnard and fellow students, and inevitably they formed impressions of their professors. In the fall of 1869, Samuel Caldwell made the two-hundred-mile journey north to Oxford from his home in Hazlehurst. Caldwell would fondly recall the education he received and his professors almost fifty years later. Some may have considered Professor John Waddel overly pedantic, but it was the rare student who did not respect him. The professor of moral science invariably neatly wrote in Greek on the blackboard and urged his students to dismiss notions that poor penmanship and greatness were somehow connected. Also eliciting praise and attracting students was Landon Garland, formerly of the University of Alabama, who spoke from a deep wellspring of spiritualism at the local Methodist church. Professor Eugene Hilgard's enthusiastic energy and comprehensive knowledge, Caldwell recalled, impressed his pupils. Some affectionately considered Professor Alexander Quinche the odd but endearing academic prototype. His habitual directive to students to "proceed please" seemingly became a figure of speech. It was the source of amusement to some students when Quinche, as the Latin professor began a buggy ride to town, was overheard prevailing on his mare, "Proceed please, Arabia."[51] Over several days in February 1871, students took a series of examinations. Allowed only pencils, the pupils of metaphysics and logic professor James A. Lyon took their seats at the examination room writing tables at 10:00 a.m. Three hours of almost incessant writing followed. Nothing was audible but the steady application of lead to paper, and nothing was seen, as Lyon admitted, but "the sight of some poor fellow who has got into the fog." Several months later, in July, students steeled themselves for more examinations, and the ensuing commencement concluded the sixth academic year following the war.[52]

The lay of the higher education land was uniquely different at East Tennessee University. As Tracey McKenzie informs in his study of wartime Knoxville, secession had much divided the small city of some five thousand residents in Unionist-leaning eastern Tennessee. The university reflected that mindset. A man of inconvertible Unionist credentials, Thomas Humes had served as president since 1864. In his highly public position as the minister of St. John's Church in Knoxville, early in the war Humes made his sentiments clear by refusing to honor Jefferson Davis's call for a day of prayer and fasting. President Humes set the political tone of the university. Seven pro-Confederates on the board of trustees who had fled the area during the war when Union troops threatened Knoxville were replaced by Unionist or Republicans soon after the surrender (see chapter 2). The changing political direction of the board garnered disapproving notice. Some local residents in the summer of 1868 voiced objections to trustees "born north of the Ohio River," and the next year the *Knoxville Whig* warily noted the university's Republican direction and, citing the status of the University of Alabama, higher education's whipping boy in Southern Democratic circles, warned of mixing politics and education. The return of Milford Butler attested to the prevailing climate. A Unionist and the ancient languages professor, Butler had in 1862 abandoned his faculty post and moved to the free states. In 1869, now in a much more accommodating environment, Butler resumed his faculty post.[53]

Since reopening in 1866, East Tennessee University had moved toward stability, albeit slowly. In 1869 six buildings, two of which the growing number of students inhabited, composed the heavily war damaged but on the mend university. An increasing number of students best conveyed renewed vitality. The rivalry between the Philomathesians and Chi Delta literary societies was indicative of reawakening intellectual life. The fielding of a baseball team (see chapter 2) corroborated activity in another sense. Even so, as a university, East Tennessee University remained something of a backwater. The question of scale provides some perspective. When local efforts to increase the number of books in a library badly damaged by the war reached a thousand, the restocking effort was hailed. The library at the University of South Carolina boasted over 25,000 volumes, and the University of Virginia even more.[54]

Designation in 1869 as the agricultural school of Tennessee dramatically increased the institution's future. Congress passed and Lincoln signed the Morrill Act in 1862, extending federal funds to states for establishing a college emphasizing an agricultural and mechanical curriculum. Tennessee became the first Southern state to take advantage of the federal windfall. Gaining designation as the agricultural college promised an influx of federal funds, and students and several schools competed for the coveted prize. The choice narrowed to East Tennessee University and Union College at Murfreesboro. Republican control of the legislature crucially tilted the selection. Support for the Confederacy in the centrally located part of the state where Murfreesboro was located had been much stronger than in eastern Tennessee. And boosters of the Knoxville school promoting its designation as the land grant school argued that loyalty at Murfreesboro to the United States remained highly circumspect. Unreconstructed "rebels" at Union College reputedly dominated, and allegedly even the safety of "loyal" students was open to question. That contrasted strikingly to East Tennessee University, which a promoter pictured as a haven for all students "without regard to birthplace or political antecedents."[55] Those arguments resonated with Republican legislators in Nashville, and East Tennessee gained the agricultural college distinction.

Status as the agricultural college immediately began paying dividends. A booster-minded *Knoxville Press and Register* in the summer of 1869 reported laborers "hard at work" improving the grounds and making various building repairs.[56] Hunter Nicholson, as the newly appointed professor of agriculture and horticulture, soon set off on a fact-finding tour of other agricultural schools in the country. When the fall term began, over one hundred students enrolled. Three out of four belonged to the preparatory school, but many would soon become true college students. Putting in place an agricultural curriculum, the *Knoxville Press and Register* averred, was not "the work of a day," but the path to a better future was clear. Henry Ludlow received a gold medal for solving one hundred geometry problems as the academic year closed in 1870. Fellow students did not require such an achievement to celebrate the conclusion of exams and the year. They placed lights in campus windows, shot off skyrockets, and at a stag dance broke boisterously into college songs. A milestone at East Tennessee University lay in the near future, when the first group of true seniors since the war would collect diplomas in 1871.[57]

Education at the Louisiana State Seminary for Learning and Military Academy had resumed early in 1866. Since then, the resolute application of Superintendent David Boyd contributed to the school at Pineville avoiding a possible military administrative takeover, weathering poor financial support, and overcoming widespread yellow fever. Appearances could not carry a university, but they helped and the impressive Italianate-style building that dominated the campus remained. In the year Americans elected Ulysses Grant president for the first time, some 150 young men were pursuing degrees in what Boyd described as "one of the finest college edifices in the States."[58]

Republican direction of Louisiana dates from the administration of Henry Clay Warmoth, who became governor in July 1868. Warmoth unequivocally endorsed freedpeople's advancement but resisted being categorized as a Radical. He and Boyd developed a respectful working relationship. As did John Waddel at the University of Mississippi, Boyd worked to insulate the Louisiana State Seminary of Learning and Military Academy from potentially harmful outside political developments. Over the years he had maintained contact with William Sherman, the school's first superintendent between 1859 and 1861. Worried about Warmoth's approach, the Union general wrote Boyd that if the executive demanded "unreasonable changes" at the university, he would be glad to intercede.[59] Boyd never needed to call on his friend. Warmoth took a genuine interest in the university, and when Boyd visited him several weeks after he became governor, they discussed the university. "I had several talks with his Excellency while in N. O.," Boyd confided to Sherman, and he speculated "that he will not interfere with us, unless *party pressure* becomes greater." Neither did the board of supervisors, which provided administrative direction to the seminary, disturb the healthy status quo. In fact, much like Boyd, the board acted to allay any notions of an unreconstructed institution. In 1869 they appointed Francis V. Hopkins, a Republican, to the faculty and promoted Harry Lott, a Black man, to the board of supervisors.[60] The subject of integration pointed further to a certain amenability. The recently ratified and Republican-authored state constitution held possible peril, for the document at least theoretically permitted integration. Warmoth frankly shared Boyd's fear that the presence of Black cadets risked, if not guaranteed, the undoing of the Louisiana State Seminary for Learning and Military Academy. Integrating the school under the circumstances did not gain serious momentum. "I have been conciliatory and courteous to the Radical leaders which may possibly have something to do with their conciliatory course towards us," Boyd wrote to an ally on the board of supervisors. "A little politeness does not cost much," the superintendent explained, "and often brings a rich return." Such were the words of an unapologetic ex-Confederate but also a diplomatic man. These circumstances allowed for stability at Louisiana's state university between 1868 and 1871.[61]

Cadets juggled with various degrees of skill the various demands placed on them, but they shared a blissful ignorance of these administrative matters. What could be described as a brimming number of students arrived at Alexandria on a Red River steamboat and then from Pineville made the several-mile overland trip to the school. It was the rare young man who failed to be impressed on first beholding the commanding, castle-like visage in the pine clearing. Many were beneficiaries whose tuition was forgiven on condition they agreed to teach in the state for at least two years. Whatever their academic aspirations, the present demanded for cadets' strict conformance to military regulation. Hops continued to offer a needed respite from the strict regimen. The return and effusive welcome extended to William Sherman when he visited the school in February 1869 pointed to a certain sectional reconcilement. Several months later, on June 30, extensive pageantry extended the first commencement at the university. Eight young men were extended diplomas in a ceremony featuring student oratory, a New

Orleans band, and the remarks of Boyd, who pridefully pointed to the commemorative milestone.

That bright day contrasted starkly with the catastrophic events several months later soon after fall term opened. Early on the morning of October 15, a fire broke out on the seminary's ground floor; suddenly aroused cadets and professors frantically responded to the raised alarm. They valiantly attempted to contain the rapidly spreading blaze, but poor access to water doomed their efforts and saving furniture and paintings was all that could be done. Soon the tremendous crash of the imposing structure's west half signaled what all realized—the battle had been lost. By dawn only the barest shell of the once-mighty building remained. In the numbing aftermath, the suddenly displaced cadets took temporary boarding at an Alexandria hotel and weeks later boarded the *Celeste* or the *Lizzie Hopkins* and departed by steamboat down the Red River.

David Boyd's relationship with the governor continued to serve the school well. Warmoth was instrumental in helping the university move temporarily to Baton Rouge, and it became established in the building housing the Asylum for the Deaf, Dumb, and Blind. When the governor reviewed the cadets there in December 1869, Boyd spoke to and thanked the Republican for his efforts to make relocation quickly possible. The cadets warmly cheered the Republican executive. The next year legislators in Baton Rouge changed the name of the school to Louisiana State University, and the town became the school's permanent home. In Louisiana, at least for now, higher education interests had forged mutual political cooperation.[62]

At no place did the percolating forces of Reconstruction partisanship have less impact than at the University of Virginia. Students flooded the campus in the immediate postwar period, and the brief triumph of Republicans in the state did not change that trend. A number were from Alabama. Some considered themselves principled academic refugees from a state that effectually no longer had a state university. One Alabamian arriving for the academic year's first term that began on October 1, 1869, found carefully tended grounds, whitewashed lecture rooms, and improved boarding houses, which he reported offered "abundant fare to administer to the wants of the flesh."[63] Several Republicans belonged to the board of visitors, but they did not demand changes that could be considered partisanly inspired. In his dated but comprehensive multivolume study of the school, Philip A. Bruce writes of the diplomatic "political disposition to choose men [on the board of visitors] whose sympathies were not antagonistic to the spirt of the new course of events."[64] Speculating that maybe as many as seven hundred students could be enrolled in 1869, the matriculating Alabamian who noticed the upgraded accommodations allowed they were "pouring in thick and fast."[65]

General tranquility also prevailed at the University of Georgia, which had rapidly regained its academic stride following the war. Central to progress was the leadership of Andrew Lipscomb, who as chancellor attempted to maintain a healthy distance between politics and university affairs. The vivid memory of how a student's oration at commencement in 1867 almost dearly cost the school financially had provided a well-learned lesson. Even so, political sanitization had its limitations. Some students took an interest in presidential-election-year politics, and they heartily cheered at a local Democratic rally in March 1868. A week later, when a prominent state Republican named Jonathan E. Bryant visited the town, some riled students went to his hotel with intentions of tarring and feathering him. The interdiction of the hotel owner, pleading that his daughter was sick and required quiet, prevented that possible recourse. Bryant left town the next morning, well aware of his standing among students, who hissed the departing Republican. Julius L. Brown also felt the uncomfortable edge of disfavor. His father, Joseph E. Brown, had been the state's governor during the war. The former governor had recently drawn criticism across the state for acting with the Republican Party. Intending to flog and then force Julius from the school, students assembled one night, but the intervention of Nathaniel Harris, a fellow student legitimized by a sterling Confederate record, turned back the masked young men. Walter Hill did not belong to that group of vigilantes. In revealing letters to his family between 1868 and 1871, the exemplary student depicted college life and addressed a variety of subjects ranging from recitation demands in Greek to assuming a debate position granting the vote to women. At the end of Hill's junior year in 1869, he was picked to speak at commencement. Before the honored student did so, however, Andrew Lipscomb screened the speech. On receiving the remarks Hill planned to make, the wary chancellor immediately inquired, "My son, have you any politics in it?"[66]

Although the trend of progress established at some schools after the war was interrupted when Republicans gained political control, education continued unaffected at others. The state universities in Georgia and Virginia flourished, and progress could be marked in Louisiana and Mississippi, in particular at the latter, despite Democratic-generated turbulence. John Waddel was central to advance at the Oxford school. The chancellor succeeded in defusing partisanship despite the detractors, who, he recalled, were sure that "the University was going to be radicalized." A mutual concern for the Louisiana State Seminary of Learning and Military Academy made for a transcending entente between David Boyd and Henry Warmoth. East Tennessee University continued to forge a path forward and, designated a land grant school, was well positioned for the future.[67]

Developments at the University of South Carolina are described by a more precarious narrative. And a critical situation at the University of North Carolina would soon deteriorate further. Democrats drew a picture of trustees, presidents, and professors feeding at the state educational trough. Sometime the faculty attracted the most wrath, and on other occasions the trustees assumed the villain's role. At both these schools, and elsewhere, the vision of integration inspired apoplectic anxiety. At a historical juncture when egalitarian imperatives suddenly commanded deference, admitting young Black men to these schools crystallized fears. Yet, in point of fact, few Republicans positioned to influence educational policy called for integrating state universities, and the subject mustered little support. When Governor William Holden spoke at commencement in 1869, he counseled against Black students attending the University of North Carolina. The board of trustees recommended a type of co-state university—but not at Chapel Hill—for Black students. The envisioned school did not materialize due to a lack of legislative enthusiasm. Providing freedmen in Louisiana an opportunity for higher education resulted in the creation of Straight University in 1870; keeping freedmen out of the state university contributed to that development. Governor James Alcorn opposed integrating the University of Mississippi, but he strongly promoted setting up a higher institution of learning for Black students. In 1870 the Mississippi legislature established Revels University—later renamed Alcorn University. The vision of young Black men at the established state universities in reality provided the circling Democratic wolves considerable grist but took on a reality far out of proportion to likelihood. And Black students never sat at a desk at East Tennessee University, although Republican legislators clearly foresaw that possibility. When legislators conferred agricultural-school status on the school, they expressly forbade denying admission on the grounds of race and, anticipating young Black males enrolling, specified that separate learning accommodations be established for those matriculates. The will to establish even this segregated arrangement did not exist. A legislative committee investigating the University of East Tennessee's compliance soon concluded that absolutely no steps had been taken to provide for any Black students who might attend. The outcry regarding integration amounted to a tempest.[68]

Chapter 7

The circumstances at the University of North Carolina uncannily paralleled those at the University of Alabama. The school at Chapel Hill, once damned as a "child of Radicalism," was by 1870 not far from shutting down. Cornelia Spencer had been the university's most outspoken critic. She had lived with her husband for a time in Alabama and retained an interest in the state's university. From afar at one point, the University of North Carolina's critic informed her brother Charles that "the scalawag President of Ala. Univ. has resigned." Spencer confused the facts, but she raised the subject of presidential leadership. Those prospering Southern universities shared in common a president or chancellor who maneuvered diplomatically. A far smoother relaunching was highly plausible at the University of Alabama if an individual who could command some consensus had presided. Superintendent Noah Cloud understood that finding such an individual was pivotal. In the summer of 1870, he placed his latest hopes in William Russell Smith, who became the fifth man in the span of two years to be named president.[69]

Chapter 8

"We Have a University to Resuscitate"

IN JUNE 1870, AFTER WHAT MIGHT BE DESCRIBED AS SIX MONTHS OF A quasi-administration, Nathaniel Lupton resigned as the president of the University of Alabama. His stepping aside represented yet another low-water point for the school. Moving the university had been proposed and shutting its doors had also been suggested. Relocating the school never advanced any further than soliciting bids from various places that served as suitors, and closing the recently reborn university was a highly undesirable option. In the summer of 1870, a year and a half removed from its reincarnation, the university continued to cast a funereal gloom. About the time that Lupton resigned, a visitor to Tuscaloosa noted the impressive oak trees and fine homes and also ventured out to the university campus. He admired the Tudor-Gothic building but, as for the school, regretted the "blighting and fatal influences of its present Radical carpet-bag administration."[1] His diagnosis of the underlying causes for the state of affairs was open to debate, but the fact of corrosion was not. An anonymous young man in nearby Shelby County provided the prism through which many viewed the institution. The prospective student was seeking confirmation of what he considered a highly favorable development. He had heard secondhand that professors had been "turned out" and replaced by "none but Democrats," and under the revamped arrangement, "myself and brother are anxious to go to college in your town if we can do so honorably." That no self-respecting white Alabamian could attend unless the highly objectionable faculty had been vanquished provided the clear inference. Stability would continue to be elusive.[2]

Within days of Lupton's resignation, meeting at Montgomery late in June 1870, the regents named a new president. They turned again to a man with strong Alabama ties. In fact, William Russell Smith lived in Tuscaloosa. His designation as president offered a certain symmetry—Smith had walked

FIGURE 8.1. William Russell Smith, president of the University of Alabama, 1870–1871. Neither the knowledge that William Russell Smith had of the university as a resident of Tuscaloosa nor his stature as a man of letters enabled him to arrest the school's decline. Smith resigned in 1871 with the university at a low ebb. University of Alabama Libraries Special Collections.

the campus as a student when the school opened almost forty years earlier. If an ability to draw upon a variegated background contributed to success, the selection held promise. The school's latest president had led a remarkable life. Ever comfortable with the written word, he had authored novels, drafted poems, composed a play concerning Aaron Burr, established the first literary magazine in the state, and, as a keen classicist, translated the fifth book of the *Iliad*, among other literary accomplishments. Smith was also a man of somewhat frustrated martial ambitions. He raised troops to oppose the Creek Indians resisting removal in the 1830s; however, the fighting ended before Smith arrived. That same decade he started out to Texas, again belatedly, to join the struggle for the future state's independence. Warning against secession did not prevent him from ultimately supporting Southern independence, and Smith raised a regiment, but election to the Confederate Congress deterred him from field service. At one time or another, Smith had acted with the Whig, Democratic, and Know Nothing/American parties. The very public man had served as a state legislator and between 1850 and 1856 sat in Congress. As a delegate to the convention that resulted in Alabama's secession, Smith dissented and refused to sign the ordinance cutting the state's ties with the Union. Out of that crucible came his most significant literary contribution; Smith recorded much of the voluble proceedings in *The History and Debates of the Convention of the People of Alabama*. Following a war, which he referred to as "the great wreck," he ran unsuccessfully for governor in 1865 and took no active role in politics as Reconstruction began. The latest president could, at the time of his election, be described as a man who resisted absolute Republican or Democratic categorization. The author-editor-lawyer-politician now turned his hand to reviving a prostrate university.

William Russell Smith moved into the president's mansion sometime over the summer of 1870. As a local resident, he possessed an understanding of the school's recent troubles. In fact, Smith had been part of the law team that defended William Smith the previous spring. Gaining conversance with the financial status of the school much concerned him. The annual state pecuniary allotment offered some encouragement, as did the prospect of tuition-driven revenue in the event of increased enrollment. On balance, however, extreme financial problems beset the school. Greatly concerned about the fiscal predicament, one regent had recently advocated banning hiring any new professors. Another proposed that the president and faculty receive half their salaries until one hundred students were enrolled. As concerning as they were, Smith realized fiscal challenges were not the most critical impediment to the university's advancement. The transcending dilemma concerned the university's image. And that was crucially tied to the perception of the professors.[3]

The composition of the faculty, although not contemplated in inspiring terms, at least projected increased stability as Smith's administration began. For the last several months of the previous spring term, Nathan Chambliss and David Peck had somehow shouldered the teaching burdens until the school recessed in June. Both men remained on the faculty. When the regents elected William Russell Smith as president, they also added two men to the faculty. Both were familiar with the university. One of them, DeForest Richards, was reappointed as the professor of natural sciences and astronomy, and the other, Hampton Whitfield, the local lawyer, became the professor of English literature. The teaching corps problematically also included William Russell Smith, eminently qualified and not averse to instructing.

Conceding the faculty's central function of classroom instruction, more can be understood about the university by considering the professors less as educators and more as individuals who adopted widely contrasting methods of dealing with the public approbation that a connection to the university assured. DeForest Richards claimed seniority as the only professor whose tenure dated to the school's reopening. Accepted by a few local white residents, viewed unfavorably by more, Richards was perhaps loathed by most. More than any other professor, Richards qualified as an unapologetic and unswerving Radical. William M. Evarts, New York Republican and United States attorney general between 1868 and 1869, commended Richards to President Grant as a man who went South to "maintain the new order of society produced by emancipation." Derision seems not to have phased him.[4] In stark contrast, Hampton Whitfield cared deeply about how he stood locally. Whitfield offers the rare example of a white man who largely maintained his social standing despite Republican affiliation. The man described nominally as a Republican had previously supported Raphael Semmes's elevation to the university's presidency and had assured the Confederate hero, "Your election would be hailed with delight here and everywhere else." By way of building support for his candidacy, Whitfield had advised Semmes to gain favor with a Republican in Mobile whom Whitfield described as "a radical but a decent one." In his view, many so-called radicals were not decent. The Tuscaloosa resident was marginally fixed for much of his life. Anticipating the public's disapproval for occupying a professorship at the university, Whitfield published a note diplomatically asking forgiveness and citing need of the $2,500 salary.[5]

Richards invited opprobrium and Whitfield assiduously attempted to avoid it. What, though, best captured the deep local adversity that faculty status could bring were the experiences of Nathan Chambliss. His standing as a former Confederate officer and son-in-law of General William Hardee had for a time afforded him local acceptance. By the spring of 1870, however, even these credentials did not insulate the commandant. Some townspeople began to view Chambliss as a chameleon-like figure attempting to socialize in respectable circles even as he acted with the unpopular regime at the university. Attracting criticism was his decision to allow the Richards family to continue to reside on campus, although at the time Harriet's husband did not belong to the faculty. So did a perceived deference toward Vernon Vaughn and William Smith during their incarceration. Randolph predictably took exception to the commandant in the *Independent Monitor*. Chambliss grew increasingly disillusioned with the situation. "After the surrender the occupation of the Southern soldier was gone," the former commandant reflected years later. "He had to create a new capacity for something else," Chambliss rationalized, adding, "Luckily for me, my lines have fallen in pleasant places." Yet, in the spring and summer of 1870, Tuscaloosa had become distinctly unpleasant. Nathan Chambliss was a proud man of rectitude, mindful of his social standing, and he concluded the situation had become personally unsustainable. Caught in Reconstruction's undertow, the commandant resigned on July 30.[6]

Chambliss held Randolph in low regard, but it was another newspaper editor whom he confronted before leaving Tuscaloosa. Joseph W. Taylor edited the *Whig and Observer* in nearby Eutaw. He had recently attacked the university and grouped Chambliss with President Smith and Hampton Whitfield as pseudo-Republicans who exchanged their integrity for salary and power. According to Taylor, Nathanial Lupton had acted honorably by resigning rather than accepting Radical direction of the university, but in stark contrast, Chambliss maintained his affiliation with the corrupt regime and so deserved the ignominy of a collaborator. Taylor editorialized that Nathan Chambliss, William Russell Smith, and Hampton Whitfield were "either Radicals in disguise, or are in the process of conversion to Radicalism," but, regardless, they were "in the market for sale to the Radicals."[7]

The accusations incensed Chambliss, and just several days after resigning, he made the thirty-five-or-so-mile trip to Eutaw on August 3. Thomas Roy, close friend and soon-to-be brother-in-law, accompanied the man who had handed in his resignation days before. Acting as an intermediary, Roy delivered a note to Taylor in which Chambliss demanded a retraction of the references to him made in the *Whig and Observer,* which he considered "offensive and insulting." In his reply, written immediately and returned by Roy, Taylor justified the charges and refused. A fading but still sometimes observed practice, that of the code duello, had accounted for men settling matters of honor with pistols. Chambliss may have determined to do so, and he composed a short note indicating as much. Roy backtracked and delivered the message, requesting that Taylor designate a "time and place" when and where the two could meet so "this matter may be further discussed." Whatever Chambliss's exact intent, there was no encounter, and the episode ended without further event.[8] Robert McKee, editor of the *Southern Argus* in Selma, personally knew Chambliss from his time in the town. He respected Chambliss as a person and an upstanding Democrat. McKee was also acquainted with Joseph Taylor. Following the contretemps, the *Southern Argus*'s editor wrote Taylor and defended Chambliss as a reputable and fine man. Refusing to alter his take on the commandant, Taylor replied that "*he is in bad company & is aiding the Radicals to run the University in the interest of the Radical party.*" Chambliss cut his relationship with the university as July ended. Eight months in Tuscaloosa must have seemed much longer, and he, Anna, and their infant daughter returned to Selma. An objective appraisal determines that Chambliss carried out his duties wisely and with an even hand. But the times leaned heavily against objectivity.[9]

And so it was, just weeks into the tenure of William Russell Smith, the university lost a figure of almost foundational importance. In the lead up to the October reopening, Ryland Randolph continued to spew his brand of hatred. The editor's physical limitations, forcing him to maneuver with a crutch, grated severely on the man who gloried in a masculine, even martial combativeness. He blamed his diminished physical condition on the university. "You shall have no peace and quiet in your usurped dominions," he promised the faculty as the term began. "Without mercy or restriction," the virulent editor vowed to "pitch into you individually and collectively."[10] In his second stint at the university, if possible, DeForest Richards's standing fell further. A local chronicler made reference to detractors who had earlier cut the tail of Richards's horse and observed that the flinty Republican drives "his shave-tailed horse through the streets as impudently as ever." Richards was only the most visible target.[11] Even young boys understood who constituted the enemy. Later that fall, they pelted Professor David Peck with snowballs as he rode his pony to town. One's physical presence at or even association with the university was not required to attract vituperation. Vernon Vaughn's efforts to find another livelihood as a government official had been awarded. President Grant appointed him as secretary of the Utah Territory. When random furniture pieces from Vaughn's former campus home were auctioned, an unknown local wryly alleged that numerous whisky bottles (all empty) were found among "Tanglefoot's" belongings.[12]

Breaking a cycle of failure posed the central dilemma. Cadets had left pell-mell following the Smith/Randolph shootout, and enrollment expectations were discouraging for the upcoming fall term of 1870. An early rehabilitative step involved attempting to attract students by advertising accommodating entrance requirements and promoting the financial savings offered to attending students. Nobody had quite the perspective regarding the school as did Noah Cloud. His connection to the university dated from a dramatic opening act, the ill-fated rendezvous with Arad Lakin in the summer of 1868 at Tuscaloosa. In his tenure as superintendent of education, well over a year now, the embroiled status of the university left him disillusioned. But at least publicly, Cloud understood, optimism must be projected. As the fall term began, the superintendent issued a pronouncement citing a "good and competent" faculty and generously estimated the number of cadets as "fair." He stressed that students paid no tuition, as recently decreed by the regents, and the only required expenses remitted for lodging and board amounted to less than $150. "Without the fear of disappointment," Cloud assured, the faculty would deliver a "thorough scholarly education, equal to any to be had in any college in the Southern states." President Smith also attested to advantages and further encouraged prospective students against becoming discouraged by personal academic shortcomings. He assured those not meeting the entrance requirements that they could find a place in the preparatory program. Signaling a fresh and new day remained the hope. The realist considered it a forlorn one.[13]

In October 1870, truly with little ado, the academic year began with somewhere between twenty and thirty students. Some of them, as had been the case since the school reopened, were from Republican families. David Smith, a son of Governor William Hugh Smith, was among them. The son of Alabama's Republican governor would soon be made to feel distinctly unwelcome. So would a young cadet named Charles Munsell who had recently arrived in Tuscaloosa. His father, Joel Munsell, was an Albany, New York, printer and had recently printed *Reports of Decisions in the Supreme Court of the State of Alabama*, authored by William Russell Smith. That connection accounted for Charles's enrollment. The young man had been associating with friends whom his father considered undesirable, and Joel Munsell decided the discipline imposed by a military school would benefit his son. By the fall, having made the trip of over one thousand miles from Albany, Charles reached Tuscaloosa. Finding his way to a second- or third-story room and unpacking his belongings were presumably among the first acts of the reorienting cadet. It would not take long for Charles to learn the names of the finite number of fellow cadets and, as it turned out, gain the enmity of some.[14]

From October to June 1871, the first full academic year at the university since the war, education haltingly proceeded. Instead of Professor Loomis, cadets recited Latin and Greek for Professor David Peck. In view of Nathan Chambliss's abrupt resignation, Hampton Whitfield took over mathematics instruction, and returning to the classroom, DeForest Richards resumed his efforts to advance an understanding of the certainties and uncertainties of the galaxies. William Russell Smith assumed direction of English literature. Seeking the governorship back in 1865, Smith acknowledged the state's immediate postwar fragility and judged righting Alabama "a great work of recuperation." Five years later, albeit on a smaller stage, he confronted an equally daunting challenge.[15]

What can be determined about the cadets, even something as basic as how many were enrolled at a given time, is limited by a lack of existing records. A dearth of sources does not preclude making some reasonable assumptions. It is certain that differences, as previously mentioned, developed among a collection of boys/young men straddling adolescence and manhood. That some of the cadets were from Democratic families and others had a Republican background exacerbated the situation. Contrasting perspectives shaped by political predisposition contributed to their differing opinions regarding Vernon Vaughn. After the previously referenced fourteen cadets signed their names to the public letter defending the professor, a fellow student, anonymously designating himself "S," provided a dissenting rejoinder. He pointed out that a majority of students "refused positively to have anything to do with" the petition, and they viewed Vaughn differently. A certain frame of reference also accounted for the mistreatment of Charles Munsell. The "Yankee" drew unwanted attention; among other indignities some cadets refused to pass him food at the mess hall. The situation would take a more serious turn for Charles and others identified with Republicanism.[16]

The resumption of classes coincided with an extremely high-spirited general election in Alabama. Democrats were determined in the fall 1870 elections to take back control of state government and banish the thoroughly condemned Republican foe. Robert Lindsay headed the Democratic state ticket and Republicans renominated William Hugh Smith. The stakes were high for the new party. Surrendering the state's direction risked stunting the

"We Have a University to Resuscitate"

gains of freedpeople, stalling economic advancement, and dealing a crippling blow to the young state Republican Party.

The election also held potentially profound implications for the University of Alabama. Democrats contended that nothing less than rescuing the university from shutting down depended on unseating Noah Cloud. The party placed their hopes of defeating the superintendent of education in the person of Joseph Hodgson, a fiery Democratic apostle who edited the *Montgomery Mail*. Gaining influence on a board of education totally controlled by Republicans was also possible because several seats would be contested. Democrats in the fall campaign connected Republicans to a litany of transgressions ranging from excessive taxation to graft, and their indictment included what they considered the rank mismanagement of the floundering state university. Joseph Hodgson emphatically made that case. In a printed address, Hodgson maintained Republican direction of the school had resulted in a campus inhabited by a handful of students and idle professors. He described the faculty as "seedy or crack-brained parasites" luxuriating in their rent-free homes under "Radical party" misdirection. Neither was the Democratic candidate above ignoring the court verdict absolving Vernon Vaughn of guilt in the William Smith/Ryland Randolph altercation. In Hodgson's version of events, Vaughn had conspired with a cadet to commit murder. "If the University of Alabama is ever to be restored," Hodgson allowed, "it must be when the school system passes out of the hands of the present ruling party." As it was, he labeled the conduct of affairs at Tuscaloosa "simply a disgrace."[17] A widely ranging broadside authored by the Democratic State Executive Committee further allowed that Republicans had "destroyed" the university and inflicted on the state overpaid, characterless, and often "incompetent" instructors.[18]

Noah Cloud offered a far different script. He described Hodgson's attack as a "diatribe" and pointed to "solid progress" at the university, whose problems he attributed to "the foolish actions of Democrats." The superintendent outlined the daunting situation he inherited on coming to the office two years earlier. The university building was incomplete, professors' homes were in disrepair, and no faculty or president in place, but order had been restored despite "the most violent, senseless opposition from the Democratic press of the state." Campaigning throughout the state, Republicans connected Governor Smith's administration to improving finances, extending railroad track, and setting the table for future progress and recovery from a tragic war they blamed on Democrats. Any list of accomplishments, no matter how optimistically presented, did not include successfully relaunching the state university. Its status reflected poorly on the Republican record, and party spokesmen taking their case to the people studiously avoided the school's mention.[19]

In Tuscaloosa, as election day approached, Republicans rallied on October 27 at the courthouse. Among those present were men locally identified with the party since its establishment—David Woodruff, Elisha Peck, and Shandy Jones, the latter seeking reelection to the legislature. Professors DeForest Richards and David Peck, true to their political affiliation, represented the university contingent. The absence of Hampton Whitfield might be attributed to a studious intent to avoid drawing attention to his Republican loyalties. Freedpeople easily outnumbered whites, and they planned in several days to cast Republican ballots.

What Democrats branded an aberration, Radical control of state government, made the contest one of the Alabama's most tumultuous. In the weeks before the election, night riders threatened, beat, whipped, shot, and otherwise persecuted Republicans. The terror and election-day Democratic fraud crucially influenced the verdict. On November 8, in an election in which Black and white Alabamians cast over 157,000 ballots, Robert Lindsay prevailed by fewer than two thousand votes. The extent of the irregularities caused Republicans to legally challenge the outcome. The protest took its most extraordinary form when William Hugh Smith barricaded himself in the governor's office and refused for almost two weeks to step down. The gambit ultimately failed, and Democrats returned to political control in Alabama.[20]

With the election of Robert Lindsay, Democrats celebrated their conception of a redeeming deliverance. In fact, Lindsay's administration proved disappointing, and the party would lose faith in him and in 1872 nominate another candidate (who lost to a Republican). But for the moment, at least, Lindsay's election accounted for boundless optimism. Intentions of the Democrats included lowering taxes, eliminating public offices the party considered unnecessary, and, in general, practicing retrenchment. Many also envisioned restoring the University of Alabama.[21]

The verdict seriously affected the university in the short and the long term. In the glow of victory, the *Montgomery Mail* declared, "We have a University to resuscitate." Democrats won four seats on the board of education, and Joseph Hodgson narrowly defeated Noah Cloud and became superintendent of education. In 1870 he was forty-two years old, a University of Virginia graduate, and a former Confederate who had risen in rank from captain to colonel of the Seventh Alabama Cavalry. After the war Hodgson became associated with the *Montgomery Mail* and soon took over as its primary editor. Acquaintances knew him as sociable, intelligent, and fiercely anti-Republican. He would make reviving the university a high priority.[22] Much of what Hodgson had said and written about the university was exaggerated or patently false. Existing problems at the university, admittedly deep and underlying, deserved qualification. Hodgson's view of an incompetent Radical faculty much oversimplified the case. None of this mattered. As Michael Fitzgerald observed in his recent overview of Reconstruction, Democrats controlled the public discourse. That changes were coming the *Alabama State Journal* conceded in an election postmortem editorial. Democrats had made political capital by demonizing the university and by so doing kept students from enrolling, and the "almost deserted" campus testified to the campaign's success.[23]

Late in November, several weeks after the election, Superintendent Hodgson convened the board of education at the capitol. He spoke in terms of restoring the University of Alabama to its former status and convincing Alabamians at distant schools to come home and enroll at the state university. The political complexion of the board had changed significantly since the last meeting. Eight Republicans continued to count a majority, but four Democrats now joined them. Their voices and increasing resignation among Republican regents contributed to a consensus that major adjustments were desperately demanded at the university. President William Russell Smith appeared before the board of education at Montgomery. Six months had passed since Smith assumed the presidency. That was sufficient time to convince him that recovery was dependent on appointing a faculty more acceptable to a white establishment who had traditionally sent their sons to the school. Smith's recommendation to reorganize the faculty was received favorably. Joseph Speed, elected to the board in the recent contest, quickly became a forceful presence. The Republican introduced a resolution that offered short-term stability yet held out the promise for fundamental change. Fellow regents agreed to Speed's proposal that the present Professors Peck, Richards, and Whitfield retain their positions through the academic year and then hold new elections once the term closed. With that purpose in mind, the board determined to meet six months later in June at Tuscaloosa. University business would command the agenda. Anticipating better days, the *Montgomery Advertiser* noted the decision to gather at Tuscaloosa and to "enter upon a complete reformation of the University."[24]

The man whom Joseph Hodgson succeeded, Noah Cloud, returned to private life. His overseeing of the university and generally tenure as superintendent of education Democrats portrayed as a time of studied failure. That evaluation represents a distortion. For one thing, Cloud's power in regard to the university was limited. He could preside when regents discussed university policy, but the superintendent could not vote. He might cajole, even upbraid, as Cloud did, but as for real power, the superintendent had little. When Nathan Whitfield advised Raphael Semmes about his candidacy for university presidency, he encouraged the *Alabama*'s former commander to cultivate regents behind the scenes. As for Cloud, he discouraged Semmes from making any efforts, for the superintendent had no influence with the regents. Two years after leaving office, Cloud was elected to the legislature and served one term. What he enjoyed much more, his real love, involved promoting agricultural knowledge. On that subject, in contrast to his tenure as a Republican official, Noah Cloud attracted widespread respect.

Joseph Hodgson envisioned changes of a wholesale nature at the university. Among those was a change in leadership. He considered William Russell Smith a Republican, or at least as a man whose sympathies skewed in that direction. At the outset of his administration, the superintendent wrote Henry Tutwiler to gauge his possible interest. The widely respected educator was not, however, his first choice. Matthew Maury was. Hodgson determined to convince the renowned scientist and author to accept the presidency. With a successor to Smith clearly in his sights, Hodgson, within weeks of taking office, quietly began luring Maury from his professorship at Virginia Military Institute. Efforts to bring him to Tuscaloosa dated to the summer of 1869, when Maury had first been contacted regarding the presidency. He had then decided against pursuing the position, and the regents ultimately extended the offer to Cyrus Northrop. Hodgson revived the flirtation by writing Maury at Lexington in the last month of 1870 and then following up early the next year. Confiding as one Democrat to another, he likened the plight of the school at Tuscaloosa to what had transpired at other Southern universities "under the usurping governments set up by Congress." Hodgson assured the Virginia Military Institute professor that his presidency would dramatically reverse the decline. By way of selling the post, the superintendent praised Tuscaloosa as a place of high society and soon a destination connected by an approaching railroad (the Alabama and Chattanooga line). Hodgson pronounced the presidential mansion and grounds superior to those at the University of Virginia and pledged to raise the executive's salary from $3,000 to $3,500. Hiring a president, he admitted, lay with the Republican-controlled board of education, but he also related his confidence in convincing them "to leave the University in your hands."[25] The offer interested Maury. Early in February 1871, he informed a friend that representatives of the Alabama school "are again making passes at me about the Presidency of their University." He leaned toward remaining at Virginia Military Institute but confided if they raised the salary to $5,000, "I may go." An extended effort to convince him to do so lay ahead. In the meantime, Henry Tutwiler had learned of Maury's possible candidacy and made known to Hodgson his disinclination to pursue the office.[26]

About the same time, at the behest of Hodgson, Joseph L. Tait visited the university over the course of several days in January 1871. Tait had been elected as the superintendent of industrial resources. Collecting information concerning the observatory's condition accounted for his turn in Tuscaloosa. The most symbolically important structure to survive John Croxton's raiders was the presidential mansion, but the observatory housing high-powered telescopes represented the most valuable building to escape destruction. On reaching the campus and getting his physical bearings, Tait theorized that the observatory's somewhat removed location from the other university buildings accounted for its fortunate fate. Accurate or not, what he found on inspection alternately pleased and distressed him. Tait inventoried various types of telescopes, the largest astronomical telescope mounted on a revolving table, two astronomical clocks, and a bewildering variety of scientific instruments, fossils, examples of conchology, and specimens of natural history. The superintendent realized fabulous promise even as he documented dereliction. Telescopes in bad need of repair reflected a state of general disarray. As 1871 began the status of the observatory—a place of potential enlightenment that had fallen on bad times—well described the university.[27]

Within weeks of becoming superintendent, Joseph Hodgson provided Governor Robert Lindsay with a survey of the university's condition. He described a dysfunctional but redeemable school. Among the bedrock strengths were facilities, a substantial financial endowment, and a healthy setting at Tuscaloosa. Hodgson maintained that an admittedly "deplorable situation" could be rectified by "a good laborious faculty." That would make a critical goal—convincing young men who were enrolling at other universities to stay in Alabama—imminently achievable. As it was, Hodgson regretted the "untoward circumstances which have destroyed the usefulness of the University." He plainly stated that all which stood between reestablishing a thriving university was the regents' agreement to "select as professors men who have the highest confidence and sympathy of the people." Hodgson's observation presumed the present faculty did not meet that standard.[28]

Robert Lindsay was willing to believe the worst of Republicans. Only recently, in the successful campaign for the governorship, he had denounced the party in campaign appearances throughout the state. In the early 1840s, while attending the University of St. Andrews in his native Scotland, the future Alabama governor formed his notions of an institution of higher learning. Nothing about the school at Tuscaloosa reminded him of that hallowed university. The governor attributed the prevailing situation to Republican mismanagement. "Whence springs this calamity," he cryptically asked, "to this once noble institution?" And by strong inference, he made disparaging reference to the faculty's "intellectual capacity, or moral obliquities" and, in general, "political harlequinism." The proponent of a stringent financial approach floated the idea of withholding state revenue due the school until "a more auspicious era of the Institution." Left unsaid was that members of his party had done their best to make the timing inauspicious.[29]

Following a Christmas recess, as the new year opened, the campus began stirring again. Graphing the school's trajectory in the first half of 1871 is to chart a sharply descending linear plunge. A new president and altered faculty did nothing to invigorate or elevate the university's standing. DeForest Richards had written the Reverend Asa Smith of a spirit of progress as the school had opened in the spring of 1869, but the intervening two years of attrition dealt cruelly with the bright vista Richards had once imagined. Yet this man of conviction, further sustained by his deep faith, is easily visualized purposefully striding across the campus. He remained determined to enlighten students, instilling in them lasting principles of work and right, but in his most honest private moments, Richards knew time was short. Although their experiences at the school were much shorter, Professors Peck and Whitfield also understood the lay of the land. And so did President William Russell Smith. In the first month of 1871, he communicated to Joseph Hodgson, "It is unnecessary to refer to the embarrassed condition of the institution when I took charge of it." He described the number of cadets, standing at twenty-one, as "meagre" and frankly admitted, "There is not much probability of an increase to any great extent, under present auspices." The man of letters pointed with particular pain to a paltry library with but approximately 1,200 books. By way of comparison, the University of South Carolina had over 25,000 volumes. As for a path expediting the school's fortunes, Smith promised to provide a masterplan at a later date. The deferral represented a tacit admission that he did not know of one.[30] Smith could provide no magical restorative elixir. Recalling his time in the Confederate Congress at Richmond as the war turning against the South, Smith favored some type of negotiated peace with the Lincoln government, for "I could not conceal from myself the downward tendency of our affairs." The university's plight offered a fitting parallel to the crumbling Confederacy.[31]

The inhospitable and harsh environment that faculty and some students faced at Tuscaloosa had earlier raised the possibility of moving the university. Joseph Speed, recently elected to the board of education, understood the dark climate locally. The Perry County Republican summed up the situation. "There has not been given to the university for its assistance and success," Speed understated, "that aid and encouragement which are usually given to an institution of that kind by the town in which it is located." The situation deteriorated in the first months and spring of 1871.[32] That was because some most dangerous opponents of the university, possibly emboldened by the recent political victory, stepped up their opposition. They aimed to run off cadets with Republican and/or Northern connections. The efforts took the form of sending threatening letters to those targeted students. Soon after the election, correspondence was found attached to a university door in an envelope marked "K.K.K., Students University," ominously secured by a dagger. Among the cadets receiving the anonymous notes was David Smith, the son of the former governor. He was informed, "You nor no other d—d son of a d—d radical traitor shall stay at our university." The author(s) reminded him that the Democrats had returned to power in Alabama and declared, "The State is ours and so shall our university." Smith was put on notice to leave in ten days or face certain retribution. A young man addressed as "Seavey" (no further identification exists) was informed, "We will be out in force in less than ten days, and it will not be good for you to be found out there," and promised furthermore the university "shall not be carried on under the present faculty." Charles Munsell received a letter giving him a ten-day grace period to pack his belongings and leave, or "look out for hell." The New York state matriculate received emphatic instructions: "You had better get back from where you came from," for "we don't want any d—d Yank at our Colleges." The grim correspondence, collected by Professor Hampton Whitfield, apparently represented only the most recent round of letters. "You have received one notice from us to leave," cadet Seavey was reminded, and the latest directive promised, "This is the last." A fellow student, John Harton, had also not complied with his evil-wishers' instructions. "They say you are of good democrat family," but "we will have good southern men there or none."[33]

A true appreciation of the correspondence requires some context. Nightriding aimed at Republicans had been widespread during the recent election campaign. Across the state from Tuscaloosa, vigilantes hanged four

Black men and a white man who taught freedpeople, following a shooting skirmish in July at Cross Plains. Much closer, at Gainesville and Eutaw, both within forty miles of the university, white supremacy advocates murdered a Black man on separate occasions and for political cause. Eutaw also provided the setting for the campaign's most emblematic event. When Republican congressman Charles Hays attempted to speak there on October 25, 1870, local rowdies fired shots, setting off bedlam and causing what became known as the Eutaw Riot. Several freedmen died and many more were wounded. Men of the same mindset, who would seemingly stop at nothing to impose their definition of right, lived in Tuscaloosa. It was a setting that since Reconstruction's outset had been and continued to be one of the most trouble-plagued places in the state. Several months before the recent election, Governor Smith issued a proclamation singling out three counties as places of extraordinary unrest. Tuscaloosa was one of them. Even a local Democrat, taking pains to identify himself as no friend of Republicans and personally opposed to Black equality, wrote to Smith of politically inspired crimes. He listed twenty-two men who were likely complicit in these activities. The author did not sign the letter for fear of the personal consequences and urged the governor, after taking down the names, to "burn this letter." In this light, existentially considered, the threatening letters addressed to the cadets represent part of a frightening mosaic aimed at Alabama Republicans.[34]

A willingness on the part of the authors to carry out their threats raises a subjective question. Maybe the best answer is suggested by the reaction of those cadets who received the warnings. They withdrew from the university. The governor's son, David Smith—admonished to leave, or "we will visit the place and it will not be well for you to be found out there"—concluded his brief time in Tuscaloosa. The cadet referred to as "Seavey" felt a distinct sense of jeopardy and did likewise. "Some have been wise enough to take our warning," his unknown antagonists advised, closing with, "Do the same." John Harton had also received foreboding warnings: "We don't intend that the concern [the university] shall run any longer." He was left to contemplate the allowed ten-day period. He, too, departed. As for Charles Munsell, he envisioned leaving Alabama for a new start in the West. Yet, rather early in 1871, he was back in Albany, New York, working in his father's printing trade.[35]

The fact of these threats became part of the public record following the establishment of the Joint Committee to Inquire into the Condition of Affairs in the Late Insurrectionary States. Created by Congress in 1871 to assess the situation in the South, the committee took testimony relating to affairs in six Southern states. Joseph Speed was one of over 150 Alabamians who testified. Asked about the recourse of the cadets who had received the letters, Speed responded they had left the university and reasoned, "They were smart enough for that." The regent posed that the cadets did so for fear of consequences if they did not. When a Democrat on the congressional committee by way of absolution skeptically postulated that the young men might simply have wanted to quit school, Speed dissented. "If you had lived in that country, and knew what has been said about the university, and what has been done in regard to it," he retorted, "you would think as I do in reference to this matter." Nothing about the authors who claimed to represent the Ku Klux Klan is known, but it is highly likely the correspondence had local origins. Intermittently since the war, a company (or less) of federal troops had been stationed in Tuscaloosa for purposes of keeping order. The post, commanded by Captain William Mills, had after the recent election been broken up and the soldiers had departed. Their exit now seemed premature.[36]

What lay beyond all possible doubt was the university's continuing decline. DeForest Richards understood that. When sitting in the legislature in January 1871, Richards introduced a bill providing state financial assistance to the school. Robert Somers, visiting Tuscaloosa that same month, captured the university's faint pulse in a different way. The Scotsman's stopover formed part of extensive travels in the South between 1870 and 1871, the trip soon described in a book Somers authored, *The Southern States Since the War*. After arriving in Tuscaloosa and a perusal of the former capital, Somers decided the town's appearance lived up to its mellifluous name. Conditions at the university provided the exception to what he described "as beautiful and spirited a country-town as one could hope to see anywhere." In conversation with a man whose Scottish brogue they surely found novel, residents related to Somers that outside political forces had resulted in the replacement of capable professors with men of inferior talents. Somers admired the campus building and appealing grounds but noted the lack of students and queried, "Where is the fruit?" Those cadets who left for fear of their safety were not the only ones to do so. Others disillusioned with a sinking ship did likewise. As the term wore down, three professors instructed fewer than a dozen students. One of the sons of DeForest and Harriet Richards, Jarvis Richards, was among them. The University of Alabama was that spring a university in name only. A type of academic rigor mortis had set in.[37]

The status of the school was hardly the public preoccupation of Tuscaloosans in the first months of 1871. Any number of diversions drew attention. Many enjoyed the deception of Wyman the Magician during a two-night stand early in February. Two weeks later a large audience took vicarious satisfaction when a visiting lecturer recounted the *Merrimack* and *Monitor*'s ironclad engagement at Hampton Roads. It was undoubtedly a Confederate acolyte who concluded, "Never before did we comprehend the extraordinary power of the Merrimack."[38]

Easily sustaining the most anticipation was construction of the approaching Alabama and Chattanooga Railroad. Residents of the railroad-starved town monitored the progress, expressed fascination with the Chinese laborers who passed in large numbers through the town, and eagerly looked forward to the end of Tuscaloosa's isolation. From a makeshift depot at the foot of Greensboro Street, workers extended track toward the business district to accommodate another novelty—a streetcar. About noon on March 6, 1871, an excited crowd witnessed an Alabama and Chattanooga locomotive pull into town, thus concluding "the dark era of stage-coaches."[39]

Some also placed hopes in regeneration out at the university. In several months, the board of education would meet at Tuscaloosa. Conducting the university's business would take total precedence, and plans for a major shake-up formed the expectation. At the previous fall meeting, convened by Joseph Hodgson, the regents had commissioned three university alumni to solicit ideas from fellow graduates about returning the school to its former status. These circumstances accounted for regents Joseph Speed, E. F. Comegys Jr., and B. J. Harrison drafting a public letter inviting alumni to attend the Tuscaloosa summit. In the call for action, the regents lamented the school's "empty walls and a silent campus." Citing widespread distrust of the faculty since the university reopened, they asked the board to install professors who would inspire confidence.[40]

Graduates who resided in Tuscaloosa best understood the university's low ebb, and none more so than Henderson Somerville. The Tuscaloosa lawyer and university graduate had also taught during the war at the school. Somerville had more recently been part of the team prosecuting William Smith. He grimly viewed the university's decline and in May drafted with other local graduates a letter appealing for alumni to return to Tuscaloosa when the board of education met. The authors cited the school's "languishing" state and posed that the graduates' presence and advice would emphasize a determination to right a badly off course ship. Their appeal was sent to individual alumni and also reprinted in newspapers. The unstated but understood intent involved assembling a block of alumni and so forming a lobbying group and forcing out the incumbent professors.[41]

In anticipation of positive change, one Autauga County resident heralded the university "is soon to be redeemed and reconstructed."[42] The school's seeming notoriety had spread to the smallest of outposts. Evergreen was a mere village far to the south of Tuscaloosa in the state's Piney Woods region. Certain where blame lay, the *Evergreen Observer*'s editor argued that the last two years' experience proved that a state university cannot preach "a political sense and represent a political creed."[43] Never missing an opportunity, Ryland Randolph urged, "A clean sweep of this Augean Stable" and leaving "no vestige of the present ignorant and disgusting faculty."[44] Surely the future promised more than the recent past, reasoned the *Tuscaloosa Observer*'s editor. John Warren recalled the regents passing over well-known Southern professors for Northern faculty who had "no more sympathies in common with our people than the wolf has for the lamb."[45]

In the weeks before the Tuscaloosa summit, assumptions that the board would increase the number of professors partly accounted for the jousting for place in the envisioned new arrangement. One observer positioned leaving the university in the hands of its own graduates and promoted Benjamin Meek, who was teaching at Wesleyan University in Florence, Alabama. William Parker, described as a "thorough classical scholar," fluent in several languages and in part European-educated, came highly recommended.[46] James Murfee had served as commandant during the war, and a nominator championed him as the "very man" for that position. Academic prowess was not the only consideration. A connection to the Confederacy and the Lost Cause already enshrined as gallantly futile might stand one in favorable stead. That formed part of the appeal of G. A. Woodward, the man envisioned as the Latin professor and the son of a Confederate officer who had lost his life defending Richmond.[47]

Events during the week of the board of education meeting, June 12–19, 1871, may have caused some residents to recall the bustling activity that occurred when the state legislature had deliberated at the former Alabama capital. Visitors noticeably increased the pace of the normally somnolent town. Among them was William Wyman, formerly associated with the school but recently instructing at the University of Mississippi. Between fifty and sixty alumni had responded to the invitation from Henderson Somerville, and his two colleagues, along with the returning alumni, met for the first of several times on Tuesday, June 13. William Wyman addressed them that night at the Baptist church. Not all coming to Tuscaloosa were selfless. Personal advancement was their god. Making a case for employment, individuals lobbied to become quartermaster, university tailor, indeed any association with the school. Most of those on the make aspired for faculty positions. The Mansion House served as unofficial headquarters. After putting down his bags there, one visitor meandered about the crowded town and decided that "every stranger in town was called 'professor.'"[48] Another observer allowed the "log-rolling was tremendous."[49] It was impossible to miss Joseph Hodgson. Speaking at the courthouse, the superintendent of education urged for "placing the University on a sound basis." The campaigning for advancement continued relentlessly, and aspiring faculty and their supernumeraries staked their claims—sometimes openly, on other occasions privately. And in the spirit of horse trading, some were surely not above offering lubrication for favorable consideration. Money, spirits, and promises of future favorable treatment in part provided the coin of the realm. Each of the sitting professors, David Peck, DeForest Richards, and Hampton Whitfield, desired retaining their appointments, but doing so seemed unlikely, for a cresting tide of irresistible change and turn overflowed heavily against them. And in the meantime, the prospects of candidates "were fully canvassed by the sundry squads of earnest talkers at the different street corners." Rumors of forming alliances and caucuses surreptitiously convening at the insane asylum and the Mansion House hinted at intrigue and clandestine maneuvering.[50]

Decisions lay with the board of education. Ten of its twelve members, six Republicans and four Democrats, came to Tuscaloosa, but it was color, not political affiliation, that most obviously identified one of them. Peyton Finley was tall, Black, and a formerly enslaved person. He had been elected to the board in the recent general election. Meeting first and inconsequentially on June 13 in the Mansion House parlor, the regents two days later moved out to the university. Among them was Joseph Speed, who expressed hope that the public would not be "blinded" by political considerations and admit that wise choices could "come from a Republican."[51] Few could claim the perspective of Jesse Booth; the Autauga County Republican had sat on the board since its creation in 1868. It seemed in the intervening turmoil that an eon had passed since he had warned against installing a faculty with no previous background in Alabama. Measured in terms of events—four university presidents, the national airing of a woodcut promising the lynching of Republican officials connected to the school, a shootout between a cadet and the school's most outspoken detractor—it had. A witness to past missteps, Booth determined "to cut loose from, and act independently of, partisan feeling and mere party interest."[52] Thomas A. Cook was also present. An Episcopal minister living in Talladega, he had recently been elected to the board of education. Several weeks earlier Cook had written privately, "I feel mortified to see the condition of the State Institution," and vowed to "do anything in my power to put it on a proper basis."[53]

Appropriately enough, at the university, the board began serious deliberations on Thursday morning, June 15. Henderson Somerville and two others presented a series of resolutions making the alumni case for reorganization. The regents' response, requesting specification regarding what lines reorganization should take, the alumni interpreted positively, and plans were agreed upon for several designated regents to meet with a like number of university graduates. On Monday, June 19, somewhere in the university building recesses, what would be extensive discussions began. A guiding tenet admitted the necessity of a major overhaul, but that presumption did not preclude disagreements. Political loyalties inevitably figured. Some Republicans regarded the assembled alumni as a Democratic juggernaut intent on expunging all Republican influence from the university. Settling on a mutually acceptable corps of professors consumed four hours. Jesse Booth would relate that he and other regents "tried to rise above party."[54] At the critical June 19 meeting, the regents at times sharply dissented. "Every member voted as he thought best," Booth assured. What was "best" represented a matter of open interpretation.[55]

The regents ended up dramatically increasing both the scope and size of the faculty. They elected eleven professors. Four of them had previously attended or taught at the university. William Wyman, Benjamin Meek, William J. Vaughan, David Peck, William Parker, and Eugene A. Smith joined the faculty, and together these men taught a range of rigorous subjects, such as pure and applied mathematics, English literature, Greek, Latin, geology, and mineralogy. Some regents continued to hold Nathaniel Lupton's previous course against him, but that did not prevent him from being awarded the professorship of chemistry. Completing the expanded faculty were Algernon S. Garnett, professor of natural history and campus physician; Reverend Telfair Hodgson, professor of moral philosophy; J. G. Griswold, professor of modern languages; and General George P. Harrison, professor of military engineering and commandant.[56]

In the selection process, inevitably, the political persuasion of candidates factored. One regent referred to "the inside workings of the Board" and allowed that David Peck's selection represented a "compromise" and concession to hire one Republican professor. A determination of some Republican regents to reappoint Hampton Whitfield also caused conflict. Joseph Speed strenuously attempted to keep Whitfield on the faculty. His failure to do so pleased a Democratic regent who feared "being saddled with both Peck and Whitfield." In the end, however, six Republicans and four Democrats belonging to the board of education did largely cooperate.[57]

Chapter 8

The question of who would lead the school as president hung over the gathering. The tenure of William Russell Smith was coming to a close. On June 17 he presented a report (not extant) regarding the university's status. Two days later, Smith resigned, effective on June 30. Whether he did so of his own volition cannot be established, but Smith's exit likely represented a mutual understanding. The president's decision gained far less attention than the announcement of his successor. The wooing of Matthew Maury had apparently met with success. Circulating rumors of the Virginia Military Institute's professor's expected designation as president were confirmed following his election on June 21.

That the University of Alabama had reached a pivoting juncture was assumed. With new faculty in place, the *Montgomery Advertiser and Mail* decided, "Every young man, about to take a collegiate course, should at once resolve to go to Tuscaloosa."[58] The *Selma Times* hinted at the seeming political coup d'état. The newspaper appropriated the term "redeemed"—already employed to reference the return of Democrats to power and the vanquishment of Republicans—to describe what had occurred.[59] John Warren was among the most relieved. Conceding that Republicans controlled the board of education and making further allowance that one member, Peyton Finley, was a freedman, the *Tuscaloosa Observer*'s editor admitted, "We must say of them . . . they have acted with a view to the prosperity of the University."[60]

William Russell Smith's tenure of almost exactly a year was over. Nearly a century and a half later, a chronicler would refer to him as the university's "forgotten president." It was surely with relief that he put down his teaching and administrative duties and returned to practicing law. A year after resigning, on more solid ground than he had ever commanded as university president, Smith completed a *Key to the Iliad of Homer*. By parallel construction, this man of letters would have conceded, he had not discovered any blueprint for navigating the university back to prosperity. Matthew Maury, the strong consensus assured, would accomplish that task.[61]

Chapter 9

Courting the Commodore

The University of Alabama Lures a President

EMPHATIC SATISFACTION GREETED THE ANNOUNCEMENT OF MATTHEW Maury's ascension to the presidency and created the expectation that the famed scientist would reinvigorate the all but comatose university. Democrats charted a timeline of dissolution from the summer of 1868 when William Wyman resigned in protest after the board of education had replaced the sitting faculty. President Arad Lakin's single-day visit several weeks later to the campus dissuaded him from assuming the presidency, and the subsequent administration of Robert Harper ended before it effectually began early in 1869. By default, inheriting direction as president pro tempore, DeForest Richards then began a tortured tenure. An attempt to name a permanent executive collapsed when Cyrus Northrop rejected the preferment, and the stewardship of Richards continued until Nathaniel Lupton, hailed as a savior, took over as 1869 closed, but the university's downward spiral worsened during his six-month quasi-presidency. Since June 1870, spanning the yearlong administration of William Russell Smith, the school retained the feel of a picked-over carcass. Against this dismal background, the coming of Matthew Maury heralded a new day and foretold progress for what was quite possibly the most beleaguered state university in the country. "Your very name would like the bugle of Rederic Dhee," one Alabama admirer wrote Maury, and "put new life into us." The bugle had sounded.[1]

The presumptive president was in the sixty-sixth year of a life marked by spectacular achievement and resulting national and even international praise.[2] Born in Virginia in 1806, Maury gained a respectable education, but he never attended college. He was drawn to the sea and at the age of nineteen became a midshipman in the United States Navy. By then he had reached his physical maturity, standing five feet six inches tall. Much of the next dozen years Maury spent on a ship, developing an understanding of the ocean and whetting a lifelong fascination for the sea. He belonged to the first expedition by a United States Naval vessel to circle the world. In 1836, Maury authored a textbook addressing sea currents and their relationship to winds, advancing mariners' navigating knowledge and marking the beginning of a prolific publishing career. In the person of Matthew Maury an insatiable curiosity was met by a conceded brilliance. He absorbed mathematic principles, made deductive calculations, and, from a deep scientific framework, promoted what would become the field of oceanography. Maury also exhibited a strong conversance with astronomy. In other respects, his life had gained an anchor in 1834 when he married Ann Hull Herndon, and the first of eight children soon arrived.

At the age of thirty-three, in 1839, Maury was involved in a stagecoach accident resulting in severe damage to his right leg. The injury left him permanently lame and ended his active sea duty. But the coming man was hardly slowed. Maury became in 1842 the superintendent of the Navy Depot of Charts and Instruments in Washington, DC, and two years later the first superintendent of the United States Naval Observatory, also in the nation's capital. After touring the observatory and spending time with its superintendent, a visiting English author described her guide as "a man of science, equally well versed in the secrets of the sea and of the sky; an accomplished mariner, an admirable astronomer, and mathematician and a superior author on many subjects."[3] Maury's time at sea had impressed on him the critical advantages of navigators possessing accurate information regarding wind and water currents. His exhaustive study of ship logs provided the research grist for the pathbreaking *Explanations and Sailing Directions Accompany the Wind and Current Charts*; a captain of a clipper sailing the high seas later admitted to him, "Until I took up your work I had been traversing the ocean blindfold." Attracting a wider reading audience, Maury addressed among other subjects the Gulf Stream and the depths of the ocean in *The Physical Geography of the Sea*. Earlier, the National Observatory superintendent had contributed to the overdue establishment of the Naval Academy in 1845 and, over a decade later, to laying the Atlantic cable, which in 1858 resulted in electronically connecting the United States and England.[4]

Thirty-six years of naval service ended, including seventeen as the National Observatory superintendent in April 1861, when Maury resigned his superintendency and offered his services to the Confederate States of America. That decision was made with regret, for he accepted secession reluctantly and out of a sense of loyalty to Virginia. Once a Confederate, however, the man who knew and admired Robert E. Lee turned his mind to the cause of Southern independence. He developed the first successful electronic torpedoes utilized for defense purposes in rivers and harbors. Maury also designed a gunboat, and his appointment to their problematic command meant that he would often be addressed as "Commodore." In another capacity, he represented the Confederacy diplomatically in England.[5]

Following the South's defeat, fearing possible imprisonment for his role during the war, Maury in 1865 relocated to Mexico, where the archduke of Austria, Ferdinand Maximilian, was attempting to revive the Mexican Empire. Maury envisioned establishing a "New Virginia" and attracting ex-Confederates dispirited by the war's outcome and bleak prospects in the South. Maximilian made Maury the imperial commissioner of immigration. The emperor's plans proved chimerical, Maury's efforts at establishing a "New Virginia" came to little, and the short-lived empire collapsed. The year was 1866. In his last two endeavors—acting with the Confederacy and Maximilian's regime—Maury had uncharacteristically been part of a failure. His fortunes soon improved. The Commodore passed much of the next two years in England, and no longer worried about punishment, the Virginian returned home in the year Ulysses Grant was elected president.

In these explosive Reconstruction years, Maury avoided taking a public political stance, but his loyalties lay firmly with the Democratic Party. He contemplated an academic life at a university. Early in 1868, Maury seriously considered an offer to become the vice chancellor of the University of the South at Sewanee, Tennessee, and later that year, he did accept the professorship of physics at Virginia Military Institute at Lexington. Part of the attraction, it seems, was the presence of his friend Robert E. Lee, president of Washington College, also located in Lexington. Although far less catastrophically than the University of Alabama, Virginia Military Institute had also been harmed by Union troops. Such was the damage done that repairs to the home the Maury family would reside in delayed their moving in. The Commodore did not teach but gave several lectures and memorably delivered in July 1869 the commencement graduation address.[6]

Yet by the summer of 1871, seemingly, he had determined to leave. Maury's acceptance of the University of Alabama presidency inspired celebration. Maury's Confederate past-and-present status as a Democrat most gratified some. Others placed a premium on the president-in-waiting's professional portfolio. Following a summary of his accomplishments, John Warren at the *Tuscaloosa Observer* rhetorically asked, "Could our Regents have done better than to secure such a man for President?" Lazarus had risen from the dead.

Hercules had held up the sky for Atlas. And in a temporal world, Matthew Maury could accomplish similar feats at the University of Alabama.[7]

In June 1871, when Maury conditionally accepted the presidency, his knowledge of the university was completely secondhand. He had never visited Tuscaloosa. While superintendent of the National Observatory, Maury had corresponded with the university's professor of mathematics and natural philosophy. Frederick Barnard had in 1844 written him regarding the recently constructed observatory on the Tuscaloosa campus. Much more recently, in the summer of 1869, Noah Cloud attempted to lure him to the school. Then and in the future, as he weighed the opportunity, the quotient of financial renumeration was important. Maury had never remotely received monetary compensation commensurate with his reputation and contributions. Referring to the possibilities at Tuscaloosa, he playfully informed his son-in-law that he would respond to the university entreaties by proposing, "Give me full swing and $10m [i.e., $10,000] a year for 5 years and I'll try to build you up."[8] Some acquaintances realized that Maury was seriously thinking about removing to Alabama. A friend warned against attempting to "build up broken down Universities" and advised that it was "too late to enter upon new schemes of life." Maury was uncomfortable in the summer of 1869 with leaving Virginia Military Institute, where he had recently put down stakes. The timing was bad, and he did not pursue the presidency, an appointment that he probably could have had. Ultimately, the regents extended the invitation to Cyrus Northrop.[9]

And so it was that previous efforts to entice Maury failed, and he remained in Lexington. Always driven to work, he remained busy, devoting most of his energies to the project that would result in the *Physical Survey of Virginia*. Not the least of his amenities was a fine study in the residence provided for the family. It was here that the man—whom Maury's masterful biographer, Frances L. Williams, describes as "one of the last universal scientists"—called on his broad knowledge and powers. Yet he worried increasingly about Robert E. Lee, who lived nearby. On October 12, 1869, the general died, and several days later Maury participated in the funeral procession at Lexington.[10]

Although deciding against pursuing the presidency of Alabama's state university, thoughts of the school fleetingly returned late in 1869 when he received a letter from Calvin Loomis. Putting the university on a much firmer footing accounted for the ancient language professor's efforts to bring Maury to Tuscaloosa. Loomis realized all too well the university's uncertain status. As a professor desirous of maintaining his teaching appointment, he

FIGURE 9.1. Matthew Maury, renowned scientist and prospective president of the University of Alabama, 1871. The appointment of Matthew Maury as president in 1871 was received with joy by Democrats. His credentials as a scientist, author, educator, and Southerner with a Confederate past promised much, but circumstances caused the Maury administration to end before it started. University of Alabama Libraries Special Collections.

understood the critical boost a man of Maury's stature could generate to a university badly in need of cadets. Loomis encouraged the scientist, "Your name would be a tower of strength and that your reputation would bring in hosts of students!" A hypothetical Maury administration, he qualified, was contingent on certain realities. Loomis explained that the Democratic press had been so critical of the board of education that its members would never turn to an ex-Confederate unless that individual categorically endorsed the altered society associated with Reconstruction. Under the correct impression that Maury was a Democrat, Loomis cautioned that the regents must be sure that he concurred with the maxim that the "*law* ought to make no distinction between white and black." Beside recognizing the nation's new racial arrangement, Loomis continued, lay any prospective president's repudiation of violence, a not-so-veiled reference to the widespread physical intimidation aimed at Republicans throughout the South. If he assumed the school's direction, the professor further posed, Maury must embrace the principle that a teacher's merit rather than their politics was paramount.[11] Maury counted Elias Loomis as a professional friend, but he failed to make the connection between the recognized Yale professor and his comparatively unknown brother. Scribbling a short and dismissive note on the back of Loomis's letter, Maury denied knowing the author but concluded, "I take him to be a Yankee. No Southerner would write such a letter." That Loomis received a reply is highly unlikely.[12]

Matthew Fontaine Maury's eventual receptiveness to the University of Alabama overtures had nothing to do with dissatisfaction at Virginia Military Institute. What did contribute, however, was the changed political landscape in Alabama. The triumph of state Democrats in the general election of 1870 created a more inviting political environment. Maury was a committed but not publicly outspoken Conservative who had no use for Republicans. He viewed Joseph Hodgson replacing Noah Cloud as superintendent of education as a highly favorable development.

In the weeks ahead Hodgson would play the role of a persistent suitor. When Hodgson became superintendent, William Russell Smith was a half-year into his tenure as president. Hodgson did not view him as the man to take the school forward in the long term. On the contrary, he was confident that Maury was that person. While attending the University of Virginia, Hodgson roomed with one of Maury's sons and in 1858 had visited the family at their Washington, DC, residence located on the grounds of the impressive domed National Observatory. On that occasion, as was the superintendent's wont, Maury probably directed a tour of the observatory and invited young Hodgson to gaze into the heavens. The University of Virginia student was not even twenty years old, but Maury made a first and lasting positive impression. Over a decade had passed since meeting Maury, but Hodgson considered him uniquely qualified to arrest the University of Alabama's descent and move the school in a positive direction. Neither was he blind to the personal accruing benefits for making that resurrection possible. The superintendent was a young man on the make with political ambitions. One who knew Hodgson well would inform Maury that he "expects naturally and very justly to make much reputation by organizing the university under your presidency." What remained, for a welter of reasons, was the revival of a campaign designed to bring Matthew Fountain Maury to Alabama.[13]

In the first month of 1871, only weeks after taking office, Hodgson wrote to the Commodore at Lexington and inquired of his interest. Hodgson explained that the university had dissipated under Republican domination. Understanding that he was corresponding with a man of like political thinking, the newly elected Democrat added, "The history of the University for two years past has been the history of all our universities under the usurping governments." In fact, assuming more power than he possessed, Hodgson all but offered Maury the presidency. Hodgson intended "reform" and predicted he could convince the board of education "to leave the University in your hands." He promised to raise the president's salary from $3,000 to $3,500. By way of further inducement, Hodgson described the executive mansion and grounds as "superior to those at our Virginia University." Tuscaloosa provided a healthy location, boasted an intelligent and gracious society, the superintendent elaborated, and within months the place would be connected by railroad to the outside world.[14]

Maury had in 1869 given some thought to the school before indicating his intention to remain at the Virginia Military Institute. Well over a year had passed since then, and altered circumstances now compelled him to entertain the overtures more seriously. Democratic control of Alabama provided but one consideration. Part of the recalibrated equation also involved his health. Maury had for years endured pain related to his carriage accident of many years past, restricting mobility and requiring sometimes the use of crutches. And recently, and more pertinently, rheumatism caused him acute suffering. Even writing, given his swelled and stiffened fingers, had become highly difficult. Cold weather exacerbated the debilitation. Doctors had advised him to go south during the winter season, and trading the harsh Virginia weather for warmer temperatures, he did so during the winter of 1870–1871. The sabbatical brought extreme physical relief. In fact, when

Hodgson initially wrote to him, Maury was wintering in the South. A significant salary increase provided further temptation. Writing an acquaintance from New Orleans in February 1871, Maury allowed, "They are again making passes at me about the Presidency of their state University." He considered the offer of $3,500 inadequate but admitted if that sum was raised to $5,000, "I may go."[15] Corresponding in early February with Hodgson from Thibodaux, Louisiana, Maury raised the possibility of visiting Montgomery and discussing the situation. The superintendent quickly responded positively and mentioned "the pleasing hope that you may be prevailed upon to make your home with us."[16]

At some point in February 1871, Matthew Maury and Joseph Hodgson met in Montgomery. Their mutual Democratic loyalties, interest in education, and ties to the University of Virginia provided the foundation of a friendship. Hodgson was hardly the young undergraduate that Maury hosted in 1858 at his Washington home. Thirteen years had passed, and since then Hodgson had led men into battle, assumed the editorial helm of a major state newspaper, and been elected to a powerful statewide office. Maury laid out his requirements. They included a $5,000 salary and expansive administrative powers. Ever cognizant of the time necessary for pursuing research interests and scholarship, the prospective president further stipulated that he be relieved of any teaching duties. If these conditions were met, Maury informed a much-encouraged Hodgson, he would take the offer under close consideration.

Various contingencies, even so, stood in the way of bringing the Virginian to Alabama. That the presidency was presently held by another man was not, however, one of them. It was certain that William Russell Smith would willingly give up the office or that he could be pressured to do so. The composition of the board of education at least theoretically posed a more serious roadblock. Four Democrats now sat on the board, and they could be relied on to support Maury, but Republicans composed the majority. Maury was an acknowledged Democrat, yet the regents had already exhibited a willingness to entrust the university's direction to a Conservative when they hired Nathaniel Lupton. Neither did Maury have the reputation as a doctrinaire ideologue. His candidacy had earlier attracted support, and Hodgson believed he could convince the regents to hire a man of such stature. Nothing was certain until the board convened. Early in 1871, at Montgomery, the groundwork had been laid when the two men met, talked of their expectations regarding the presidency, and given their shared political perspective, surely commiserated about what they viewed as the malevolent Radical misdirection of the university. The superintendent of education would persist in the months ahead, and other advocates of the school would make their case as well to the acclaimed scientist. Forthrightly writing Maury in mid-April, Hodgson inquired, "Will you accepted the Presidency of the University of Alabama, with a salary of $3,500?"[17]

Some signs indicated that Maury's time in Virginia was short. In the months before the board of education met in June 1871 at Tuscaloosa, Maury heard from various individuals. Among those wooing him was Thomas Cook, the Talladega minister who had recently been elected to the board of education. "Let me beg of you not to refuse," and the Episcopal pastor extolled the virtues of Tuscaloosa, promising a suitable faculty, a fine home, enchanting campus grounds, and, maybe most crucially, that "there would be no trouble in raising the salary high enough to satisfy you." Cook entreated, "Help us to revive our unfortunate University."[18] James Murfee joined the recruitment campaign. Having played a major role in the school's resurrection, Murfee noted the unfulfilled "beautiful promise" of a university, which "only needed your wisdom and influence to reach."[19] Replying to Thomas Cook, Maury reiterated terms under which he would presumably become the executive. Rev. Cook replied the conditions seemed "reasonable enough" and endorsed providing him "*carte blanche* [powers] to manage the Institution as you think expedient." The prospect of the celebrated Commodore becoming president left him positively giddy. Cook identified himself as the son of a sea captain and responded, "Delighted to see you demand full control of the ship. 'Aye, aye sir,' Is my motto until your surrender."[20]

The possibility of a Maury administration gained notice that spring in circles far removed from Tuscaloosa. Some individuals, presuming his presidency only a matter of time, wrote the Commodore at Lexington and promoted themselves or others for faculty positions. Among the correspondents was Catesby ap Roger Jones, formerly an officer in the Confederate Navy who for a time commanded the *Merrimack* in its duel with the *Monitor*. Living now in Selma, where word had spread of Maury's apparent installation as president, Jones noted local residents' "great satisfaction." Jones recommended for commandant a distant relation who was presently a cadet, ironically, at the Virginia Military Institute.[21] Another prospective colleague, presently teaching at Hampden-Sydney College, made known his interest in the Latin chair, and the president of William and Mary College recommended a modern languages professor. Commending not one but two candidates, yet another acquaintance wrote, "I have heard that you were much interested in the reorganization of the Alabama University on a Conservative basis." Even so, much remained unsure, and corresponding in May with another inquiring about employment, Maury made clear that his presidency represented only a possibility.[22]

A quiet but persistent campaign to bring the Virginia Military Institute professor to Alabama had been underway for six months when the board of education met in June 1871 at Tuscaloosa. And it was there, when a new and more numerous faculty was settled upon, that Matthew Maury's seeming acceptance became public knowledge. Joseph Hodgson expressed confidence to the regents of Maury's consent if they agreed to his requested conditions regarding authority and compensation. On June 21, congregating at the university building, the regents unanimously elected him. In celebration, beginning a letter "My Dear Commodore," Hodgson informed Maury of his selection and that the terms he had outlined in his earlier visit to Montgomery had been met. That list included total control of university funds, the option of teaching or not doing so, a $5,000 salary, presidential mansion accommodations, and in short "you have been given every thing you asked." Well aware that Maury continued to have mixed feelings, he added that Alabamians "have set their hearts upon having you." Hodgson raised the stakes further by interposing that declining at this stage would be "disastrous" for the university and, in a personal aside, would "place me, individually, in a most awkward situation." Hodgson asked Maury to telegraph him a decision and that "we expect you to accept." Maury remained, true to character, very cautious. To a relative, the month he was elected, Maury expressed serious reservations about working with a Republican-dominated board of education.[23]

At Tuscaloosa, as the regents had deliberated, questions elicited different answers among the board members. The composition of the faculty provoked considerable contention. More controversy arose after the meeting; some faulted the financial wisdom of hiring so many professors, and the appointment of Hodgson's brother, Telfair Hodgson, as professor of moral philosophy also raised questions of propriety and conflict of interest. Even the new faculty's almost universal affiliation with the Episcopalian Church gained negative attention. In contrast, however, little or no dissent attended the selection of Matthew Maury. John Warren rhapsodized as to what would surely follow, leaping to the grandiose and predicting three hundred students, and projected the resulting financial windfall would allow expanding and enclosing the university building as James Murfee had originally intended. From throughout Alabama and the entire South, the *Montgomery Advertiser and Mail* echoed, the "luster of his splendid reputation will draw students."[24] Over in Mississippi, a University of Alabama graduate adopted a similar tone. Taking the self-satisfied view that one good thing led to another, he volunteered, "Alabama is wrested from the hands of Radicalism and so is her University." What was largely lost on all celebrants was a critical distinction: Matthew Maury had not definitively consented.[25]

Less than a month after his election, Maury returned to Montgomery. The trip purposefully coincided with a meeting of the Alabama Education Association that took place over several days in mid-July. Questions regarding public schools of a nuts-and-bolts variety demanded attention, but so did a subject that reflected an emerging national debate regarding higher education. The traditional heavy reliance on a classical curriculum at colleges and universities had increasingly come under fire. Ministers, lawyers, professors, and physicians benefitted from studying the classics, but the traditional approach had far less application for the farmer, manufacturer, or mechanic, essentially the man who worked with his hands. James Tait belonged to the ranks of those in Alabama advocating revision. The commissioner of industrial resources, who had earlier in the year visited the university observatory, spoke and emphasized integrating the application of science with the traditional classical curriculum. Maury listened with approval, and then he took the floor. A curious audience noted the short, rather stout, balding individual who approached the speaking platform with the slight limp he had lived with since the stage accident thirty years earlier. But this was no compromised man. It was a supremely confident Maury who heartily concurred with Tait and provided specific cases when the avid pursuit of science had translated into advancement for the entire country. He contended that the long-honored classics emphasis was somewhat irrelevant to a wide cross section of society. As president of the University of Alabama, he planned to pursue that line of philosophy.[26]

Montgomery's visitor found far less satisfying an informal faculty meeting that convened with most of the recently appointed professors. What Maury came to understand alarmed him. On one level, he was troubled by a new curriculum format that had been adopted at the recent board of education meeting at Tuscaloosa. The president considered the masterplan overly permissive and flawed, for it failed to take into account a student's aptitude. To one of his daughters, whom he had long ago nicknamed Nannie, he would soon complain that the arrangement effectually conveyed the unrealistic message that "you have paid your money, take your choice." But it was the university's financial standing that caused the president-in-waiting the greatest anxiety. Maury learned that the anemic status of the state treasury likely meant that the university could not draw some $11,000 due upon its annual interest. Although he had not so much as walked the campus or viewed the facilities, Maury realized that funds were critically needed for infrastructural repairs and outfitting the military department. It was sobering that the anticipated money due the university owed upon the school's annual interest would not be immediately forthcoming. He also understood that little revenue would be generated by an expected influx of students because tuition fees were so small. The sum of these circumstances caused Maury to make a shocking announcement to those assembled: he could not undertake reviving a school so gravely compromised. Immediate consternation greeted that statement. "*Hy-falutin* speeches followed," he would relate to Nannie, "and from the floor professors worried about consequences and decried 'what shall I do?'" That Maury would assume the helm they had not questioned, and the possibility that the great man might renege provoked panic, histrionically expressed. Without the figure who had taken on savior proportions, the university's revival seemed beyond hope and, not incidentally, their appointments in sudden peril. One professor exclaimed he had "given up his house," another forfeited "his practice," a third "his business," and one more decried passing on an appointment from another college. Even more dramatically, another academic allowed the sudden and unexpected development placed in jeopardy his recent marriage engagement. Acting immediately to reassure Maury, Joseph Hodgson arranged for several prominent local men and state supreme court judges to intercede. They promised that the legislature, as Maury later recalled to Nannie, "Black & white radicals & all," would be forthcoming with supporting funds. Professors who pledged part of their salary toward a supportive fund further testified to resolve—and desperation. Equilibrium was restored when Maury agreed to assume the presidency under certain conditions. Those stipulations included establishing a generous "launching fund," scrapping the recently constructed curriculum plan, and raising fees for students, and therefore university revenue. Everything ultimately would ride on the regents' reaction to his conditions. Joseph Hodgson would poll them by mail.[27]

Tuscaloosa's status as a seemingly fabled destination had been made abundantly clear to Maury, and he hoped to visit the town. While in Montgomery, some thought was given to making the one-hundred-mile trip to Alabama's former capital. Over three weeks had passed since William Russell Smith resigned, but he had not yet vacated the president's mansion. Smith's delayed departure kept Maury from undertaking the trip. As the Commodore soon privately and caustically observed, "My radical predecessor, with his three students" had not moved out.[28]

Maury returned to Lexington in a conflicted state of mind. A deliberate man who approached situations with clinical detachment, even those unrelated to science, he rejected impulse and risk-taking. Prior to Maury joining the faculty at Virginia Military Institute, officials at the University of the South had attempted to make him the school's vice chancellor. "It is wisest & best to go surely and slowly & step by step," Maury reasoned in correspondence with those wooing him, and to address "ourselves at each stage to the circumstances by which we may then find ourselves surrounded." And not long thereafter he turned down their invitation.[29] Maury similarly considered prospects regarding the University of Alabama. He wrote Nannie that not only was money lacking in the state treasury to "fit up the Univ. but there was nothing to keep it a-goin." The recent gathering at Montgomery hardly resembled the expected joyous coronation. Yet, despite doubts, the overt adulation was flattering, and Maury admitted to his daughter that his promoters' promises "to rally around me" and their emphatically expressed wish "for me to take charge of their Univ. was gratifying." All things considered, he confirmed, "my going to Tuscaloosa is still in abeyance." In his fine stone home on the Virginial Military Institute campus, Maury awaited the telegram providing the regents' response. Chances remained better that he would leave than stay. The presumed president informed Nannie of "working *like a Turk*" and collecting materials to take to Alabama. His tenure was scheduled to begin with a faculty meeting on September 1, 1871. If a majority of regents agreed to his stipulations, Maury planned to be present.[30]

One month before the anticipated gathering of the new faculty at Tuscaloosa, Hodgson telegraphed him of the regents' consent, and Maury forthrightly replied by wire, "I will come." And on the next day, July 30, he formally accepted in writing the presidency.[31] Some two weeks had expired since the disturbing meeting at Montgomery. Signs indicated the rescue and revitalization of the university was at hand. "Now that Radicalism has been swept from the University of Alabama, and Commodore Maury placed at its head," a Black Belt editor observer predicted, enrollment problems would be over.[32]

It was a man plainly set on relocating who soon inquired of progress regarding the highly deliberate efforts of William Russell Smith in Tuscaloosa to leave the presidential residence. Maury even handled a few executive administrative functions while at Virginia Military Institute. Some persons concerned for the interests of the university advocated abandoning the guiding straight jacket military arrangement or at least allowing students to enroll who had no desire to be cadets or conform to the regulations that living on campus required. In a letter to Hodgson, Maury agreed to adjustments on a limited basis, making an exception for those enrolling who resided in Tuscaloosa. They could live at home, attend the university, and, in his words, "these we can receive as students—not as cadets." Hodgson no doubt appreciated Maury's use of the collective word "we."

Maybe the clearest indication of his plans to become president involved drafting and issuing an inaugural salutation. Michael Cohen in *Reconstructing the Campus* writes of curriculum changes in Southern universities following the war, best expressed by courses of a more utilitarian nature, such as engineering. Similarly in his prospectus, Maury outlined a direction he intended to take the school. Allowing that the university must adapt to a changing world, Maury called for emphasizing new physical discoveries and their practical application. The president noted the "progress of the age" and posed that the university curriculum should correspondingly evolve and reflect adjustment, meaning the classical fields would necessarily forfeit "a little of their ancient prominence" in deference to "physical science." A humanities curriculum would continue to dominate, but a "polytechnic" dimension should prepare students for "the mechanical arts or industrial callings." Maury made no reference to the school's travails and prudently avoided any political statement or allusion. He mixed inspiration with realism, predicting the university's ultimate but not overnight return to its former prominence, and in a better and more relevant guise.[33]

The implementation of Maury's vision, even so, soon became increasingly doubtful. Several days into August, within a week of agreeing to become president, he received a highly disturbing letter from Hodgson. Although the superintendent confirmed the "launching fund," he advised that in light of "the load of debt upon the state from Radical misrule, you will ask for the very least sum necessary to start the wheels."[34] In reply, on August 8, Maury expressed concern as to having sufficient funds to carry out the improvements he considered necessary. Enlarging and better equipping the laboratories, repairing buildings, and providing textbooks, uniforms, and weapons for drilling to students dominated that list. Much of the foregoing, he believed, could not wait. Under the circumstances, Maury proposed delaying the university's opening for a month and thereby allowing time for the legislature to convene and provide absolute financial underwriting. On August 12, in reply, Hodgson attempted to allay those fears. Maury seems to have misapprehended that the "launching fund" could be immediately tapped into. With a trace of exasperation, Hodgson informed him otherwise, adding, "I thought that was understood." What the incoming president did have at his disposal, $5,500 cash and a state warrant for $11,000, he maintained would suffice in the short term. An additional $20,000, generated by a projected one hundred students (the tuition of sixty-five cadets assumed by the state), would be realized as the term began in early October. Until the legislature met in late November and provided the "launching fund" money, he reasoned those funds will "float you comfortably." Postponing the semester's start, Hodgson continued, was out of the question, for doing so would cost the school badly needed students. Conceding that "you may not commence with everything as you want it," the superintendent reasoned, "By the time the boys are uniformed, classified & drilled a little you will have all the money you need."[35]

William Wyman also joined the discourse. Three years had passed since he had, in protest, resigned the presidency. At the recent meeting in Tuscaloosa, the regents had elected him professor of Latin. As a man long moored to the university, the returning professor claimed a special influence. The state treasury was empty, Wyman admitted to Maury, and he regretted that it would remain so until replenishing taxes arrived late in November. Even so, he expressed confidence in the school's ability to "feed the boys and to give them a place to sleep when they come in October."[36]

As he weighed options at Lexington, President Maury grew more skeptical. The financial resources he assumed would be available had increasingly taken on an evanescent quality. One month had passed since his July visit to the Alabama capital, when he picked up his pen on August 17 at Lexington and wrote Wellford Corbin, Nannie's husband. He complained to his son-in-law, "I was to have had $40,000 to begin with & have got $16,000 *maybe*." He added, "It bothers me enough."[37] On that same day, clearly perturbed, the Commodore directed a letter to Hodgson calling into question both the amount and availability of funds. "When you were here," Hodgson back-pedaled in reply a week later, "I did not know that the financial condition of the State was as bad as it is," and he reasoned, "The Radicals left the state in a terrible condition." The superintendent nevertheless laid out a fiscal blueprint that he assured would allow the university to open as scheduled and move forward until late November when the legislature could provide the promised funds. "If I did not feel sure that you would have all the money you would need by December 1 or 10," Hodgson closed, "I would feel like giving up."[38] These words failed to reassure Maury. He increasingly doubted the state treasury's ability, in a timely manner, to set the university up on the basis he considered necessary. Time was growing short. In a matter of days, on September 1, he was expected to preside over a faculty meeting. Less than ten days before his duties officially began, Maury received from William

Wyman gloomy notice that "the out look begins to darkin again." Wyman informed the $11,000 warrant would not be honored until early October. Maury was completely outdone. Remaining in Virginia, he seems to have gradually concluded, was the safer option. And so, the Commodore decided against the presidency. He made that known presumably by telegraph to Alabama's superintendent of education.[39]

Hodgson's worst fears, that Maury would change his mind and leave the school in the lurch, had been confirmed. It was not entirely unexpected. Several weeks earlier, Hodgson had written Maury, "I am distressed at your letter." He considered the news as cataclysmic but not final. Hodgson remained undeterred, and he and other university boosters determined on convincing Maury to reconsider.[40] Among those prevailing on him was Daniel S. Troy. The Montgomery attorney and entrepreneur had spent time with the scientist when, weeks earlier, Maury had visited the city. Troy proposed that he consent to serve on a trial basis for one year. "If you find from experience that the difficulties are really insufferable," Troy rationalized, "you can then retire without damage to your own reputation or to the University." In the meantime, Hodgson pledged to travel to Tuscaloosa and privately raise $10,000 from private parties.[41]

It soon became clear that Maury had firmly set his mind. At Lexington, on September 11, he composed a formal letter of resignation directed to Joseph Hodgson and the board of education. Maury maintained that his acceptance had been contingent upon the state's responsibility of furnishing the school with what he referred to as "apparatus and appliances." The failure to honor this pledge partly accounted for altering his plans. Maury also cited the poor financial standing of the university. "My acceptance was conditional," justifying not providing the required six months' notice of his decision to resign, "and when conditions lapse, obligations cease."[42]

The about-face provoked widespread reaction. The *Montgomery Advertiser and Mail* printed Maury's formal resignation and prefaced, "Nothing could afford us more sincere regret than to publish the following letter."[43] Republicans also rued the turn of events. Maury's rationale for backing off was dismissed as a "trifling misunderstanding" by the *Alabama State Journal*, which had counted on him to reverse the university's "sad condition."[44] Others reacted with far less equanimity. Ryland Randolph conveniently forgot his previous fawning praise, declared Maury's reasoning "quite lame" and, branding him "too old," ridiculed the Commodore's educational philosophy.[45] A somewhat contrary Robert McKee of the *Southern Argus* conceded Maury's "greatness" but attributed his hiring to the "the influence of his name," and speculated that his reputation would have attracted only a paltry number of students to the university.[46] Raphael Semmes had long known Maury, and he took a different perspective. Betraying no bitterness about being passed over earlier for the presidency in 1869, Semmes wrote a Virginia friend that Maury had resigned after accepting the presidency following "inspecting our State University, its endowment, surroundings, and prospects."[47]

Presuming Maury's thoughts is an uncertain exercise, but some of his thinking seems sure. The challenge of reviving a discredited institution intrigued a man who valued achievement throughout his life. And the prospect of a significantly increased salary and diminishing arthritic pain further pushed him toward coming south. Other considerations ultimately weighed heavier. Maury was sixty-six years old, and his duties were light at the Virginia Military Institute, where he was much appreciated, if not lionized. He was a Virginian and cherished ties to the Commonwealth state, and various members of his family lived in close proximity. And the justification for resigning that the Commodore publicly referred—inadequate financial and physical resources—registered significantly. What the university lacked distressed Maury, and those concerns protestations should not be dismissed as a convenient excuse to remain in Virginia. Much about the University of Alabama was discouraging and the path to stability far from certain. George Harrison understood as much. He had been elected commandant, and Harrison soon made his way to the university. On inspection, the former Confederate colonel found a shocking lack of the most basic items—arms, uniforms, and expected accoutrements. A short acquaintanceship with the school revealed what Harrison termed the military department's "utter disregard," and he resigned rather than try and run a "wooden-gun" system.[48] And, moreover, future financial support from the state was highly tenuous. When the Wilcox County superintendent of education had applied recently to the state secretary of treasury for much needed funds, that official replied, "The Treasury is empty" and admitted prospects were "rather gloomy."[49] Maury likely felt no guilt at reneging at the late hour, but he worried about how his decision would be received. He expressed those concerns in writing to Daniel Troy. "The people very readily believe that the king always has a good reason for everything he does," the prominent Montgomerian reassured him, "and with one holding your position in science and literature there would be very few who would believe for a moment that your resignation was capricious."[50]

And so an extended courtship of over two years ended. Among others, state officials, private citizens, entrepreneurs, at least one minister, regents, two superintendents of education representing opposite political parties had wooed the famed Commodore. Pages of correspondence were exhausted, and telegraph messages heated the wires between Montgomery and Lexington. University boosters coaxed with flattery, and appeals to vanity were dolloped out copiously. Others preyed on Maury's sense of noblesse oblige by acknowledging the university's woeful situation and his restorative powers. The much-pursued man had been promised a generous salary, freedom from teaching, congenial society, a beautiful home, and unquestioned power. All the cajoling, in fact abject supplication, had failed in the effort, as one Virginian wrote, "to coax him into Alabama." Some may have reflected on a supreme irony. Matthew Fontaine Maury had never stepped foot on the University of Alabama campus.[51]

Chapter 10

Aftermath

In June 1871, when the board of education gathered at Tuscaloosa and elected Matthew Maury, universal acclaim greeted the appointment. The fall had come quickly. By September the Commodore's resignation seemed to foretell an extension of the university's difficulties, which dated either from late 1868 or, measured by another calendar, from the harrowing visit of John Croxton's raiders as the Civil War ended. William H. C. Price was a graduate of the school. Writing Maury from New York in October 1871, Price recorded his disappointment at seeing notice of the reversal, for he "felt very much encouraged to believe it [his alma mater] would succeed again." The heralded promise of a Maury administration proved false. The University of Alabama stood jilted at the altar. In fact, the school would regain its footing, and much sooner than many considered possible.[1]

Although George Harrison had resigned the commandant's position and Maury's decision triggered far more remonstrances, the faculty selected at the June meeting otherwise remained in place. Those professors promoted confidence and respect. In September, the month the Maury vigil ended, they began arriving. William Vaughn and his family moved into the campus home that had previously been inhabited by the DeForest Richards family. An Alabamian who had graduated from the university in 1857, sympathized with the Confederacy, and had tutored at the school before and during the war, Vaughn offered a dramatically different profile than the home's previous occupant. Local white residents considered the abode infinitely better filled. When notice of Richards's intentions to sell some belongings circulated, Ryland Randolph bid expurgated farewell to "the hoary headed Yankee Vagabond."[2] And by contrast the new faculty were heartily welcomed. These were men with Southern backgrounds who were loyal to the Democratic Party creed. John Warren pronounced with satisfaction that some have "clung to the banner of the 'lost cause.'"[3]

Chapter 10

Joseph Hodgson had feared that Maury's withdrawal would discourage attendance by reinforcing the public's image of a mismanaged and sinking school. The Virginian's decision did cost the university some students, but the effect was not calamitous. Algernon Garnett, the surgeon and professor of natural history, came to Tuscaloosa before his wife joined him and began setting up housekeeping. Writing to Alice Garnett from Tuscaloosa, he doubted that Maury's resignation would "injure the prosperity of the University." Professor Garnett was right. Word circulated throughout the state of renewed interest in the school. One witness from the Lowndes County seat of Hayneville noted the enrolling intentions of a half-dozen young local men. On September 21, at the first meeting of the faculty, Nathaniel Lupton was elected chairman of the faculty and ex officio president. He took satisfaction in recent financial advances on the state warrant that allowed for some of the refurbishments of which Maury had despaired.[4]

In early October 1871, as the term's opening neared, the noticeable numbers of young men arriving in Tuscaloosa represented a highly encouraging trend. Almost sixty cadets were soon circulating on the campus, and one observer concluded, "Every train increased the number."[5] In the meantime, moving into their new quarters, each cadet signed a document agreeing to regulations that included pledging not to "carry a pistol, bowie knife, swordcare or any other deadly weapon."[6] That a local tailor was making uniforms for the students and the prospects of guns to drill with also foretold a new day. When Professor William Vaughn's son found a long-missing "magnifying glass," which was essential to powerful telescope in the observatory, Nathaniel Lupton celebrated the "valuable discovery."[7] Only weeks after school began, a visitor testified to stability. His optimistic appraisal included mention of sixty to seventy cadets "hard at work" and that "the whole machine of the institution" conformed to a "thorough military organization."[8] Likewise, at the capitol in Montgomery, when Joseph Hodgson convened the board of education late in 1871, he celebrated, "I congratulate you also upon the prospects of the state university." At the meeting the regents elected Lupton president, and his second stint in the office would be longer and more gratifying. The route to the university's resurrection was set. The University of Alabama now possessed what it had lacked since that April day almost three years earlier when the school reopened—the imprimatur of legitimacy.[9]

The faculty originally entrusted with taking the resurrected university forward back in 1869 had scattered well before then. Rather than a rewarding future career, their experiences at the University of Alabama provided a tormented and brief professional detour that ended badly. In the future,

Jasper Callan and Calvin Loomis found stability, teaching in secondary schools in Alabama and Georgia, both living into the 1890s. Nathan Chambliss never taught again. He was thirty-six years old when he left Tuscaloosa and returned to Selma. With his wife, Anna, and a growing family, Major Chambliss (as he was called) led a comfortable life as a planter and a respected member of the local gentry. Death came dramatically while visiting Baltimore; Chambliss collapsed during an Episcopalian service on March 7, 1897. He was remembered as a "Southern gentleman of the old school."[10] On the basis of his Republican credentials, Vernon Vaughn was appointed secretary of the Utah Territory in 1870, and after the death of the territory's governor later that year, he became its governor. Vaughn's executive tenure, understood from the outset to be temporary, ended five months later in February 1871. He and his wife, Cornelia, moved to San Francisco with their four children, where the transplanted Alabamian practiced law, which he had done before teaching at the University of Alabama. He remained a Republican advocate and spoke publicly for Ulysses Grant's reelection in 1872. Other aspects of the former professor's past, specifically an extreme overindulgence in alcohol, also followed Vaughn West, to the point of seriously impairing his health. Only forty years old, he died on December 11, 1878. And so a fascinating life, beginning in humble Mount Meigs, Alabama, concluded prematurely in a room at the International Hotel in Sacramento, California. Although DeForest Richards lost his faculty post in 1871, he remained briefly a state senator. In that capacity, he proved what white Democrats already well knew—that he was a committed Radical Republican. As the legislature met in Montgomery, Richards powerfully spoke on behalf of integrating colleges and universities in Alabama. Rising from his seat on January 22, 1872, Richards proclaimed that institutions of higher learning should be open to all races, and for that matter, the Republican advocate hoped "at some day not far in the distant future, some negroe would apply for admission into the class walls of the University of the State." If Black students attending the flagship state university was highly problematic (this was not achieved until 1963 under extreme duress), so was Richards's future livelihood. The former professor of natural sciences was sixty-two years old and without employment, and he and his wife, Harriet, were supporting several children. With the influence of William Evarts, a close confidant of President Grant, Richards gained a civil service position in Mobile, where he died not long after on December 2, 1872. In some senses, peace had been elusive during his years in Alabama. Jonas DeForest Richards was interred, appropriately enough, in his native Vermont.[11]

Conclusion

Saturday, February 6, 1869, broke cold in Tuscaloosa, and that brisk morning several men stepped from the steamboat that had ferried them up the Black Warrior River. The *Reindeer* was a familiar packet to Tuscaloosans, but the disembarking visitors were not. Several were professors accompanying Superintendent of Education Noah Cloud and intending to gain some familiarity with the University of Alabama, where they would soon begin teaching. In small towns such as Tuscaloosa, strangers attracted attention, and the stovepipe hats several wore, preferred by Northerners, further marked the party as outsiders. Whether the men sensed a certain coolness directed toward them cannot be known. Whatever the case, after settling in Tuscaloosa several weeks later, the professors became keenly aware of their disfavor. Unlike John Croxton's federal troops in 1865, this second wave of perceived intruders was not garbed in blue uniforms, brandishing weapons, or wielding torches, but much of the local white population, nevertheless, viewed them as highly unwelcome despoilers.[1]

It was spring 1869, just months earlier Republicans in Alabama had seized political power, and Reconstruction-forced adjustments were reverberating throughout the state and the former Confederacy. The reconfigured relationship of the races uprooted Alabama, and on a smaller stage, the tense strains were on full display at Tuscaloosa, where the challenge to cultural shibboleths in the former slave haven and Confederate bastion accounted for unprecedented political havoc. That scenario describes wide swaths of the Reconstruction South. Making the situation at Tuscaloosa crucially different, singularly unique in respects, were the presence of the state university and the Reconstruction-generated controversy enveloping the school's revival. Stoking the fires was Ryland Randolph, arguably the most incendiary editor in the South, who had recently gained national notoriety by publishing woodcuts depicting the hypothetical Ku Klux Klan lynching of both the state superintendent of education and the University of Alabama president. It would have been hard to find a more combustible location for establishing what many whites condemned as a "Radical" university.

Comprehending how the resurrection of a proud university in gleaming new dress turned so disastrously is predicated upon acknowledging the bitter forces unleashed by Reconstruction's distemper. Like Conservatives elsewhere in the South, Alabama Democrats viewed Republicans less as ideological opponents and more as reprehensible enemies. In this hostile environment, Democrats quickly reached for the pejorative, and violently disposed elements for the whip, club, rope, and gun. The "scalawag" who from courthouse perches outlined Republicanism's promise to freedpeople became a blasphemous target, as did the "carpetbagger" who summoned blinding enmity. This mindset framed what took place at the University of Alabama, where the timing of the school's reopening and the paralleling Republican takeover of state government made for a jarring historical intersection. At the university, the book-toting outsider, often a Republican, widely regarded as a masquerading professor, inspired shrill derision and frank malice. Exacerbating the situation was Tuscaloosa's status as among the most politically scorching places in the state. It was here, where the capital had been lost and white residents clung proudly to the state university, that conceptual differences over the remastered school raised sharp conflict. Before the first cadet was prevailed upon to attempt a recitation, the faculty faced withering fire from a hostile newspaper press that set the university's negative image. And so it was that Calvin Loomis warily took stock and likened the residents' "irritable feelings standing out in every direction" to "quills upon the fretful porcupine."[2] Detractors painted a subterranean world, a dark lair inhabited by "bats" and" owls," a "doomed" school infested with Republican pariahs. Even a man possessing Nathan Chambliss's seeming impeccable social and military credentials failed to pass muster. Such was the strafing that the board of education considered relocating the university.

In the expansive view of Southern higher education, the turmoil did not represent an anomaly, but neither could the consternation at Tuscaloosa be described as pervasive. In fact, among the eight state universities in the region, experiences during Reconstruction varied widely. In the first years following the war, progress ranged from incremental at East Tennessee University to spirited at the University of Virginia. The establishment of Republican governments by 1868 and the subsequent party direction of state universities interrupted stability at some places but had no effect elsewhere.

Accounting for the comparative lack of contention at some universities and explosive pyrotechnics at others involves following various leads—some false. The simple fact of geography provides no insight. In the Upper South, the University of Virginia rapidly reclaimed its prewar popularity, but in neighboring North Carolina, the state university deteriorated rapidly. In Georgia and Alabama, although sharing Lower South status and a common border, their state universities understood diametrically different experiences. Examining the role of the most important political officer in each state—the governor—to gain understanding is more instructive regarding casualty. William Holden in 1868 was the driving force in the temporary shutting down of the University of North Carolina, cashiering sitting professors and reopening with a Republican faculty. Yet Mississippi's Republican governor, James Lusk Alcorn, proceeded far more cautiously, as did Louisiana's Republican executive, Henry Clay Warmoth, and their approach contributed to the stability of universities in those two states. Even so, a governor's involvement, or lack thereof, was not necessarily determinative. William Hugh Smith did not add to or detract from the shrill acrimony at Tuscaloosa. Alabama's executive between 1868 and 1870 never visited the university and does not seem to have made a public statement concerning the school.

What did, then, contribute to or mitigate against tumult and conflict in the early period of adjustment as Republicans assumed direction of state universities? An examination of the faculty's composition at each institution is instructive. At the universities of Georgia, Mississippi, South Carolina, and Virginia, professors who had taught at those institutions before the war, or had Southern backgrounds, promoted a certain reassuring continuity. Indeed, the high regard conceded to the University of South Carolina faculty for a time warded off the renting confrontation to come, and the professors' public esteem also guarded against decline at the University of Mississippi. By contrast, where outsiders, sometimes Republicans, dominated the faculty, most notably at Chapel Hill and Tuscaloosa, certain turmoil ensued. Further intertwined with stability or strife was the course and outlook of those directly making policy, referred variously to as the board of trustees, the board of supervisors (Louisiana), or board of visitors (Virginia). Some of these officials scrupulously avoided the appearance of political investment. At the University of Mississippi, Republican and Democratic trustees labored with demonstrative harmony. The debate became voluble at other places where the presence of forceful and ideologically committed individuals accounted for confrontation. James Neagle, for instance, served as the state comptroller and also as a University of South Carolina trustee. Achieving consensus was

Conclusion

less crucial to him than was advancing changes in keeping with the spirit of Reconstruction, and Neagle attempted as early as 1869 to throw over the existing faculty and enroll Black students.

Making any overarching conclusions regarding higher education during Reconstruction is precluded by the limited range of this study, which concludes in 1871. What followed at the state universities after 1871 varied widely. Easily ranking as the most significant single event occurred at the University of South Carolina when Black students enrolled in 1873. For the next several years, young Black men studying there outnumbered their white peers, and Tyler Parry in *Invisible No More* describes congenial racial interactions between the students. Elsewhere, the state universities of Georgia, Mississippi, and Virginia continued to thrive and attract students, and East Tennessee University, established as the land grant school, moved forward on a steady path. In stark contrast, confrontation continued at the University of North Carolina and accounted for the school's closure between 1871 and 1875. The delicate equilibrium achieved under President David Boyd at what in 1870 had become Louisiana State University was interrupted after the tenure of Governor Henry Clay Warmoth. During the following administration of Governor William P. Kellogg, the university's relationship with the legislature deteriorated, financial problems beset the school, enrollment fell sharply, and by the mid-1870s the image of Louisiana State University had dimmed dramatically. In the meantime, at the University of South Carolina, the school came under heavy fire and lost stature and support. Democrats regained control of state government and in 1877 closed the University of South Carolina for three years. An overview of circumstances at the state universities in the decade following the war would fill a significant void.[3]

What transpired at the University of Alabama is at once distinctive from and similar to the adversity at other schools struggling to overcome the Radical brand. By way of brief review, when a Republican-dominated board of education removed the standing professors in 1868, the state university was plunged into the stormy Reconstruction maelstrom. What I have referred to as the battle for the University of Alabama raged for the next three years. Poor enrollment, a revolving door of faculty and presidents, and financial distress severely tarnished the image of Alabama's flagship university. After the state general election of 1870, now largely under Democratic direction, the school regained its footing and reputation. This synopsis does not denote blame or credit.

Best understood, the seeming imperatives of Reconstruction exponentially complicated the school's revival. Unlike any period in the nation's past, excepting that of the Republic's establishment, a sense of aspirational regeneration was apparent in the Civil War's wake. Slavery was over and the Union saved, but the realization of a Reconstruction-sired interracial democracy was far from certain. That was undisputedly true in Alabama, where in the recent presidential election, the Democratic presidential candidate running on a white-supremacy platform and rejecting the mandates of the Reconstruction settlement came within several thousand votes of carrying the state. These circumstances derivatively imparted to the University of Alabama's revival a special pertinence. Imagined from a Republican vantage, the historical juncture demanded that the school reflect a reforged and enlightened nation. What setting could be more appropriate to project what one Northern contemporary termed "moral Reconstruction" than the intellectual summit of the state? But the university's past discouraged that progression of thought.[4]

In his probing study of slavery and Southern institutions of higher learning, Alfred Brophy identifies how colleges and universities provided intellectual underpinnings to the institution of slavery and its necessary perpetuation. The University of Alabama's relationship with the peculiar institution could be described as long, one-sided, and sometimes brutal. After an enslaved person balked at the instructions of Basil Manly, the president of the school allowed, "I whipped him a second time, very severely."[5] The recent promotion of treason at the university also contributed to anxiety. Young men had trained on the campus to fight for the Confederate States of America. The university's past could not be rewritten, but its future might be shaped. A certain engineering by regents, understood in terms of board of education's interposition, is clearly evident in policy regarding the university. Gustavus Adolphus Smith was representative of those regents determined that Alabama bend with the age. Others sharing a sense of historical determinism joined the faculty. DeForest Richards offers the purest example. Writing the Reverend Asa Smith within weeks of the school's reopening, the president pro tempore celebrated reviving the university under "loyal Republican auspices."[6]

Where Republicans visualized promise and reform in this most recent iteration of the school, Democrats foresaw peril. As Alabama's state university, the school commanded an exalted status ever since the first students arrived in 1831. In his classic study of the institution, James Sellers recalled the pride and optimism, and the feeling of "making a University rise out of the new earth of a new state."[7] The school's destruction was of far less military significance than the fall of Mobile and other Confederate reverses in Alabama, but the university's torching arguably left a deeper and more extended void. Calculating the loss could only partly be appraised in dollars and cents. The University of Alabama was not only the final Southern state university to open after the war but, by three years, easily the last to do so. In the spring of 1869, following four years of dormancy, the resumption of life at the cherished institution was tantalizing close. At that point, in Democrats' view, Republicans crassly sprang a political trapdoor. The facsimile of the University of Alabama that emerged, according to the quickly forming legion of detractors, insulted the school's memory just as surely as it jeopardized its future. The battle had been joined.

It became far easier to attack than to defend the school. And the Democratic establishment had the means, employing the party newspaper press as a medieval battering ram used to knock down the school's recently raised walls. The assault completely ignored the impartial efforts of regents who took a vital interest in reviving the university. A board of education that asked three Democrats to direct the university—William Wyman, Nathaniel Lupton, and Matthew Maury—resists a doctrinaire stamp. Neither did preferment of faculty appointments betray a Republican machine. Jasper Callan, Nathan Chambliss, John Forney, and William McConnell, and possibly Calvin Loomis, were Democrats. Attributing a blind determination to impose a monolithic Republican ethos on the school represents a far too facile interpretation. Preventing the state university from projecting a repudiated past more accurately describes the regents' course. Yet the fierce practice of politics in Reconstruction Alabama did not admit qualification or recognize nuance. Democrats controlled the discourse, and their judgment of the university came to represent conventional thinking. Writing of an earlier period in the state's past, J. Mills Thornton identifies the power and salience of "subjective perceptions."[8] What white Alabamians *thought* about the University of Alabama was what crucially mattered. And so the university entered into an extended period of freefall. How to boost a flagging university without ceding the school's direction to unreconstructed elements provided the conundrum. As events devolved, the dilemma defied a solution.

Above and beyond the embroiling debate were a shifting and fluid group of cadets who carried on with general detachment from the firestorm around them. Given a paucity of sources describing their experiences, I have taken some liberties in attempting to provide a sense of those young men who walked the campus. In keeping with that license, speculatively considered, how would a former student respond if years later asked about his time at the reborn school? Such an account, to my knowledge, does not exist. Yet, reasonably constructed, the former cadet would recall the small number of fellow students. Among others, Commandant McConnell and Professors Callan, Chambliss, Loomis, Vaughn, and certainly Richards stirred varying recollections. And if some classmates had faded from memory, others had not. William Smith made a lasting impression. His shooting of Ryland Randolph, subsequent escape from jail and flight, and the following frenzy at the university could not have been forgotten. As for the quality of education he received, our mythical student probably provided a mixed account. Former cadets W. G. Butler, M. A. Kendrick, M. H. Mahan, O. R. Bell, T. W. Denny, and their classmates would have recounted their experiences with a perspective and appreciation they could not have possessed when they attended as boys or young men. They spent their campus days at a uniquely freighted time in the university's existence.

And so did their professors. To belong to the faculty at the University of Alabama, as we have seen, meant accepting a tightly circumscribed world. The professors worked but also lived on the campus and in the shadow of a town where controlling opinion largely held them in contempt. A very small faculty, and sometimes abrupt turnover, required professors to suddenly pivot and presume command of subjects that largely lay outside their academic field. The question of the quality of instruction persists. In quantifiable measures, years of teaching experience and advanced degrees, the faculty suffered when compared with other Southern state universities. Yet, if the rather universal laws of pedagogy hold, and there is no reason to assume otherwise, their effectiveness varied and possibly widely. With the exception of DeForest Richards, the professors were relatively young men. They would not have later looked back nostalgically at their time in Tuscaloosa.

What is certain—even granting teaching deficiencies or individual peccadillos such as Vernon Vaughn's drinking, for example—is the inescapable truth. Any faculty shortcomings, perceived or accurate, did not seal the university's fate. Just before the board of education met at Tuscaloosa in the summer of 1871 and chartered a new course, the *Alabama State Journal* sensed the coming change. Its Republican editor admitted the university's weak standing but posed that condition was not due to ineffective professors, uninspired students, or incompetent regents. Neither was the school's situation explained by a lack of supportive resources of a physical or financial nature. What accounted, rather, for the institution's plight, the Republican editor correctly decided, was a fierce determination of Democrats to "ruin it."[9]

In his recent study of the period, Michael Fitzgerald dates Reconstruction's end as starting from when Democrats authoring a new state constitution in 1875, accompanied by the rapid decline of the state Republican Party. What Bourbons referred to as "redemption" had arrived. Similarly, the purported redemption of the University of Alabama's had taken place a few years earlier. By way of that reductive reasoning, Radical influence had been expunged, faculty competence restored, and nothing less than the triumph of good over evil served. The university's unshakable torpor in fact lay far less in poor administrative and professorial execution than in a fierce resolve to derail the institution as presently composed. What could have offered a classic narrative of a pristine university rising from the literal ashes of war, inverted into a brutal, downward spiraling disaster. Attending the university, an honor before the Civil War, became distinctly dishonorable in its sullied postwar guise. Returning to an earlier advanced thesis, the overriding question of autonomy drove confrontation between 1868 and 1871. Accounting for that transcending conflict were *fears* raised by the precepts of Reconstruction. Some Republicans *feared* a reversion to a neo-slaveocracy and pseudo-secessionist mentality at the university. An understanding of the school's past, the searing conflict of the present, and the hopes of a liberal future informed their thinking. Taking wide exception, Democrats *feared* a sharp dilution of academic standards and inferior professors recommended by their political affiliation presiding over the revered school's desecration. Both scenarios were unlikely. Democrats anticipated a rebuilt university, but Republicans demanded a reimagined one. The victor in the battle for the University of Alabama was a foregone conclusion. The admixture of emotions raised by Reconstruction—conflict understood in cultural, socioeconomic, ideological, and political terms—knew no precedent and has known none since. What took place at the University of Alabama provided a unique battleground that was revelatory of the Reconstruction South.[10]

Notes

Introduction

1. The standard treatment of Reconstruction is Eric Foner, *Reconstruction: America's Unfinished Revolution 1863–1877* (New York: Harper & Row, 1988). See also Kenneth M. Stampp, *The Era of Reconstruction* (New York: Alfred Knopf, 1965). For a more recent study see Mark W. Summers, *The Ordeal of the Reunion: A New History of Reconstruction* (Chapel Hill: University of North Carolina Press, 2014). For Reconstruction historiography see Michael W. Fitzgerald, "Reconstruction Politics and the Politics of Reconstruction," in *Reconstruction: New Perspectives on the Postbellum United States*, ed. Thomas J. Brown, 91–116 (New York: Oxford University Press, 2006).

2. James D. Sellers, *History of the University of Alabama. Volume 1, 1818–1902* (Tuscaloosa: University of Alabama Press, 1953), 258–87; Suzanne Rau Wolfe, *The University of Alabama: A Pictorial History* (Tuscaloosa: University of Alabama Press, 1983), 38–62; Helen Eckinger, "The Militarization of the University of Alabama," *Alabama Review* 66, no. 13 (July 2013), 163–85.

3. *Independent Monitor*, March 2, 1869. Please note that throughout this text the direct quotations are as they appear in the original source. Incorrect spellings and grammatical errors have not been changed by the author.

4. *Daily Sentinel*, April 6, 1869.

5. *Weekly Clarion*, August 18, 1870.

6. J. G. de Roulhac Hamilton, *Reconstruction in North Carolina* (New York: Columbia University Press, 1914), 626–27. See also John S. Reynolds, *Reconstruction in South Carolina, 1865–1877* (Columbia, SC: State Co., 1905), 231–38; Walter L. Fleming, *Civil War and Reconstruction in Alabama* (New York: Columbia University Press, 1905), 611–16; Lawrence A. Cremin, *American Education, The National Experience, 1783–1876* (New York: Harper & Row, 1980); Frederick Rudolph, *The American College and University: A History* (New York: Alfred Knopf, 1962).

7. Tyler D. Parry, "'Irrespective of Race or Color': Examining Desegregation at the Reconstructed University of South Carolina, 1868–1877," in *Invisible No More: The African American Experience at the University of South Carolina*, eds. Robert Greene II and Tyler D. Parry (Columbia: University of South Carolina Press, 2021), 37; T. R. C. Hutton, *Bearing the Torch: The University of Tennessee, 1794–2010* (Knoxville: University

Notes to Chapter 1

of Tennessee Press, 2022); Michael David Cohen, *Reconstructing the Campus: Higher Education and the American Civil War* (Charlottesville: University of Virginia Press, 2014).

CHAPTER 1

1. For general histories of Tuscaloosa, see G. Ward Hubbs, *Tuscaloosa: 200 Years in the Making* (Tuscaloosa: University of Alabama Press, 2019); G. Ward Hubbs, *Tuscaloosa: Portrait of an Alabama County* (Northridge, CA: Windsor Publications, 1987). See also, James Robert Maxwell, *Autobiography of James Robert Maxwell of Tuskaloosa, Alabama* (New York: Greenberg, 1926); John W. Quist, *Restless Visionaries: The Social Roots of Antebellum Reform in Alabama and Michigan* (Baton Rouge: Louisiana State University Press, 1998). Estimates of Tuscaloosa's size vary. Census records indicate a place pushing four thousand residents in 1860, but approximations later in the decade reveal a smaller town, with somewhere between two thousand and three thousand people. Quist, *Restless Visionaries*, 9; G. Ward Hubbs, *Searching for Freedom after the Civil War: Klansman, Carpetbagger, Scalawag, and Freedman* (Tuscaloosa: University of Alabama Press, 2015), 2; *Independent Monitor*, November 29, 1870; *Pickens County Herald and West Alabamian*, July 19, 1871.

2. Maxwell, *Autobiography*, 20–45; Hubbs, *Searching for Freedom*, 1–2, 134, 138, 142; Quist, *Restless Visionaries* 7, 155, 159, 165; Benjamin Buford Williams, *A Literary History of Alabama: The Nineteenth Century* (Rutherford, NJ: Farleigh Dickinson University Press, 1979), 21–24. For a visitor's impressions of Tuscaloosa in 1854, see *Daily National Intelligencer*, November 22, 1854; *Independent Monitor*, April 26, 1871.

3. *Daily National Intelligencer*, November 22, 1854. For more on the campus, see Robert O. Mellown, *The University of Alabama: A Guide to the Campus and Its Architecture* (Tuscaloosa: University of Alabama Press, 2013), 1–7; Sellers, *History of the University of Alabama*, 32–36; Wolfe, *The University of Alabama*, 8–13; A. James Fuller, *Chaplain of the Confederacy: Basil Manly and Baptist Life in the Old South* (Baton Rouge: Louisiana State University Press, 2000), 154–81; William J. Chute, *Damn Yankee! The First Career of Frederick A. P. Barnard, Educator, Scientist, Idealist* (Port Washington, NY: Kennikat Press, 1978), 76–144; *Republican Banner*, September 4, 1868; Montgomery *Weekly State Journal*, August 28, 1869; *Tuscaloosa Observer*, April 1, 1871; *Independent Monitor*, March 7, 1869, April 6, 1869; Thomas M. Clinton, "A Hundred Years of Catholicity in Tuscaloosa," Tuscaloosa, 1922.

4. *Tuscaloosa Observer*, July 3, 1861; *Daily National Intelligencer*, November 22, 1854; Quist, *Restless Visionaries*, 7, 22, 304–12. See also Louis F. Herzberg, "Negro Slavery in Tuscaloosa County, Alabama, 1818–1865" (master's thesis, University of Alabama, 1955).

5. *Southern Argus*, January 20, 1871; *Reconstructionist*, June 6, 1868; *Republican Banner*, October 9, 1868, October 16, 1868; *Independent Monitor*, March 4, 1868, May 10, 1871; *Daily National Intelligencer*, November 22, 1854; Chute, *Damn Yankee!*, 78; Mellown, "Early Photography," 24–33; Sarah Woolfolk Wiggins, "J. DeForest Richards, a Vermont Carpetbagger in Alabama," *Vermont History* 51 (Spring 1983): 104.

6. *Tuscaloosa Observer*, March 8, 1865; *Independent Monitor*, May 10, 1861; Eckinger, "The Militarization of the University of Alabama," 169–78; Hubbs, *Tuscaloosa: 200 Years in the Making*, 38–50; Clarence P. Denman, *The Secession Movement in Alabama* (Montgomery: Alabama State Department of Archives and History, 1933), 155; Moses Coit Tyler, "The Burning of Alabama University," *The Independent . . . Devoted to the Consideration*

Notes to Chapter 1

of Politics, Social and Economic Tendencies, History, Literature, and the Arts 21 (October 28, 1869): 1; Christopher Lyle McIlwain Sr., *Civil War Alabama* (Tuscaloosa: University of Alabama Press, 2016), 254; Sellers, *History of the University of Alabama*, 281–88; *Independent Monitor*, December 29, 1868, July 5, 1870; United States, War Department, *The War of the Rebellion: A Compilation of the Official Records of the Union and Confederate Armies* (Washington, DC: Government Printing Office, 1880–1901) series 1, vol. 49 (part 1), 419.

7. Tyler, "The Burning of Alabama University," 1.

8. Landon Garland to Caroline Garland, May 30, 1865, in the Robert T. Lagemann Papers, Vanderbilt University Special Collections and University Archives, Nashville, TN, hereafter cited as Lagemann Papers; McIlwain, *Civil War Alabama*, 254; Sellers, *History of the University of Alabama*, 286. For Garland, see Willis Brewer, *Alabama: Her History, Resources, War Record, and Public Men: From 1540 to 1872* (Montgomery: Barrett & Brown, 1872), 565–66, hereafter cited as *Alabama: Her History*.

9. Christopher L. McIlwain, *1865 Alabama: From Civil War to Uncivil Peace* (Tuscaloosa: University of Alabama Press, 2017), 66–67, 145–47, 149–50, 265.

10. Sarah Woolfolk Wiggins, ed. *The Journals of Josiah Gorgas 1857–1878* (Tuscaloosa: University of Alabama Press, 1995), 175; Peter Kolchin, *First Freedom: The Responses of Alabama's Blacks to Emancipation and Reconstruction* (Westport, CT: Greenwood Press, 1972), 14–15.

11. Whitelaw Reid, *After the War: A Southern Tour, May 1, 1865 to May 1, 1866* (London, UK: Sampson Low, 1866), 389; Kolchin, *First Freedom*, xvi, 4–7.

12. Basil Manly Diary, Manly Family Papers, W. S. Hoole Special Collections Library, University of Alabama, entry for June 20, 1865, 75; Peter Bryce to Lewis Parsons, September 11, 1865, Lewis E. Parsons Papers, 1831–1891, Government Records Collections, Alabama Department of Archives and History, Montgomery. For Basil Manly, see Fuller, *Chaplain to the Confederacy* and, by the same author, "'I Whipped Him a Second Time, Very Severely': Basil Manly, Honor, and Slavery at the University of Alabama," in *Slavery and the University Histories and Legacies*, eds. Leslie M. Harris, James T. Campbell, and Alfred L. Brophy (Athens: University of Georgia Press, 2019), 114–30; McIlwain, *Civil War Alabama*, 2.

13. Jno. Gibbs to Lewis Parsons, August 2, 1865, Parsons Papers; Hubbs, *Searching for Freedom*, 3.

14. Landon Garland to Caroline Garland, May 30, 1865, Parsons Papers; James Murfee to building committee, June 1, 1867, University of Alabama Commandant's Book 1867–1887, 13, in the W. S. Hoole Special Collections Library, University of Alabama; Sellers, *History of the University of Alabama*, 89–90, 127, 286; William Garrett, *Reminiscences of Public Men in Alabama, for Thirty Years* (Atlanta, GA: Plantation Publishing, 1872), 799.

15. *Independent Monitor*, April 20, 1869, May 25, 1869, July 27, 1869; *Mobile Daily Advertiser and Register*, October 31, 1865; *Montgomery Advertiser*, March 19, 1867; *Alabama Beacon*, July 21, 1865; Sellers, *History of the University of Alabama*, 291–92.

16. For Andrew Johnson, see Eric L. McKitrick, *Andrew Johnson and Reconstruction* (New York: Oxford University Press, 1960). The best source for the army's role remains James Sefton, *The United States Army and Reconstruction, 1865–1877* (Baton Rouge: Louisiana State University Press, 1967). For general histories of the period, see Foner,

Reconstruction: America's Unfinished Revolution; Mark W. Summers, *The Ordeal of the Reunion: A New History of Reconstruction* (Chapel Hill: University of North Carolina Press, 2014); Michael W. Fitzgerald, *Splendid Failure: Postwar Reconstruction in the American South* (Chicago: Ivan R. Dee, 2007).

17. John Kennedy to Lewis Parsons, December 1, 1865; Alfred Battle et al., to Lewis Parsons, Parsons Papers; William Peck to O. D. Kinsman, October 7, 1866, reel 8, Records of the Assistant Commissioner for the State of Alabama, Bureau of Refugees, Freedmen and Abandoned Lands, 1865–1869, records group 105, National Archives, Morrow, GA, hereafter cited as Records of the Assistant Commissioners, Alabama. For Parsons, see Sarah Woolfolk Wiggins, "Lewis E. Parsons, June–December 1865," in *Alabama Governors: A Political History of the State*, eds. Samuel L. Webb and Margaret Armbrester (Tuscaloosa: University of Alabama, 2001), 77–80. For Kennedy, see Brewer, *Alabama: Her History*, 569.

18. Charles Manly to Basil Manly, May 28, 1866, Manly Family Papers, W. S. Hoole Special Collections Library, University of Alabama. For Charles Manly, see Fuller, *Chaplain to the Confederacy*, 234, 289.

19. *Reconstructionist*, October 5, 1867; Paul M. Pruitt Jr., "Scalawag Dreams: Elisha Wolsey Peck's Career, and Two of His Speeches, 1867–1869," *Alabama Review* 66, no. 3 (July 2013): 211–32; Joel D. Kitchens, "E. W. Peck: Alabama's First Scalawag Chief Justice," *Alabama Review* 54, no. 1 (January 2001): 4, 8, 17–18; *Independent Monitor*, February 5, 1868, February 12, 1868.

20. Hubbs, *Searching for Freedom*, xiv–xv, 159–63.

21. William H. Peck to O. D. Kinsman, May 14, 1866, in Unregistered Letters Received December 1865–July 1870, reel 3, Records of the Superintendent of Education for the State of Alabama, Bureau of Refugees, Freedmen and Abandoned Lands, records group 105, National Archives, Morrow, GA; *Independent Monitor*, September 28, 1869; entry for June 24, 1866, Basil Manly Diary, 83–84, Manly Family Papers; Hubbs, *Searching for Freedom*, 144–47; Hermione Dannelly, "The Life and Times of Robert Jemison, Jr. during the Civil War and Reconstruction" (master's thesis, University of Alabama, 1942), 94.

22. *Republican Banner*, September 4, 1868; *Independent Monitor*, November 10, 1868, August 17, 1869; *Southern Argus*, April 28, 1870. For Jones, see Hubbs, *Searching for Freedom*, 133–57.

23. William Peck to C. Cadle, April 18, 1866, Peck to [?], October 12, 1866, reel 8, Records of the Assistant Commissioner, Alabama. For Berry, see Michael Fitzgerald, *Urban Emancipation: Popular Politics in Reconstruction Mobile, 1860–1890* (Baton Rouge: Louisiana State University Press, 2002), 62, 79; William Warren Rogers Jr. *Reconstruction Politics in a Deep South State: Alabama, 1865–1874* (Tuscaloosa: University of Alabama Press, 2021), 37, 42, 48; Hubbs, *Searching for Freedom*, 32–33.

24. William Peck to O. D. Kinsman, April 1866, reel 8, Records of the Assistant Commissioner, Alabama.

25. *Livingston Journal*, December 2, 1868; Records of the Proceedings of the Executive and Building Committee of the Trustees of the University of Alabama, 1866, 17, W. S. Hoole Special Collections Library, University of Alabama, hereafter cited as Proceedings of the Executive and Building Committee; University of Alabama Minutes of Board of Trustees, April 2, 1866 to June 12, 1868, 8–9, 13, Special Collections and Archives,

Notes to Chapter 1

Auburn University, hereafter cited as Minutes of Board of Trustees, 1866–1868. Restitution in some form was provided by Congress in 1884, largely through the efforts of Senator John Tyler Morgan. Some forty-six thousand acres of public lands were given to the state of Alabama to compensate for the university's destruction. See Joseph A. Fry, *John Tyler Morgan and the Search for Southern Autonomy* (Knoxville: University of Tennessee Press, 1992), 69; George H. Denny, "Universities and Colleges of the South," in *The South in the Building of the Nation: History of the Social Life of the South, Volume 10*, ed. Samuel C. Mitchell (Richmond, VA: Southern Historical Publication Society, 1909), 237–38.

26. *Mobile Daily Advertiser and Register*, January 19, 1866, March 1, 1866. For Patton, see William Warren Rogers Jr., "Robert M. Patton, December 1865-March 1867," in *Alabama Governors: A Political History of the State*, eds. Samuel L. Webb and Margaret Armbrester (Tuscaloosa: University of Alabama Press, 2001), 80–83; Sellers, *History of the University of Alabama*, 293.

27. *Selma Daily Messenger*, July 25, 1866; Proceedings of the Executive and Building Committee, 19, 21; Minutes of the Board of Trustees, 1866–1868, 45–46, 58, 69; William Warren Rogers Jr., *Confederate Home Front: Montgomery During the Civil War* (Tuscaloosa: University of Alabama Press, 1999), 26, 30.

28. John Massey, *Reminiscences Giving Sketches of Scenes through which the Author Has Passed and Pen Portraits of People Who Have Modified His Life* (Nashville, TN: M.E. Church, South, 1916), 136; James Murfee, "A New Scheme of Organization, Instruction, and Government for the University of Alabama, with Report on Construction of Building" (Tuscaloosa, AL: John F. Warren, 1867), 13, 66–67, hereafter cited as "A New Scheme of Organization"; Minutes of Board of Trustees, 1866–1868. Garland soon joined the faculty at the University of Mississippi and in 1874 became the Chancellor of Vanderbilt University. For Murfee, see Wolfe, *The University of Alabama*, 56; and Joseph W. Matthews Jr., "The Military College of Alabama Marion Military Institute," *Alabama Heritage* 115 (Winter 2015): 39–45.

29. James Murfee to Building Committee of University of Alabama, February 15, 1867, Minutes of the Board of Trustees, 1866–1868, 92; Murfee, "A New Scheme of Organization," 3–4; James Murfee to George Figh, April 17, 1869, Commandant's Book 1867–1887. For Figh, see *Montgomery Advertiser*, October 8, 1868; Rogers, *Confederate Home Front*, 5, 89; Robert Gamble, *Historic Architecture in Alabama: A Primer of Styles and Types, 1810–1930* (Tuscaloosa: University of Alabama Press, 1990), 84–85.

30. *Reconstructionist*, October 5, 1867; *Independent Monitor*, March 4, 1868, May 31, 1871; Alfred L. Brophy, *University, Court, and Slave: Pro-slavery Thought in Southern Colleges and Courts and the Coming of Civil War* (New York: Oxford University Press, 2016), 148–50; Sellers, *History of the University of Alabama*, 38–41. For recent reconciliation efforts that have taken the form of a slavery apology marker at a campus cemetery where formerly enslaved peoples are interred, see Hilary Green, "The Slave Cemetery and the Apology Marker at the University of Alabama," in *Final Resting Places Reflections on the Meaning of Civil War Graves*, eds. Brian Matthew Jordan and Jonathan W. White (Athens: University of Georgia Press, 2023), 248–56.

31. J. H. Fitts to Robert Patton, May 30, 1867, Patton Papers.

32. Murfee, "A New Scheme of Organization," 5; *Alabama Beacon*, August 10, 1867; *Montgomery Advertiser*, December 24, 1867. For description of completed building, see

Notes to Chapter 1

Robert Gamble, *Historic Architecture in Alabama: A Primer of Styles and Types, 1810–1930* (Tuscaloosa: University of Alabama Press, 1990), 84–85; Mellown, *The University of Alabama*, 63–64; *Selma Times and Messenger*, April 26, 1868.

33. Murfee, "A New Scheme of Organization," 10.

34. Murfee, "A New Scheme of Organization," 5–6.

35. Thomas P. Clinton, "The Military Operations of General John T. Croxton in West Alabama, 1865," *Transactions of the Alabama Historical Society 1899–1903* 4 (1904): 457.

36. Tyler, "The Burning of Alabama University," 1; *Montgomery Mail*, May 1, 1868; *Montgomery Advertiser*, June 16, 1868; *Independent Monitor*, April 21, 1868, May 12, 1868; Message of Robert M. Patton, Governor of Alabama, to the General Assembly, November 12, 1866 (Montgomery: Reid & Screws, 1866), 3, Government Records Collections, Alabama State Department of Archives and History, Montgomery; James Murfee to Building Committee of University of Alabama, February 15, 1867, June 1, 1867, Minutes of the Board of Trustees, 1866–1868, 79–81, 94; Proceedings of the Executive and Building Committee, 13; *Montgomery Mail*, May 1, 1868; G. Ward Hubbs, "'Dissipating the Clouds of Ignorance': The First University of Alabama Library, 1831–1865," *Libraries & Culture* 27, no. 1 (Winter 1992): 20–35.

37. Foner, *Reconstruction*, 251–60, 267, 271–77, 282–303; Allen W. Trelease, *White Terror: The Ku Klux Klan Conspiracy and Southern Reconstruction* (New York: Harper & Row, 1971), xxv–xlviii.

38. *Independent Monitor*, February 5, 1868, February 12, 1868, November 10, 1868, August 17, 1869; *Reconstructionist*, October 7, 1867; *Daily State Sentinel*, September 25, 1867, December 23, 1867; *Alabama Beacon*, August 31, 1867; *Alabama State Journal*, November 4, 1868; George Cox to J. C. Keffer, June 24, 1867, Wager Swayne Papers, Alabama Department of Archives and History, Montgomery; Edwin Beecher to O. D. Shepherd, April 13, 1868, reel 1, 14; Records of the Assistant Commissioner, Alabama; *Memorial Record of Alabama: A Concise Account of the State's Political, Military, Professional and Industrial Progress, Together With the Personal Memoirs of Many of Its People* (Spartanburg, SC: Reprint Company, 1976), 2:176.

39. Sterling Wood to Robert Patton, September 30, 1867, Patton Papers; *Independent Monitor*, January 15, 1868, January 29, 1868; *Alabama Beacon*, March 18, 1871. For Wood, see Brewer, *Alabama: Her History*, 569.

40. *Independent Monitor*, February 12, 1868.

41. "Ryland Randolph's Scribbles" [c. 1894], reel 2, 10, unpublished manuscript in Ryland Randolph Papers, Samford University Special Collections, Birmingham, Alabama, hereafter cited as "Ryland Randolph's Scribbles."

42. *Independent Monitor*, September 1, 1868.

43. For Randolph, see Hubbs, *Searching for Freedom*, 9–56; Trelease, *White Terror*, 84–87; Nancy Anne Sindon, "The Career of Ryland Randolph: A Study in Reconstruction Journalism," (master's thesis, Florida State University, 1965).

44. *Reconstructionist*, October 5, 1867; Hubbs, *Searching for Freedom*, 31; Rogers, *Partisan Politics in a Deep South State*, 56–69.

45. *Independent Monitor*, March 11, 1868, March 18, 1868, April 28, 1868, October 16, 1868. For the scalawag stereotype, see James Alex Baggett, *The Scalawags: Southern Dissenters in the Civil War and Reconstruction* (Baton Rouge: Louisiana State University

Notes to Chapter 2

Press, 2003), 1–6. For how carpetbaggers have been regarded, see Richard N. Current, *Those Terrible Carpetbaggers* (New York: Oxford University Press, 1988), 422–25.

46. US Congress, House, 42nd Congress, second session, *Testimony Taken by the Joint Select Committee to Inquire into the Condition of Affairs in the Late Insurrectionary States*, Alabama Testimony, Elisha Peck, 1850, hereafter cited as "Alabama Testimony"; Robert Blair to R. Harper, May 2, 1868; Allen Williams to Henry Bush, February 10, 1868, April 6, 1868, reel 2, Records of the Superintendent of Education for the State of Alabama, Bureau of Refugees, Freedmen, and Abandoned Lands, 1865–1870, Letters Received, reel 2, records group 105, National Archives, Morrow, Georgia, hereafter cited as Records of the Superintendent of Education, Alabama; Hubbs, *Searching for Freedom*, 32–33.

47. Elisha Peck to George Meade, March 31, 1868, in Third Military District 1867–1868, Letters Received, Records of the United States Army Continental Command, Third Military District, 1867–1868, records group 393, National Archives.

48. "Ryland Randolph's Scribbles," 85; Hubbs, *Searching for Freedom*, 32–33; Trelease, *White Terror*, 84.

49. Ellen Benton to Henry Bush, March 28, 1868, reel 2, Records of the Superintendent of Education, Alabama. For Benton, see Loren Schweninger, "The American Missionary Association and Philanthropy in Reconstruction," *Alabama Historical Quarterly*, 32, nos. 3 and 4 (Fall and Winter 1970): 135. For opposition to American Missionary Association teachers, see Joe M. Richardson, *Christian Reconstruction: The American Missionary Association and Southern Blacks, 1861–1890* (Athens: University of Georgia Press, 1986), 213–26, 227–29.

50. Robert Blair to R. Harper, April 1, 1868, reel 2, Records of the Superintendent of Education, Alabama.

51. James Murfee to Building Committee of the University of Alabama, June 1, 1868, Minutes of the Board of Trustees, 1866–1868, 147; *Independent Monitor*, May 5, 1868, June 16, 1868.

52. Murfee, "A New Scheme of Organization," 13.

53. George Figh to the Honorable Building Committee of the Board of Trustees of the University of Alabama, January 16, 1868, Minutes of Board of Trustees, 1866–1868, 118.

Chapter 2

1. Cohen, *Reconstructing the Campus*, 29, 32–33, 36; Clement Eaton, *A History of the Old South* (New York: Macmillan Company, 1949), 482; Daniel Walker Hollis, *University of South Carolina, Volume 1, South Carolina College* (Columbia: University of South Carolina College, 1951), 212–16.

2. William D. Armes, ed. *The Autobiography of Joseph Le Conte* (New York: D. Appleton, 1903), 179. For LeConte, see Lester Stephens, *Joseph LeConte, Gentle Prophet of Evolution* (Baton Rouge: Louisiana State University Press, 1982); Joseph M. Stetar, "In Search of a Direction: Southern Higher Education after the Civil War," *History of Education Quarterly* 2, no. 3 (Autumn 1985), 341–43; Kemp P. Battle, *History of the University of North Carolina: From Its Beginning to the Death of President Swain, 1789–1868* (Raleigh, NC: Edwards & Broughton, 1907), 1:72; Phillip A. Bruce, *History of the University of Virginia: The Lengthened Shadow of One Man* (New York: Macmillan, 1921), 3:262.

Notes to Chapter 2

3. Paul E. Hoffman, *Louisiana State University and Agricultural and Mechanical College, 1860–1869: A History* (Baton Rouge: Louisiana State University Press, 2020), 1, 20; David G. Sansing, *The University of Mississippi: A Sesquicentennial History* (Jackson: University Press of Mississippi, 1999), 112–16; Thomas G. Dyer, *The University of Georgia: A Bicentennial History, 1785–1985* (Athens: University of Georgia Press, 2004), 107–09; Hollis, *South Carolina College*, 1, 220; Daniel Hollis *University of South Carolina, Volume 2, College to University* (Columbia: University of South Carolina Press, 1956), 4–5; Bruce, *History of the University of Virginia*, 3:262.

4. US Congress, Senate, "Relief of East Tennessee University," (42 Congress, second session), Senate Report No. 17; James Riley Montgomery, Stanley J. Folmsbee, and Lee Seifert Greene, *To Foster Knowledge: A History of the University of Tennessee, 1794–1970* (Knoxville: University of Tennessee Press, 1984), 66. For the extend efforts to gain reparations for damage sustained by the school, see Earl Hess, *The Knoxville Campaign: Burnside and Longstreet in East Tennessee* (Knoxville: University of Tennessee Press, 2012), 273–74.

5. Maximilian LaBorde, "Report of the Chairman of the Faculty," South Carolina College, November 26, 1865, 193, University of South Carolina Board of Trustees Minutes, vol. 7, 1858–1869, South Carolina Library, University of South Carolina; Germaine M. Reed, *David French Boyd, Founder of Louisiana State University* (Baton Rouge: Louisiana State University Press, 1977), 55–56; Allen Cabaniss, *The University of Mississippi; Its First Hundred Years* (Hattiesburg: University & College Press of Mississippi, 1971), 57–59; Hollis, *South Carolina College*, 22–25.

6. Dyer, *The University of Georgia*, 111. For an example of state appropriations lost, see Bruce, *History of the University of Virginia*, 3: 346–48.

7. Charles Phillips to J. B. Killebrew, March 12, 1866, Cornelia Phillips Spencer Papers, Southern Historical Collection, Wilson Library, University of North Carolina, hereafter cited as Spencer Papers; Mary Boykin Miller Chesnut, *Mary Chesnut's Civil War*, ed. C. Vann Woodward (New Haven: Yale University Press, 1981), 92, 99–110, 252–53; Bruce, *History of the University of Virginia*, 3:9, 285; Battle, *History of the University of North Carolina*, 1:750.

8. Michael Sugrue, "'We Desired Our Future Rulers to Be Educated Men': South Carolina College, the Defense of Slavery, and the Development of Secessionist Politics," in *The American College in the Nineteenth Century*, ed. Roger Geiger (Nashville, TN: Vanderbilt University Press, 2000), 94–95; Laurence R. Veysey, *The Emergence of the American University* (Chicago: University of Chicago Press, 1965), 36–38. For a student's description of the recitation, see Lyman H. Bagg, *Four Years at Yale* (New Haven, CT: Charles C. Chatfield, 1871), 550–53; Noah Porter, *The American Colleges and the American Public* (New Haven, CT: Charles C. Chatfield, 1870), 39–40, 73, 119–21; John N. Waddel, *Memorials of Academic Life: Being an Historical Sketch of the Waddel Family Identified through Three Generations with the History of the Higher Education in the South and Southwest* (Richmond, VA: Presbyterian Committee of Publication, 1891), 448–49; Stetar, "In Search of a Direction: Southern Higher Education after the Civil War," 344–48; Thomas Perkins Abernethy, *Historical Sketch of the University of Virginia* (Richmond, VA: Dietz Press, 1948), 25; T. C. Karns, "The University of Tennessee," in *Higher Education in Tennessee*, ed. Lucius S. Merriam (Washington: Government Printing Office, 1893), 69; Phillip Alexander Bruce, *History of the University of Virginia 1819–1919*, 4:23.

Notes to Chapter 2

9. Daniel Walker Hollis, *College to University*, 4–9, 22–23; Robert Barnwell, "Report of the Chairman of the Faculty," University of South Carolina Board of Trustees, vol. 7, 1858–1869, May 9, 1866, 207, South Carolina Library, University of South Carolina; J. T. Trowbridge, *A Picture of the Desolated States; and the Work of Restoration, 1865–1868* (Hartford, CT: L. Stebbens, 1868), 564; Cohen; *Reconstructing the Campus*, 44–46.

10. W. J. Rivers, "Report of Ancient Languages and Literature," William J. Rivers Papers, University of South Carolina April 30, 1866, 209; (Barnwell or LaBorde) "Report of the Chairman of the Faculty," University of South Carolina, May 9, 1866, 208, University of South Carolina Board of Trustees, vol. 7, 1858–1869, South Carolina Library, University of South Carolina. For Porter during the Civil War, see Edward Porter Alexander, *Fighting for the Confederacy: The Personal Recollections of General Edward Porter Alexander*, ed. Gary W. Gallagher (Chapel Hill: University of North Carolina Press, 1989); Hollis, *College to University*, 2:15, 20–21, 25–26.

11. "Report of Prof. Jos. LeConte," South Carolina College, November 28, 1865, 194; University of South Carolina Board of Trustees, vol. 7, 1858–1869; South Carolina Library, University of South Carolina; E. P. Alexander, "Report of the Professor of Mathematics, Civil and Military Engineering & Construction," May 6, 1866, 212, University of South Carolina Board of Trustees, vol. 7, 1858–1869, South Carolina Library, University of South Carolina.

12. Robert Barnwell, "Report of the Chairman of the Faculty," University of South Carolina, May 9, 1866, 207, University of South Carolina Board of Trustees, vol. 7, 1858–1869, South Carolina Library, University of South Carolina.

13. Robert Barnwell, "Report of the Chairman of the Faculty," University of South Carolina, May 9, 1866, 208, South Carolina Library, University of South Carolina; Frederick Rudolph, *The American College and University: A History* (New York: Alfred Knopf, 1962), 138–39; Hollis, *College to University*, 32, 29–40.

14. John LeConte to R. W. Barnwell, May 5, 1866, John LeConte Papers, South Carolina Library, University of South Carolina; "Catalogue of the University of South Carolina 1867–68–69," 7–9, 17–19; *Charleston Daily Courier*, September 3, 1869; *Columbia Phoenix*, July 2, 1867, June 28, 1867, May 17, 1868; *Yorkville Enquirer*, January 31, 1867, July 4, 1867; Cohen, *Reconstructing the Campus*, 81–82.

15. "Minutes of the Board of Trustees and Minutes 1860–1882," vol. 2, 52–56, University of Mississippi Libraries, Department of Archives and Special Collections; Sansing, *The University of Mississippi*, 116.

16. Waddel, *Memorials of an Academic Life*, 448, 474; *Oxford Falcon*, June 21, 1866, July 5, 1866, October 11, 1866, November 24, 1866. For Waddel, see Allen Cabaniss, *The University of Mississippi: Its First Hundred Years* (Hattiesburg: University & College Press of Mississippi, 1971), 61–62; *Oxford Falcon*, June 19, 1869; Sansing, *The University of Mississippi*, 117–20; Don H. Doyle, *Faulkner's County: The Historical Roots of Yoknapatawpha* (Chapel Hill: University of North Carolina, 2001), 94.

17. J. S. Averit to Eugene Hilgard, October 8, 1866, A. Mayus to Eugene Hilgard, January 13, 1866, John A. Binford to Eugene Hilgard, August 29, 1866, W. Walker to Eugene Hilgard, December 12, 1866, Eugene W. Hilgard Papers, Mississippi Department of Archives and History, Jackson, MS; S. C. Caldwell to "Dear Doctor," May 4, 1927, Allen Cabaniss Collection, University of Mississippi Libraries, Archives and Special

Notes to Chapter 2

Collections. For Hilgard, see Cabaniss, *History of the University of Mississippi*, 41–42, 63, and also for Sears, 62.

18. *Oxford Falcon*, October 4, 1866, December 8, 1866, March 27, 1867; *Daily Clarion*, June 30, 1868.

19. John C. Inscoe, "To Do Justice to North Carolina: The War's End According to Cornelia Philips Spencer, Zebulon B. Vance, and David L. Swain," in *North Carolinians in the Era of the Civil War and Reconstruction*, ed. Paul D. Escott (Chapel Hill: University of North Carolina Press, 2008), 143–44; Battle; *History of the University of North Carolina*, 1:741–44.

20. Cornelia Spencer to E. Summerell (1866), Cornelia Phillips Spencer Papers; Battle, *History of the University of North Carolina*, 1:751, 754.

21. Charles Phillips to J. B. Killebrew, March 12, 1866, Spencer Papers; Battle, *History of the University of North Carolina*, 1:754–56.

22. *Hillsborough Recorder*, October 3, 1866; *Catalogue of the Trustees, Faculty and Students of the University of North Carolina, 1866–67* (Raleigh, NC: Nichols, Gorman & Neathery, 1867), 10–14; *Catalogue of the Trustees, Faculty and Students of the University of North Carolina, 1869–70* (Raleigh, NC: Standard Steam, 1870), 10; *Raleigh Sentinel*, June 28, 1869; William S. Powell, *The First State University: A Pictorial History of The University of North Carolina* (Chapel Hill: University of North Carolina, 1992), 85.

23. Charles Phillips to J. B. Killebrew, March 12, 1866, Spencer Papers; Battle, *History of the University of North Carolina*, 1:763.

24. Bruce, *History of the University of Virginia*, 3:272–340.

25. Charles to Pa, April 29, July 8, 1866, January 8, 1867, Septimus Cabiness Papers, University of Alabama Special Collections Library; *New York Herald*, June 5, 1867. For Jefferson and Washington societies, see Phillip Alexander Bruce, *History of the University of Virginia: The Lengthened Shadow of One Man 1819–1919* (New York: Macmillan, 1920), 2: 355–60; Phillip Alexander Bruce, *History of the University of Virginia 1819–1919* (New York: Macmillan, 1921), 4:84–86, 133–34.

26. *Daily Dispatch*, July 2, 1866, July 6, 1866.

27. *Daily Dispatch*, October 4, 1867; *Alexandria Gazette*, July 3, 1867.

28. Ward W. Briggs Jr., *Soldier and Scholar Basil Lanneau Gildersleeve and the Civil War* (Charlottesville: University of Virginia, 1998), 11, 18, 48. For Gildersleeve, see Bruce, *History of the University of Virginia*, 3:85–88.

29. John F. Marszalek, *A Soldier's Passion for Order* (New York: Free Press, 1993), 124. For Sherman's tenure, see Marszalek, 123–39; Reed, *David French Boyd*, 5, 17–18; Walter L. Fleming, *Louisiana State University 1860–1896* (Baton Rouge: Louisiana State University Press, 1936), 132.

30. William Sherman to David Boyd, April 12, 1866, William T. Sherman Papers, Louisiana State University Archives, LSU Libraries, Baton Rouge, Louisiana; Hoffman, *Louisiana State University*, 23; Reed, *David French Boyd*, 55–56. "Beneficiaries" were students whose college expenses were assumed by the state.

31. James M. Garnett, "Reminiscences of the Louisiana State Seminary and Military Academy in 1867," 5, 8, Louisiana State University, Offices of the Chancellor Records, Louisiana State University Archives, LSU Libraries, Baton Rouge, Louisiana; Samuel Lockett to Cornelia Lockett, March 31, 1867, Samuel Lockett Papers, Southern

Notes to Chapter 2

Historical Collection, Wilson Library, University of North Carolina, hereafter cited as Lockett Papers. For Lockett, see Lauren C. Post, "Samuel Henry Lockett (1837–1891): A Sketch of his Life and Work," *Louisiana History* 5 (Fall 1964), 421–41; Fleming, *Louisiana State University, 1860–1896*, 171–73; Hoffman, *Louisiana State University*, 15–16.

32. Garnett, "Reminiscences of the Louisiana State Seminary and Military Academy," 6, 8; Reed, *David French Boyd*, 16; Lee Kennett, *Sherman: A Soldier's Life* (New York: Harper Collins, 2001), 87.

33. Samuel Lockett to Cornelia Lockett, March 31, 1867, Lockett Papers.

34. Boyd to Semmes, November 24, 1866, Semmes Family Papers, Alabama Department of Archives and History, hereafter cited as ADAH, Montgomery, Alabama; Samuel Lockett to Cornelia Lockett, April 29, 1867, Lockett Papers; Garnett, "Reminiscences of the Louisiana State Seminary and Military Academy," 7; Warren Spencer, *Raphael Semmes: The Philosophical Mariner* (Tuscaloosa: University of Alabama Press, 1997), 197–98.

35. Samuel Lockett to Cornelia Lockett, March 31, 1867, Lockett Papers; William T. Sherman to Ulysses Grant, August 6, 1867, in *The Papers of Ulysses S. Grant*, ed. John Y. Simon (Carbondale: Southern Illinois University Press, 1991), 17: 479; Samuel Lockett to Cornelia Lockett, March 31, 1867, Lockett Papers; Joseph G. Dawson III, *Army Generals and Reconstruction: Louisiana, 1862–1877* (Baton Rouge: Louisiana State University Press, 1982), 46–58.

36. Raphael Semmes to David Boyd, April 6, 1867, in "Eleven Letters of Raphael Semmes, 1867–1868," ed. Elisabeth Doyle, *Alabama Review* 5 (July 1952), 227–28; Spencer, *Raphael Semmes*, 197–98.

37. David Boyd to James Gresham, November 24, 1867, David Boyd Letterbooks; Post, "Samuel Henry Lockett (1837–1891)," 421–41; Reed, *David French Boyd*, 66–71; David Boyd to W. H. Freret, November 27, 1867, David Boyd Letterbooks, LSU Archives, Baton Rouge, Louisiana.

38. *New Orleans Republican*, August 11, 1867; Reed, *David French Boyd*, 62–64.

39. *New Orleans Republican*, August 24, 1867.

40. David Boyd to James Gresham, November 24, 1867, David Boyd Letterbooks; Reed, *David French Boyd*, 66.

41. David Boyd to W. H. Freret, November 27, 1867, David Boyd Letterbooks; Fleming, *Louisiana State University, 1860–1896*, 204; Reed, *David French Boyd*, 69–70; David M. Jordan, *Winfield Scott Hancock: A Soldier's Life* (Bloomington: Indiana University Press, 1988), 201–02.

42. "Minutes of the Proceedings of the Board of Trustees of the University of Georgia" (November 6, 1858–July 1871), 4:92. For Lipscomb, see Dyer, *The University of Georgia*, 99–100.

43. *Southern Banner*, November 15, 1865, December 5, 1866.

44. "Minutes of the Proceedings of the Board of Trustees of the University of Georgia," 101; Dyer, *History of the University of Georgia*, 112–18.

45. Nathaniel E. Harris, *Autobiography: The Story of An Old Man's Life with Reminiscences of Seventy-five Years* (Macon, GA: J. W. Burke, 1925), 151–52.

46. Walter Hill to Barnard Hill, September 18, pp. 1, 120; Walter Hill to Mary Clay Hill, January 15, January 24, pp. 17, 19–20; Hill to Barnard Hill, September 18, 1869;

Notes to Chapter 2

Hill to Mary Clay Hill, April 1868, in G. Ray Mathis, ed. *College Life in the Reconstruction South: Walter B. Hill's Student Correspondence, University of Georgia, 1869–1871* (Athens: University of Georgia Libraries Miscellanea Publications, No. 10, 1974), 38–39. For a biography of Hill, see the same, 1–9; "Minutes of the Proceedings of the Board of Trustees of the University of Georgia," 151; Harris, *Autobiography*, 160, 164–65.

47. John Pope to Ulysses Grant, October 22, 1867, in *The Papers of Ulysses S. Grant*, ed. John Y. Simon (Carbondale: Southern Illinois University Press, 1991), 18: 12–13; Dyer, *The University of Georgia*, 113–15; "Minutes of the Proceedings of the Board of Trustees of the University of Georgia," 146, Walter Hill to Barnard Hill, May 13, 1868, *College Life in the Reconstruction South*, 44; Joseph H. Parks, *Joseph E. Brown of Georgia* (Baton Rouge: Louisiana State University Press, 1977), 366–92.

48. Charles Phillips to J. B. Killebrew, March 12, 1866, Spencer Papers; *New York Herald*, June 5, 1867; Spencer, *Raphael Semmes*, 197.

49. Karns, "The University of Tennessee," 69; *Brownlow's Knoxville Whig*, August 11, 1866; Montgomery, Folmsbee, and Greene, *To Foster Knowledge*, 64–70.

50. *Knoxville Press and Register*, April 16, 1868, June 18, 1868, May 26, 1869; *Brownlow's Knoxville Whig*, January 30, 1867, August 28, 1867; Montgomery, Folmsbee, and Greene, *To Foster Knowledge*, 53, 72–73; Karns, "The University of Tennessee," 70.

51. "Message of Gov. Brownlow to 1st session of the General Assembly April 1865," reel 2, Governor William G. Brownlow Papers, Tennessee State Library and Archives, Nashville, TN; Thomas B. Alexander, *Political Reconstruction in Tennessee* (Nashville, TN: Vanderbilt University Press, 1950), 110–12. For Brownlow, see E. Merton Coulter, *William G. Brownlow: Fighting Parson of the Southern Highlands* (Chapel Hill: University of North Carolina Press, 1937); Kyle Osborn, "Reconstructing Race: Parson Brownlow and the Rhetoric of Race in Postwar East Tennessee," in *Reconstructing Appalachia the Civil War's Aftermath*, ed. Andrew L. Slap (Lexington: University of Kentucky Press, 2010), 163–84.

52. *Brownlow's Knoxville Whig and Rebel Ventilator*, December 26, 1866; Student File (Frederic DeForest Allen), Alumni & Development Records, Oberlin College Archives, Oberlin, Ohio; *Knoxville Press and Register*, February 15, 1868; Hutton, *Bearing the Torch*, 24–29; Moses White, *Early History of the University of Tennessee, Address before the Alumni Association* (Knoxville, TN: Board of Trustees, 1879), 70–71; Folmsbee, *East Tennessee University 1840–1879*, 50.

53. *Southern Banner*, December 13, 1865.

54. Trowbridge, *A Picture of the Desolated States*, 564.

55. *Brownlow's Knoxville Whig*, October 9, 1867; A. C. Haskell to Porter Alexander, January 9, 1866, Edward Porter Alexander Papers, Southern Historical Collection, Wilson Library, University of North Carolina, hereafter cited as Edward Porter Alexander Papers, SHC; James Lusk Alcorn, "Special Message Hon. James L. Alcorn on the Subject of Establishment of a University for the Colored People, [e]tc." (Jackson, MS: Kimball, Raymond, 1871), 1–3, Mississippi Department of Archives and History, Jackson, Mississippi; Waddel, *Memorials of Academic Life*, 446, 456; Fleming, *Louisiana State University, 1860–1896*, 139, 142–43; *Daily Dispatch*, July 1, 1868.

56. "Minutes of the Proceedings of the Board of Trustees of the University of Georgia," 92.

Notes to Chapter 3

57. LeConte, *Autobiography of Joseph LeConte*, 235; Cohen, *Reconstructing the Campus*, 53–54.

CHAPTER 3

1. *Daily Dispatch*, October 3, 1867; Bruce, *History of the University of Virginia*, 4:105, 133.

2. Karns, "The University of Tennessee," 70; *Catalogue of the Officers and Alumni at the Washington and Lee University, Lexington, Virginia, 1749–1888* (Baltimore, MD: John Murphy & Co., 1888), 129–53, Special Collections & Archives, James G. Leyburn Library, Lexington, Virginia; *Catalogue of the Trustees, Faculty and Students of the University of North Carolina 1867–68* (Raleigh, NC: Nichols Gorman, & Neathery, 1868), 12–13; *Historical Catalogue of the Trustees, Faculties, and Alumni of the University of Mississippi from the Original Organization 1869–70* (Oxford, 1870), 26–30; Arthur B. Chitty, *Reconstruction at Sewanee: The Founding of the University of the South and Its First Administration, 1857–1872* (Sewanee, TN: University Press, 1954), 83, 175; *Montgomery Advertiser*, July 9, 1867.

3. Robert Patton, "Address to the People of Alabama, by Governor Robert M. Patton," July 11, 1868 (Montgomery, AL: Barrett & Brown, 1868), Government Records Collections, Alabama State Department of Archives and History, Montgomery.

4. *Montgomery Mail*, May 1, 1868.

5. *Independent Monitor*, June 23, 1868; Proceedings of the Executive and Building Committee, 142–45. For description of completed building, see Mellown, *The University of Alabama: A Guide to the Campus and Its Architecture*, 63–64.

6. For Henry Tutwiler, see Alfred F. Brophy, *University, Court, and Slave: Pro-Slavery Thought in Southern Colleges and Courts and the Coming of Civil War* (Oxford, UK: Oxford University), 97.

7. Elisha W. Peck to E. F. Bouchello, April 4, 1868, E. F. Bouchello to William Hugh Smith, July 20, 1868, William Hugh Smith Papers, Alabama State Department of Archives and History, Montgomery, Alabama. For Henry Tutwiler, see Paul M. Pruitt Jr., *Taming Alabama Lawyers and Reformers, 1804–1929* (Tuscaloosa: University of Alabama Press, 2010), 32–35; Charles William Dabney, *Universal Education in the South* (Chapel Hill: University of North Carolina Press, 1936), 307–9; *Montgomery Advertiser*, September 18, 1868; Abernethy, *Historical Sketch of the University of Virginia*, 8.

8. "Proclamation of Governor Lewis E. Parsons," in *Livingston Journal*, July 20, 1865; Brophy, *University, Court, and Slave*, 49–50, 61–71, 78–80, 84; Alfred L. Brophy, "Proslavery Political Theory in the Southern Academy, 1832–1861," in *Slavery and the University Histories and Legacies*, eds. Leslie M. Harris, James F. Campbell, and Alfred L. Brophy (Athens: University of Georgia Press, 2019), 65–83. Also see Sugrue, "We Desired Our Future Rulers to Be Educated Men," 102–09.

9. Robert Lanier, May 28, 1868, in Sidney Lanier, *The Centennial Edition of the Works of Sidney Lanier Letters 1857–1868*, edited by Charles R. Anderson, vol. 7 (Baltimore, MD: Johns Hopkins Press, 1945), 348.

10. Thomas M. Owen, ed., "Report of the Alabama History Commission to the Governor of Alabama. December 1, 1900," in *Publications of the Alabama Historical Society, Miscellaneous Collections* (Montgomery, AL: Brown Printing Co., 1901), 1:125; Minutes of the Board of Trustees, 1866 to 1868, 155–58; Sellers, *History of the University of Alabama*, 297–98.

Notes to Chapter 3

11. For Smith, see Michael W. Fitzgerald, "William Hugh Smith, July 1868–December 1870," in *Alabama's Governors: A Political History of the State*, eds. Samuel L. Webb and Margaret E. Armbrester (Tuscaloosa: University of Alabama, 2001), 87–90; Rogers, *Reconstruction Politics in a Deep South State*, 79–82.

12. "Report of the Superintendent of Public Instruction of the State of Alabama for the Fiscal Year Ending 30th September, 1869," (Montgomery: Jno. G. Stokes & Co., 1870), 17, in Records of the United States of America, Property of the Library of Congress in Association with the University of North Carolina, Alabama, reel 1 (1868–1877), Ilah Dunlap Little Memorial Library University of Georgia, hereafter cited as "Report of the Superintendent of Public Instruction (1869)." For Cloud, see Hubbs, *Searching for Freedom*, 99–131.

13. Fitzgerald, *Reconstruction in Alabama*, 230–32; Rogers, *Reconstruction Politics in a Deep South State*, 87, 114–15, 220–21.

14. "Report of the Superintendent of Public Instruction (1869)," 17.

15. "Report of the Superintendent of Public Instruction (1869)," 15.

16. *Daily State Sentinel*, February 6, 1868; Sellers, *History of the University of Alabama*, 297–98.

17. *Sun*, April 26, 1870. For Smith, see Ezra J. Warner, *Generals in Blue: Lives of the Union Commanders* (Baton Rouge: Louisiana State University, 1981), 458–59; *Pittsburgh Gazette*, September 18, 1868.

18. *Montgomery Mail*, August 26, 1868; University of Alabama Minutes of the Board of Regents, August 1, 1868 to August 24, 1869, 160–67, hereafter cited as Minutes of the Board of Regents, 1868–1869; *Daily State Sentinel*, January 3, 1868; *Montgomery Mail*, August 24, 1868, August 26, 1868; *Independent Monitor*, September 15, 1868.

19. *Montgomery Mail*, August 7, 1868, August 11, 1868; William Wyman to William Hugh Smith, January 4, 1869, William Hugh Smith Papers. For Lakin, see Hubbs, *Searching for Freedom*, 57–98.

20. *Montgomery Advertiser*, August 8, 1868.

21. *Democrat* quoted in *Montgomery Mail*, August 20, 1868.

22. *Montgomery Mail*, August 7, 1868.

23. *Montgomery Mail*, August 7, 1868, August 20, 1868.

24. *Independent Monitor*, September 15, 1868.

25. *Montgomery Mail*, August 7, 1868; *Tuskegee News* quoted in the *Montgomery Advertiser*, August 15, 1868; *Independent Monitor*, September 15, 1868; "Alabama Testimony," Joseph Speed, 427.

26. Calvin Loomis to Matthew Maury, October 1, 1869, Matthew Fontaine Maury Papers, 1825–1960, Manuscript Division, Library of Congress, Washington, DC, hereafter cited as "Matthew Maury Papers, LOC."

27. *Independent Monitor*, August 11, 1869.

28. "Alabama Testimony," Arad S. Lakin, 134, 127–35, 157; Lionel W. Day, 594, 616; Nicholas Davis, 784. For a biography of Lakin, see Hubbs, *Searching for Freedom*, 57–98.

29. "Alabama Testimony," Arad Lakin, 114; Robert Lindsay, 180; Hubbs, *Searching for Freedom*, 57–80.

30. "Alabama Testimony," Turner Reavis, 332, 339; Lewis Parsons, 94; "Ryland Randolph's Scribbles," 84–85.

Notes to Chapter 4

31. "Alabama Testimony," Arad Lakin, 112; William Wyman to William Hugh Smith, January 4, 1869, William Hugh Smith Papers; *Independent Monitor*, May 31, 1871; Hubbs, *Searching for Freedom*, 1–6.

32. William Wyman to William Hugh Smith, January 4, 1869, William Hugh Smith Papers.

33. *Independent Monitor*, August 18, 1868.

34. "Alabama Testimony," Arad Lakin, 136; Hubbs, *Searching for Freedom*, 1:65–66.

35. *Republican Banner*, September 4, 1868, September 25, 1868; *Independent Monitor*, September 22, 1868; Rogers, *Black Belt Scalawag*, 40.

36. R. Blair to Edwin Beecher, September 14, 1868, Records of the Assistant Commissioners, Alabama; *Republican Banner*, September 18, 1868.

37. *Independent Monitor*, September 1, 1868. For full text, see Hubbs, *Searching for Freedom*, 177–78; Trelease, *White Terror*, 86–87. The woodcut remains perhaps the most quintessential example of printed/illustrated Southern Reconstruction defiance. It appears on the cover of Hubbs, *Searching for Freedom*, opposite the title page of Wiggins, *The Scalawag in Alabama Politics*, and in Walter Fleming's *Civil War and Reconstruction in Alabama*.

38. *Cincinnati Commercial*, September 19, 1868; Foner, *Reconstruction*, 224–25, 262–63, 342; William Gillette, *Retreat from Reconstruction, 1869–1879* (Baton Rouge: Louisiana State University Press, 1979), 4–5. For Halstead, see Donald W. Curl, *Murat Halstead and the Cincinnati Commercial* (Boca Raton: University Presses of Florida, 1980).

39. *Buchanan County Bulletin and Guardian*, October 2, 1868; *Chicago Tribune*, September 29, 1868; *Burlington Weekly Free Press*, October 2, 1868; *Daily Missouri Democrat*, October 8, 1868; *Pittsburgh Gazette*, September 21, 1868; *Daily Ohio Statesman*, September 28, 1868; *Detroit Tribune*, September 25, 1868; Hubbs, *Searching for Freedom*, 39–42.

40. *Independent Monitor*, November 10, 1868; Rogers, *Reconstruction Politics in a Deep South State*, 99–100.

41. "Alabama Testimony," Arad Lakin, 112.

42. Basil Manly Jr. to Basil Manly Sr. (1868), Manly Family Papers. For Basil Manly Jr., see Fuller, *Chaplain to the Confederacy*, 211, 276–77, 309; *Historical Catalogue of the Officers and Alumni of the University of Alabama, 1821 to 1870* (Selma, AL: Armstrong, Duval & Martin, 1870), 12.

43. *Republican Banner*, October 23, 1868. For Dykous, see Sarah Woolfolk Wiggins, "The Life of Ryland Randolph as Seen through His Letters to John W. DuBose," *Alabama Historical Quarterly* 30, nos. 3 and 4 (Fall and Winter 1968), 164, 166, hereafter cited as Wiggins, "Life of Ryland Randolph as Seen through His Letters"; *Memorial Record of Alabama*, 2:176.

44. *Independent Monitor*, December 28, 1868; Williams, *A Literary History of Alabama*. Benjamin's much better-known brother was Alexander B. Meek, who was involved in various literary endeavors, including poetry, served in various offices in Alabama and was an accomplished orator.

Chapter 4

1. *Tuscaloosa Observer*, June 19, 1869, June 12, 1869, August 28, 1869; *Republican Banner*, October 9, 16, 1868.

Notes to Chapter 4

2. *Tuscaloosa Observer*, January 2, 1869.

3. *Reconstructionist*, June 6, 1868; *Tuscaloosa Observer*, March 27, 1869, April 1, 1871; *Independent Monitor*, August 17, 1869, May 4, 1869; Clinton, "A Hundred Years of Catholicity in Tuscaloosa," 9; *New Catholic Encyclopedia* (New York: McGraw Hill, 1967), 8:1110.

4. Charles Manly to children, September 13, 1868, Manly Family Papers.

5. "Report of the Superintendent of Public Education of the State of Alabama to the Governor from the Fiscal Year Ending 30 September 1869," 15. The building was named Woods Hall for the school's first president, Alva Woods; Sellers, *History of the University of Alabama*, 357.

6. Robert Harper to Edwin Beecher, October 19, 1868, "Press Copies of Letters Sent (September 16, 1868–July 1, 1870)," in Records of the Superintendent of Education for the State of Alabama, Bureau of Refugees, Freedmen and Abandoned Lands, records group 105, National Archives, Morrow, Georgia; for summary of his career, see *Indianapolis Journal*, January 6, 1890.

7. *Mobile Register* quoted in *Alabama State Journal*, December 13, 1868; *Independent Monitor*, December 22, 1868.

8. Minutes of Board of Trustees, 1866–1868, 169–90; *Sun*, October 26, 1869.

9. *Catalogue of the Officers and Students of Cumberland University at Lebanon, Tennessee for the Academic Year, 1855–56*, (Nashville, TN: A. A. Stitt, 1856), 6, 11; *Catalogue of the Officers and Students of Cumberland University at Lebanon, Tennessee for the Academic Year 1858–9* (Lebanon, TN: Neal & Spillers, 1859), 4, 10, Stockton Archives, Cumberland University, Lebanon, Tennessee; *Weekly State Journal*, August 28, 1869; Owen, *Dictionary of Alabama Biography*, 3:287–88; Caroline Winterer, *The Culture of Classicism Ancient Greece and Rome in American Intellectual Life, 1780–1910* (Baltimore, MD: Johns Hopkins University Press, 2002), 25; *Birmingham News*, March 21, 1936.

10. Calvin Loomis to Elias Loomis, May 26, 1854, June 8, 1848, October 18, 1850, November 26, 1856, Loomis Papers; *Independent Monitor*, November 2, 1869; *Catalogue of the Officers and Students of the Western Reserve College, 1836–37* (Cleveland, OH: Penniman & Bemis, 1838), 9; *Catalogue of the Officers and Students of the Western Reserve College. Hudson, Ohio, November 1840* (Hudson, OH: Charles Aiken, 1840), 8, Case Western University Archives, Cleveland, Ohio.

11. Calvin Loomis to Elias Loomis, February 5, 1857, Loomis Papers.

12. Calvin Loomis to Elias Loomis, March 8, 1857, Loomis Papers.

13. Calvin Loomis to Elias Loomis, January 10, 1869, July 29, 1850, October 10, 1856, January 9, 1860, May 13, 1860, Loomis Papers; *Sun*, October 6, 1869. For Elias Loomis, see Timothy Dwight, *Memories of a Yale Life and Men, 1845–1899* (New York: Dodd, Mead and Co., 1903), 348, 386, 388, 391. For Centenary College, see Brophy, *University, Court, and Slave*, 85; Lynda F. Worley, "A History of Centenary Institute, Selma, Alabama," *The Wesleyan Quarterly Review* 11 (February 1965), 30–33.

14. *Alabama State Journal*, January 2, 1869.

15. DeForest Richards to wife, December 5, 1865, Richards Family Papers (1800–1982), American Heritage Center, University of Wyoming, Laramie, Wyoming. For Richards, see Wiggins, "J. DeForest Richards, a Vermont Carpetbagger in Alabama," 98–106; Bartlett Richards Jr. and Ruth Van Ackeren, *Bartlett Richards Nebraska Sandhills*

Notes to Chapter 4

Cattleman (Lincoln: Nebraska State Historical Society, 1980), 32–36; *General Catalogue of the Theological Seminary Andover, Massachusetts 1808–1908* (Boston, MA: Thomas Todd, 1908), 182; *Sun*, October 6, 1869; Rogers, *Reconstruction Politics in a Deep South State*, 81–82.

16. *Daily State Sentinel*, June 21, 1867, November 1, 1867; *Montgomery Advertiser*, September 10, 1867; *Weekly Advertiser*, April 30, 1867; *Alabama State Journal*, February 2, 1869; *Sun*, October 6, 1869; *Catalogue of the University of North Carolina, 1857–58*, (Chapel Hill, NC: Gazette Office, 1858), 20; *Catalogue of the Trustees, Faculty and Students, of the University of North Carolina, 1859–1860*, (Chapel Hill, NC: John B. Neatherly, 1860), 12; Wiggins, "Life of Ryland Randolph as Seen through His Letters," 175–76; Battle, *History of the University of North Carolina*, 2:685, 705.

17. Ezra J. Warner, *Generals in Gray: Lives of the Confederate Commanders* (Baton Rouge: Louisiana State University Press, 1959), 90–91.

18. *Catalogue of the Officers and Students of the University of Alabama, 1869–70*, 9, W. S. Hoole Special Collections Library, University of Alabama, hereafter cited as *Catalogue of the Officers and Students, 1869–1870*; Cohen, *Reconstructing the Campus*, 53, 59–60, 68–69, 73; John A. Wyeth, *History of La Grange Military Academy and the Cadet Corps, 1857–1862* (New York: The Brewer Press, 1907), 66, 73, 148; *Sun*, October 6, 1869. For Southerners leaving for Mexico, see Andrew F. Folle, *The Lost Cause: The Confederate Exodus to Mexico* (Norman, OK: University of Oklahoma Press, 1965).

19. *Tuscaloosa Observer*, February 13, 1869; *Republican Banner*, October 16, 1868; for Warren see *Tuscaloosa Observer*, November 28, 1868; Quist, *Restless Visionaries*, 198, 204–11.

20. *Tuscaloosa Observer*, January 5, 1869.

21. *Independent Monitor*, January 5, 1869.

22. *Independent Monitor*, January 12, 1869; one individual traveling through the swamp in 1871 noted "briars, brambles and logs, under overlapping trees" and advised anyone doing likewise, "Have your lives, your bones and your good clothes insured before you undertake a trip thro' Sipsey Swamp." Carrollton *Pickens County Herald and West Alabamian*, July 19, 1871. For presidential mansion, see Gamble, *Alabama Catalog*, 357–58.

23. *Independent Monitor*, January 12, 1869; Rogers, *Reconstruction Politics in a Deep South State*, 80–81.

24. Barbara Little to John Little, February 9, 1869, Little Family Papers, W. S. Hoole Special Collection Library; *Independent Monitor*, January 26, 1869, February 9, 1869, October 5, 1869; *Tuscaloosa News*, March 11, 1928; Wiggins, "The Life of Ryland Randolph as Seen through His Letters," 175.

25. Calvin Loomis to Elias Loomis, March 3, 1869, Loomis Papers.

26. *Independent Monitor*, March 23, 1869.

27. DeForest Richards to Asa Smith, June 4, 1869, DeForest Richards Alumni File, Manuscript Collection, Dartmouth College, Rauner Special Collections Library, Hanover, New Hampshire. For Asa Smith, see Baxter Perry Smith, *The History of Dartmouth College* (Boston, MA: Houghton, Osgood & Co., 1878), 177, 189.

28. *Alabama State Journal*, August 25, 1869; *Independent Monitor*, February 5, 1869.

29. DeForest Richards to Asa Smith, June 14, 1869, Frederick DeForest Allen in Student File Alumni & Development Records, Oberlin College Archives, Oberlin, Ohio.

Notes to Chapter 4

30. Calvin Loomis to Elias Loomis, February 5, 1857, March 3, 1869, April 1, 1869, April 13, 1869; Barbara Little to John Little, February 9, 1869, Little Family Papers; *Jacksonville Republican*, March 6, 1869; *Tuscaloosa Observer*, March 3, 1869, March 30, 1869.

31. *Alabama State Journal*, August 12, 1869; *Cincinnati Daily Gazette*, September 14, 1868; *Indianapolis Journal*, January 6, 1890; Kolchin, *First Freedom*, 95–97.

32. Calvin Loomis to Elias Loomis, April 1, 1869, Loomis Papers; DeForest Richards to Asa Smith, June 14, 1869; *Independent Monitor*, February 9, 1869.

33. James Murfee to Building Committee, February 29, 1868, Proceedings of the Executive and Building Committee, 122–26.

34. *Catalogue of the Officers and Students, 1869–1870*, 7; *Independent Monitor*, March 30, 1869. The minimum age of admittance was fifteen years old.

35. *Moulton Advertiser*, May 7, 1869; *Catalogue of the Officers and Students, 1869–1870*, 5–6; *Independent Monitor*, April 6, 1869, June 8, 1869.

36. Minutes of the Board, 1866–1868, 187; *Independent Monitor*, April 20, 1869, August 30, 1870; Pace, Robert F. *Halls of Honor: College Men in the Old South* (Baton Rouge: Louisiana State University Press, 2004), 4, 16–17.

37. *Independent Monitor*, April 13, 1869; *Southern Republican*, April 7, 1869.

38. DeForest Richards to Asa Smith, June 14, 1869, DeForest Richards Alumni File; *Catalogue of the Officers and Students, 1869–1870*, 5–6.

39. Lyman H. Bagg, *Four Years at Yale* (New Haven, CT: Charles C. Chatfield, 1871), 552; Noah Porter, *The American Colleges and the American Public* (New Haven, CT: Charles C. Chatfield & Co., 1870), 119–21; Murfee, "A New Scheme of Organization," 8, 10; Winterer, *The Culture of Classicism*, 1–2, 36, 78; Veysey, *The Emergence of the American University*, 37–38.

40. *Catalogue of the Officers and Students, 1869–1870*, 40.

41. *Sun*, October 26, 1869; Murfee, *A New Scheme of Organization*, 39; Green, *Military Education*, 62–63, 65–67, 251, 253; Veysey, *Emergence of the American University*, 32–35; Eckinger, *The Militarization of the University of Alabama*, 171, 173–74. For the symbolic role of military colleges in the South after the Civil War, see Rod Andrew Jr., "Soldiers, Christians, and Patriots: The Lost Cause and Southern Military Schools, 1865–1915," *Journal of Southern History* 64, no. 4 (November 1998): 677–710.

42. Calvin Loomis to Elias Loomis, April 13, 1869, Loomis Papers.

43. *Independent Monitor*, March 2, 1869, January 5, 1869.

44. *Independent Monitor*, March 23, 1869.

45. *Independent Monitor*, March 2, 1869, April 6, 1869, November 2, 1869; Randolph's antipathy did not wane. Some thirty years later, he recalled that Vaughn at the university had spent most of his time "drinking whisky and hunting quails." Wiggins, "Life of Ryland Randolph as Seen through His Letters," 176.

46. *Independent Monitor*, March 9, 1869, April 13, 1869, May 25, 1869, June 8, 1869; Sarah Woolfolk Wiggins describes Richards as a service-minded legislator rather than an "avaricious carpetbagger" in "J. DeForest Richards, a Vermont Carpetbagger in Alabama," 105.

47. *Independent Monitor*, March 23, 1869, April 6, 1869.

48. *Independent Monitor*, June 1, 1869; Richards, *Bartlett Richards Nebraska Sandhills Cattleman*, 3–4.

Notes to Chapter 5

49. "Ryland Randolph's Scribbles," reel 2, 109–12; Hubbs, *Searching for Freedom*, 45–56; *Independent Monitor*, April 13, 1869, April 20, 1869.

50. *Independent Monitor*, April 13, 1869, May 25, 1869, June 8, 1869.

51. Calvin Loomis to Elias Loomis, April 19, 1869, Loomis Papers; *The Morning Star and Catholic Messenger*, August 6, 1871.

52. Hubbel Lomas to Elias Loomis, April 1, 1869, Loomis Papers.

53. T. P. Lewis to William Hugh Smith, December 13, 1868, William Hugh Smith Papers; *Weekly Alabama State Journal*, May 29, 1869; *Tuscaloosa Observer*, August 21, 1869; Rogers, *Partisan Politics in a Deep South State*, 101.

54. T. P. Lewis to William Hugh Smith, May 5, 1869, Smith Papers; Diary of Joshua Hill Foster, entries for April 20–21, 23–24, W. S. Hoole Special Collections Library, University of Alabama; *Weekly Alabama State Journal*, May 15, 1869; "Ryland Randolph's Scribbles," reel 2, 129–30; *Tuscaloosa Observer*, May 1, 1869; *Cincinnati Commercial Tribune*, April 26, 1871.

55. Colored Citizens of Tuscaloosa to William Hugh Smith April 22, 1869, Smith Papers.

56. *Alabama State Journal*, April 29, 1869.

57. William Hugh Smith to D. L. Dalton, May 20, 1869; J. J. Pegues to William Hugh Smith, May 14, 1869; Sterling Moore to David Dalton, May 20, 1869, William Hugh Smith Papers; *Independent Monitor*, March 25, 1869, May 11, 1869. For Pegues, see Owen, *Dictionary of Alabama Biography*, 4:1338–39. For Mills, see William Warren Rogers and Ruth Pruitt, *Stephen S. Renfroe, Alabama's Outlaw Sheriff* (Tallahassee, FL: Sentry Press, 1972), 52, 81, 85.

58. Calvin Loomis to William Hugh Smith, May 11, 1869, Smith Papers.

59. David Dalton to Calvin Loomis, May 17, 1869, William H. Smith Letterbooks, Government Records Collections, Alabama Department of Archives and History.

60. DeForest Richards to William Hugh Smith, June 10, 1869, Smith Papers; *Alabama State Journal*, November 27, 1869.

61. DeForest Richards to Elisha Peck, June 22, 1869, Smith Papers.

62. S. A. M. Wood to William Hugh Smith, May 5, 1869; William Miller to D. L. Dalton, May 22, 1869, Smith Papers; *Alabama State Journal*, May 22, 1869; Dannelly, "Life and Times of Robert Jemison," 137. For Wood, see Brewer, *Alabama: Her History*, 569.

63. Robert Jemison to David Dalton, June 21, 1869, Smith Papers. For Jemison, see McIlwain, *Civil War Alabama*, 31, 42, 58, 132–33; Brewer, *Alabama: Her History*, 563–64; Dannelly, "Life and Times of Robert Jemison," 89–90.

64. Barbara Little to George Little, February 9, 1869, Little Family Papers.

CHAPTER 5

1. *Independent Monitor*, August 24, 1868.

2. *Mobile Register*, August 15, 1869. For Cochran, see John T. Morris and Barbara Ann McClary, *Jerome Cochran: His Life, His Works, His Legacy* (Cullman, AL: Mulberry River Press, 1998), 26–37; *Monroe Eagle* quoted in the *Independent Monitor*, September 28, 1869.

3. Frederick Rudolph, *The American College and University: A History* (New York: Alfred Knopf, 1962), 165; DeForest Richards to Ava Smith, June 14, 1869, Richards Alumni File.

Notes to Chapter 5

4. *Alabama State Journal*, July 6, 1869.

5. *Alabama State Journal*, July 13, 1869; *Southern Republican*, July 21, 1869. For a masterful biography of Maury, see Frances Leigh Williams, *Matthew Fontaine Maury: Scientist of the Sea* (New Brunswick, NJ: Rutgers University Press, 1963). A short summary is Dumas Malone, ed., *Dictionary of American Biography* (New York: Charles Scribner's Sons, 1933), 8:428–31. For a biography of Semmes, see Warren Spencer, *Raphael Semmes: The Philosophical Mariner* (Tuscaloosa: University of Alabama Press, 1997), 197–201. And for Hardee, see Nathaniel C. Hughes Jr., *General William J. Hardee: Old Reliable* (Baton Rouge: Louisiana State University Press, 1965), 41–50, 55–66.

6. Matthew Maury to S. Wellford Corbin, June 7, 1869, Matthew Fontaine Maury Papers, Virginia Military Institute Archives, Lexington, Virginia, hereafter cited as VMI Archives; Williams, *Matthew Fontaine Maury*, 464–65.

7. *Montgomery Mail*, August 7, 1868; Rogers, *Reconstruction Politics in a Deep South State*, 87.

8. S. O. Scroggs to Raphael Semmes, August 5, 1869, Semmes Family Papers, Alabama State Department of Archives and History, Montgomery, Alabama; Doyle, "Eleven Letters of Raphael Semmes, 1867–1868," 222–32.

9. Minutes of the Board of Trustees (1868–1869), 193–202; Hampton Whitfield to Raphael Semmes, July 3, 1869, Semmes Family Papers; Calvin Loomis to Elias Loomis, July 5, 1869, Loomis Papers; Rogers, *Reconstruction Politics in a Deep South State*, 51–52, 111–12, 138–39.

10. Hampton Whitfield to Raphael Semmes, July 3, 1869, Semmes Family Papers; Minutes of the Board of Regents, (1868–1869), 191. For Putnam, see Fitzgerald, *Urban Reconstruction*, 127, 144–45.

11. "Alabama Testimony," Newton Whitfield, 1876; *Historical Catalogue of the Officers and Students of the University of Alabama, 1831–1870*, 13.

12. *Montgomery Advertiser*, February 5, 1885.

13. David Woodruff to D. L. Dalton, May 26, 1869; Dennis Dykous to William Hugh Smith, August 8, 1868, William Hugh Smith Papers; *Montgomery Mail*, August 7, 1868; *Independent Monitor*, September 25, 1868, August 16, 1870; *Alabama State Journal*, May 22, 1869.

14. *Montgomery Advertiser* quoted in the *Tuscaloosa Observer*, July 17, 1869.

15. *Gadsden Times* quoted in the *Independent Monitor*, October 5, 1869.

16. *Southern Argus*, September 15, 1869. For McKee, see Samuel Webb, "A Jacksonian Democrat in Postbellum Alabama: The Ideology and Influence of Journalist Robert McKee, 1869–1896," *Journal of Southern History* 62, no. 2 (May 1996): 239–74.

17. *Tuscaloosa Observer*, August 14, 1869.

18. *Southern Republican*, July 21, 1869; Richard H. Abbott, *For Free Press and Equal Rights: Republican Newspapers*, 85–87; Rogers, "'Politics is Mighty Uncertain': Charles Hays Goes to Congress," *Alabama Review* 30 (July 1977): 168.

19. *Alabama State Journal*, August 12, 1869.

20. H. L. Owen to Matthew Maury, July 16, 1869; William Byrd to Matthew Maury, July 22, 1869, Matthew Maury Papers, LOC; *Alabama State Journal*, July 13, 1869. For Byrd, see Owen, *Dictionary of Alabama Biography*, 3:277.

21. Elias Loomis to Calvin Loomis, July 5, 1869, Loomis Papers; Minutes of the

Notes to Chapter 5

Board of Regents, (1868–1869), 218–21; *The College Courant* (Yale), September 4, 1869, Manuscripts and Archives, Yale University Library; *Alabama State Journal*, August 17, 1869, August 18, 1869; Oscar W. Firkins, *Cyrus Northrop: A Memoir* (Minneapolis: University of Minnesota Press, 1925), 221, 246.

22. Minutes of the Board of Regents (1868–1869), 226–27. For Chambliss, see *Selma Morning Times*, March 9, 1897.

23. *Weekly State Journal*, August 28, 1869; *The College Courant* (Yale), September 4, 1869; Calvin Loomis to Elias Loomis, October 18, 1869, Loomis Papers.

24. *Mobile Daily Register*, August 25, 1869.

25. *Tuscaloosa Observer*, August 28, 1869.

26. *Alabama Beacon*, September 4, 1869.

27. Oscar Firkins, *Cyrus Northrop*, 266, 261, 273, 303–4; *Montgomery Advertiser*, September 19, 1869.

28. "Report of the Superintendent of Public Instruction of the State of Alabama, to the Governor, for the Fiscal Year Ending 30th September 1869" (Montgomery, AL: J. G. Stokes, 1870), 16.

29. *Montgomery Advertiser*, September 19, 1869, September 21, 1869.

30. *Southern Republican*, September 22, 1869; *Independent Monitor*, May 4, 1869, August 24, 1869; *Montgomery Advertiser*, September 2, 1869.

31. *Alabama State Journal*, August 28, 1869.

32. *Mobile Register*, September 5, 1869.

33. *Tuscaloosa Observer*, August 21, 1869.

34. *Southern Argus*, September 15, 1869.

35. *Independent Monitor*, August 18, 1870; *Alabama State Journal*, May 5, 1869; Calvin Loomis to Elias Loomis, April 19, 1869, Loomis Papers.

36. Dick Riser to Cousin Mattie, October 17, 1870, Mary Anne Norton-Black Papers, Special Collections and Archives, Auburn University, Auburn, Alabama; *Alabama State Journal*, April 8, 1871; Rogers, *Reconstruction Politics in a Deep South State*, 145.

37. "Affairs in Alabama," Benjamin Gardner, 300–301.

38. *Southern Republican*, October 20, 1869.

39. *Sun*, November 9, 1869.

40. Basil Manly to Charles, April 23, 1867, Basil Manly Jr. Papers, Southern Historical Collection, University of North Carolina; *Independent Monitor*, April 6, 1869.

41. *Sun*, November 9, 1869; Minutes of the Board of Regents (1868–1869), 209–11, 216; *Southern Republican*, October 20, 1869.

42. *Moulton Advertiser*, May 7, 1869; *Independent Monitor*, March 30, 1869; *Southern Republican*, May 5, 1869; Calvin Loomis to Elias Loomis, October 18, 1869, Loomis Papers; *Weekly Alabama State Journal*, August 28, 1869; Jennifer R. Green, *Military Education and the Emerging Middle Class in the Old South* (Cambridge, UK: Cambridge University Press, 2008), 66–68, 110.

43. Calvin Loomis to Elias Loomis, September 4, 1870, Loomis Papers; *Sun*, October 6, 1869; Murfee, *A New Scheme of Organization*, 31; *Catalogue of the Officers and Students, 1869–1870*, 5.

44. *Sun*, October 26, 1869; Green, *Military Education*, 63–66; Handlin, *The American College*, 36–38.

Notes to Chapter 5

45. "Military Commandant's Book 1869–1871," October 31, 1869; Wiggins, "The Life of Ryland Randolph as Seen through His Letters," 175; *Independent Monitor*, April 13, 1869. For discipline in Southern military schools see Jennifer R. Green, *Military Education and the Emerging Middle Class in the Old South* (Cambridge, UK: Cambridge University Press, 2008), 66–68, 110.

46. Handlin, *The American College*, 38–39.

47. *Independent Monitor*, April 20, 1869. For discussion of the psychological environment created by students living in close conditions, see Green, *Military Education*, 86, 98–99, 128; Pace, *Halls of Honor*, 39–40, 44; Rudolph, *The American College and University: A History*, 96–97.

48. Calvin Loomis to Elias Loomis, November 16, 1869, July 20, 1869, Loomis Papers; *Independent Monitor*, March 2, 1869, July 5, 1870, August 7, 1870; Wiggins, "The Life of Ryland Randolph as Seen through His Letters," 174–76; Bartlett, *Bartlett Richards: Nebraska Sandhills Cattleman*, 10, 12, 15, 22–23.

49. Wiggins, "The Life of Ryland Randolph as Seen through His Letters," 173; Calvin Loomis to Elias Loomis, April 19, 1869, Loomis Papers; *Independent Monitor*, April 20, 1869, September 7, 1869; *Alabama State Journal*, January 23, 1871.

50. DeForest Richards to Bartlett Richards, May 10, 1872, Richards Family Papers.

51. Calvin Loomis to Elias Loomis, September 4, 1870, Loomis Papers, Yale University Library, Manuscripts, and Archives, New Haven, Connecticut, hereafter cited as Loomis Papers. Elias Loomis was a prolific and highly successful author of textbooks and at his death willed $300,000 to Yale University for the support of an observatory. Brooks Mather Kelly, *Yale: A History* (New Haven, CT: Yale University Press, 1974), 247; Bartlett, *Bartlett Richards: Nebraska Sandhills Cattleman*, 18.

52. Hubbel Loomis to Elias Loomis, October 12, 1869, Loomis Papers; Hubbel Loomis to Elias Loomis, January 1, 1870, Loomis Papers.

53. Calvin Loomis to Elias Loomis, April 19, 1869, Loomis Papers.

54. Wiggins, "The Life of Ryland Randolph as Seen through His Letters," 175.

55. Wiggins, "The Life of Ryland Randolph as Seen through His Letters," 176. This statement was a slight that referenced Cornelia Vaughn's husband.

56. *Independent Monitor*, August 16, 1870, August 23, 1870. For Read, see G. Ward Hubbs, "John B. Read's Okra Paper," *Alabama Review* 43 (October 1990), 288–92; and by the same author, *Tuscaloosa: 200 Years in the Making*, 43–44; Rogers, *Black Belt Scalawag*, 5.

57. Calvin Loomis to Elias Loomis, October 18, 1869, Loomis Papers.

58. Calvin Loomis to Elias Loomis, November 16, 1869, Loomis Papers.

59. *Independent Monitor*, October 19, 1869.

60. *Independent Monitor*, November 2, 1869.

61. *Independent Monitor*, April 6, 1869, August 16, 1870, October 5, 1869; Minutes of the Board of Trustees, 1866–1868, 81; Veysey, *The American College and University*, 101–2; Pace, *Halls of Honor*, 45–56; Murfee, "A New Scheme of Organization," 11–12.

62. Minutes of the State Board of Education, 1869–1871, 1–2; Alabama State Department of Archives and History, Montgomery, hereafter cited as Minutes of the State Board of Education, 1869–1871; *Independent Monitor*, January 18, 1870.

63. Minutes of the State Board of Education, 1869–1871, 9, 16; *Selma Daily Messenger*, April 5, 1867. For Lupton, see Owen, *History of Alabama and Dictionary of Alabama*

Notes to Chapter 6

Biography (Chicago: S. J. Clarke, 1921), 4:1077; Wiggins, ed., *The Journals of Josiah Gorgas 1857–1878*, 189; *Nashville Banner*, July 4, 1883.

64. *Independent Monitor*, November 8, 1870; Nathan Chambliss to Nathan Lupton, February 5, 1870, Commandant's Book 1867–1887; Minutes of the State Board of Education, 1869–1871, 16–19; Minutes of the Board of Regents, 1866–1869, 225.

65. Calvin Loomis to Elias Loomis, January 2, 1870, Loomis Papers; Minutes of the State Board of Education, 1869–1871, 16–17, 19.

66. *Southern Argus*, December 16, 1869; *Marion Commonwealth*, January 20, 1870; *Alabama Beacon*, December 18, 1869.

CHAPTER 6

1. Thomas Wolfe, *The Web and the Rock* (New York: Harper & Brothers, 1939), 169.

2. Calvin Loomis to Elias Loomis, January 10, 1869, Loomis Papers.

3. David Peck to father, June 8, 1867, Elisha Peck Papers, William R. Perkins Library, Duke University, Durham, North Carolina; "Obituary, David Peck," *Trinity Tablet* (April 7, 1888), 47, Trinity College Archives, Watkinson Library, Hartford Connecticut; *Selma Times*, July 1, 1871.

4. *Independent Monitor*, July 5, 1870.

5. Nathan Chambliss to Nathan Lupton, February 5, 1870, Commandant's Book 1867–1887, 114–16; Minutes of the State Board of Education, 1869–1871, 16–17; *Alabama Beacon*, December 16, 1869.

6. T. Roy to Sallie Hardee, October 9, 1868, William Hardee to T. B. Roy, August 31, 1868, Hardee Family Papers; *Annual Reunion of the Association of Graduates of the United States Military Academy at West Point, New York* (Saginaw, MI: Seemann & Peters, 1897), 69–73, Archives and Special Collections, United States Military Academy Library, West Point, New York; Elizabeth Burgess Buford, "The Last Roll Call: Col. Nathan Rives Chambliss," *Confederate Veteran Magazine* (May 1897), 203; Minutes of the State Board of Education, 1869–1871, 16; Nathan Chambliss to Robert Patton, October 1, 1867, Patton Papers; *Selma Times*, March 17, 1866; *Selma Morning Times*, March 9, 1867; *Independent Monitor*, July 5, 1870; Ralph Kirsher, *The Class of 1861 Custer, Ames, and Their Classmates after West Point* (Carbondale: Southern Illinois University Press, 1999), 54. For Roy, see Hughes, *Old Reliable*, 116, 310–11, 314.

7. Nathan Chambliss to Nathan Lupton, February 5, 1870, Commandant's Book 1867–1887.

8. Nathan Chambliss to Nathan Lupton, February 5, 1870, March [1870?], May 14, 1870, Commandant's Book 1867–1887.

9. University of Alabama Cadet's Ledger 1870–1872, 5, Military Department, W. S. Hoole Special Collections Library, University of Alabama, hereafter cited as Cadet Ledger; Commandant's Book 1867–1887, 114–16, 145–46.

10. Cadet's Ledger, 1870–1872, 10–11, 20.

11. Cadet's Ledger, 1870–1872, 15.

12. Cadet's Ledger, 1870–1872, 13.

13. Cadet's Ledger, 1870–1872, 9.

14. Nathan Chambliss to Nathan Lupton, February 5, 1870, March 1870, Commandant's Book 1867–1887; Nathan Chambliss to Stollenwerck & Bros., March 22,

Notes to Chapter 6

1870; *Names of Citizens of Mobile, A Business Directory, and a Variety of Other Useful Information, 1869* (Mobile, Alabama: Henry Farrow & Co., 1869), 91, City Directories Collection, The Doy Leale McCall Rare Book & Manuscript Library, University of South Alabama, Mobile, Alabama.

15. Nathan Chambliss to Nathan Lupton, February 5, 1870, Commandant's Book 1867–1887; *Southern Republican*, February 2, 1870.

16. Major Nathan Chambliss to Lieutenant Colonel J. R. Waddy, December 29, 1863, Official Records of the Rebellion, series 1, no. 28, 575.

17. Nathan Chambliss to Nathan Lupton, February 5, 1870, March 1870, Commandant's Book 1867–1887.

18. Nathan Chambliss to F. E. Stollenwerck, February 13, 1870; Nathan Chambliss to Nathan Lupton, February 5, 1870, March 1870, Commandant's Book 1867–1887.

19. *Independent Monitor*, March 15, 1870.

20. *Southern Republican*, April 13, 1870.

21. "Ryland Randolph's Scribbles," reel 2, 117–21; *Southern Republican*, April 13, 1870; *Montgomery Mail*, April 17, 1870; *Independent Monitor*, May 3, 1870; Wiggins, "The Life of Ryland Randolph as Seen through His Letters," 169–70; Maxwell, *Autobiography*, 39.

22. *Independent Monitor*, April 26, 1870; *Montgomery Mail*, April 17, 1870, April 18, 1870; *Southern Argus*, April 28, 1870; *Santa Fe New Mexican*, December 28, 1904; Thomas Waverly Palmer, ed., *A Register of the Officers and Students of the University of Alabama, 1831–1901* (Tuscaloosa: University of Alabama, 1901), 463.

23. *Independent Monitor*, July 6, 1869, July 20, 1869, November 8, 1870.

24. Cadet's Ledger, 1870–1872, 3–4, 6, 9, 14, 19, 21–22; Ward W. Briggs Jr., ed., *The Letters of Basil Lanneau Gildersleeve* (Baltimore, MD: Johns Hopkins, 1987), 42.

25. *Selma Press*, May 14, 1870; *Independent Monitor*, April 26, 1870; Gustavus Smith to William Hugh Smith, April 20, 1870, William Hugh Smith Papers.

26. Cornelia Vaughn to William Hugh Smith, April 20, 1870, William Hugh Smith Papers; *Independent Monitor*, May 3, 1870.

27. Gustavus Smith to William Hugh Smith, April 16, 1870, William Hugh Smith Papers; Warner, *Generals in Blue*, 458–59.

28. *Tuscaloosa Observer*, April 23, 1870, April 30, 1870; *Independent Monitor*, April 26, 1870, May 10, 1870; *Selma Press*, May 14, 1870.

29. Cornelia Vaughn to William Hugh Smith, April 20, 1870, William Hugh Smith Papers; *Independent Monitor*, April 26, 1870.

30. Nathan Chambliss to Nathan Lupton, May 14, 1870, Commandant's Book 1867–1887.

31. *Selma Press*, May 14, 1870.

32. Nathan Chambliss to Nathan Lupton, May 14, 1870; Nathan Chambliss to W. S. Mudd, May 25, 1870, Commandant's Book 1867–1887; *Alabama Beacon*, April 30, 1870; *Montgomery Mail*, May 5, 1870; *Independent Monitor*, May 3, 1870, April 19, 1871; *Sun*, April 19, 1870. For T. Osborne, see Palmer, *Register of the Officers and Students of the University of Alabama, 1831–1901*, 457.

33. William Hugh Smith to Josiah Pegus, April 28, 1870, Alabama Governor Secretary Letterbooks 1870–February 1870 to October 1870, Alabama State Department

Notes to Chapter 7

of Archives and History, Montgomery, Alabama; *Tuscaloosa Observer*, April 30, 1870; *Independent Monitor*, April 19, 1870, April 26, 1870, April 19, 1871; *Montgomery Mail*, May 5, 1870.

34. Nathan Chambliss to Nathan Lupton, May 14, 1870, Commandant's Book 1867–1887.

35. Nathan Chambliss to Horace Osborne, May 25, 1870, Commandant's Book 1867–1887.

36. *Independent Monitor*, March 15, 1870; "Ryland Randolph's Scribbles," reel 2, 117–24; Hubbs, *Searching for Freedom*, 48–50; Wiggins, "The Life of Ryland Randolph as Seen through His Letters," 169–71. To date, the author was unable to locate this source.

37. Nathan Chambliss to Noah Cloud, April 21, 1870, Commandant's Book 1867–1877.

38. William Smith obituary, December 1904, Gustavus Adolphus Smith Papers, 1841–1920, Abraham Lincoln Presidential Library, Springfield, Illinois; *Sun*, April 19, 1870; "Ryland Randolph's Scribbles," reel 2, 121; *Independent Monitor*, April 26, 1870.

39. *Montgomery Mail* quoted in *Marion Commonwealth*, May 5, 1870.

40. *Alabama State Journal*, April 8, 1870, May 4, 1870.

41. Nathan Chambliss to Noah Cloud, May 30, 1870, Commandant's Book 1867–1887; Sir Paul Harvey, ed., *The Oxford Companion to English Literature* (Oxford, UK: Clarendon Press, 1967), 620.

42. Nathan Chambliss to Noah Cloud, May 30, 1870, May 14, 1870, Commandant's Book 1867–1887; Nathan Chambliss to Nathan Lupton, May 14, 1870, Commandant's Book 1867–1887; Handlin, *The American College*, 29–30; Cohen, *Reconstructing the Campus*, 29–30.

43. *Shelby County Guide*, May 24, 1870.

44. *Tuscaloosa Observer*, May 28, 1870.

45. Nathan Chambliss to Vernon Vaughn, June 24, 1870, 153; Nathan Chambliss to Nathan Lupton, May 14, May 30, 154–57, Commandant's Book 1867–1887; *Independent Monitor*, June 28, 1870; *Mobile Register*, April 30, 1870; John Simon, ed., *The Papers of Ulysses S. Grant* (Carbondale: Southern Illinois Press, 1998), 21:107.

46. *Independent Monitor*, July 12, 1870, December 28, 1869; *Alabama Beacon*, July 2, 1870; *Alabama State Journal*, July 8, 1870; Minutes of the State Board of Education, 1869–1871, 23, 25.

47. *Alabama Beacon*, July 2, 1870; *Independent Monitor*, July 5, 1870.

48. *Alabama State Journal*, July 8, 1870.

49. *Southern Argus*, January 13, 1871; *Times-Argus*, February 24, 1871; *Marion Commonwealth*, April 13, 1871.

50. Minutes of the State Board of Education, 1869–1871, 25.

Chapter 7

1. Lillian A. Pereya, *James Lusk Alcorn: Persistent Whig* (Baton Rouge: Louisiana State University Press, 1966), 123–24; Hollis, *College to University*, 44–53; Kemp P. Battle, *History of the University of North Carolina 1868–1912* (Raleigh, NC: Edwards & Broughton, 1912), 2:3–12.

2. The standard biography of William Holden is William C. Harris, *William Woods*

Notes to Chapter 7

Holden: Firebrand of North Carolina Politics (Baton Rouge: Louisiana State University Press, 1967); Battle, *History of the University of North Carolina*, 2:2–8.

3. Solomon Pool to John Pool, August 15, 1868, Governor W. W. Holden Papers, State Archives, Raleigh, North Carolina; *Raleigh Sentinel*, January 29, 1869; Harris, *William Woods Holden*, 264–65; Battle, *History of the University of North Carolina*, 2:10–11. For the economic relationship between a university and town, see Don H. Doyle, *Faulkner's County: The Historical Roots of Yoknapatawpha* (Chapel Hill: University of North Carolina Press, 1991), 94–99.

4. *Raleigh Sentinel*, January 29, 1869, February 9, 1869; Deborah Beckel, *Radical Reform: Interracial Politics in Post-Emancipation North Carolina* (Charlottesville: University of Virginia, 2011), 68–69, 71.

5. *Raleigh Sentinel*, April 6, 1869.

6. *Raleigh Sentinel*, May 6, 1869, June 3, 1869. For Brewer and Martling, see Battle, *History of the University of North Carolina, Vol. 2*, 10–11. For Fisk Brewer, see Fisk Parsons Brewer and William P. Vaughn, "'South Carolina University—1876' of Fisk Parsons B. Brewer." For Vaughn, see William P. Vaughn in *The South Carolina Historical Magazine*, vol. 76, no. 4 (October 1975): 225–28.

7. Alexander McIver to Cornelia Spencer, 1869, Spencer Papers. For McIver and Patrick, see Battle, *History of the University of North Carolina*, 2:10.

8. Alexander McIver to Cornelia Spencer, 1869, Spencer Papers.

9. Battle, *History of the University of North Carolina*, 2:9.

10. Battle, *History of the University of North Carolina*, 2:35; William D. Snider, *Light on the Hill: A History of the University of North Carolina at Chapel Hill* (Chapel Hill: University of North Carolina Press, 1992), 75.

11. Cornelia Spencer to Mrs. Laura [Charles] Phillips, June 14, 1869, Spencer Papers; *Raleigh Sentinel*, March 12, 1869, April 8, 1869; Battle, *History of the University of North Carolina*, 2:24.

12. For a biography of Cornelia Spencer, see John C. Inscoe, "To Do Justice to North Carolina: The War's End According to Cornelia Phillips Spencer, Zebulon B. Vance, and David L. Swain," in *North Carolinians in the Era of the Civil War and Reconstruction*, ed. Paul D. Escott (Chapel Hill: University of North Carolina Press, 2008), 133–34; Cornelia Pamela Blair Gwin, "'Poisoned Arrows' from a Tar Heel Journalist: The Public Career of Cornelia Phillips Spencer, 1865–1890," (PhD. diss., Duke University, 1983), 87–125.

13. *Raleigh Sentinel*, May 6, 1869; Vaughn, ed., "Brewer, South Carolina University—1876," 226–28; Fisk Brewer, *Roman Family Coins in the Yale College Collection* (New Haven, CT: Tuttle, Morehouse & Taylor, 1860).

14. Cornelia Spencer to Charles Phillips, April 26, 1869, Spencer Papers; Gwin, "Poisoned Arrows," 87, 108–09.

15. *Raleigh Sentinel*, April 16, 1871, March 24, 1871.

16. Cornelia Spencer to Mrs. Laura, [Charles] Phillips, August 6, 1869, Spencer Papers; Battle, *History of the University of North Carolina*, 2:19.

17. Cornelia Spencer to Mrs. Laura [Charles] Phillips, June 14, 1869, Spencer Papers; *Raleigh Sentinel*, June 12, 1869; *North Carolina Standard*, June 12, 1869; Battle, *History of the University of North Carolina*, 2:34–35.

Notes to Chapter 7

18. *Raleigh Sentinel*, August 27, 1869, November 12, 1869, February 3, 1870; Battle, *History of the University of North Carolina*, 2:20–25.

19. Battle, *History of the University of North Carolina*, 2:11; *Raleigh Sentinel*, February 3, 1870.

20. *Raleigh Sentinel*, February 3, 1870; Cornelia Spencer to Laura, December 18, 1869, Spencer Papers.

21. Cornelia Spencer to Laura, August 6, 1869, Spencer Papers.

22. *Wilmington Journal* quoted in *Charleston Daily Courier*, September 23, 1869.

23. *Charleston Daily Courier*, December 4, 1868, December 17, 1868, January 7, 1869, July 8, 1869, July 17, 1869; *Charleston Daily News*, December 18, 1868, January 7, 1869; Parry, "Examining Desegregation at the University of South Carolina," 32–34; Hollis, *College to University*, 46–50. For Whipper, see Hyman Rubin III, *South Carolina Scalawags* (Columbia: University of South Carolina Press, 2006), 33, 60.

24. "Prof. Rivers Report," May 2, 1867, in University of South Carolina Board of Trustees, vol. 7, 1858–1869, 261.

25. "University of South Carolina Department of Mathematics. Intermediate Examination. Senior Class—February 1869," Edward Porter Alexander Papers, 1852–1910, Southern Historical Collection, University of North Carolina, Chapel Hill, North Carolina; *Columbia Phoenix*, August 7, 1867; Hollis, *College to University*, 40, 50–51.

26. William D. Armes, ed., *The Autobiography of Joseph Le Conte* (New York: D. Appleton, 1903), 239; *Charleston Daily News*, January 18, 1869; Stephens, *Joseph LeConte: Gentle Prophet of Evolution*, 104–08.

27. Porter Alexander to father, January 5, 1869, Adam Leopold Alexander Papers, David M. Rubenstein Rare Book & Manuscript Library, Duke University; *Charleston Daily News*, November 26, 1868, January 7, 1869.

28. *Charleston Daily Courier*, July 17, 1869; Robert Barnwell, "Report of the Chairman of the Faculty," in University of South Carolina Board of Trustees, vol. 7, 1858–1869, 324; Stephens, *Joseph LeConte*, 10; Hollis, *College to University*, 47.

29. *Columbia Phoenix* quoted in *Charleston Daily Courier*, September 22, 1869, September 23, 1869; Hollis, *College to University*, 50–52.

30. *Chester Reporter* quoted in *Charleston Daily Courier*, September 25, 1869; Hollis, *College to University*, 54.

31. *Charleston Daily Courier*, October 1, 1869; Hollis, *College to University*, 57–58.

32. *Charleston Daily Courier*, October 1, 1869; Hollis, *College to University*, 57–58.

33. *Sumter Watchman* quoted in *Charleston Daily Courier*, October 1, 1869.

34. *Charleston Daily Courier*, October 1, 1869, December 17, 1859.

35. *Weekly Mississippi Pilot*, December 10, 1870; Waddel, *Memorials of Academic Life*, 474–75.

36. Pereyra, *James Lusk Alcorn*, 106–07, 115–16, 128–30; Harris, *Day of the Carpetbagger*, 343–46.

37. *Weekly Clarion*, September 1, 1870; Harris, *Day of the Carpetbagger*, 345.

38. *Weekly Clarion*, August 18, 1870.

39. Harris, *Day of the Carpetbagger*, 345–46; *Weekly Mississippi Pilot*, April 27, 1870, August 27, 1870; Waddel, *Memorials of Academic Life*, 469–70, 474. For Quinche, see

Notes to Chapter 7

Cabaniss, *A History of the University of Mississippi*, 60–61, 63. For Tarbell, see Harris, *Day of the Carpetbagger*, 70, 183, 202.

40. *Weekly Clarion*, September 15, 1870; Harris, *Day of the Carpetbagger*, 345. For Warner, see Harris, *Day of the Carpetbagger*, 54, 61.

41. *Independent Monitor* quoted in *Weekly Clarion*, September 29, 1870. For Clarke, see Harris, *Day of the Carpetbagger*, 70, 92, 106–07.

42. *Weekly Mississippi Pilot*, September 17, 1870; Abbott, *For Free Press and Equal Rights*, 40, 58, 75–77.

43. *Weekly Mississippi Pilot*, October 15, 1870; Sansing, *The University of Mississippi*, 130.

44. Waddel, *Memorials of Academic Life*, 469; Pereyra, *James Lusk Alcorn*, 123–24.

45. *Testimony Taken by the Joint Select Committee to Inquire into the Condition of Affairs in the Late Insurrectionary States*, Mississippi, 1: 88; *Weekly Mississippi Pilot*, October 15, 1870; Jackson *Weekly Clarion*, October 6, 1870. For Flourney, see Harris, *Day of the Carpetbagger*, 94, 104, 232, 347; and Abbott, *For Free Press and Equal Rights*, 53, 121.

46. *Fayette Chronicle* quoted in *Weekly Clarion*, September 15, 1870; *Historical Catalogue of the Trustees, Faculties, and Alumni of the University of Mississippi* (Oxford, 1870), 26–30; *Catalogue of the Officers and Students of the University of Mississippi for the Session of 1870–71* (Oxford, 1871), 5–7.

47. *Weekly Clarion*, September 8, 1870, September 15, 1870.

48. *Weekly Clarion*, September 1, 1870, September 15, 1870. For Pegues, see Doyle, *Faulkner's County*, 97, 183, 245, 275.

49. Samuel C. Caldwell to Doctor, May 4, 1927, Allen Cabaniss Collection, Archives and Special Collections, J. D. Williams Library, University of Mississippi, Oxford, Mississippi, 5, hereafter cited as Allen Cabaniss Collection; Harris, *Day of the Carpetbagger*, 345.

50. Robert Barnard to father, November 15, 1870, F. A. P. Barnard Collection, Archives and Special Collections, J. D. Williams Library, University of Mississippi, Oxford, Mississippi.

51. S. C. Caldwell to "Doctor," May 4, 1927, Allen Cabaniss Collection, Archives and Special Collections, 3–4, 16–18; *Weekly Clarion*, August 25, 1870.

52. *Weekly Clarion*, March 29, 1871.

53. *Brownlow's Knoxville Whig*, July 29, 1868; *Knoxville Press and Register*, June 23, 1869, October 13, 1869, September 22, 1869; *Knoxville Whig* quoted in *Nashville Union and American*, October 31, 1869. For Humes, see Hutton, *Bearing the Torch*, 24, and Robert Tracy McKenzie, *Lincolnites and Rebels: A Divided Town in the American Civil War* (New York: Oxford University Press, 2006), 6–7, 142–43; John Bell Brownlow to Governor Andrew Johnson, June 26, 1871, in *The Papers of Andrew Johnson*, eds. Leroy P. Graf and Ralph Haskins (Knoxville: University of Tennessee Press, 1976), 4: 517–18.

54. *Brownlow's Knoxville Whig*, December 30, 1868; *Knoxville Press and Register*, April 16, 1868, June 18, 1868, June 23, 1869, October 13, 1869; *Charleston Daily News*, April 10, 1868; Bruce, *History of the University of Virginia*, 4: 51.

55. *Brownlow's Knoxville Whig*, December 30, 1868; Montgomery, Folmsbee, and Greene, *To Foster Knowledge*, 74–75.

56. *Knoxville Press and Register*, June 9, 1869.

Notes to Chapter 8

57. *Knoxville Press and Register,* October 13, 1869, December 2, 1869; *Knoxville Daily Chronicle,* June 12, 1870.

58. Boyd to Semmes, November 24, 1866, Semmes Family Papers; Hoffman, *Louisiana State University,* 27. For Warmoth, see Richard N. Current, "The Carpetbagger as Corruptionist: Henry Clay Warmoth," in *Reconstruction an Anthology of Revisionist Writings,* eds. Kenneth M. Stampp and Leon Litwack (Baton Rouge: Louisiana State University Press, 1969), 241–63.

59. William Sherman to David Boyd, August 17, 1868, William Sherman Papers; Hoffman, *Louisiana State University,* 31; Ted Tunnell, *Crucible of Reconstruction War, Radicalism and Race in Louisiana, 1862–1877* (Baton Rouge: Louisiana State University Press, 1984), 161–62, 167–69; Henry Clay Warmoth, *Politics and Reconstruction Stormy Days in Louisiana* (New York: Macmillan, 1930), 88–89.

60. Boyd to Sherman, July 29, 1868, David Boyd Letterbooks; Hoffman, *Louisiana State University,* 30–31; Reed, *David French Boyd,* 69–71.

61. Reed, *David French Boyd,* 71; Hoffman, *Louisiana State University,* 30–31; Tunnell, *Crucible of Reconstruction,* 169; Fleming, *Louisiana State University 1860–1896,* 150–54.

62. *Louisiana Democrat,* October 20, 1869, November 3, 1869; *Daily Picayune,* December 17, 1869; Fleming, *Louisiana State University 1860–1896,* 168, 184–85; Reed, *David French Boyd,* 87–88.

63. *Daily Dispatch,* September 30, 1869.

64. Phillip Alexander Bruce, *History of the University of Virginia 1819–1919* (New York: Macmillan, 1921), 4:196.

65. *Daily Dispatch,* September 30, 1869.

66. Walter Hill to Barnard Hill June 27, 1869; Walter Hill to Mary Clay Hill, March 28, 1868, April 4, 1868; Walter Hill to Mary Clay Hill, May 16, 1868; Walter Hill to Mary Clay Hill, 27, 1870, in Gerald R. Mathis, ed., *College Life in the Reconstruction South: Walter B. Hill's Student Correspondence, University of Georgia, 1869–1871* (Athens: University of Georgia Libraries Miscellanea Publications, 1974), 46, 94, 146; Harris, *Autobiography,* 153–55. For Bryant, see Ruth Currie-McDaniel, *Carpetbagger of Conscience: A Biography of John Emory Bryant* (Athens: University of Georgia Press, 1987); Joseph H. Parks, *Joseph E. Brown of Georgia* (Baton Rouge: Louisiana State University Press, 1977), 406–33.

67. Waddel, *Memorials of Academic Life,* 470.

68. Warmoth, *Politics and Reconstruction Stormy Days in Louisiana,* 92–93; Horace W. Raper, *William Holden: North Carolina's Political Enigma* (Chapel Hill: University of North Carolina Press, 1985), 125–26, 265–66; Pereyra, *James Lusk Alcorn,* 124–28; Harris, *Day of the Carpetbagger,* 347–49; Montgomery, Folmsbee, and Greene, *To Foster Knowledge,* 75, 80; Fleming, *Louisiana State University,* 155–58; *Journal of the House of Representatives of the State of Tennessee Thirty-Sixth General Assembly, Convened at Nashville, on Monday, October 1869* (Nashville, TN: Jones, Purvis & Co., 1869), 616–19; Snider, *Light on the Hill,* 75–84; Foner, *Reconstruction,* 368–72.

69. Cornelia Spencer to Charles Phillips, Spencer Papers, April 26, 1869.

CHAPTER 8

1. *Tuscaloosa Observer,* September 4, 1870.

2. *Independent Monitor,* August 16, 1870.

Notes to Chapter 8

3. *Livingston Journal*, October 28, 1865; Minutes of the State Board of Education, 1869–1871, 25–26. For Smith, see Williams, *A Literary History of Alabama*, 28–39; *Independent Monitor*, September 27, 1870.

4. Simon, ed., *The Papers of Ulysses S. Grant*, 22: 360.

5. Hampton Whitfield to Raphael Semmes, July 3, 1869, Semmes Family Papers; Minutes of the State Board of Education, 1869–1871, 25–26; *Independent Monitor*, July 12, 1870; *Montgomery Advertiser*, February 5, 1885.

6. Buford, "The Last Roll Call: Col. Nathan Rives Chambliss," 203; Chambliss to Lupton, May 14, 1870, Commandant's Book 1867–1887; *Independent Monitor*, July 5, 1870, July 12, 1870; Wiggins, "Life of Ryland Randolph as Seen through His Letters," 175.

7. *Independent Monitor*, August 23, 1870. For Taylor, see Rogers, *Black Belt Scalawag*, 35, 57.

8. *Independent Monitor*, August 16, 1870, August 23, 1870, April 26, 1871.

9. Joseph Taylor to Robert McKee, July 31, 1870, Robert McKee Papers, Alabama State Department of Archives and History; *Southern Argus*, August 12, 1869, August 25, 1870.

10. *Independent Monitor*, July 5, 1870.

11. *Independent Monitor*, August 2, 1870.

12. *Independent Monitor*, July 5, 1870, August 2, 1870, November 29, 1870; Simon, ed. *Papers of Ulysses Grant*, 21: 107.

13. *Alabama State Journal*, October 7, 1870; *Independent Monitor*, August 30, 1870; *Minutes of the State Board of Education, 1869–1871*, 218.

14. David S. Edelstein, *Joel Munsell: Printer and Antiquarian* (New York: Columbia University Press, 1950), 365; Palmer, ed., *Register of the Officers and Students of the University of Alabama*, 456.

15. *Livingston Journal*, October 28, 1865; William R. Smith to Joseph Hodgson, January 25, 1871, in *Special Report of Joseph Hodgson, Superintendent Public Instruction of the State of Alabama, to the Governor, January 1871* (Montgomery, AL: W. W. Screws, 1871), 45–46, hereafter cited as *Special Report of Joseph Hodgson*.

16. *Independent Monitor*, April 20, 1870; Edelstein, *Joel Munsell*, 365.

17. *Independent Monitor*, September 27, 1870; *Weekly Alabama State Journal*, August 26, 1870. For Lindsay, see Samuel L. Webb and Margaret E. Armbrester, eds., *Alabama Governors: A Political History of the State* (Tuscaloosa: University of Alabama Press, 2001); Michael W. Fitzgerald, "Robert B. Lindsay, 1870–1872," 90–93. For Hodgson, see Owen, *Dictionary of Alabama Biography*, 3:823–24.

18. *Montgomery Daily Mail*, September 3, 1870.

19. *Weekly Alabama State Journal*, October 7, 1870; *Weekly Huntsville Advocate*, September 16, 1870; Rogers, *Partisan Politics in a Deep South State*, 147–52.

20. *Independent Monitor*, November 8, 1870; Fitzgerald, *Reconstruction in Alabama*, 239–48.

21. Fitzgerald, "Robert B. Lindsay, 1870–1872," in *Alabama Governors*, eds. Webb and Armbrester (Tuscaloosa: University of Alabama, 2001), 90–93; Rogers, *Reconstruction Politics in a Deep South State*, 186–89.

22. *Montgomery Daily Mail*, December 11, 1870; *Daily State Sentinel*, October 7, 1867; "Alabama Testimony," James H. Clanton, 248.

23. *Weekly Alabama State Journal*, December 16, 1870; *Daily State Sentinel*, October 7, 1867; Michael W. Fitzgerald, *Reconstruction in Alabama: From Civil War to Redemption in the Cotton South* (Baton Rouge: Louisiana State University Press, 2017), 330, 335.

24. *Montgomery Advertiser*, December 17, 1870; Minutes of the State Board of Education, 1869–1871, 29–31; *Independent Monitor*, December 13, 1870.

25. Joseph Hodgson to Matthew Maury, January 28, 1871, Matthew Maury Papers, LOC; Hampton Whitfield to Raphael Semmes, July 3, 1869, Semmes Papers; *Independent Monitor*, July 12, 1871; *Alabama Beacon*, July 15, 1871; *Alabama State Journal*, November 7, 1875.

26. Maury to My Dear Friend, February 10, 1871, Mathew Maury Papers, LOC; *Independent Monitor*, July 12, 1871.

27. Joseph Tait to Joseph Hodgson, January 14, 1871, in *Special Report of Joseph Hodgson*, 49–52. For Tait, see *Alabama State Journal*, June 10, 1871. Conchology is the study of shells.

28. Hodgson, *Special Report of Joseph Hodgson*, 45–47.

29. Robert Lindsay to "Gentlemen of the Senate," *Journal of the Session of 1870–71 of the Senate of Alabama*, 168–69. For Lindsay, see Fitzgerald, "Robert B. Lindsay, 1870–1872," in *Alabama Governors*, eds. Webb and Armbrester (Tuscaloosa: University of Alabama, 2001), 90–93.

30. William Rufus Smith to Joseph Hodgson, January 25, 1871, in *Special Report of Joseph Hodgson*, 45–47; *Charleston Daily News*, April 10, 1868.

31. *Livingston Journal*, October 28, 1865.

32. "Alabama Testimony," Joseph Speed, 426.

33. "Alabama Testimony," Joseph Speed, 418. The author has been unable to confirm the attendance of a cadet with the last name of "Seavey." For Harton, Muncell, and Smith, see Palmer, *A Register of the Offices and Students of the University of Alabama*, 446, 456, 463; Edelstein, *Joel Munsell*, 365.

34. [?] to William Hugh Smith, May 1, 1870, William Hugh Smith Papers; *Independent Monitor*, April 19, 1870; *Tuscaloosa Observer*, November 26, 1870; Rogers, *Black Belt Scalawag*, 68–71. For murders in Calhoun County, see Gene L. Howard, *Death at Cross Plains: An Alabama Reconstruction Tragedy* (Tuscaloosa: University of Alabama Press, 1984), 23, 46–48, 76–79.

35. "Alabama Testimony," 418, Joseph Speed, 423; Edelstein, *Joel Munsell*, 365.

36. "Alabama Testimony," Joseph Speed, 423; *Tuscaloosa Observer*, November 26, 1870.

37. Robert Somers, *The Southern States since the War, 1870–71* (London, UK: MacMillan, 1871), 159–60; *Journal of the Session of 1870–71 of the Senate of Alabama, Held in the City of Montgomery. Commencing on the 21st November 1870* (Montgomery, AL: W. W. Screws, 1871), 351; *Independent Monitor*, April 26, May 10, 1871.

38. *Tuscaloosa Observer*, February 4, 1871, February 18, 1871.

39. *Independent Monitor*, January 31, 1871, March 7, 1871, March 14, 1871, March 21, 1871, March 28, 1871.

40. *Bluff City Times*, March 23, 1871.

41. *Independent Monitor*, May 24, 1871, July 5, 1871. For Somerville, see *Livingston Journal*, March 3, 1871.

42. *Independent Monitor*, April 26, 1871.

43. *Evergreen Observer* quoted in *Independent Monitor*, April 11, 1871.
44. *Independent Monitor*, June 7, 1871.
45. *Tuscaloosa Observer*, April 1, 1871.
46. *Evergreen Observer* quoted in *Independent Monitor*, April 11, 1871; *Tuscaloosa Observer*, April 29, 1871; *Independent Monitor*, May 24, 1871.
47. *Independent Monitor*, May 17, 1871; *Alabama State Journal*, May 25, 1871.
48. *Independent Monitor*, July 5, 1871.
49. *Independent Monitor*, June 21, 1871.
50. *Tuscaloosa Observer*, June 21, 1871; *Independent Monitor*, June 21, 1871.
51. *Tuscaloosa Observer*, May 27, 1871, June 17, 1871; Minutes of the State Board of Education, 1869–1871, 38; *Independent Monitor*, July 19, 1871; *Alabama State Journal*, June 20, 1871.
52. *Independent Monitor*, July 19, 1871.
53. Thomas Cook to Matthew Maury, April 4, 1871, Matthew Maury Papers, LOC.
54. *Independent Monitor*, July 19, 1871.
55. *Independent Monitor*, June 14, 1871; July 19, 1871, July 26, 1871; August 2, 1871.
56. *Tuscaloosa Observer*, June 24, 1871; *Independent Monitor*, June 21, 1871.
57. *Independent Monitor*, July 26, 1871.
58. *Montgomery Advertiser and Mail* quoted in *Independent Monitor*, July 5, 1871; *Independent Monitor*, June 21, 1871; Minutes of the State Board of Education, 1869–1871, 43–44, 48.
59. *Selma Times* quoted in *Independent Monitor*, July 5, 1871.
60. *Tuscaloosa Observer*, June 24, 1871.
61. Robert H. McKenzie, "William Russell Smith: Forgotten President of the University of Alabama," *Alabama Review*, vol. 37 (July 1984): 174–77; *Independent Monitor*, June 21, 1871; Williams, *A Literary History of Alabama*, 37.

Chapter 9

1. Thomas Cook to Matthew Maury, April 14, 1871, Matthew Maury Papers, LOC; *Alabama Beacon*, July 1, 1871; *Tuscaloosa Observer*, July 22, 1871; *Selma Times and Messenger*, July 1, 1871.
2. For a fine, brief summary of Maury's career, see *Dictionary of American Biography*, 12:428–31. An interesting angle is provided by Peter C. Thomas, "Matthew Fontaine Maury and the Problem of Virginia's Identity, 1865–1873," *The Virginia Magazine of History and Biography* 90, no. 2 (April 1982), 213–37. The definitive biography is Williams, *Matthew Fontaine Maury: Scientist of the Sea* (New Brunswick, NJ: Rutgers University Press, 1963).
3. Sarah Mytton Maury, *The Statesmen of America in 1846* (Philadelphia, PA: Carey & Hart, 1847); *Dictionary of American Biography*, 12:428–31.
4. Williams, *Matthew Maury*, 192.
5. Williams, *Matthew Maury*, 348–420.
6. Williams, *Matthew Maury*, 422–58. For Maury in Mexico, see Rolle, *The Lost Cause*, 131–54; Thomas, "Maury and the Problem of Virginia's Identify," 215–21.
7. *Tuscaloosa Observer*, June 24, 1871.
8. Matthew Maury to Welford Corbin, June 17, 1869, Matthew Maury Papers, LOC; Williams, *Matthew Maury*, 159.

Notes to Chapter 9

9. Francis W. Tremlett to Matthew Maury, July 29, 1869, Matthew Maury Papers, LOC; Williams, *Matthew Maury*, 465–66.

10. Williams, *Matthew Maury*, 344, 176, 183, 458–68.

11. Calvin Loomis to Matthew Maury, October 1, 1869, Matthew Maury Papers, LOC.

12. Note to Loomis, Lexington, 1869, Matthew Maury Papers, LOC; Williams, *Matthew Maury*, 177, 346.

13. Daniel Troy to Matthew Maury, September 1, 1871; Joseph Hodgson to Matthew Maury, January 28, 1871, Matthew Maury Papers, LOC; Williams, *Matthew Maury*, 158, 183, 311, 333.

14. Joseph Hodgson to Matthew Maury, January 28, 1871, Matthew Maury Papers, LOC.

15. Matthew Maury to My Dear Friend, February 10, 1871, Matthew Maury Papers, LOC; Williams, *Matthew Maury*, 466–69.

16. Joseph Hodgson to Matthew Maury, February 5, 1871, Matthew Maury Papers, LOC.

17. Joseph Hodgson to Matthew Maury, April 15, 1871, Mathew Maury Papers, LOC.

18. Thomas Cook to Matthew Maury, April 14, 1871, Matthew Maury Papers, LOC. For Cook, see E. Grace Jemison, *Historic Tales of Talladega* (Montgomery, AL: Paragon Press, 1959), 250–51, 261.

19. James Murfee to Matthew Maury, May 1, 1871, Matthew Maury Papers, LOC.

20. Thomas Cook to Matthew Maury, May 19, 1871, Matthew Maury Papers, LOC.

21. Catesby ap Roger Jones to Matthew Maury, May 5, 1871; John Gilmer to Matthew Maury, April 4, 1871, Matthew Maury Papers, LOC. For Jones, see Maxine Turner, *Navy Gray: A Story of the Confederate Navy on the Chattahoochee and Apalachicola Rivers* (Tuscaloosa: University of Alabama Press, 1988), 62–65.

22. [?] to Maury, May 25, 1871; Benjamin Ewell to Matthew Maury, March 30, 1871; Walter Blair to Matthew Maury, May 12, 1871, Matthew Maury Papers, LOC.

23. Hodgson to Matthew Maury, June 21, 1871; Rutson Maury to Matthew Maury, June 21, 1871, Matthew Maury Papers, LOC. Rutson was a cousin of Maury. See Williams, *Matthew Maury*, 124; *Independent Monitor*, June 21, 1871.

24. *Montgomery Advertiser and Mail* quoted in *Independent Monitor*, July 5, 1871; *Tuscaloosa Observer*, July 22, 1871; *Alabama Beacon*, July 15, 1871.

25. *Weekly Clarion*, August 17, 1871.

26. *Alabama State Journal*, July 8, 1871, July 21, 1871; *Montgomery Advertiser*, July 18–21, 1871; Williams, *Matthew Maury*, 140, 167, 375, 402.

27. Matthew Maury to Nannie, July 26, 1871, Matthew Maury Papers, VMI Archives; "Report of Joseph Hodgson, Superintendent of Public Instruction, of the State of Alabama, for the Scholastic Year, January 1, 1871, to September 30, 1871" (Montgomery, AL: W. W. Screws, 1871), 27, hereafter cited as Report of Joseph Hodgson; *Alabama State Journal*, June 20, 1871; *Tuscaloosa Observer*, September 23, 1871; Williams, *Matthew Maury*, 119.

28. Matthew Maury to Nannie, July 26, 1871, Maury Papers, VMI Archives; William Wyman to Maury, August 17, 1871, "General Correspondence of 1871–1872 (Acting) President Wyman," 1–3, W. S. Hoole Special Collections Library, University of Alabama.

Notes to Chapter 10

29. Matthew Maury to Charles Todd Quintard, January 4, 1868, Charles Todd Quintard Papers, William R. Laurie University Archives and Special Collections, University of the South, Sewanee, Tennessee; Chitty, *Reconstruction at Sewanee* (Sewanee, TN: University Press, 1954), 105–07.

30. Matthew Maury to Nannie, July 26, 1871, Maury Papers, VMI Archives.

31. Williams, *Matthew Maury*, 469; copy of Western Union telegram, July 29, 1871, "Hodgson to Maury," Matthew Maury Papers, LOC.

32. *West Alabamian*, July 19, 1871.

33. *Independent Monitor*, August 23, 1871; Cohen, *Reconstructing the Campus*, 16, 73–75.

34. Joseph Hodgson to Matthew Maury, July 29, 1871, Matthew Maury Papers, LOC.

35. Joseph Hodgson to Matthew Maury, August 12, 1871, Matthew Maury Papers, LOC.

36. William Wyman to Maury, August 17, 1871, "General Correspondence of 1871–1872 (Acting) President Wyman," 1–3.

37. Matthew Maury to Wellford Corbin, August 17, 1871, Matthew Maury Papers, LOC.

38. Joseph Hodgson to Matthew Maury, August 24, 1871, Matthew Maury Papers, LOC.

39. William Wyman to Matthew Maury, August 22, 1871, "General Correspondence of 1871–1872 (Acting) President Wyman," 4.

40. Joseph Hodgson to Matthew Maury, August 24, 1871, Matthew Maury Papers, LOC.

41. Daniel Troy to Matthew Maury, September 1, 1871, Matthew Maury Papers, LOC. For Troy, see Owen, *Dictionary of Alabama Biography*, 4:1685–86.

42. *Tuscaloosa Observer*, September 23, 1871.

43. *Montgomery Advertiser and Mail* quoted in *Tuscaloosa Observer*, September 23, 1871.

44. *Alabama State Journal*, September 22, 1871.

45. *Independent Monitor*, June 21, 1871, July 13, 1871, September 27, 1871.

46. *Southern Argus* quoted in *Tuscaloosa Observer*, September 30, 1871.

47. Raphael Semmes to Frank Tremlett, January 5, 1872, Frank W. Tremlett Papers, Virginia Museum of History and Culture, Richmond, Virginia.

48. *Mobile Register*, October 5, 1871; Williams, *Matthew Maury*, 176, 183, 327, 343.

49. *Independent Monitor*, August 23, 1871.

50. Daniel Troy to Maury, September 1, 1871, Matthew Maury Papers, LOC.

51. M. Scheles de Vere to Miss Mary, October 6, 1871, Matthew Maury Papers, LOC.

Chapter 10

1. William H. Price to Matthew Maury, October 11, 1871, Matthew Maury Papers, LOC.

2. *Independent Monitor*, September 13, 1871, September 20, 1871, October 4, 1871.

3. *Tuscaloosa Observer*, June 24, 1871.

4. Algernon Garnett to wife, September 21, 1871, Alice and Algernon Garnett

Papers, W. S. Hoole Special Collections Library, University of Alabama; Hodgson, "Report of Joseph Hodgson," 27; *Independent Monitor*, August 23, 1871.

5. *Tuscaloosa Observer*, October 14, 1871; *Independent Monitor*, October 11, 1871; *Catalogue of the University of Alabama, Session of 1871–72* (Selma, AL: Jas. P. Armstrong, 1872), 9–12.

6. Faculty Minutes 1871–1879, 2.

7. *Tuscaloosa Observer*, October 28, 1781, November 11, 1871; *Historical Catalogue of the Officers and Alumni of the University of Alabama, 1821 to 1870*, 20, 29; Sellers, *History of the University of Alabama*, 266, 310, 312; Hodgson, "Report of Joseph Hodgson," 27. Not all were impressed by martial ardor. A critic of the university's military connection would in 1873 write that he knew "noting more provocative of ridicule than to see a set of boys dressed in brass buttons and bob-tail coats, paraded around like a set of monkeys for the amusement of an idle crowd." *Birmingham News* quoted in *Tuscaloosa Blade*, August 21, 1873.

8. *Southern Argus*, October 20, 1871.

9. *Tuscaloosa Observer*, December 2, 1871; Journal of the Proceedings of the Board of Education of the State of Alabama, 233–34, 242–43; Sellers, *History of the University of Alabama*, 312–13.

10. *Selma Morning Times*, March 9, 1897; Buford, "The Last Roll Call: Col. Nathan Rives Chambliss," 203; *Scottsboro Citizen*, September 5, 1879; *Henry County Register*, April 15, November 19, 1871.

11. *Moulton Advertiser*, March 3, 1872; Wiggins, "J. DeForest Richards, a Vermont Carpetbagger in Alabama," 105; *Sacramento Bee*, October 1, 1878, December 2, 1878; *Ogden Semi-Weekly Junction*, December 4, 1878; *Salt Lake Daily Telegraph*, October 25, 1926.

CONCLUSION

1. *Tuscaloosa Observer*, December 17, 1870; *Independent Monitor*, February 9, 1869; Richard Nelson Current, *Those Terrible Carpetbaggers: A Reinterpretation* (New York: Oxford University Press, 1988), 154; Hubbs, *Searching for Freedom*, 181.

2. Calvin Loomis to Elias Loomis, April 19, 1869, Loomis Papers.

3. Recent relevant scholarship is Michael David Cohen, *Reconstructing the Campus Higher Education and the American Civil War* (Charlottesville: University of Virginia Press, 2012), 204; Robert Greene II and Tyler D. Parry, eds., *Invisible No More: The African American Experience at the University of South Carolina* (Columbia: University of South Carolina Press, 2021); T. R. C. Hutton, *Bearing the Cross: The University of Tennessee, 1794–2010* (Knoxville: University of Tennessee Press, 2022).

4. Stephen V. Ash, *When the Yankees Came: Conflict and Chaos in the Occupied South* (Chapel Hill: University of North Carolina Press, 1995), 172.

5. Harris, Campbell, and Brophy, *Slavery and the University*, 117.

6. DeForest Richards to Asa Smith, June 14, 1869, DeForest Richards Alumni File.

7. Sellers, *History of the University of Alabama*, 42.

8. J. Mills Thornton, *Politics and Power in a Slave Society Alabama, 1800–1860* (Baton Rouge: Louisiana State University Press, 1978), xv.

9. *Alabama State Journal*, June 6, 1871.

10. Fitzgerald, *Reconstruction in Alabama*, 325, 330.

Bibliography

Primary Sources
Unpublished

Abraham Lincoln Presidential Museum and Library, Springfield, Illinois
Gustavus Adolphus Smith Papers

Alabama Department of Archives and History, Montgomery, Alabama
Hardee Family Papers
Governor Lewis E. Parsons Papers, 1831–1891
Governor Robert M. Patton Papers
Governor William H. Smith Papers
Governor William H. Smith Letterbooks (July 1868–July 1869)
Governor William H. Smith Letterbooks (February 1870–October 1871)
Minutes of the State Board of Education, 1869–1871
Robert McKee Papers
Semmes Family Papers
Wager Swayne Papers

American Heritage Center, University of Wyoming, Laramie, Wyoming
Richards Family Papers

Doy Leale McCall Rare Book and Manuscript Library, University of South Alabama, Mobile, Alabama
Names of Citizens of Mobile, A Business Directory and A Variety of Other Useful Information. Mobile, AL: Henry Farrow & Co., 1869.

Hargrett Rare Book and Manuscript Library, University of Georgia, Athens, Georgia
Minutes of the Proceedings of the Board of Trustees of the University of Georgia, Volume 4

J. D. Williams Library Archives and Special Collections, Oxford, Mississippi
Allen Cabaniss Papers
Frederick Augustus Porter Barnard Papers
University of Mississippi Minutes of the Board of Trustees, 1860–1872, Volume 2

Bibliography

Library of Congress, Washington, DC
Matthew Fontaine Maury Papers, 1825–1960, Manuscript Division

Louisiana State University Archives, LSU Libraries, Baton Rouge, Louisiana
David Boyd Letterbooks
Reminiscences of the Louisiana State Seminary and Military Academy in 1867
Samuel Lockett Papers
William Sherman Papers

Mississippi Department of Archives and History, Jackson, Mississippi
Eugene W. Hilgard Papers

National Archives, Washington, DC
Records of the United States Army Continental Commands, Third Military District, Records Group 60

National Archives, Morrow, Georgia
Records of the Assistant Commissioner for the State of Alabama, Bureau of Refugees, Freedmen, and Abandoned Lands, 1865–1869, Records Group 105
Records of the Superintendent of Education for the State of Alabama, Bureau of Refugees, Freedmen, and Abandoned Lands, Records Group 105

North Carolina State Archives, Raleigh, North Carolina
Governor William W. Holden Papers

Oberlin College Archives, Oberlin, Ohio
Student File [Frederick DeForest Allen] Alumni & Development Records

Rauner Special Collections Library, Dartmouth College, Hanover, New Hampshire
Jonas DeForest Richards Papers

Samford University Special Collections, Birmingham, Alabama
Ryland Randolph Papers

South Carolina Library, University of South Carolina, Columbia, South Carolina
Charles Todd Quintard Papers
John LeConte Papers
University of South Carolina Board of Trustees Minutes, Volume 7 (1858–1869)
William J. Rivers Papers

Southern Historical Collection, Wilson Library, University of North Carolina, Chapel Hill, North Carolina
Basil Manly Jr. Papers
Cornelia Phillips Spencer Papers
Edward Alexander Porter Papers
University of North Carolina Faculty Minutes, 1856–1885

Special Collections and Archives, Auburn University, Auburn, Alabama
Mary Anne Norton-Black Papers
University of Alabama Minutes of Board of Regents (1868–1869)
University of Alabama Minutes of Board of Trustees (1866–1868)

Bibliography

Special Collections and Archives, James G. Leyburn Library, Washington and Lee University, Lexington Virginia
Catalogue of the Officers and Alumni at the Washington and Lee University, 1749–1888

Special Collections and University Archives, Vanderbilt University, Nashville, Tennessee
Robert T. Lagemann Papers

Tennessee State Library and Archives, Nashville, Tennessee
Governor William C. Brownlow Papers

Vanderbilt University Special Collections and University Archives, Nashville, Tennessee
Landon Cabell Garland Papers

Virginia Military Institute Archives, Lexington, Virginia
Matthew Maury Papers

Virginia Museum of History and Culture, Richmond, Virginia
Frank W. Tremlett Papers

W. S. Hoole Special Collections Library, University of Alabama, Tuscaloosa, Alabama
Alice and Algernon Sydney Garnett Papers
Basil Manly Family Papers
Department of Education Minutes of the State Board of Education, 1869–1871
Joshua Hill Foster Diary
Records of the Proceedings of the Executive and Building Committee of the Trustees of the University of Alabama, 1866
Septimus Cabaniss Papers
University of Alabama Cadet Ledgers, 1870–1872
University of Alabama Commandant's Book, 1867–1887

William R. Perkins Library, Duke University, Durham, North Carolina
Adam Leopold Alexander Papers

Yale University Library, Manuscripts and Archives, New Haven, Connecticut
Elias Loomis Papers

Published
Alcorn, James Lusk. *Special Message Hon. James L. Alcorn on the Subject of Establishment of a University for the Colored People, Etc.* Jackson, MS: Kimball, Raymond, 1871.
Andover Theological Seminary. *General Catalogue of the Theological Seminary Andover, Massachusetts 1808–1908.* Boston: Thomas Todd, 1908.
Annual Reunion of the Association of Graduates of the United States Military Academy at West Point, New York. Saginaw, MI: Seemann & Peters, 1897.
Armes, William D. *The Autobiography of Joseph Le Conte.* New York: D. Appleton and Company, 1903.
Bagg, Lyman H. *Four Years at Yale.* New Haven, CT: Charles C. Chatfield, 1871.
Battle, Kemp P. *History of the University of North Carolina: From Its Beginning to the Death*

of President Swain, 1789–1868. Vol. 1. Raleigh, NC: Edwards & Broughton Printing Company, 1907.

———. *History of the University of North Carolina: From 1868 to 1912*. Vol. 2. Raleigh, NC: Edwards & Broughton Printing Company, 1912.

Bergeron, Paul H., ed. *The Papers of Andrew Johnson, Volume 16, May 1869–July 1875*. Knoxville: University of Tennessee Press, 2000.

Brewer, Willis. *Alabama: Her History, Resources, War Record, and Public Men, from 1540 to 1872*. Montgomery, AL: Barrett & Brown, 1872.

Buford, Elizabeth Burgess. "The Last Roll Call: Col. Nathaniel Rives Chambliss." *Confederate Veteran Magazine*, May 1897, 203.

Chesnut, Mary Boykin. *Mary Chesnut's Civil War*, edited by C. Vann Woodward. New Haven, CT: Yale University Press, 1981.

Clinton, Thomas P. "A Hundred Years of Catholicity in Tuscaloosa." Tuscaloosa, AL: n.p., 1922.

———. "The Military Operations of General John T. Croxton in West Alabama, 1865." *Transactions of the Alabama Historical Society 189–1903* 4 (Montgomery: Publications of the Alabama Historical Society, 1904): 449–63.

Denny, George H. "Universities and Colleges of the South." In *The South in the Building of the Nation: History of the Social Life of the South*, vol. 10, edited by Samuel C. Mitchell, 237–58. Richmond, VA: Southern Historical Publication Society, 1909.

Doyle, Elisabeth Joan, ed. "Eleven Letters of Raphael Semmes, 1867–1868." *Alabama Review* 5, no. 3 (July 1952): 222–32.

Dwight, Timothy. *Memories of a Yale Life and Men, 1845–1899*. New York: Dodd, Mead, 1903.

Garrett, William. *Reminiscences of Public Men in Alabama for Thirty Years*. Atlanta, GA: Plantation Publishing, 1872.

Graff, Leory P., and Ralph Haskins, eds. *The Papers of Andrew Johnson, Volume 4, 1860–1861*. Knoxville: University of Tennessee Press, 1976.

Gunby, A. A., and J. C. Eagan. *Life and Services of David French Boyd*. New Orleans: T. H. Thomason, 1904.

Harris, Nathaniel E. *Autobiography: The Story of An Old Man's Life with Reminiscences of Seventy-Five Years*. Macon, GA: J. W. Burke, 1925.

Journal of the House of Representatives of the State of Tennessee. Thirty-Sixth General Assembly, Convened at Nashville Convened at Nashville, on Monday, October 4, 1869. Nashville, TN: Jones, Purvis, 1869.

Laborde, Maximilian. *History of the South Carolina College, from Its Incorporation, December 19, 1801, to December 19, 1865, Including Sketches of Its Presidents and Professors*. Charleston, SC: Walker, Evans & Cogswell, 1874.

Massey, John. *Reminiscences Giving Sketches of Scenes through which the Author Has Passed and Pen Portraits of People Who Have Modified His Life*. Nashville, TN: M. E. Church, South, 1916.

Mathis, Gerald R., ed. *College Life in the Reconstruction South: Walter B. Hill's Student Correspondence, University of Georgia, 1869–1871*. Athens: University of Georgia Libraries Miscellanea Publications, 1974.

Maury, Sarah Mytton. *The Statesmen of America in 1846*. Philadelphia: Carey & Hart, 1847.

Bibliography

Maxwell, James Robert. *Autobiography of James Robert Maxwell of Tuskaloosa, Alabama.* New York: Greenberg, 1926.

McKitrick, Eric L. *Andrew Johnson and Reconstruction.* Chicago: University of Chicago Press, 1960.

Memorial Record of Alabama: A Concise Account of the State's Political, Military, Professional and Industrial Progress, Together with the Personal Memoirs of Many of the People. Vol. 2. Spartanburg, SC: Reprint Company, 1976.

Murfee, James. *A New Scheme of Organization, Instruction, and Government for the University of Alabama, with Report on Construction of Building.* Tuscaloosa, AL: John F. Warren, 1867.

Names of Citizens of Mobile, a Business Directory, and a Variety of Other Useful Information (1869). Mobile, AL: Henry Farrow, 1869.

Owen, Thomas B. *History of Alabama and Dictionary of Alabama Biography.* Vol. 4. Chicago: S. J. Clarke, 1921.

Owen, Thomas M., ed. *Publications of the Alabama Historical Society Miscellaneous Collections.* Vol. 1 (1900). Montgomery, AL: Brown Printing Co., 1901.

Palmer, Thomas Waverly. *A Register of the Offices and Students of the University of Alabama.* Tuscaloosa: University of Alabama, 1901.

Porter, Noah. *The American Colleges and the American Public.* New Haven, CT: Charles C. Chatfield, 1870.

Reid, Whitelaw. *After the War: A Southern Tour. May 1, 1865, to May 1, 1866.* London, UK: Sampson Low, 1866.

Simon, John Y., ed. *The Papers of Ulysses S. Grant.* 31 vols. Carbondale: Southern Illinois Press, [1967]–2012.

Smith, William Russell. *Reminiscences of a Long Life: Historical, Political, Personal and Literary.* Washington, DC: W. R. Smith, 1889.

Somers, Robert. *The Southern States since the War, 1870–71.* London, UK: Macmillan, 1871.

Trinity College. "David Peck Obituary." *Trinity Tablet.* Hartford, Connecticut, April 7, 1888.

Trowbridge, J. T. *A Picture of the Desolated States: And the Work of Restoration 1865–1868.* Hartford, CT: L. Stebbens, 1868.

Tyler, Moses Coit. "The Burning of the University of Alabama." *The Independent . . . Devoted to the Consideration of Politics, Social and Economic Tendencies, History, Literature and the Arts* 21 (October 1869): 1.

Waddel, John N. *Memorials of Academic Life Being an Historical Sketch of the Waddel Family Identified through Three Generations with the History of the Higher Education in the South and Southwest.* Richmond, VA: Presbyterian Committee of Publication, 1891.

Ward, W. Briggs, ed. *The Letters of Basil Lanneau Gildersleeve.* Baltimore, MD: Johns Hopkins, 1987.

Warmoth, Henry Clay. *Politics and Reconstruction: Stormy Days in Louisiana.* New York: Macmillan, 1930.

White, Moses. *Early History of the University of Tennessee. Address before the Alumni Association.* Knoxville, TN: Board of Trustees, 1879.

Wiggins, Sarah Woolfolk, ed. *The Journals of Josiah Gorgas, 1857–1878*. Tuscaloosa: University of Alabama Press, 1995.

———, ed. "The Life of Ryland Randolph as Seen through His Letters to John W. DuBose." *Alabama Historical Quarterly* 30, nos. 3 and 4 (Fall and Winter 1968): 145–80.

Wyeth, John A. *History of La Grange Military Academy and the Cadet Corps, 1857–1862*. New York: Brewer Press, 1907.

Alabama Newspapers
Columbiana *Shelby County Guide*, 1870
Demopolis *Southern Republican*, 1869–1870
Eufaula *Bluff City Times*, 1871
Greensboro *Alabama Beacon*, 1865, 1867, 1869, 1871
Henry County Register, 1871
Livingston Journal, 1865, 1871
Marion Commonwealth, 1870
Mobile Daily Advertiser and Register, 1866
Mobile Register, 1869–1871
Montgomery Advertiser, 1867, 1868, 1885
Montgomery *Daily State Sentinel*, 1867
Montgomery Mail, 1867–1870
Moulton Advertiser, 1869
Pickens County Herald and West Alabamian, 1871
Scottsboro Citizen, 1879
Selma Daily Messenger, 1866
Selma Morning Times, 1867
Selma Press, 1870
Selma *Southern Argus*, 1870–1871
Selma Times, 1866
Selma Times and Messenger, 1871
Talladega *Sun*, 1869–1870
Tuscaloosa *Independent Monitor*, 1861, 1865, 1868–1871
Tuscaloosa News, 1928
Tuscaloosa *Observer*, 1865, 1869–1871
Tuscaloosa *Reconstructionist*, 1868
Tuscaloosa *Republican Banner*, 1868
Weekly Montgomery Advertiser, 1867

Out-of-State Newspapers
Alexandria *Louisiana Democrat*, 1869
Athens *Southern Banner*, 1865
Brownlow's Knoxville Whig, 1867, 1868
Brownlow's Knoxville Whig and Rebel Ventilator, 1866
Burlington Weekly Free Press, 1868
Charleston Daily Courier, 1869

Bibliography

Charleston Daily News, 1868, 1869
Chicago Tribune, 1866
Cincinnati Commercial, 1868
Cincinnati Commercial Tribune, 1871
Columbus *Daily Ohio Statesman*, 1868
Detroit Tribune, 1868
Hillsborough Recorder, 1867
Indianapolis Journal, 1890
Jackson *Weekly Clarion*, 1870–1871
Jackson *Weekly Mississippi Pilot*, 1870
Knoxville Register, 1868
Missouri *Daily Democrat*, 1868
New Orleans *Daily Picayune*, 1869
New Orleans *Morning Star and Catholic Messenger*, 1871
Ogden Semi-Weekly Junction, 1878
Oxford Falcon, 1866, 1867
Pittsburgh Gazette, 1868
Raleigh *North Carolina Standard*, 1869
Raleigh Sentinel, 1869–1871
Richmond *Daily Dispatch*, 1867
Sacramento Bee, 1878
Salt Lake Daily Telegraph, 1926
Santa Fe New Mexican, 1904
Washington *Daily National Intelligencer*, 1854

United States Government Documents
US Congress. House. "Affairs in Alabama." 43rd Congress, second session. House Report 262.
———. "Testimony Taken by the Joint Select Committee to Inquire into the Condition of Affairs in the Late Insurrectionary States." 42nd Congress, second session. House Report 22.
———. Senate. "Relief of East Tennessee University." 42nd Congress, second session. Senate Report 17.
———. War Department. *The War of the Rebellion: A Compilation of the Official Records of the Union and Confederate Armies. 128 vols*. Washington, DC: Government Printing Office, 1880–1901.

Alabama Documents
Department of Education Minutes of the State Board of Education, 1869–1871.
Journal of the Session of 1870–71 of the Senate of Alabama, Held in the City of Montgomery, Commencing on the 21st November 1870. Montgomery: W. W. Screws, 1871.
Patton, Robert. *Address to the People of Alabama, by Governor Robert M. Patton*. Montgomery, AL: Barrett & Brown, 1868.
———. *Message of Robert M. Patton, Governor of Alabama, to the General Assembly, November 12, 1866*. Montgomery, AL: Reid & Screws, 1866.

Bibliography

"Report of Joseph Hodgson Superintendent of Public Instruction, of the State of Alabama for the Scholastic Year, January 1, 1871, to September 30, 1871." Montgomery, AL: W. W. Screws, 1871.

"Report of the Superintendent of Public Instruction for the State of Alabama for the Fiscal Year Ending September 30, 1869." Montgomery, AL: Jno. G. Stokes, 1870.

"Special Report of Joseph Hodgson, Superintendent Public Instruction of the State of Alabama, to the Governor, January, 1871." Montgomery, AL: W. W. Screws, 1871.

University Catalogs

Catalogue of the Officers and Alumni at the Washington and Lee University, Lexington, Virginia, 1749–1888. Baltimore, MD: John Murphy & Co., 1888.

Catalogue of the Officers and Students of Cumberland University at Lebanon, Tennessee for the Academic Year, 1855–56. Nashville, TN: A. A. Stitt, 1856.

Catalogue of the Officers and Students of Cumberland University at Lebanon, Tennessee for the Academic Year 1857–58. Lebanon, TN: Neal & Spillers, 1858.

Catalogue of the Officers and Students of Cumberland University at Lebanon, Tennessee for the Academic Year 1858–59. Lebanon, TN: Neal & Spillers, 1859.

Catalogue of the Officers and Students of the University of Alabama, 1869–70.

Catalogue of the Officers and Students of the University of Mississippi for the Session of 1870–71. Oxford, MS, 1871.

Catalogue of the Officers and Students of the Western Reserve College 1836–37. Cleveland, OH: Penniman & Bemis, 1838.

Catalogue of the Officers and Students of the Western Reserve College. Hudson, OH: Charles Aiken, 1840.

Catalogue of the Trustees, Faculty and Students of the University of North Carolina, 1859–60. Chapel Hill, NC: John B. Neathery, 1860.

Catalogue of the Trustees, Faculty and Students of the University of North Carolina 1867–68. Raleigh, NC: Nichols, Gorman & Neathery, 1868.

Catalogue of the University of Alabama, Session of 1871–72. Selma, AL: Jas. P. Armstrong, 1872.

Catalogue of the University of North Carolina, 1857–58. Chapel Hill, NC: Gazette Office, 1858.

Historical Catalogue of the Officers and Alumni of the University of Alabama, 1821 to 1870. Selma, AL: Armstrong, Duval & Martin, 1870.

Historical Catalogue of the Trustees, Faculties, and Alumni of the University of Mississippi: From the Original Organization 1869–70. Oxford, MA, 1870.

Historical Catalogue of the University of Mississippi: 1859–1909. Nashville, TN: Marchall & Brown, 1910.

PUBLISHED SECONDARY SOURCES

Articles, Books, Dissertations, and Theses

Abbott, Richard. *For Free Press and Equal Rights: Republican Newspapers in the Reconstruction South*. Athens: University of Georgia Press, 2004.

———. *The Republican Party and the South, 1855–1877*. Chapel Hill: University of North Carolina, 1986.

Bibliography

Abernethy, Thomas Perkins. *Historical Sketch of the University of Virginia*. Richmond, VA: Dietz Press, 1948.

Alexander, Edward Porter. *Fighting for the Confederacy: The Personal Recollections of General Edward Alexander Porter*. Edited by Gary W. Gallagher. Chapel Hill: University of North Carolina Press, 1989.

Alexander, Thomas B. *Political Reconstruction in Tennessee*. Nashville, TN: Vanderbilt University, 1950.

Andrew, Rod, Jr. "Soldiers, Christians, and Patriots: The Lost Cause and Southern Military Schools, 1865–1915." *Journal of Southern History* 64, no. 4 (November 1998): 677–710.

Ash, Stephen V. *When the Yankees Came: Conflict and Chaos in the Occupied South, 1861–1865*. Chapel Hill: University of North Carolina Press, 1995.

———, ed. *Secessionist and Other Scoundrels Selections from Parson Brownlow's Book*. Baton Rouge: Louisiana State University Press, 1999.

Baggett, James Alex. *The Scalawags: Southern Dissenters in the Civil War and Reconstruction*. Baton Rouge: Louisiana State University Press, 2003.

Beckel, Deborah. *Radical Reform: Interracial Politics in Post-Emancipation North Carolina*. Charlottesville: University of Virginia, 2011.

Brewer, Fisk. *Roman Family Coins in the Yale College Collection*. New Haven, CT: Tuttle, Morehouse & Taylor, 1860.

Brewer, Fisk Parsons, and William P. Vaughn. "'South Carolina University: 1876' of Fisk Parsons Brewer." *The South Carolina Historical Magazine* 76, no. 4 (1975): 225–31.

Brophy, Alfred L. *University, Court, and Slave: Pro-slavery Thought in Southern Colleges and Courts and the Coming of Civil War*. New York: Oxford University Press, 2016.

———. "Proslavery Political Theory in the Southern Academy, 1832–1861." In *Slavery and the University Histories and Legacies*, edited by Leslie M. Harris, James F. Campbell, and Alfred L. Brophy, 65–83. Athens: University of Georgia Press, 2019.

Bruce, Philip Alexander. *History of the University of Virginia, 1819–1919: The Lengthened Shadow of One Man*. Vol. 2. New York: Macmillan, 1920.

———. *History of the University of Virginia, 1819–1919: The Lengthened Shadow of One Man*. Vol. 3. New York: Macmillan, 1921.

———. *History of the University of Virginia, 1819–1919: The Lengthened Shadow of One Man*. Vol. 4. New York: Macmillan, 1921.

Cabaniss, Allen. *A History of the University of Mississippi*. Oxford: University of Mississippi, 1949.

———. *The University of Mississippi: Its First Hundred Years*. Hattiesburg: University & College Press of Mississippi, 1971.

Chitty, Arthur B. *Reconstruction at Sewanee: The Founding of the University of The South and Its First Administration, 1856–1872*. Sewanee, TN: University Press, 1954.

Chute, William J. *Damn Yankee! The First Career of Frederick A. P. Barnard: Educator, Scientist, Idealist*. Port Washington, NY: Kennikat Press, 1978.

Cohen, Michael David. *Reconstructing the Campus: Higher Education and the American Civil War*. Charlottesville: University of Virginia, 2012.

Coulter, E. Merton. *William G. Brownlow, Fighting Parson of the Southern Highlands*. Chapel Hill: University of North Carolina, 1937.

Cremin, Lawrence A. *American Education, the National Experience, 1783–1876*. New York: Harper & Row, 1980.

Curl, Donald W. *Murat Halstead and the Cincinnati Commercial*. Boca Raton: University Presses of Florida, 1980.

Current, Richard Nelson. "The Carpetbagger as Corruptionist: Henry Clay Warmoth." In *Reconstruction: An Anthology of Revisionist Writings*, edited by Kenneth Stampp and Leon Litwack, 241–63. Baton Rouge: University of Louisiana Press, 1969.

———. *Those Terrible Carpetbaggers: A Reinterpretation*. New York: Oxford University Press, 1988.

Currie-McDaniel, Ruth. *Carpetbagger of Conscience: A Biography of John Emory Bryant*. Athens: University of Georgia Press, 1987.

Dabney, Charles W. *Universal Education in the South*. Chapel Hill: University of North Carolina Press, 1963.

Dannelly, Hermione. "The Life and Times of Robert Jemison, Jr. during the Civil War and Reconstruction." Master's thesis, University of Alabama, 1942.

Dawson, Joseph G., III. *Army Generals and Reconstruction: Louisiana, 1862–1877*. Baton Rouge: Louisiana State University Press, 1982.

Denman, Clarence Phillips. *The Secession Movement in Alabama*. Montgomery: Alabama State Department of Archives and History, 1933.

Doyle, Don H. *Faulkner's County: The Historical Roots of Yoknapatawpha*. Chapel Hill: University of North Carolina Press, 1991.

Dyer, Thomas G. *The University of Georgia: A Bicentennial History, 1785–1985*. Athens: University of Georgia Press, 1985.

Eaton, Clement. *A History of the Old South*. New York: Macmillan, 1949.

Eckinger, Helen. "The Militarization of the University of Alabama." *Alabama Review* 66, no. 3 (July 2013): 163–85.

Edelstein, David. S. *Joel Munsell: Printer and Antiquarian*. New York: Columbia University Press, 1950.

Firkins, Oscar W. *Cyrus Northrop: A Memoir*. Minneapolis: University of Minnesota Press, 1925.

Fischer, Roger A. *The Segregation Struggle in Louisiana, 1862–1877*. Urbana: University of Illinois Press, 1974.

Fitzgerald, Michael W. *Reconstruction in Alabama: From Civil War to Redemption in the Cotton South*. Baton Rouge: Louisiana State University Press, 2017.

———. "Reconstruction Politics and the Politics of Reconstruction." In *Reconstruction: New Perspectives on the Postbellum United States*, edited by Thomas J. Brown, 91–116. New York: Oxford University Press, 2006.

———. "Robert B. Lindsay, 1870–1872." In *Alabama Governors: A Political History of the State*, edited by Samuel L. Webb and Margaret E. Armbrester, 90–93. Tuscaloosa: University of Alabama Press. 2001.

———. *Splendid Failure: Postwar Reconstruction in the American South*. Chicago, IL: Ivan R. Dee, 2007.

———. "The Steel Frame of Walter Lynwood Fleming." In *The Dunning School: Historians, Race and the Meaning of Reconstruction*, edited by John David Smith and J. Vincent Lowery, 157–72. Lexington: University of Kentucky Press, 2013.

Bibliography

———. *Urban Emancipation: Popular Politics in Reconstruction Mobile, 1860–1890*. Baton Rouge: Louisiana State University Press, 2002.

———. "William Hugh Smith, July 1868–December 1870." In *Alabama Governors: A Political History of the State*, edited by Samuel L. Webb and Margret E. Armbrester, 87–90. Tuscaloosa: University of Alabama Press, 2001.

Fleming, Walter L. *Louisiana State University, 1860–1896*. Baton Rouge: Louisiana State University Press, 1936.

Foner, Eric. *Reconstruction: America's Unfinished Revolution 1863–1877*. New York; Harper & Row, 1988.

Fry, Joseph A. *John Tyler Morgan and the Search for Southern Autonomy*. Knoxville: The University of Tennessee Press, 1992.

Fuller, A. James. *Chaplain to the Confederacy: Basil Manly and Baptist Life in the Old South*. Baton Rouge: Louisiana State University Press, 2000.

———. "'I Whipped Him a Second Time, Very Severely': Basil Manly, Honor, and Slavery at the University of Alabama." In *Slavery and the University Histories and Legacies*, edited by Leslie M. Harris, James T. Campbell, and Alfred L. Brophy, 114–30. Athens: University of Georgia Press, 2019.

Gamble, Robert. *The Alabama Catalog: Historic American Buildings Survey: A Guide to the Early Architecture of the State*. Tuscaloosa: University of Alabama Press, 1987.

———. *Historic Architecture in Alabama: A Primer of Styles and Types, 1810–1930*. Tuscaloosa: University of Alabama Press, 1990.

Gillette, William. *Retreat from Reconstruction, 1869–1879*. Baton Rouge: Louisiana State University Press, 1979.

Green, Hilary. *Educational Reconstruction African American Schools in the Urban South, 1865–1890*. New York: Fordham University Press, 2016.

———. "The Slave Cemetery and the Apology Marker at the University of Alabama." In *Final Resting Places Reflections on the Meaning of Civil War Graves*, edited by Brian Matthew Jordan and Johnathan W. White, 248–56, Athens: University of Georgia Press, 2023.

Green, Jennifer R. *Military Education and the Emerging Middle Class in the Old South*. Cambridge, UK: Cambridge University Press, 2008.

Gwin, Pamela Blair. "'Poisoned Arrows' from a Tar Heel Journalist: The Public Career of Cornelia Spencer, 1865–1890." PhD diss., Duke University, 1983.

Hamilton, J. G. de Roulhac. *Reconstruction in North Carolina*. New York: Columbia University Press, 1914.

Handlin, Oscar, and Mary Handlin. *The American College and American Culture: Socialization as a Function of Higher Education*. New York: McGraw Hill, 1970.

Harris, William C. *The Day of the Carpetbagger: Republican Reconstruction in Mississippi*. Baton Rouge: Louisiana State University Press, 1979.

———. *William Woods Holden: Firebrand of North Carolina Politics*. Baton Rouge: Louisiana State University Press, 1967.

Harvey, Paul, ed. *The Oxford Companion to English Literature*, 4th ed. Oxford, UK: Clarendon Press, 1967.

Herzberg, Louis. F. "Negro Slavery in Tuscaloosa County, Alabama, 1818–1865." Master's thesis, University of Alabama, 1955.

Hess, Earl J. *The Knoxville Campaign: Burnside and Longstreet in East Tennessee*. Knoxville: University of Tennessee Press, 2012.

Hoffman, Paul E. *Louisiana State University and Agricultural and Mechanical College, 1860–1919: A History*. Baton Rouge: Louisiana State University Press, 2020.

Hollis, Daniel Walker. *University of South Carolina. Volume 1, South Carolina College*. Columbia: University of South Carolina Press, 1951.

———. *University of South Carolina. Volume 2, College to University*. Columbia: University of South Carolina Press, 1956.

Howard, Gene L. *Death at Cross Plains: An Alabama Reconstruction Tragedy*. Tuscaloosa: University of Alabama Press, 1984.

Hubbs, G. Ward. "'Dissipating the Clouds of Ignorance': The First University of Alabama Library, 1831–1865." *Libraries & Culture* 27, no. 1 (Winter 1992): 20–35.

———. "John B. Read's Okra Paper." *Alabama Review* 42, no. 4 (October 1990): 289–96.

———. *Searching for Freedom after the Civil War: Klansman, Carpetbagger, Scalawag, and Freedman*. Tuscaloosa: University of Alabama, 2015.

———. *Tuscaloosa: Portrait of an Alabama County: An Illustrated History*. Northridge, CA: Windsor Publications, 1987.

———. *Tuscaloosa: 200 Years in the Making*. Tuscaloosa: University of Alabama Press, 2019.

Hughes, Nathaniel C., Jr. *General William J. Hardee: Old Reliable*. Baton Rouge: Louisiana State University Press, 1965.

Hutton, T. R. C. *Bearing the Torch: The University of Tennessee, 1794–2010*. Knoxville: University of Tennessee Press, 2022.

Hyman, Rubin, III. *South Carolina Scalawags*. Columbia: University of South Carolina Press, 2006.

Inscoe, John C. "To Do Justice to North Carolina: The War's End According to Cornelia Philips Spencer, Zebulon B. Vance, and David L. Swain." In *North Carolinians in the Era of the Civil War and Reconstruction*, edited by Paul D. Escott, 129–53. Chapel Hill: University of North Carolina Press, 2008.

Jemison, E. Grace. *Historic Tales of Talladega*. Montgomery, AL: Paragon Press, 1959.

Jordan, David M. *Winfield Scott Hancock: A Soldier's Life*. Bloomington: University of Indiana Press, 1988.

Karns, T. C. "The University of Tennessee." In *Higher Education in Tennessee*, edited by Lucius S. Merriam, 63–106. Washington, DC: Government Printing Office, 1893.

Kelley, Brooks Mather. *Yale: A History*. New Haven: Yale University Press, 1974.

Kennett, Lee B. *Sherman: A Soldier's Life*. New York: Harper Collins, 2001.

Kirsher, Ralph. *The Class of 1861: Custer, Ames, and Their Classmates after West Point*. Carbondale: Southern Illinois University Press, 1999.

Kitchens, Joel D. "E. W. Peck: Alabama's First Scalawag Chief Justice." *Alabama Review* 54, no. 1 (January 2001): 3–32.

Kolchin, Peter. *First Freedom: The Responses of Alabama's Blacks to Emancipation and Reconstruction*. Westport, CT: Greenwood Press, 1972.

Lanier, Sydney. *The Centennial Edition of the Works of Sidney Lanier, Letters 1857–1868*. Vol. 7. Edited by Charles R. Anderson. Baltimore, MD: Johns Hopkins Press, 1945.

Malone, Dumas, ed. *Dictionary of American Biography*. Vol. 8. New York: Charles Scribner's Sons, 1933.

Marszalek, John F. *Sherman: A Soldier's Passion for Order.* New York: Free Press, 1993.
Matthews, Joseph W., Jr. "Marion Military Institute: The Military College of Alabama." *Alabama Heritage* 115 (Winter 2015): 39–45.
McIlwain, Christopher L. *Civil War Alabama.* Tuscaloosa: University of Alabama Press, 2016.
———. *1865 Alabama: From Civil War to Uncivil Peace.* Tuscaloosa: University of Alabama Press, 2017.
McKenzie, Robert H. "William Russell Smith: Forgotten President of the University of Alabama." *Alabama Review* 37 (July 1984): 163–82.
McKenzie, Robert Tracy. *Lincolnites and Rebels: A Divided Town in the American Civil War.* New York: Oxford University Press, 2006.
McKitrick, Eric L. *Andrew Johnson and Reconstruction.* New York: Oxford University Press, 1960.
Mellown, Robert Oliver. "Early Photography, F. A. P. Barnard, the University of Alabama." *Alabama Review* 32, no. 1 (January 1984): 24–33.
———. *The University of Alabama: A Guide to the Campus and Its Architecture.* Tuscaloosa: University of Alabama Press, 2013.
Montgomery, James R., Stanley J. Folmsbee, and Lee S. Greene. *To Foster Knowledge: A History of the University of Tennessee 1794–1970.* Knoxville: University of Tennessee Press, 1984.
Morris, John T., and Ann McClary. *Jerome Cochran: His Life, His Works, His Legacy.* Cullman, AL: Mulberry River Press, 1998.
Osborn, Kyle, "Reconstructing Race: Parson Brownlow and the Rhetoric of Race in Postwar East Tennessee." In *Reconstructing Appalachia: The Civil War's Aftermath,* edited by Andrew L. Slap, 163–83. Lexington: University of Kentucky Press, 2010.
Pace, F. Robert. *Halls of Honor: College Men in the Old South.* Baton Rouge: Louisiana State University Press, 2004.
Parks, Joseph H. *Joseph E. Brown of Georgia.* Baton Rouge: Louisiana State University Press, 1977.
Pereyra, Lillian A. *James Lusk Alcorn: Persistent Whig.* Baton Rouge: Louisiana State University Press, 1966.
Post, Lauren C. "Samuel Henry Lockett (1837–1891): A Sketch of His Life and Work." *Louisiana History* 5, no. 4 (Autumn 1964): 421–41.
Powell, Lawrence N. "The Politics of Livelihood: Carpetbaggers in the Deep South." In *Region, Race and Reconstruction: Essays in Honor of C. Vann Woodward,* edited by J. Morgan Kousser and James M. McPherson, 315–47. New York: Oxford University Press, 1982.
Powell, William S. *The First State University: A Pictorial History of the University of North Carolina.* Chapel Hill: University of North Carolina Press, 1992.
Pruitt, Paul. "Scalawag Dreams: Elisha Wolsey Peck's Career, and Two of His Speeches, 1867–1869." *Alabama Review* 66, no. 3 (July 2013): 211–32.
———. *Taming Alabama Lawyers and Reformers, 1804–1929.* Tuscaloosa: University of Alabama Press, 2013.
Quist, John W. *Restless Visionaries: The Social Roots of Antebellum Reform in Alabama and Michigan.* Baton Rouge: Louisiana State University Press, 1998.

Rable, George C. *But There Was No Peace: The Role of Violence in the Politics of Reconstruction*. Athens: University of Georgia Press, 1984.

Raper, Horace W. *William W. Holden: North Carolina's Political Enigma*. Chapel Hill: University of North Carolina Press, 1985.

Reed, Germaine M. *David French Boyd, Founder of Louisiana State University*. Baton Rouge: Louisiana State University Press, 1977.

Reynolds, John S. *Reconstruction in South Carolina, 1865–1877*. Columbia, SC: State Co., 1905.

Richards, Bartlett, Jr., and Ruth Van Ackeren. *Bartlett Richards, Nebraska Sandhills Cattleman*. Lincoln: Nebraska State Historical Society, 1980.

Richardson, Joe Martin. *Christian Reconstruction: The American Missionary Association and Southern Blacks, 1861–1890*. Athens: University of Georgia Press, 1986.

Rogers, William Warren. "'Politics Is Mighty Uncertain': Charles Hays Goes to Congress." *Alabama Review* 39, no. 3 (July 1977): 163–90.

Rogers, William Warren, and Ruth Pruitt. *Stephen S. Renfroe, Alabama's Outlaw Sheriff*. Tallahassee, FL: Sentry Press, 1972.

Rogers, William Warren, Jr. *Black Belt Scalawag: Charles Hays and the Southern Republicans in the Era of Reconstruction*. Athens: University of Georgia Press, 1993.

———. *Confederate Home Front: Montgomery during the Civil War*. Tuscaloosa: University of Alabama Press, 1999.

———. *Reconstruction Politics in a Deep South State: Alabama, 1865–1874*. Tuscaloosa: University of Alabama Press, 2021.

———. "Robert Patton, December 1865–March 1867." In *Alabama Governors: A Political History of the State*, edited by Samuel L. Webb and Margaret E. Armbrester, 80–83. Tuscaloosa: University of Alabama Press. 2001.

Rolle, Andrew F. *The Lost Cause: The Confederate Exodus to Mexico*. Norman: University of Oklahoma Press, 1965.

Rudolph, Frederick. *The American College and University: A History*. New York: Alfred Knopf, 1962.

Sansing, David G. *The University of Mississippi: A Sesquicentennial History*. Jackson: University Press of Mississippi, 1999.

Schweninger, Loren. "The American Missionary Association and Philanthropy in Reconstruction." *Alabama Historical Quarterly* 32, nos. 3 and 4 (Fall and Winter 1970): 129–56.

Sefton, James. *The United States Army and Reconstruction, 1865–1877*. Baton Rouge: Louisiana State University Press, 1967.

Sellers, James B. *History of the University of Alabama. Volume 1, 1818–1902*. Tuscaloosa: University of Alabama Press, 1953.

Sindon, Nancy Anne. "The Career of Ryland Randolph: A Study in Reconstruction Journalism." Master's thesis, Florida State University, 1965.

Smith, Baxter Perry. *The History of Dartmouth College*. Boston: Houghton, Osgood & Co., 1878.

Smith, John David, and J. Vincent Lowery, eds. *The Dunning School: Historians, Race, and the Meaning of Reconstruction*. Lexington: University of Kentucky Press, 2013.

Bibliography

Snider, William D. *Light on the Hill: A History of the University of North Carolina at Chapel Hill*. Chapel Hill: University of North Carolina Press, 1992.

Spencer, Warren. *Raphael Semmes: The Philosophical Mariner*. Tuscaloosa: University of Alabama Press, 1997.

Stampp, Kenneth M. *The Era of Reconstruction*. New York: Alfred A. Knopf, 1965.

Stephens, Lester. *Joseph LeConte, Gentle Prophet of Evolution*. Baton Rouge: Louisiana State Press, 1982.

Stetar, Joseph M. "In Search of a Direction: Southern Higher Education after the Civil War." *History of Education Quarterly* 25, no. 3 (Fall 1985): 341–67.

Sugrue, Michael. "'We Desired Our Future Rulers to Be Educated Men': South Carolina College, the Defense of Slavery, and the Development of Secessionist Politics." In *The American College in the Nineteenth Century*, edited by Roger L. Geiger, 91–114. Nashville, TN: Vanderbilt University Press, 2000.

Summers, Mark W. *The Ordeal of the Reunion: A New History of Reconstruction*. Chapel Hill: University of North Carolina Press, 2014.

Thomas, Peter C. "Matthew Fontaine Maury and the Problem of Virginia's Identity, 1865–1873." *The Virginia Magazine of History and Biography* 90, no. 2 (April 1982): 213–37.

Thornton, J. Mills. *Politics and Power in a Slave Society Alabama, 1800–1860*. Baton Rouge: Louisiana State University Press, 1978.

Trelease, Allen W. *White Terror: The Ku Klux Klan Conspiracy and Southern Reconstruction*. New York: Harper & Row, 1971.

Tunnell, Ted. *Crucible of Reconstruction: War, Radicalism, and Race in Louisiana, 1862–1877*. Baton Rouge: Louisiana State University Press, 1984.

Turner, Maxine T. *Navy Gray: A Story of the Confederate Navy on the Chattahoochee and Apalachicola Rivers*. Tuscaloosa: University of Alabama Press, 1988.

Veysey, Lawrence R. *The Emergence of the American University*. Chicago: University of Chicago Press, 1965.

Warner, Ezra J. *Generals in Blue: Lives of the Union Commanders*. Baton Rouge: Louisiana State University, 1964.

———. *Generals in Gray Lives of the Confederate Commanders*. Baton Rouge: Louisiana State University Press, 1959.

Webb, Samuel L. "A Jacksonian Democrat in Postbellum Alabama: The Ideology and Influence of Journalist Robert McKee, 1869–1896." *Journal of Southern History* 62, no. 2 (May 1996): 239–74.

Wiggins, Sarah Woolfolk. "J. DeForest Richards, a Vermont Carpetbagger in Alabama." *Vermont History* 51 (Spring 1983): 98–106.

———. "Lewis E. Parsons, June–December 1865." In *Alabama Governors: A Political History of the State*, edited by Samuel L. Webb and Margaret E. Armbrester, 77–80. Tuscaloosa: University of Alabama Press. 2001.

———. "The Life of Ryland Randolph as Seen through His Letters to John W. DuBose," *Alabama Historical Quarterly* 30, nos. 3 and 4 (Fall and Winter, 1968), 145–80.

———. *The Scalawag in Alabama Politics, 1865–1881*. Tuscaloosa: University of Alabama Press, 1977.

Bibliography

Williams, Benjamin Buford. *A Literary History of Alabama: The Nineteenth Century*. Rutherford, NJ: Farleigh Dickinson University Press, 1979.

Williams, Frances Leigh. *Matthew Fontaine Maury: Scientist of the Sea*. New Brunswick, NJ: Rutgers University Press, 1963.

Winterer, Caroline. *The Culture of Classicism Ancient Greece and Rome in American Intellectual Life, 1780–1910*. Baltimore, MD: Johns Hopkins University Press, 2002.

Wolfe, Suzanne Rau. *The University of Alabama, a Pictorial History*. Tuscaloosa: University of Alabama Press, 1983.

Wolfe, Thomas. *The Web and the Rock*. New York: Harper & Row, 1939.

Worley, Lynda F. "A History of Centenary Institute, Selma, Alabama." *The Wesleyan Quarterly Review* 2 (February 1965): 21–39.

Index

Page numbers in italics refer to figures.

Aberdeen *Examiner*, 139–40
abolitionism, 9, 10
Adams, John, 16
African Americans. *See* Blacks
agriculture, stability provided by, 11
Alabama, 40, 43, 162
Alabama, 11, 22, 47, 115, 147, 198; changing political landscape in, 178; education in, 52; election of 1870 and, 158–60, 178, 197; exodus of students from, 47–48; political upheaval in, 22, 24; postwar fragility of, 158; readmission process and, 26, 51; readmitted to the Union, 2, 51; Reconstruction Acts and, 51; Reconstruction timetable in, 140; Republican control over state government in, 52, 76; Republicans take power in, 52, 136, 194; secession of, 10; state constitution and, 49, 51–52, 76, 201; state government in, 89; state universities, 142 (*see also* University of Alabama)
Alabama and Chattanooga Railroad, 66, 92, 97, 162, 168
Alabama Beacon, 99, 130
Alabama Central Female College, 66, 128
Alabama Education Association, 183

Alabama Female Institute, 9, 66
Alabama State Journal, 97, 98–99, 100, 125, 127, 130, 161, 188, 200
"Alabamians," 47
Alcorn, James Lusk, 140, 141–42, 149, 196
Alcorn University, 149
Alexander, Edward Porter, 33, 45, 137, 138
Alexandria, Louisiana, 37, 39, 146, 147
Allen, Frederic W., 44
American Cotton Planter, The, 52
American Missionary Association, 27
amnesty proclamation, possibility of, 109
Andalusia, Alabama, 82
Andover, Massachusetts, 70
Andover Theological Seminary, 70
Appomattox Court House, surrender at, 1
Arkansas, 3, 53
Army of the Cumberland, 68
Army of the Tennessee, 30, 75
Asylum for the Deaf, Dumb, and Blind, 147
Asylum for the Deaf and Dumb, 43
Athens, Georgia, 11, 32, 42–43, 45
Atlanta, Georgia, 42, 75
Autauga County, Alabama, 55

Index

Barge, Minerva Traweek, 69
Barge, Thomas, 82, 103
Barnard, Frederick A. P., 10, 176
Barnard, M. L., 82
Barnard, Robert, 142–43
Barnwell, Robert W., 31, 138, 139
Bates, A. S., 82
Baton Rouge, Louisiana, 40, 147
Battle, Kemp W., 136
Battle House Hotel, Mobile, 28
Beaufort, South Carolina, 137
Bell, O. R., 200
Benton, Ellen L., 27, 28
Berry, Lawrence, 17
Bibb, Cornelia Dandridge, 74
Birmingham, Alabama, 100. *See also* Elyton, Alabama
Black Americans, citizenship of, 16
Black Belt, 7, 70
Black legislators, 136–38
Black men: education of, 103, 135, 141–42, 149 (*see also* integration; segregation); on juries, 74
Blacks, 8, 12–16; education of, 103, 135, 141–42, 149 (*see also* integration; segregation); enfranchisement of, 24; on juries, 74; in the legislature, 160; possibility of admitting, 102–3; registration to vote, 26; seeking advancement, 17; at University of South Carolina, 197; whippings of, 90
Black students: possibility of admitting, 102–3; at University of South Carolina, 197
Black Warrior River, 7, 9, 10, 11, 61, 66, 67, 76, 79, 89, 97, 109, 119, 194; Northport side of, 88
Blair, Francis P., 61
Blair, Robert, 24, 27–28
Bledsoe, Thomas, 29
Booth, Jesse H., 54, 55, 56, 58, 93, 98, 170, 171
Boseman, Benjamin A., 136

Bouchello, E. F., 49–50
Boyd, David, 37–38, 39, 40, 41, 145–47, 149, 197
Bradford, Sarah Elizabeth, 69
Brewer, Fisk P., 133–35
Broad (Main) Street, Tuscaloosa, 7
Brophy, Alfred, 50, 198
Brott, C. S., 82
Brown, Joseph E., 42, 148
Brown, Julius L., 148
Brownlow, William "Parson," 44
Bruce, Philip A., 147–48
Bryant, Jonathan E., 148
Bryce, Peter H., 12, 18, 24
Bunsen, Robert, 109
Burton, Pierce, 100
Burton, Pierre, 96–97
Bush, Henry M., 27
Butler, Milford, 144
Butler, W. G., 82, 200
Byrd, William, 97, 120–23, 126–27

Cabiness, Charles, 36–37
cadets, 79–84, 90–91, 102–5, 108–9, 117–18, 127–28, 157–58, 165–67, 185–86, 192, 199–200; adjusting to new, 165–67; uniforms of, 84, 103, 119, 192
Caldwell, Samuel C., 142, 143
Callan, Sarah, 105
Callan, William Jasper, 68–69, 76–78, 82, 98, 104, 111, 113, 114, 116–17, 193, 199, 200
Cardozo, Francis L., 136
"carpetbaggers," 22, 58, 63, 64, 75, 111, 133, 134, 139, 151, 195
Carter House, Montgomery, 97
Catholic sisters, Tuscaloosa, 66–67
Celeste, 147
Centenary College, 69–70
Central Female College, 9
Chambliss, Anna, 108, 116, 156, 193
Chambliss, Martha "Mattie" Matthews, 116

Chambliss, Nathan Rives, 98, 106, 108, 111, 114–19, 124–29, 154, 195, 199, 200; accused of being a pseudo-Radical, 155–56; cuts off relations with University of Alabama, 156, 158; life after University of Alabama, 193
Chancellorsville, battle of, 17
Chapel Hill, North Carolina, 31, 35–36, 132, 134–35, 196. *See also* University of North Carolina
Charleston, South Carolina, 115–16
Charleston Arsenal, 115–16, 119
Charleston Courier, 138
Charleston Harbor, 10
Charlottesville, Virginia, 32, 36, 37, 47
Chattanooga, Tennessee, 75
Cheney, W. B., 117
Cherokee County, Alabama, 81–82
Chester *Reporter*, 139
Chicago, Illinois, 61, 141
Chi Delta Society, 44, 144
Cincinnati Commercial, 63
Citadel, South Carolina, 137
"City of Oaks," 62, 63
Civil Rights Act, 15
Civil War, 4, 10–12, 114, 136; aspirational regeneration after, 198; "Decoration Day," 66; surrender at Appomattox Courthouse, 1
Clarion, 140
Clariosophic Society, 33–34, 137
Clarke, Charles, 141
Clayton, William H., 54, 55, 93, 94
Clinton, Thomas, 21
Cloud, Noah B., 52–53, 55, 56, 58, 91, 109, 126–29, 194; Chambliss and, 126, 127–28; on daily drills, 84; Hodgson and, 159–62, 178; Lakin and, 59–63, 67–68, 157; Lupton and, 129; Maury and, 97, 176; McConnell and, 104; Northrop and, 98–99; at opening ceremonies, 82; search for president and, 93–95, 98–99,

109, 150, 176; treatise on university drafted by, 101–2
Cochran, Jerome, 92
Cochrane, W. G., 123
Cochrane, William, 88, 122, 125
Cohen, Michael, 74
Cohen, Michael David, 4, 34, 186
Coleman, Aaron, 88
Coleman, Lewis M., 31
Collins, Andrew, 94
Columbia, South Carolina, 30–33, 45, 137–38
Columbia Phoenix, 139
Columbus, Georgia, 82
Columbus Democrat, 142
Comegys, E. F., Jr., 168
Confederate bonds, universities' investment in, 31
Confederate States of America, 10, 11, 13, 31, 169, 174–75, 194, 198; capitulation of, 12; Congress of, 42; empathy for, 43; provisional governments in, 14; readmission to the Union, 14–15, 22, 26; support for, 144–45. *See also specific states*
Congressional Reconstruction, 42, 50, 61
Cook, Thomas A., 170, 181
Cooper, Thomas, 50
Cooperationists, 10
Copeland, Aaron, 89
Corbin, Nannie, 183–85, 187
Corbin, Wellford, 187
Corinth, Mississippi, 125
Courtland, Alabama, 53, 82, 121
Cox, Albert H., 42
Crossland, Merdy, 88
Cross Plains, Alabama, 166
Croxton, John T., 1–2, 11, 21, 67, 82–83, 96, 163, 164, 191, 194
Cumberland University, 69, 114

Dalton, David L., 89, 90
Dantzler, D. Z., 34

Index

Dartmouth College, 70, 83
Davidson College, 133
Davis, Jefferson, 12, 19, 43, 44, 141, 143
Decatur Republican, 57
Democratic Party, 2, 4, 5, 14, 42, 53, 56, 58, 61, 76; election of 1870 and, 158–60, 178; loyalty to, 191; Maury and, 175. *See also* Democrats
Democratic press, 99–100, 102, 133, 159, 178, 199
Democratic State Executive Committee, 159
Democrats, 26, 40, 57–58, 99, 130, 132–33, 142, 166, 195, 198–201
Demopolis, Alabama, 10, 96–97, 100
Demosthenian Society, 41–42
Denny, T. W., 200
Dhee, Rederic, 173
Dialectic Society, 36
Dick, M., 82
Dickinson College, 109
Dix, Dorothea, 12
"Dixie Club," 42
Dixon, George, 136
Dranesville, battle of, 74
Duck Hill, Mississippi, 35
Dunning, William A., 3
Dyer, Tom, 31
Dykous, Dennis, 64

East Tennessee University, 30, 43–45, 46, 47, 131, 143–44, 149; board of trustees, 144; College Hill, 43; designated as agricultural school of Tennessee, 144–45; enrollment at, 144; experience of Reconstruction, 195; library, 144; possible integration of, 149; rebuilding of, 43–44; reopening of, 144; success, 197; war damage, 144
education, 148–49; after the war, 32; in Alabama, 52; of Blacks, 103, 135, 141–42, 149 (*see also* integration; segregation); Republicanism and, 52; segregation and, 149
Elyton, Alabama, 47, 100, 125
emancipation, 14, 16
enslaved persons, 8, 12; escaped, 9; freed (*see* freedmen; freedpeople)
Episcopalian Church, 182
Eufaula, Alabama, 47, 101
Euphradian Society, 33–34, 137, 138
Eutaw, Alabama, 155–56, 166
Eutaw Riot, 166
Evarts, William M., 154, 193
Evergreen, Alabama, 70, 169
Evergreen Observer, 169
Exchange Hotel, Montgomery, 19

F. E. Stollenwerck & Bros., 118, 127
faculty, at University of Alabama, 49–51, 53–56, 66–78, 82–85, 96, 98, 109, 111, 154–55, 159, 171, 182–83, 191–94, 199–200; appointments of, 94, 96; attacks on, 84–87, *85*, *86*; composition of, 49–51, 98, 129, 154, 182–83; disagreements among, 106; enlisted in war, 31; exiting to battlefield, 29, 31; experiences of, 105–6; faculty appointments, 54–56, 66–75; families of, 105–6; insular living and working arrangements of, 105; Maury meets with, 183–84, 185; numbers reduced by regents, 109, 111; past, 192–93; public backlash to appointments, 66–91; Randolph's attacks on, 84–87, *85*, *86*; regents reduce numbers of, 109, 111; Republican affiliation of, 106; residences of, 105; return of, 76–78, 82, 84–85; seen as owing positions to Republican loyalties, 133; selection of, 5, 54–56, 66–75, 96, 171; size of, 171; taunted by KKK, 87
faculty residences, at University of Alabama, 77, 105
faculty wives, 95

Index

Fayette Chronicle, 142
Ferdinand Maximilian, Archduke, 175
Fifth Military District, 39, 41
Figh, George, 19, 20, 28, 51, 104
Finley, Peyton, 170, 172
Finley, William, 88
Fiquet, Dominique D., 123
First Baptist Church, Tuscaloosa, 15
First Reconstruction Act, 2, 22, 26, 39
Fitzgerald, Michael, 161, 200–201
Florence, Alabama, 47
Florida, 3
Flourney, Robert W., 142
Forney, John H., 51, 53, 55, 57–58, 68, 74, 76–79, 98, 199
Forsyth, John, 99
Fort Monroe, 43
Fort Sumter, 19
Foster, Charles M., 24
Fourteenth Amendment, 2, 21–22, 24, 50, 52, 72, 73
Fourth Military Reconstruction Act, 51
Franklin, battle of, 34
Franklin Hall, 9
Fredericksburg, Battle of, 31
Freedman's Bureau, 15, 16, 17, 24, 41, 61, 68, 79; schools of, 27
freedmen, 24, 64; altercations and, 88–89; education of, 149; possibility of admitting, 102–3. *See also* freedpeople
"freedom," definitions of, 16
freedpeople, 12, 14–18, 22, 24, 27, 64, 133, 145, 160, 170; advancement of, 145; citizenship granted to, 15; colonization of Liberia by, 16; education of, 52; juries and, 24, 74, 83; killed in Eutaw Riot, 166; violence against, 22–24, 88–90, 165–66
free persons of color, 8

Gadsden Times, 96
Gainesville, Alabama, 166
Galt, Alexander, 45

Gardener, Benjamin, 101
Garland, Landon C., 11, 13, 18, 19, 21, 51, 53, 143
Garnett, Algernon S., 171, 192
Garnett, Alice, 192
Garnett, James, 38
Gaylesville, Alabama, 69
Geary, Joseph, 55, 56, 68
Georgia, 3, 46, 50, 82; legislation to cover tuition of ex-soldiers, 41; state university in, 99, 131
Gettysburg, Pennsylvania, 27; battle at, 30
Gibbs, Jonathan, 12–13
Gildersleeve, Basil, 37
Giles College, 114
Glascock, John, 17, 24
Glascock's Corner, 61
Goodfellow, Thomas M., 56, 68
Gorgas, Josiah, 12, 109
Grace, F. M., 47
Grant, Ulysses S., 2, 30, 42–44, 61, 63, 64, 83, 88, 133, 141, 154; administration of, 128; election of, 145, 175; reelection campaign, 193; rumored to speak at UNC commencement, 135; Vaughn and, 156–57
Green, Jennifer, 103
Greene County, Alabama, 61
Greene Springs School, 49
Greensboro, Alabama, 10, 99, 109, 129, 130
Greenville, South Carolina, 102
Griswold, J. G., 171
Grove Hill, Alabama, 82
"Guard Room," 13

Halstead, Murat, 63
Hampden-Sydney College, 181
Hancock, Winfield S., 41
Handlin, Mary, 104
Hardee, Anna Dummett, 116. *See also* Chambliss, Anna

Hardee, William J., 93, 95, 97, 99, 106, 116, 155
Harper, Robert David, 67–68, 75, 76, 79, 92–93, 99, 173
Harris, Claiborne, 21
Harris, Nathaniel E., 41, 148
Harrison, B. J., 168
Harrison, George P., 171, 189, 191
Hartford, Connecticut, 113
Harton, John, 165, 166
Hausman, J., 20
Havana, Alabama, 49
Haynesville, Alabama, 192
Hays, Charles, 61, 166
Hazlehurst, Mississippi, 143
higher education, 3, 51, 94; relevance of providing, 45; slavery and, 198; Southern, 30–31, 45, 94 (*see also* Southern state universities); war's consequences for, 30–31
Hilgard, Eugene W., 34–35, 140, 143
Hill, Benjamin H., 42
Hill, Walter B., 41, 42, 148
Hodgson, Joseph, 159–64, 168, 170, 178–81, 184, 185–88, 192
Hodgson, Telfair, 171, 182
Holden, William, 132, 135, 140, 149, 196
Hopkins, Francis V., 146
Howells Crossroads, 81–82
Hubbs, G. Ward, 16, 60
Hudson, Robert S., 141, 142
Humes, Thomas W., 43–45, 143–44
Humphreys, David, 55, 56, 57, 68
"Hunki Gory" club, 44
Huntsville, Alabama, 12, 59, 68, 82
Huntsville *Democrat*, 56, 68
Huntsville Road, 79
Hutton, T. R. C., 4, 45

Independent Monitor, 3, 24–25, 49, 58, 60, 62, 75, 84–87, 120, 125, 155
integration, of Southern universities, 2, 193, 197; denial of, 102–3; fears of, 137, 141–42, 149; prospect of, 131, 137, 141–42

Jackson, Andrew, 11
Jackson, Mississippi, 64, 140
Jackson, Thomas F., 54, 55, 56, 58, 93
Jacksonville, Alabama, 74, 77, 78
Jarvis, Harriet Bartlett, 70
Jarvis, William, 70
Jefferson, Thomas, 36, 45, 49, 70
Jefferson Hall, 9
Jefferson Society, 36, 43
Jemison, Robert, Jr., 90
Jenkins, Ike, 88, 89
Jennie Rogers, 79
Johnson, Andrew, 12, 14, 42–43
Johnston, Joseph, 66
Joint Committee to Inquire into the Condition of Affairs in the Late Insurrectionist States, 166–67
Jones, Catesby ap Roger, 181
Jones, Shandy, 16–17, 20, 24, 85, *86*, 102, 160
Jones, William Henry, 102–3
juries: Blacks on, 24, 74; Ku Klux Klan and, 89; lack of impartiality in, 89

Karns, Thomas C., 43–44
Kellogg, William P., 197
Kemper County, Mississippi, 82
Kendrick, M. A., 118, 200
Kennedy, John S., 15
Kentucky, 115
Knox County courthouse, 43
Knoxville, Tennessee, 4, 30, 43, 143–44
Knoxville Press and Register, 145
Knoxville Whig, 144
Ku Klux Klan, 22, *23*, 27, 59, 61, *62*, 63, 75–76, 78, 86–89, 165–66, 195

LaBorde, Maximilian, 33, 34, 137
Lafayette, Alabama, 47
La Grange, Georgia, 75

Index

La Grange Military Academy, 75
Lakin, Arad S., 56, 58–59, 60, 62, 64, 67, 68, 76, 87, 99, 157, 173
Lanier, Sidney, 50
Lauderdale County, Alabama, 18
Lawson, Nat, 66
Lebanon, Tennessee, 69
LeConte, John, 137
LeConte, Joseph, 29, 33, 34, 46, 137, 138
Lee, Robert E., 33, 175, 176
Lewis, Thomas P., 16, 24, 26, 88, 89
Lexington, Virginia, 47, 93, 175, 176, 181, 185, 190
Liberia, colonization in, 16
Lincoln, Abraham, 10, 44, 83; assassination of, 14; government of, 10, 164
Lindsay, Robert, 158, 160, 163–64
Lipscomb, Andrew, 41, 42–43, 46, 148
literary societies, 33, 36, 44, 137, 138, 144. *See also specific societies*
Little, Barbara, 91
Lizzie Hopkins, 147
local government officials, replaced by Republicans, 67
Lockett, Samuel H., 39–40
Longstreet, Augustus Baldwin, 50
Longstreet, James, 30
Loomis, Elias, 69, 70, 87–88, 98–99, 105, 106, 108, 113, 178
Loomis, Hubbell, 69–70, 108
Loomis, John Calvin, 68, 71, 76–79, 81–82, 103–5, 113–14, 116–18, 158, 195, 199–200; academic pedigree of, 69–70; adversity faced by, 84, 86–87; after University of Alabama, 193; assaulted by Randolph, 86–87; letters to his brother, 77–78, 79, 84, 87–88, 105, 106, 107, 108, 111, 113; letters to Smith, 78, 83, 89; letter to Maury, 176, 178; loses post, 111, 113–14; Northrop and, 97–98; at opening ceremonies, 82

Loomis, Minerva, 76, 82, 103, 105, 118
Lost Cause, 169
Lott, Harry, 146
Louisiana, 3, 30–31, 82, 94, 142–43; Republican stewardship of, 145–46; sister school in, 131
Louisiana State Seminary of Learning and Military Academy, 30, *38*, 43, 45, 46, 93, 94, 131, 145–47, 149; becomes Louisiana State University, 147; board of supervisors, 132; commencement exercises, 146–47; financial difficulties, 40, 41; lack of equipment and books, 37–39; "Loyalist" letter and, 40; military oversight at, 40; precarious status, 39–40; progress at, 148; remoteness of, 39; reopening of, 145; temporary move to Baton Rouge after fire, 147; tuition forgiveness at, 146; yellow fever quarantine at, 40, 41. *See also* Louisiana State University
Louisiana State University, 1, 147; decline of, 197; progress at, 148
Louisville, Kentucky, 44
Lowndes County, Alabama, 192
"Loyalist," 40
Ludlow, Henry, 145
Lupton, Nathaniel L., 109–11, 119, 124, 155, 171, 173, 180, 192, 199; accepts position as president, 112; administration, 111–12, 113–30; appointment, 113; board of education and, 130; conflict with board of education, 129–30; elected president for second time, 192; end of his administration, 129–30; postpones relocation, 114, 117, 119; regents and, 129–30; rejoins Southern University, 130; resignation, 151; returns to campus, 128–29
lynchings, *62*, 63, 88, 122–25, 195
Lyon, James A., 143

— 261 —

Mabry, Jesse, 124
Mackey, Albert G., 139
Macon, Georgia, 41
Macon County, Alabama, 52
Madison Hall, 9
Mahan, M. H., 117, 118, 200
Manly, Basil, Jr., 102
Manly, Basil, Sr., 12, 15, 16, 64, 198
Manly, Charles, 15–16, 24, 67
Mansion House (Tuscaloosa), 60, 169–70
Marengo County, Alabama, 70
Marion, Alabama, 47
Martin, John M., 24, 123
Martling, James A., 133, 135, 136
Mary, Queen of Scots, 34
Mary H., the, 66
Maupin, Socrates, 37
Maury, Ann Hull Herndon, 174
Maury, Edward, 82, 117
Maury, H., 82
Maury, Matthew Fontaine, 5, 93, 95, 97, 162, 163, 172, *177*, 199; ascension to the presidency, 173–90, 191; background, 174–75; campaign to bring, 178–83; conflicted about accepting position, 185; decides against the presidency, 188–90; Democratic Party and, 175; drafting of inaugural salutation, 186; Joseph Hodgson and, 178–81, 184, 185–88; letter from Loomis, 176, 178; meeting with Alabama Education association, 183, 185; meeting with faculty, 183–84, 185; in Mexico, 175; resignation of, 188–90, 191, 192
Maximilian, Emperor, 75
McConnell, William K., 74–77, 82, 98, 104, 111, 114, 116–18, 199, 200; loses post, 111; at opening ceremonies, 82
McEachin, A. B., 123
McGown, Henry, 24, 26
McIver, Alexander, 133, 134

McKee, Robert, 96, 100, 112, 156, 188–89
McKenzie, Tracey, 143
Meade, George, 27
Meek, Benjamin F., 24, 64, 169, 171
Merrimack, 168, 181
Methodist Episcopal Church, 56, 59
Mexico, 75, 175
Miller, Charles, 89, 90
Miller, William, 16, 24, 70
Mills, William, 89, 90, 122, 125, 167
Mississippi, 3, 46, 82, 115, 139–40, 182–83; Reconstruction timetable in, 140; Republican control over state government in, 140–41; Republican oversight in, 140–41; Republican State Executive Committee, 141; Republican stewardship in, 131; state universities, 131
Mississippi *Democrat*, 64
Mississippi Pilot, 141
Mobile, Alabama, 7, 12, 17, 82, 93, 119, 130, 154
Mobile County, Alabama, 95
Mobile *Nationalist*, 17
Mobile Register, 68, 99, 100
Monterey, Alabama, 69, 81
Montgomery, Alabama, 12, 50, 52, 57, 89, 93–94, 100, 107, 129, 161, 180, 190; board meetings, 19, 95, 97, 103, 109, 111, 161, 192; legislature, 2, 73; Maury in, 180, 183–84, 185; Republican convention in, 26; secession convention in, 10
Montgomery Advertiser and Mail, 56, 96, 99, 161, 172, 182, 188
Montgomery County, Alabama 74
Montgomery Mail, 48, 56, 126–27, 159, 160–61
Monticello, 49
Moody, W., 123
Morrill Act, 144
Mount Meigs, Alabama, 74

Munsell, Charles, 157–58, 165, 166
Munsell, Joel, 157
Murfee, James Thomas, 19, 20–21, 28, 49, 51, 53, 67, 81, 104, 181, 182
Murfreesboro, Tennessee, 75, 144

Nashville, Tennessee, 44, 78, 145
National Observatory, 93
Neagle, James L., 138–39, 196–97
New Haven, Connecticut, 70, 98
New Orleans, Louisiana, 39, 40, 82, 146–47
New Orleans Republican, 40
"New Virginia," 175
New York *Herald*, 12
Nichols, James, 94
Nicholson, Hunter, 145
North Carolina, 3, 35–36, 140; board of education, 132–33; Democratic press in, 133; Reconstruction timetable in, 140; Republican control over state government, 132; Republicans take power in, 136; Republican stewardship in, 131; state universities, 142; universities, 29–30
Northport, Alabama, 61, 88
Northrop, Cyrus, 97–100, 162, 173, 176; declines presidency, 99; selected as president, 98–99
North/South divide, 54

Oakland, California, 138
Odd Fellows, 74
Oglethorpe University, 50
Ohio Female Seminary at College Hill, 70
Opelika, Alabama, 100
Orr, James L., 137
Osborne, Horace, 125
Osborne, T. D., 117–18, 124, 125
Owen, H. L., 97
Oxford, Mississippi, 30, 34, 142, 143, 148
Oxford University, 45

Pace, Robert, 104
Parish, Richard C., 24
Parker, William, 169, 171
Parry, Tyler D., 4, 197
Parsons, Lewis E., 15, 17–18
Patrick, David S., 133, 134, 136
Patton, Robert M., 18, 20, 22, 24, 48, 116
Pea Ridge, battle of, 53–54
Peck, David L., 111, 113–14, 117–19, 127–28, 154, 156, 158, 160–61, 164, 170–71
Peck, Elisha Woolsey, 16, 24, 26–27, 49–50, 52, 58, 90, 96, 113, 129, 160
Peck, Lucy Randall, 113
Peck, Mary Brainerd, 113–14
Peck, William H., 17
Pegues, Josiah J., 89, 120–21, 123, 124–25
Pegus, Thomas E. B., 142
Perry, Benjamin F., 33
Perry County, Alabama, 165
Phi Kappa Society, 41–42
Philanthropic Society, 36
Philanthropic Society Hall, 134
Phillips, Charles, 31, 36, 43, 134
Phillips, James, 134
Philomathesian Society, 44, 144
Pickens County, Alabama, 49
Pickensville, Alabama, 49
Pineville, Louisiana, 30, 37, 39, 40, 145, 146
Piney Woods, 11–12
Pittsburgh Gazette, 63
Pontotoc, Mississippi, 142
Pool, Solomon, 132, 133, 134, 135
Pope, John, 42–43
Price, William H. C., 191
public education, 3, 52
Putnam, George L., 94, 95, 98, 130

Quinche, Alexander J., 140, 143
Quist, John, 9

race, 9; questions regarding, 5–6; race consciousness, 16
racial relations, changes to, 63, 194
Radical Republicanism, 24, 57, 59, 61, 64, 142, 183, 185, 195, 197, 201
"Radical" Republicans, 5, 15, 24, 111–12, 139, 154–55, 181, 193; interference by, 41; label of, 145
Raleigh, North Carolina, 132, 134–35
Raleigh Sentinel, 133, 134
Randolph, Edward Ryland, 3, *25*, 58, 96, 102, 114, 155–57, 159, 169, 188, 191; background, 24–25, 27; boycott called by, 66; in KKK, 27; as lightning rod, 194–95; Loomis and, 86–87, 108; lynching lead by, 88; physical attacks by, 87, 91, 106–8; publicizes visit of Cloud and Lakin, 60, 62; shooting of, 120–27, 200; visual/verbal attacks on faculty, 62–64, 75–76, 78, 84–87, *85*, *86*, 90
Randolph County, Alabama, 52
Read, John, 107
Reconstruction, Congressional, 27, 42, 50
Reconstruction Acts, 51; First Reconstruction Act, 2, 22, 26, 39; Fourth Military Reconstruction Act, 51
Reconstruction era, 2, 3, 4, 7–28, 49, 51, 155, 161; adjustments brought by, 4; alienation characterizing, 5; bitter forces unleashed by, 195; end of, 200–201; fears about, 201; grassroots politics during, 22, 24; partisanship, 1, 4–5; political environment, 195; Reconstruction adjustments, 15; Republican Party control of, 1–2 (*see also specific states*); Southern state universities and, 195–96 (*see also specific universities*); timetable of, 140; uncertainty of, 11–12
Reconstructionist, 24, 58, 96
Red River, 37, 146, 147
Reid, Whitelaw, 12

Reindeer, 79, 81, 194
Republican Banner, 64, 96
Republicanism, 17, 24, 42, 57, 59, 60, 61, 62, 101, 128; education and, 52; opposition to, 22, 26; resistance to, 26–27; triumph of, 52
Republican Party, 10, 14–17, 52–53, 56–57, 59, 61, 74, 76, 111–12, 142, 148, 163–64, 200; Alabama state constitution and, 76; Black minority and, 24; control of Reconstruction, 1–2; control over state governments by, 76, 131 (*see also specific states*); decline, 201; election of 1870, 158–60, 178; fear of, 40; midterm elections of 1866, 21
Republican press, 141
Republicans, 40, 49, 50, 62, 68, 166, 195, 198–99; attacks on, 22; fear of reversion to slavery and secession, 201; gathering at Waverly bookstore, 96; nightriding aimed at, 165–66; replacing local government officials, 67; whites, 26. *See also* Republican Party
Revels University, 149
Richards, Bartlett, 86, 105, 118
Richards, Harriet, 70, 76, 82, 86, 95, 105, 118, 155, 167, 193
Richards, Jarvis, 82, 167
Richards, Jonas DeForest, 72, 73, 156, 158, 160–61, 164, 167, 170, 191, 198, 200, 220n46; after University of Alabama, 193; arrival of, 76; attacks on, 85–86, *86*, 106, 122; background, 70–73; cadets and, 104; letters to Smith, 78, 89–90; loses post, 111, 113–14, 116–19; at opening ceremonies, 82; as president pro tempore, 79, 92–93, 173; pressed into teaching mathematics, 98; Read and, 107; reappointment of, 154; report outlining university's standing, 95; selection of, 68; as unapologetic Radical, 154–55

Richards, Margaret, 86, 105, 118
Riser, Dick, 101
Rivers, William J., 33, 137
Roberts, Dossie, 20
Rockford, Illinois, 114
Roy, Thomas B., 116, 155–56
Rudolph, Frederick, 92
Ryan, R. B., 74
Ryland, Robert, 94

"scalawags," 22, 64, 103, 111, 139, 150, 195
Schurz, Carl, 43
Scott, Robert K., 136, 139
"Scott's pets," 139
Sears, Claudius, 34, 35, 140
"Seavey," 165, 166
secession, 52, 53, 142, 143, 174; repudiation of, 54
segregation, 135, 137, 141–42, 149
Sellers, James, 2, 198
Selma, Alabama, 11, 47, 69, 96, 100, 116, 124, 129, 156, 181, 193
Selma and Meridian Railroad, 93, 116
Selma Morning Times, 116
Selma Press, 124
Selma Times, 172
Semmes, Raphael, 39, 40, 43, 93, 94, 95, 97, 99, 154, 162, 189
Seven Days' campaign, 17
Sewanee, Tennessee, 47, 175
Seymour, Horatio, 61, 63, 64
Sharkey, William L., 34, 45
Shelby County, Alabama, 100, 128, 151
Shelton, A. B., 82
Sheridan, Phillip, 39–40, 41, 42
Sherman, William, 30, 33, 37, 38, 66, 136, 145, 146
Shillaber, Benjamin P., 127
Sipsey Swamp, 75, 76, 88
Sixteenth Alabama Infantry, 75
slavery, 11, 29, 50, 198; debates over morality of, 137–38; end of, 14, 198; threats posed by abolitionism and Republican Party to, 10
Smith, Albert, 26
Smith, Asa, 78, 83, 89, 164, 198
Smith, David, 157, 165, 166
Smith, Eugene A., 171
Smith, Gustavus Adolphus, 53–55, *54*, 58, 94, 98, 102, 116–17, 121, 123–25, 159, 198
Smith, Martha Ellen, 75
Smith, William, 117, 120–26, 153, 155, 157, 159, 168, 200; escape of, 124–25; shooting of Randolph, 126–27
Smith, William A., 121
Smith, William Hugh, 2, 52, 60, 88–90, 157, 158, 160; administration of, 52
Smith, William Russell, 123, 150, 151–72, *152*, 173, 178, 180, 184, 185, 196; accused of being a pseudo-Radical, 155; board of education and, 161; as instructor, 154
Somers, Robert, 167
Somerville, Henderson M., 24, 123, 168, 169, 171
South Carolina, 3, 29–33, 46, 115; Black legislators in, 136; legislature, 137, 138; Reconstruction timetable, 140; Republican-authored constitution, 137; Republicans take power in, 136; Republican stewardship in, 131; sister school in, 131
South Carolina College, 29, 30, 31, 32–33, 45, 50, 131, 136
Southern Argus, 96, 100, 112, 156, 188–89
Southern Banner, 45
Southern Republican, 96–97, 100
Southern sovereignty, 50
Southern state universities: curriculum changes after the war, 186; financial realities of, 31; infrastructural weakness, 30–31; plight, 162; presidential leadership of, 150; Reconstruction

era and, 195–96; reestablishing despite adversity, 45–46; reinvigoration, 29–46
Southern University, 109, 112, 114, 130
Speed, Joseph, 161, 165–68, 170–71
Spencer, Charles, 150
Spencer, Cornelia Phillips, 35–36, 134–36, 150
state constitutions, 51, 52, 76, 201. *See also specific states*
state governments, 131, 137, 140. *See also specific states*
Stearns, H. D., 82
Stephens, Alexander, 44
Steward's Hall, 13
Straight University, 149
students: abandoning studies to enlist, 29; enrollment after the war, 32; ex-soldiers as, 36–37; injured in war, 31; regimented schedules of, 83–84; return to studies after the war, 32–33, 79–84, 90–91
Sugrue, Michael, 32
Sumter Watchman, 139
Swain, David L., 35
Swain, Eleanor (Ellie), 35
Swain, James, 132

Tait, James, 183
Tait, Joseph L., 163
Talladega, Alabama, 82, 100, 170, 181
Talladega County, Alabama, 74–75, 101
Tarbell, Jonathan, 140–41
Taylor, Joseph W., 155–56
Tennessee, 3, 4, 47, 114, 115; first state to rejoin the Union, 44; rejoins the Union, 14; sister school in, 131; Unionism in, 43
Texas, 3
Thibodaux, Louisiana, 180
Third Military District, 42
Thirteenth Amendment, 14, 15
Thompson, J. W., 9

Thornton, A. Q., 51, 53
Thornton, J. Mills, 199
Thurston, T. R., 82
Tillson, Davis, 41
Tombigbee River, 7, 10
Trawick, F. W., 81
Trinity College, 113
Trowbridge, John T., 45
Troy, Daniel S., 188, 189
Tuscaloosa, Alabama, 1–2, 5–6, 16, 24, 27, 30, 49–50, 57–60, 66, 76, 123, 192, 196; board of education meeting in, 94–95, 170–72, 181, 183, 191, 200; board of regents meeting in, 97; as fabled destination, 184; "low water" season, 66; national exposure, 62; oak trees, 7, 92, 151; opposition to opening of university, 77–78; political alienation, 88; political environment, 99–100, 124, 154–55, 159, 160, 165, 167, 194, 195; during Reconstruction, 7–28; return of faculty to, 76–78; troops sent to, 89; violence in, 88, 89–90
Tuscaloosa County, Alabama, 7, 26, 64, 90; population, 15
Tuscaloosa Female College, 128
Tuscaloosa Observer, 66, 75, 96, 99, 169, 175
Tuscumbia, Alabama, 82
Tutwiler, Henry, 49, 51, 162, 163

uniforms (for cadets), 84, 103, 108, 119, 192
Union, 2, 18; Alabama readmitted, 51, 52; fragility of, 10; readmission of ex-Confederate States, 14, 22, 51, 52; Tennessee rejoins, 44
Union Army, 11, 27
Union College, 144–45
Union Female College, 35
Unionism, 43, 52, 143–44
United States Army, 15, 39–40, 111, 114

Index

universities: adversity faced by, 29; Civil War and, 4; Northern, 4; politicization of university affairs, 131; refugees sheltering at, 33; resumption of education after war, 31–32. *See also specific universities and colleges*

"University Nine," 44

University of Alabama, 8, 17, 19, 30, 47–49, *48*, 64, *80*, 143, 144, 150; attempts to legitimize, 5; board of education and, 52–55, 93–95, 99–100, 114, 161–62, 170–72, 173, 178, 180–84, 185, 199, 200; board of trustees, 50–51, 53, 68, 74, 82, 93–94, 117, 118–19, 122, 151; cadets at, 103–5, 157 (*see also* cadets); caught in crossfire, 2; consequences of Smith/Randolph shooting on, 127–28; continued decline of, 167–69, 179, 189, 191, 192; curriculum plan, 183–84; decline of, 162, 197; declining enrollments, 161; demonized by Democratic Party, 161; destruction of, 4, 11, 198–99; discipline, 104; discussions to close, 108, 151, 173; discussions to relocate, 98, 99–100, 101, 108, 151; efforts to rebuild, 4, 28; election of 1870 and, 159–60, 197; enrollments, 98, 100–101, 103, 108, 153–54, 157–58, 161, 164, 185–86, 192, 197; experience of Reconstruction, 196, 197–98; faculty, 49–51, 53–56, 66–75, 77, 96, 98, 154–55, 159, 171, 182–83, 191–94, 199, 200 (*see also specific faculty members*); faculty composition, 49–51, 98, 154, 182–83; faculty residences, 77; faculty selection and, 54–56, 66–75, 96, 171; faculty tenure, 98; faltering renaissance, 47–65; financial difficulties, 153, 183–84, 186–88, 189, 197; financial records, 21, 67; food at, 108–9; hope for regeneration of, 168; image of, 101, 154, 192; increase in faculty size, 171; lack of infrastructure, 51–52; "launching fund," 184, 186–88; library, 21, 164; location, 98; low ebb of, 100–101; Maury ascends to presidency, 173–90; Maury conditionally accepts offer, 175–76; mission of, 103; names Smith as president, 151, 153; need to resuscitate, 151–72; Northrop declines presidency of, 99–100; North/South factionalism and, 111; notoriety of, 168–69; possible integration of, 102–3, 142; presidential leadership of, 150; presidential selection, 172; public backlash to appointments at, 66–91; public perception of, 96–97; Radical Republicans at, 3, 111–12, 120, 139, 181; rebuilding vs. reimagining, 201; during Reconstruction, 7–28; reflects poorly on Republican record, 159–60; regeneration, 4; regents reduce numbers of faculty, 109, 111; renewed interest in, 192; reopening of, 5, 13–14, 47–48, 51–52, 75–76, 77–84, 87–88, 90–91, 93, 100; Republican control over board of education, 180; Republican direction of, 65; reputation, 111–12; resuming constitutional mission as "seminary of learning" after four years of dormancy, 51; resurrection of, 192, 195; return of faculty, 76–78, 82, 84–85; return of students, 79–82, 83–84; revival of, 194, 197; scrutiny of after Randolph shooting, 126–27; search for president, 92–112, 199 (*see also specific candidates*); seen as "Radical University," 92; selection of Lupton as president, 109, 111; selection of Northrop as president, 97–99; slavery and, 198; solvency, 96–97; standing of, 103; status, 109, 111, 167–68, 198; students leaving, 127–28, 157; survey

— 267 —

of conditions, 163; target date for resuming instruction, 67–68; travails, 132; on trial, 123; uniforms at, 103; vision to restore, 160; weathering the storm, 131–50
University of California, 138
University of Georgia, 3, 30, 31, 41–42, 44, 148–49; board of trustees, 42, 43; commencement exercises, 148; experience of Reconstruction, 196; faculty composition, 196; Hill's speech supporting defiance at commencement meets with threat of lost revenue, 42–43; politics at, 148; progress at, 148; as "rebel Institution," 42; reopening of, 45; return to prewar status, 131; success at, 197
University of Heidelberg, 109
University of Minnesota, 99
University of Mississippi, 1, 3, 5, 30, 34, 35, 44, 45, 47, 139–40, 142–43, 145, 169; board of trustees, 140–42; enrollment at, 140, 142; experience of Reconstruction, 196; faculty, 140; faculty composition, 196; governor and, 140; possible integration of, 141–42, 149; progress at, 148; Republican stewardship of, 140–41; return to prewar status, 131; state government and, 140; Stewart Hall, 143; students, 140; success at, 197
University of North Carolina, Chapel Hill, 1, 3, 31, 35–36, 43, 46, 102, 131–34, 150; board of trustees, 136, 149; closure between 1871 and 1875, 197; commencement exercises, 37, 135, 149; continued confrontation, 197; damned as "child of Radicalism," 150; deterioration of situation at, 149; East, West, and South buildings, 36; enrollment at, 135, 136; experience of Reconstruction, 196; faculty, 136, 149; open during war's duration, 35–36; possible integration of, 142, 149; relationship between professors and students, 135–36; reopening of, 133; status, 134–35; students, 135; travails, 132

University of South Carolina, 1, 3, 4, 5, 33–34, 102, 136, 140; board of trustees, 149, 196–97; closure of, 197; criticism of trustees, 138–39; decline of, 197; enrollment at, 136, 137, 138, 139, 197; enrollment of Black students in 1873, 197; faculty, 138, 149; faculty composition, 196; held in disrepute by whites, 139; library, 144; possible integration of, 137, 138, 141, 149, 197; precarious status, 149; "Radical" leadership at, 139; reemergence of, 33; Republican oversight of, 136–37; standing, 138; state government and, 137; status, 138. *See also* South Carolina College

University of Tennessee, 3, 30
University of the South, 175, 185; reopening of, 47
University of Virginia, 3, 29, 31, 36–37, 43, 45, 49, 160, 178–79; board of visitors and, 132, 147; enrollment at, 147–48; experience of Reconstruction, 195, 196; faculty composition, 196; lack of partisanship at, 147–48; library, 144; progress at, 148; refugees from Alabama at, 147; reopening of, 47; Republicans on board of visitors, 147; return to prewar status, 131; success at, 197
Upper Alton, Illinois, 88
Ursuline Convent, 66–67
US Congress, 21, 76, 162; First Reconstruction Act, 2, 22, 26, 39; Fourth Military Reconstruction Act, 51; Joint Committee to Inquire into the Condition of Affairs in the Late

Index

Insurrectionist States, 166–67; Morrill Act, 144

Van Buren, Martin, 10
Vandaver, J. T., 82
Vaughn, Cornelia Spencer, 76–77, 107, 123, 124, 193
Vaughn, Vernon H., 73, 76–77, 98, 103–7, 111, 117, 119, 120–26, 158, 159, 200; acquittal of, 126; after University of Alabama, 193; appointed secretary of Utah Territory, 156–57; attacks on, 84, *85*, 91; background, 74; Lupton severs ties with, 128–29; misses opening ceremonies, 82; pronounced innocent by *Alabama State Journal*, 127; selection of, 68; and shooting of Randolph by a cadet, 120–26
Vaughn, William J., 171, 191, 192
Vicksburg, battle at, 30, 74
vigilante justice, 63, 165–66
Virginia, 89
Virginia, 3, 36–37, 46; board of visitors, 196; state universities, 99, 131; universities in, 29–30
Virginia Military Institute, 12, 19, 93, 97, 162, 163, 172, 175, 176, 178, 179, 181, 185, 189
Voltz, Caroline, 69

Waddel, John N., 34, 139–40, 141, 142, 143, 145, 148–49
Warmoth, Henry Clay, 145–46, 147, 149, 196, 197
Warner, Alexander, 141
Warren, John, 75, 96, 99, 100, 128, 169, 172, 175, 182, 191
Washington and Lee University, 47
Washington College, 47, 175
Washington Hall, 9, 12
Washington Society, 36, 43
Waverly bookstore, Tuscaloosa, 96, 108

Wells, J. Madison, 45
Western Reserve College, 69
West Point Military Academy, 93, 103, 106, 114, 116, 117, 119, 122
Whig and Observer, 155, 156
Whipper, William J., 137, 138
Whitfield, Hampton S., 24, 55–58, 95–96, 154–55, 158, 160, 161, 164, 170, 171
Whitfield, Nannie, 96
Whitfield, Nathan, 162, 165
Whitfield, Newton, 96
Wilcox County, Alabama, 72, 73, 189
William and Mary College, 181
Williams, Allen A., 26, 27
Williams, Frances L., 176
Williamson, Charles, 17, 24, 64
Wilmington Journal, 136
Wilson, J. M., 82
Wilson, John M., 118
Wolfe, Thomas, 113
Wood, Sterling A. M., 24, 90
Woodruff, David, 16, 24, 67, 87, 96, 105, 108, 160
Woodward, G. A., 169
Wyman, William, 51, 53, 55–57, 59, 60, 67, 96, 99, 102, 169, 171, 173, 187–88, 199
Wyman the Magician, 167–68

Xenia, Ohio, 68, 79

Yale College, 70, 98–99, 108, 134
Yates, Robert, 17
Yazoo City, Mississippi, 141